7th SIGdial Workshop on Discourse and Dialogue 2006

(SIGdial 06)

Held in conjunction with COLING/ACL 2006

Sydney, Australia
15-16 July 2006

ISBN: 978-1-61738-509-4

Printed from e-media with permission by:

Curran Associates, Inc.
57 Morehouse Lane
Red Hook, NY 12571
www.proceedings.com

Some format issues inherent in the e-media version may also appear in this print version.

Printed by Curran Associates, Inc. (2010)

Association for Computational Linguistics
209 N. Eighth Street
Stroudsburg, Pennsylvania 18360

Phone: 1-570-476-8006
Fax: 1-570-476-0860

acl@aclweb.org

Table of Contents

Preface

This is the proceedings of the Seventh SIGdial Workshop on Discourse and Dialogue. It is organized by SIGDial which is jointly sponsored by ACL and ISCA. The seventh workshop continues a series of successful workshops held in Hong Kong, Aalborg, Philadelphia, Sapporo, Boston and Lisbon. These workshops attract a wide range of participants, both within the dialogue community and beyond.

For this workshop, we received a total of 45 submissions of which we accepted 21. 11 of these are full papers and the rest posters. At the time of writing we are in the process of collecting demonstrations. However, due to the tight time schedule, we will unfortunately not be able to include these into the proceedings. The papers cover a number of thematic areas: spoken dialogue systems, question-answering agents, natural language generation for dialogue applications, machine learning and multimodal dialogue management.

We are very grateful to the members of the Program Committee for investing their time not only for reviewing but also for their post-review discussions.

There are a number of additional people who have been involved in the preparation of this workshop. In particular, we would like to express our gratitude to the following people: Stephan Lesch (DFKI GmbH) for setting up and management of the web page, Olivia Kwong for help producing the proceedings and Suzanne Stevenson for local organisation. We would also like to thank Microsoft for their sponsorship of the workshop. Finally, a special thanks to David Traum (ICT) and Wolfgang Minker (Ulm) from the SIGdial executive committee for their valuable advice and assistance.

We are very grateful to our invited speakers Diane Litman (Pittsburgh) and Jonathan Ginzburg (King's College, London) for contributing their expertise. It is our belief that their presence will make the workshop even more attractive. Finally, we wish all participants of the Workshop a great event.

Jan Alexandersson (DFKI GmbH) and Alistair Knott (University of Otago)
Organising Committee

Organizers

Chairs:

Jan Alexandersson, DFKI GmbH (Germany)
Alistair Knott, University of Otago (New Zealand)

Program Committee:

André Berton, DaimlerChrysler AG (Germany)
Masahiro Araki, Kyoto Institute of Technology (Japan)
Ellen Bard, University of Edinburgh (UK)
Johan Bos, La Sapienza (Italy)
Johan Boye, Telia Research (Sweden)
Dirk Bühler, University of Ulm (Germany)
Sandra Carberry, University of Delaware (USA)
Rolf Carlson, KTH (Sweden)
Jennifer Chu-Carroll, IBM Research (USA)
Mark Core, University of Edinburgh (UK)
Laila Dybkjaer, University of Southern Denmark (Denmark)
Sadaoki Furui, Tokyo Institute of Technology (Japan)
Jonathan Ginzburg, King's College, London (UK)
Iryna Gurevych, Darmstadt University of Technology (Germany)
Joakim Gustafson, Teliasonera (Sweden)
Masato Ishizaki, University of Tokyo (Japan)
Michael Johnston, AT&T Research (USA)
Arne Jönsson, Linköping University (Sweden)
Staffan Larsson, Göteborg University (Sweden)
Ramón López-Cózar Delgado, University of Granada (Spain)
Susann Luperfoy, Stottler Henke Associates (USA)
Michael McTear, University of Ulster (UK)
Wolfgang Minker, University of Ulm (Germany)
Sharon Oviatt, Oregon Health and Sciences University (Canada)
Tim Paek, Microsoft Research (USA)
Norbert Pfleger, DFKI GmbH (Germany)
Roberto Pieraccini, Tell-Eureka (USA)
Massimo Poesio, University of Essex (UK)
Norbert Reithinger, DFKI GmbH (Germany)
Laurent Romary, LORIA (France)
Alex Rudnicky, Carnegie Mellon University (USA)
David Schlangen, University of Potsdam (Germany)
Candy Sidner, Mitsubishi Electric Research Laboratories—MERL (USA)
Ronnie Smith, East Carolina University (USA)
Matthew Stone, Rutgers University (USA)
Marc Swerts, Tilburg University (The Netherlands)
David Traum, USC/ICT (USA)
Bonnie Webber, University of Edinburgh (UK)
Janyce Wiebe, University of Pittsburgh (USA)
Ingrid Zukerman, Monash University (Australia)

Invited Speakers:

Jonathan Ginzburg, King's College, London (UK)
Diane J. Litman, University of Pittsburgh (USA)

Workshop Program

Saturday, 15 July 2006

08:45–09:00 Opening remarks

Session 1: Spoken dialogue systems

09:00–09:45 *Adaptive Help for Speech Dialogue Systems Based on Learning and Forgetting of Speech Commands*
Alexander Hof, Eli Hagen and Alexander Huber

09:45–10:30 *Multi-Domain Spoken Dialogue System with Extensibility and Robustness against Speech Recognition Errors*
Kazunori Komatani, Naoyuki Kanda, Mikio Nakano, Kazuhiro Nakadai, Hiroshi Tsujino, Tetsuya Ogata and Hiroshi G. Okuno

10:30–11:00 Morning coffee break

Session 2: Question-answering agents

11:00–11:45 *Building Effective Question Answering Characters*
Anton Leuski, Ronakkumar Patel, David Traum and Brandon Kennedy

11:45–12:30 *Interactive Question Answering and Constraint Relaxation in Spoken Dialogue Systems*
Sebastian Varges, Fuliang Weng and Heather Pon-Barry

12:30–13:45 Lunch

Invited Talk I - Jonathan Ginzburg

13:45–14:45 *Content Recognition in Dialogue*
Jonathan Ginzburg

Session 3: Generation in dialogue

14:45–15:30 *Multidimensional Dialogue Management*
Simon Keizer and Harry Bunt

15:30–16:00 Afternoon coffee break

Saturday, 15 July 2006 (continued)

16:00–17:00 **Poster and demo session**

DRT Representation of Degrees of Belief
Yafa Al-Raheb

Resolution of Referents Groupings in Practical Dialogues
Alexandre Denis, Guillaume Pitel and Matthieu Quignard

Tracing Actions Helps in Understanding Interactions
Bernd Ludwig

Semantic and Pragmatic Presupposition in Discourse Representation Theory
Yafa Al-Raheb

Semantic tagging for resolution of indirect anaphora
R. Vieira, E. Bick, J. Coelho, V. Muller, S. Collovini, J. Souza and L. Rino

An annotation scheme for citation function
Simone Teufel, Advaith Siddharthan and Dan Tidhar

An Information State-Based Dialogue Manager for Call for Fire Dialogues
Antonio Roque and David Traum

Automatically Detecting Action Items in Audio Meeting Recordings
William Morgan, Pi-Chuan Chang, Surabhi Gupta and Jason M. Brenier

Empirical Verification of Adjacency Pairs Using Dialogue Segmentation
T. Daniel Midgley, Shelly Harrison and Cara MacNish

Multimodal Dialog Description Language for Rapid System Development
Masahiro Araki and Kenji Tachibana

(Titles of demos will be provided at the workshop)

Sunday, 16 July 2006

Session 4: Coherence relations and dialogue acts

09:00–09:45 *Classification of Discourse Coherence Relations: An Exploratory Study using Multiple Knowledge Sources*
Ben Wellner, James Pustejovsky, Catherine Havasi, Anna Rumshisky and Roser Saurí

09:45–10:30 *Measuring annotator agreement in a complex hierarchical dialogue act annotation scheme*
Jeroen Geertzen and Harry Bunt

10:30–11:00 Morning coffee break

Session 5: Machine learning I

11:00–11:45 *Balancing Conflicting Factors in Argument Interpretation*
Ingrid Zukerman, Michael Niemann and Sarah George

11:45–12:30 *An Analysis of Quantitative Aspects in the Evaluation of Thematic Segmentation Algorithms*
Maria Georgescul, Alexander Clark and Susan Armstrong

12:30–13:45 Lunch

Invited Talk II - Diane J. Litman

13:45–14:45 *Discourse and Dialogue Processing in Spoken Intelligent Tutoring Systems*
Diane J. Litman

Session 6: Multi-modal dialogue management

14:45–15:30 *A computational model of multi-modal grounding for human robot interaction*
Shuyin Li, Britta Wrede and Gerhard Sagerer

15:30–16:00 Afternoon coffee break

Session 7: Machine learning II

16:00–16:45 *Relationship between Utterances and "Enthusiasm" in Non-task-oriented Conversational Dialogue*
Ryoko Tokuhisa and Ryuta Terashima

16:45–17:00 Closing remarks

Adaptive Help for Speech Dialogue Systems Based on Learning and Forgetting of Speech Commands

Alexander Hof, Eli Hagen and Alexander Huber
Forschungs- und Innovationszentrum
BMW Group, Munich
alexander.hof,eli.hagen,alexander.hc.huber@bmw.de

Abstract

In this paper we deal with learning and forgetting of speech commands in speech dialogue systems. We discuss two mathematical models for learning and four models for forgetting. Furthermore, we describe the experiments used to determine the learning and forgetting curve in our environment. Our findings are compared to the theoretical models and based on this we deduce which models best describe learning and forgetting in our automotive environment. The resulting models are used to develop an adaptive help system for a speech dialogue system. The system provides only relevant context specific information.

1 Introduction

Modern premium class vehicles contain a large number of driver information and driving assistance systems. Therefore the need for enhanced display and control concepts arose. BMW's iDrive is one of these concepts, allowing the driver to choose functions by a visual-haptic interface (see Fig. 1) (Haller, 2003). In Addition to the visual-haptic interface, iDrive includes a speech dialogue system (SDS) as well. The SDS allows the driver to use a large number of functions via speech commands (Hagen et al., 2004). The system offers a context specific help function that can be activated by uttering the keyword 'options'. The options provide help in the form of a list, containing speech commands available in the current context (see dialogue 1). Currently neither the driver's preferences nor his knowledge is taken into consideration. We present a strategy to optimize the options by adaption that takes preferences and knowledge into account.

Figure 1: iDrive controller and Central Information Display (CID)

Our basic concern was to reduce the driver's memory load by reducing irrelevant information. An adaptive help system based upon an individual user model could overcome this disadvantage. In (Komatani et al., 2003) and (Libuda and Kraiss, 2003), several adaptive components can be included to improve dialogue systems, e.g. user and content adaption, situation adaption and task adaption. Hassel (2006) uses adaption to apply different dialogue strategies according to the user's experience with the SDS. In our system we concentrate on user modeling and content adaption.

In this paper, we present studies concerning learning and forgetting of speech commands in automotive environments. The results are used to develop a model describing the driver's knowledge in our SDS domain. This model is used to adapt the content of the options lists.

Proceedings of the 7th SIGdial Workshop on Discourse and Dialogue, pages 1–8,
Sydney, July 2006.

Dialogue 1

User: "Phone."
System: "Phone. Say dial name, dial number or name a list."
User: "Options."
System: "Options. Say dial followed by a name, for example 'dial Alex', or say dial name, dial number, save number, phone book, speed dialing list, top eight, last eight, accepted calls, missed calls, active calls and or or off."

2 Learning of Commands

In this section, we determine which function most adequately describes learning in our environment. In the literature, two mathematically functions can be found. These functions help to predict the time necessary to achieve a task after several trials. One model was suggested by (Newell and Rosenbloom, 1981) and describes learning with a *power law*. Heathcote et. al. (2002) instead suggest to use an *exponential law*.

$$T = B \cdot N^{-\alpha} \quad \text{(power law)} \qquad (1)$$

$$T = B \cdot e^{-\alpha \cdot N} \quad \text{(exponential law)} \qquad (2)$$

In both equations T represents the time to solve a task, B is the time needed for the first trial of a task, N stands for the number of trials and α is the learning rate parameter that is a measure for the learning speed. The parameter α has to be determined empirically. We conducted memory tests to determine, which of the the two functions best describes the learning curve for our specific environment.

2.1 Test Design for Learning Experiments

The test group consisted of seven persons. The subjects' age ranged from 26 to 43 years. Five of the subjects had no experience with an SDS, two had very little. Novice users were needed, because we wanted to observe only novice learning behaviour. The tests lasted about one hour and were conducted in a BMW, driving a predefined route with moderate traffic.

Each subject had to learn a given set of ten tasks with differing levels of complexity (see table 1). Complexity is measured by the minimal necessary dialogue steps to solve a task. The tasks were not directly named, but explained in order not to mention the actual command and thus avoid any influence on the learning process. There was no help allowed except the options function. The subjects received the tasks one by one and had to search for the corresponding speech command in the options. After completion of a task in the testset the next task was presented. The procedure was repeated until all commands had been memorized. For each trial, we measured the time span from SDS activation until the correct speech command was spoken. The time spans were standardized by dividing them through the number of the minimal necessary steps that had to be taken to solve a task.

2.2 Results

In general, we can say that learning takes place very fast in the beginning and with an increasing amount of trials the learning curve flattens and approximates an asymptote. The asymptote at $T_{\min} = 2$s defines the maximum expert level, that means that a certain task can not be completed faster.

The resulting learning curve is shown in Fig. 3. In order to determine whether equation (1) or (2) describes this curve more exactly, we used a chi-squared goodness-of-fit test (Rasch et al., 2004). The more χ^2 tends to zero, the less the observed values (f_o) differ from the estimated values (f_e).

$$\chi^2 = \sum_{i=1}^{k} \frac{(f_o - f_e)^2}{f_e} \qquad (3)$$

According to Fig. 2, the power law has a minimum ($\chi^2_{\min} = 0.42$) with a learning rate parameter of $\alpha = 1.31$. The exponential law has its minimum ($\chi^2_{\min} = 2.72$) with $\alpha = 0.41$. This means that the values of the exponential law differ more from the actual value than the power law's values. Therefore, we use the power law (see Fig. 3(a)) to describe learning in our environment.

3 Forgetting of Commands

The second factor influencing our algorithm for the calculation of options is forgetting. If a command was not in use for a long period of time, we can assume that this command will be forgotten. In this section, we determine how long commands are being remembered and deduce a function most adequately describing the process of for-

Task 1	Listen to a radio station with a specific frequency
Task 2	Summary of already used destinations
Task 3	Enter a new destination
Task 4	Start navigation
Task 5	Turn off speech hints
Task 6	3D map
Task 7	Change map scale
Task 8	Avoid highways for route calculation
Task 9	Turn on CD
Task 10	Display the car's fuel consumption

Table 1: Tasks for learning curve experiments

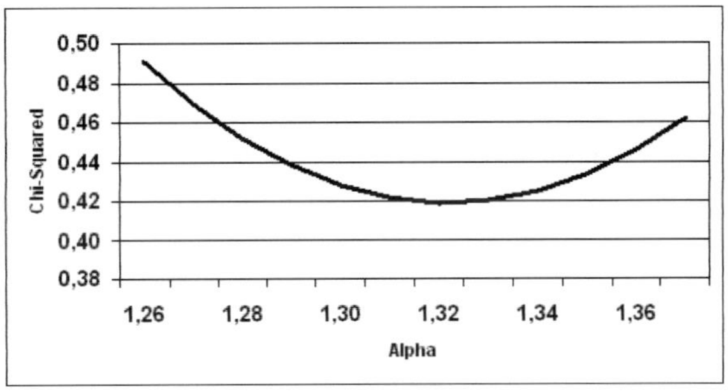

(a) χ^2 for the Power Law

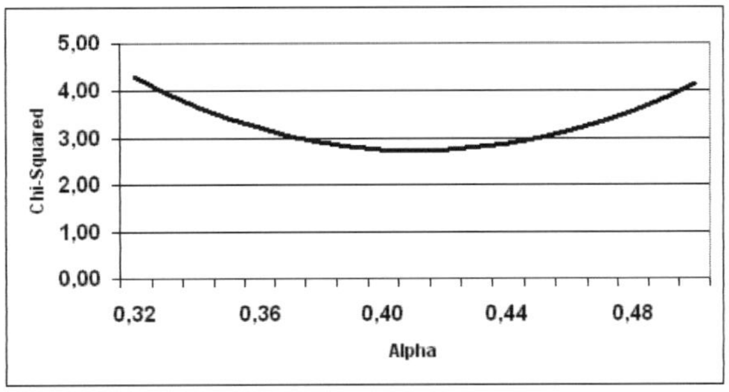

(b) χ^2 for the Exponential Law

Figure 2: Local χ^2 Minima

getting in our environment. In (Rubin and Wenzel, 1996) 105 mathematical models on forgetting were compared to several previously published retention studies. The results showed that there is no generally appliable mathematical model, but a few models fit to a large number of studies. The most adequate models based on a logarithmic function, an exponential function, a power function and a square root function.

$$\mu_{\text{new}} = \mu_{\text{old}} \cdot \ln(t+e)^{-\delta} \quad \text{(logarithmic)} \quad (4)$$

$$\mu_{\text{new}} = \mu_{\text{old}} \cdot e^{-\delta \cdot t} \quad \text{(exponential)} \quad (5)$$

$$\mu_{\text{new}} = \mu_{\text{old}} \cdot (t+\delta)^{-\delta} \quad \text{(power)} \quad (6)$$

$$\mu_{\text{new}} = \mu_{\text{old}} \cdot e^{-\delta \cdot \sqrt{t}} \quad \text{(square root)} \quad (7)$$

The variable μ represents the initial amount of learned items. The period of time is represented through t while δ defines the decline parameter of the forgetting curve. In order to determine the best forgetting curve for SDS interactions, we conducted tests in which the participants' memory skills were monitored.

3.1 Test design for forgetting experiments

The second experiment consisted of two phases, learning and forgetting. In a first step ten subjects learned a set of two function blocks, each consisting of ten speech commands (see table (2)). The learning phase took place in a BMW. The tasks and the corresponding commands were noted on

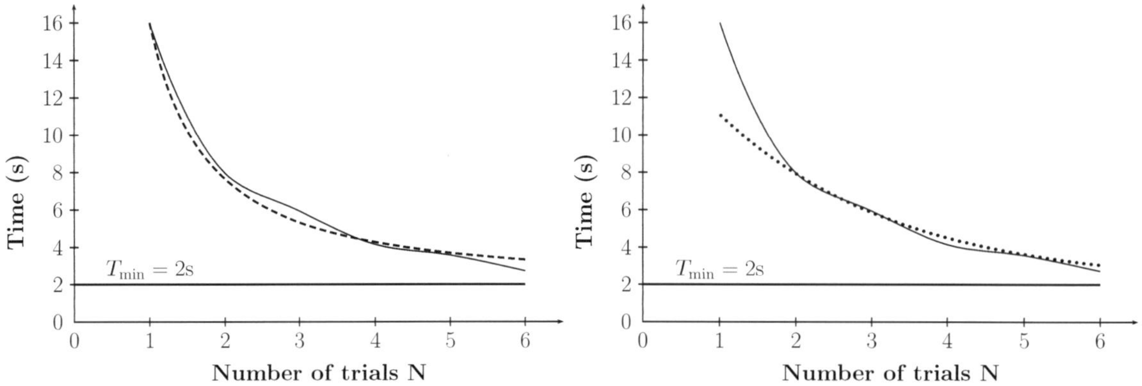

(a) Observed learning curve and power law (dashed) with $\alpha = 1.31$

(b) Observed learning curve and exponential law (dotted) with $\alpha = 0.42$

Figure 3: Learning curves

	Function block 1		Function block 2
Task 1	Start CD player	**Task 11**	Turn on TV
Task 2	Listen to CD, track 5	**Task 12**	Watch TV station 'ARD'
Task 3	Listen to tadio	**Task 13**	Regulate blowers
Task 4	Listen to radio station 'Antenne Bayern'	**Task 14**	Change time settings
Task 5	Listen to radio on frequency 103,0	**Task 15**	Change date settings
Task 6	Change sound options	**Task 16**	Change CID brightness
Task 7	Start navigation system	**Task 17**	Connect with BMW Online
Task 8	Change map scale to 1km	**Task 18**	Use phone
Task 9	Avoid highways for route calculation	**Task 19**	Assistance window
Task 10	Avoid ferries for route calculation	**Task 20**	Turn off the CID

Table 2: Tasks for forgetting curve experiments

a handout. The participants had to read the tasks and uttered the speech commands. When all 20 tasks were completed, this step was repeated as long as all SDS commands could be freely reproduced. These 20 commands built the basis for our retention tests.

Our aim was to determine how fast forgetting took place, so we conducted several memory tests over a time span of 50 days. The tests were conducted in a laboratory environment and should imitate the situation in a car if the driver wants to perform a task (e.g. listen to the radio) via SDS. Because we wanted to avoid any influence on the participant's verbal memory, the intentions were not presented verbally or in written form but as iconic representations (see Fig. 4). Each icon represented an intention and the corresponding speech command had to be spoken.

Intention $\longrightarrow$ Task $\longrightarrow$ Command $\longrightarrow$ Success

Icon $\longrightarrow$ Task $\longrightarrow$ Command $\longrightarrow$ Success

Figure 4: Iconic representation of the functions: phone, avoid highways and radio

This method guarantees that each function was

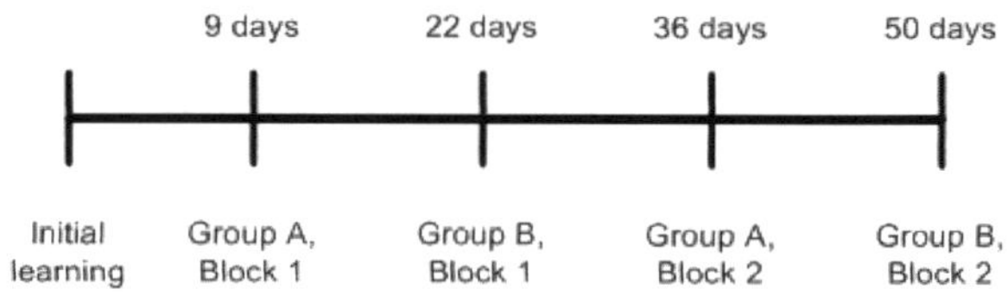

Figure 5: Test procedure for retention tests

only used once and relearning effects could not influence the results. As a measure for forgetting, we used the number of commands recalled correctly after a certain period of time.

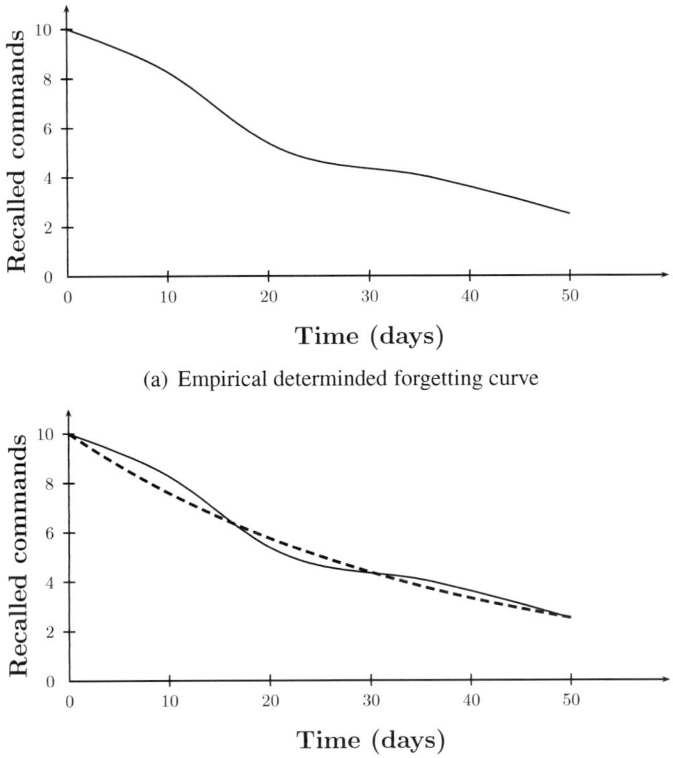

(a) Empirical determinded forgetting curve

(b) Exponential forgetting curve (dashed) with $\delta = 0.027$

Figure 6: Forgetting curves

3.2 Results

The observed forgetting curve can be seen in Fig. 6(a). In order to determine whether equation (4), (5), (6) or (7) fits best to our findings, we used the chi-squared goodness-of-fit test (cf. section 2.2). The minima χ^2 for the functions are shown in table (3). Because the exponential function (see Fig. 6(b)) delivers the smallest χ^2, we use equation (5) for our further studies.

Function	χ^2	Corresponding δ
logarithmic	2.11	0.58
exponential	0.12	0.027
power	1.77	0.22
square root	0.98	0.15

Table 3: χ^2 values

Concerning forgetting in general we can deduce that once the speech commands have been learned, forgetting takes place faster in the beginning. With increasing time, the forgetting curve flattens and at any time tends to zero. Our findings show that after 50 days about 75% of the original number of speech commands have been forgotten. Based on the exponential function, we estimate that complete forgetting will take place after approximately 100 days.

4 Providing Adaptive Help

As discussed in previous works, several adaptive components can be included in dialogue systems, e.g. user adaption (Hassel and Hagen, 2005), content adaption, situation adaption and task adaption (Libuda and Kraiss, 2003). We concentrate on user and content adaption and build a user model.

According to Fischer (2001), the user's knowledge about complex systems can be divided into several parts (see Fig. 7): well known and regularly used concepts (*F1*), vaguely and occasionally used concepts (*F2*) and concepts the user believes to exist in the system (*F3*). *F* represents the complete functionality of the system. The basic idea behind the adaptive help system is to use information about the driver's behaviour with the SDS to provide only help on topics he is not so familiar with. Thus the help system focuses on *F2*, *F3* within *F* and finally the complete functionality *F*.

For every driver an individual profile is gen-

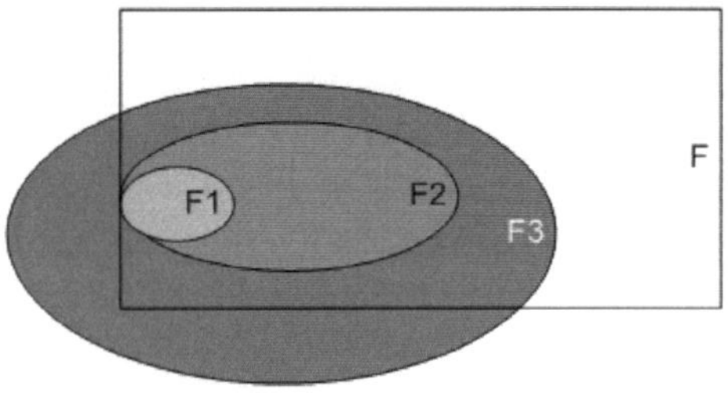

Figure 7: Model about the user's knowledge on complex systems

erated, containing information about usage frequency and counters for every function. Several methods can be used to identify the driver, e.g. a personal ID card, a fingerprint system or face recognition (Heckner, 2005). We do not further focus on driver identification in our prototype.

4.1 Defining an Expert User

In section 2 we observed that in our environment, the time to learn speech commands follows a power law, depending on the number of trials (N), the duration of the first interaction (B) and the learning rate parameter (α). If we transform equation (1), we are able to determine the number of trials that are needed to execute a function in a given time T.

$$N = \sqrt[-\alpha]{\frac{T}{B}} \tag{8}$$

If we substitute T with the minimal time $T_{\min}$ an expert needs to execute a function ($T_{\min} = 2$s, cf. section 2.2), we can estimate the number of trials which are necessary for a novice user to become an expert. The only variable is the duration B, which has to be measured for every function at its first usage.

Additionally, we use two stereotypes (novice and expert) to classify a user concerning his general experience with the SDS. According to Hassel (2006), we can deduce a user's experience by monitoring his behaviour while using the SDS. The following parameters are used to calculate an additional user model: help requests *h* (user asked for general information about the system), options requests *o* (user asked for the currently available speech commands), timeouts *t* (the ASR did not get any acoustic signal), onset time *ot* (user needed more than 3 sec to start answering) and barge-in *b* (user starts speech input during the system's speech output). The parameters are noted in a vector $\vec{UM}$.

The parameters are differently weighted by a weight vector $\vec{UM_w}$, because each parameter is a different indicator for the user's experience.

$$\vec{UM_w} = \begin{pmatrix} h & = & 0.11 \\ o & = & 0.33 \\ t & = & 0.45 \\ ot & = & 0.22 \\ b & = & -0.11 \end{pmatrix} \tag{9}$$

The final user model is calculated by the scalar product of $\vec{UM} \times \vec{UM_w}$. If the resulting value is over a predefined threshold, the user is categorized as novice and a more explicit dialogue strategy is applied, e.g. the dialogues contain more expamples. If the user model delivers a value under the threshold, the user is categorized as expert and an implicit dialogue strategy is applied.

4.2 Knowledge Modeling Algorithm

Our findings from the learning experiments can be used to create an algorithm for the presentation of the context specific SDS help. Therefore, the option commands of every context are split into several help layers (see Fig. 8). Each layer contains a

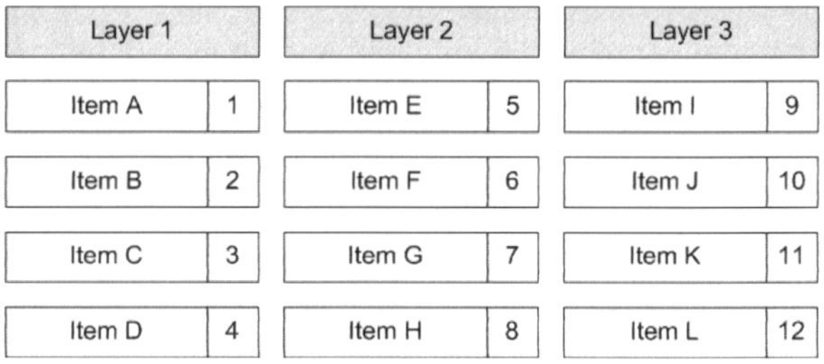

Figure 8: Exemplary illustration of twelve help items divided into three help layers

maximum of four option commands in order to reduce the driver's mental load (Wirth, 2002). Each item has a counter, marking the position within the layers. The initial order is based on our experience with the usage frequency by novice users. The first layer contains simple and frequently used commands, e.g. dial number or choose radio station. Complex or infrequent commands are put into the lower layers. Every usage of a function is logged by the system and a counter i is increased by 1 (see equation 10).

Besides the direct usage of commands, we also take transfer knowledge into account. There are several similar commands, e.g. the selection of entries in different lists like phonebook, adressbook or in the cd changer playlists. Additionally, there are several commands with the same parameters, e.g. radio on/off, traffic program on/off etc. All similar speech commands were clustered in functional families. If a user is familiar with one command in the family, we assume that the other functions can be used or learned faster. Thus, we introduced a value, σ, that increases the indices of all cammnds within the functional families. The value of σ depends on the experience level of the user.

$$i_{\text{new}} = \begin{cases} i_{\text{old}} + 1 & \text{direct usage} \\ i_{\text{old}} + \sigma & \text{similar command} \end{cases} \tag{10}$$

In order to determine the value of σ, we conducted a small test series where six novice users were told to learn ten SDS commands from different functional families. Once they were familiar with the set of commands, they had to perform ten tasks requiring similar commands. The subjects were not allowed to use any help and should derive the necessary speech command from their prior knowledge about the SDS. Results showed that approximately 90% of the tasks could be completed by deducing the necessary speech commands from the previously learned commands. Transferring these results to our algorithm, we assume that once a user is an expert on a speech command of a functional family, the other commands can be derived very well. Thus we set $\sigma_{expert} = 0.9$ for expert users and estimate that for novice users the value should be $\sigma_{novice} = 0.6$. These values have to be validated in further studies.

Every usage of a speech command increases its counter and the counters of the similar commands. These values can be compared to the value of N resulting from equation (8). N defines a threshold that marks a command as known or unknown. If a driver uses a command more often than the corresponding threshold ($i > N$), our assumption is that the user has learned it and thus does not need help on this command. It can be shifted into the lowest layer and the other commands move over to the upper layers (see Fig. 9).

If a command is not in use for a long period of time (cf. section 3.2), the counter of this command steadily declines until the item's initial counter value is reached. The decline itself is based on the results of our forgetting experiments (cf. section

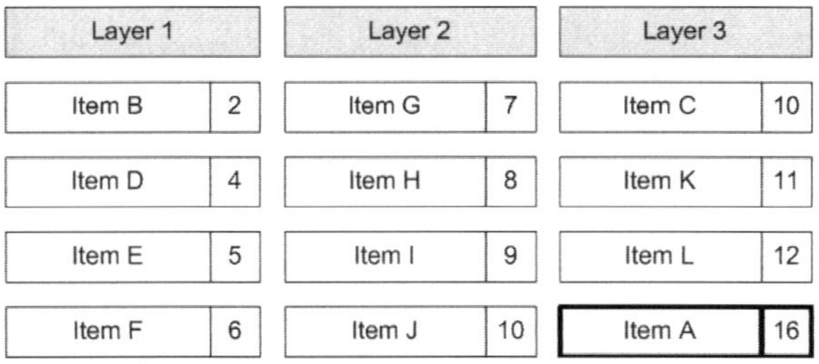

Figure 9: Item A had an initial counter of $i = 1$ and was presented in layer 1; after it has been used 15 times (i > N), it is shifted into layer 3 and the counter has a new value $i = 16$

3.2) and the behaviour of the counter is described by equation (5).

5 Summary and Future Work

In this paper we presented studies dealing with learning and forgetting of speech commands in an in-car environment. In terms of learning, we compared the power law of learning and the exponential law of learning as models that are used to describe learning curves. We conducted tests under driving conditions and showed that learning in this case follows the power law of learning. This implies that learning is most effective in the beginning and requires more effort the more it tends towards an expert level.

Concerning forgetting we compared four possible mathematical functions: a power function, an exponential function, a logarithmic function and a square root function. Our retention tests showed that the forgetting curve was described most adequately by the exponential function. Within the observed time span of 50 days about 75% of the initial amount of speech commands have been forgotten.

The test results have been transferred into an algorithm specifying the driver's knowledge of commands within the SDS. Based on the learning experiments we are able to deduce a threshold that defines the minimal number of trials that are needed to learn a speech command. The forgetting experiments allow us to draw conclusions on how long this specific knowledge will be remebered. With this information, we developed an algorithm for an adaptive options list. It provides help on unfamiliar speech commands.

Future work focuses on usability tests of the prototype system, e.g. using the PARADISE evaluation framework to evaluate the general usability of the system (Walker et al., 1997). One main question that arises in the context of an adaptive help system is if the adaption will be judged useful on the one hand and be accepted by the user on the other hand. Depending on user behaviour the help system could shift its contents very fast, which may cause some irritation. The test results will show whether people get irritated and whether the general approach for the options lists appears to be useful.

References

Gerhard Fischer. 2001. User modeling in human-computer interaction. *User Modeling and User-Adapted Interaction*, 11:65–86.

Eli Hagen, Tarek Said, and Jochen Eckert. 2004. Spracheingabe im neuen BMW 6er. ATZ.

Rudolf Haller. 2003. The Display and Control Concept iDrive - Quick Access to All Driving and Comfort Functions. *ATZ/MTZ Extra (The New BMW 5-Series)*, pages 51–53.

Liza Hassel and Eli Hagen. 2005. Evaluation of a dialogue system in an automotive environment. In *6th SIGdial Workshop on Discourse and Dialogue*, pages 155–165, September.

Liza Hassel and Eli Hagen. 2006. Adaptation of an Automotive Dialogue System to Users Expertise and Evaluation of the System.

Andrew Heathcote, Scott Brown, and D. J. K. Mewhort. 2002. The Power Law Repealed: The case for an Exponential Law of Practice. *Psychonomic Bulletin and Review*, 7:185–207.

Markus Heckner. 2005. Videobasierte Personenidentifikation im Fahrzeug – Design, Entwicklung und Evaluierung eines prototypischen Mensch Maschine Interfaces. Master's thesis, Universität Regensburg.

Kazunori Komatani, Fumihiro Adachi, Shinichi Ueno, Tatsuya Kawahara, and Hiroshi Okuno. 2003. Flexible Spoken Dialogue System based on User Models and Dynamic Generation of VoiceXML Scripts. In *4th SIGdial Workshop on Discourse and Dialogue*.

Lars Libuda and Karl-Friedrich Kraiss. 2003. Dialogassistenz im Kraftfahrzeug. In *45. Fachausschusssitzung Anthropotechnik der DGLR: Entscheidungsunterstützung für die Fahrzeug- und Prozessführung*, pages 255–270, Oktober.

Allen Newell and Paul Rosenbloom. 1981. Mechanisms of skill acquisition and the law of practice. In J. R. Anderson, editor, *Cognitive skills and their acquisition*. Erlbaum, Hillsdale, NJ.

Björn Rasch, Malte Friese, Wilhelm Hofmann, and Ewald Naumann. 2004. *Quantitative Methoden*. Springer.

David Rubin and Amy Wenzel. 1996. One hundred years of forgetting: A quantitative description of retention. *Psychological Review*, 103(4):734–760.

Marilyn Walker, Diane Litman, Candace Kamm, and Alicia Abella. 1997. Paradise: A framework for evaluating spoken dialogue agents. In *Proceedings of the eighth conference on European chapter of the Associationfor Computational Linguistics*, pages 271–280, Morristown, New Jersey. Association for Computational Linguistics.

Thomas Wirth. 2002. Die magische Zahl 7 und die Gedächtnisspanne.

Multi-Domain Spoken Dialogue System with Extensibility and Robustness against Speech Recognition Errors

Kazunori Komatani **Naoyuki Kanda** **Mikio Nakano**†
Kazuhiro Nakadai† **Hiroshi Tsujino**† **Tetsuya Ogata** **Hiroshi G. Okuno**

Kyoto University, Yoshida-Hommachi, Sakyo, Kyoto 606-8501, Japan
{komatani,ogata,okuno}@i.kyoto-u.ac.jp

† Honda Research Institute Japan Co., Ltd., 8-1 Honcho, Wako, Saitama 351-0188, Japan
{nakano,nakadai,tsujino}@jp.honda-ri.com

Abstract

We developed a multi-domain spoken dialogue system that can handle user requests across multiple domains. Such systems need to satisfy two requirements: extensibility and robustness against speech recognition errors. Extensibility is required to allow for the modification and addition of domains independent of other domains. Robustness against speech recognition errors is required because such errors are inevitable in speech recognition. However, the systems should still behave appropriately, even when their inputs are erroneous. Our system was constructed on an extensible architecture and is equipped with a robust and extensible domain selection method. Domain selection was based on three choices: (I) the previous domain, (II) the domain in which the speech recognition result can be accepted with the highest recognition score, and (III) other domains. With the third choice we newly introduced, our system can prevent dialogues from continuously being stuck in an erroneous domain. Our experimental results, obtained with 10 subjects, showed that our method reduced the domain selection errors by 18.3%, compared to a conventional method.

1 Introduction

Many spoken dialogue systems have been developed for various domains, including: flight reservations (Levin et al., 2000; Potamianos and Kuo, 2000; San-Segundo et al., 2000), train travel information (Lamel et al., 1999), and bus information (Komatani et al., 2005b; Raux and Eskenazi, 2004). Since these systems only handle a single domain, users must be aware of the limitations of these domains, which were defined by the system developer. To handle various domains through a single interface, we have developed a multi-domain spoken dialogue system, which is composed of several single-domain systems. The system can handle complicated tasks that contain requests across several domains.

Multi-domain spoken dialogue systems need to satisfy the following two requirements: (1) extensibility and (2) robustness against speech recognition errors. Many such systems have been developed on the basis of a master-slave architecture, which is composed of a single master module and several domain experts handling each domain. This architecture has the advantage that each domain expert can be independently developed, by modifying existing experts or adding new experts into the system. In this architecture, the master module needs to select a domain expert to which response generation and dialogue management for the user's utterance are committed. Hereafter, we will refer to this selecting process **domain selection**.

The second requirement is robustness against speech recognition errors, which are inevitable in systems that use speech recognition. Therefore, these systems must robustly select domains even when the input may be incorrect due to speech recognition errors.

We present an architecture for a multi-domain spoken dialogue system that incorporates a new domain selection method that is both extensible and robust against speech recognition errors. Since our system is based on extensible architecture similar to that developed by O'Neill (O'Neill et al., 2004), we can add and modify the domain

Proceedings of the 7th SIGdial Workshop on Discourse and Dialogue, pages 9–17,
Sydney, July 2006.

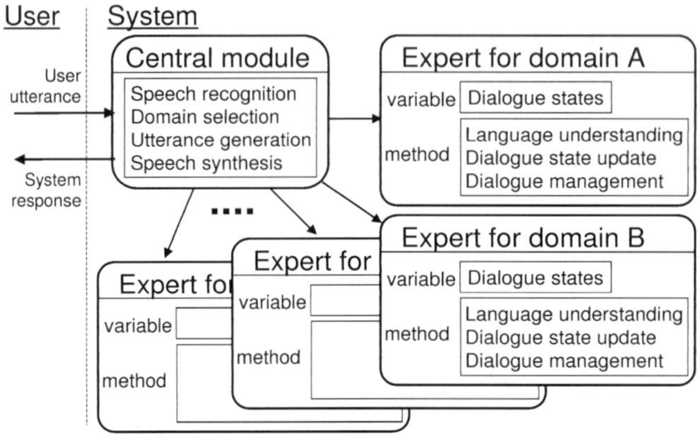

Figure 1: Distributed-type architecture for multi-domain spoken dialogue systems

experts easily. In order to maintain robustness, domain selection takes into consideration various features concerning context and situations of the dialogues. We also designed a new selection framework that satisfies the extensibility issue by abstracting the transitions between the current and next domains. Specifically, our system selects the next domain based on: (I) the previous domain, (II) the domain in which the speech recognition result can be accepted with the highest recognition score, and (III) other domains. Conventional methods cannot select the correct domain when neither the previous domain nor the speech recognition results for a current utterance are correct. To overcome this drawback, we defined another choice as (III) that enables the system to detect an erroneous situation and thus prevent the dialogue from continuing to be incorrect. We modeled this framework as a classification problem using machine learning, and showed it is effective by performing an experimental evaluation of 2,205 utterances collected from 10 subjects.

2 Architecture used for Multi-Domain Spoken Dialogue Systems

In multi-domain spoken dialogue systems, the system design is more complicated than in single domain systems. When the designed systems are closely related to each other, a modification in a certain domain may affect the whole system. This type of a design makes it difficult to modify existing domains or to add new domains. Therefore, a distributed-type architecture has been previously proposed (Lin et al., 2001), which enables system developers to design each domain independently. In this architecture, the system is composed of two kinds of components: a part that can be designed independently of all other domains, and a part in which relations among domains should be considered. By minimizing the latter component, a system developer can design each domain semi-independently, which enables domains to be easily added or modified. Many existing systems are based on this architecture (Lin et al., 2001; O'Neill et al., 2004; Pakucs, 2003; Nakano et al., 2005).

Thus, we adopted the distributed-type architecture (Nakano et al., 2005). Our system is roughly composed of two parts, as shown in Figure 1: several experts that control dialogues in each domain, and a central module that controls each expert. When a user speaks to the system, the central module drives a speech recognizer, and then passes the result to each domain expert. Each expert, which controls its own domains, executes a language understanding module, updates its dialogue states based on the speech recognition result, and returns the information required for domain selection[1]. Based on the information obtained from the experts, the central module selects an appropriate domain for giving the response. An expert then takes charge of the selected domain and determines the next dialogue act based on its dialogue state. The central module generates a response based on the dialogue act obtained from the expert, and outputs the synthesized speech to the user. Communications between the central module and each expert are realized using method-calls in the central module. Each expert is required to have several methods, such as utterance understanding or response selection, to be considered an expert

[1]Dialogue states in a domain that are not selected during domain selection are returned to their previous states.

in this architecture.

As was previously described, the central module is not concerned with processing the speech recognition results; instead, the central module leaves this task to each expert. Therefore, it is important that the central module selects an expert that is committed to the process of the speech recognition result. Furthermore, information used during domain selection should also be domain independent, because this allows easier domain modification and addition, which is, after all, the main advantage of distributed-type architecture.

3 Extensible and Robust Domain Selection

Domain selection in the central module should also be performed within an extensible framework, and also should be robust against speech recognition errors.

In many conventional methods, domain selection is based on estimating the most likely domains based on the speech recognition results. Since these methods are heavily dependent on the performance of the speech recognizers, they are not robust because the systems will fail when a speech recognizer fails. To behave robustly against speech recognition errors, the success of speech recognition and of domain selection should be treated separately. Furthermore, in some conventional methods, accurate language models are required to construct the domain selection parts before new domains are added to a multi-domain system. This means that they are not extensible.

When selecting a domain, other studies have used the information on the domain in which a previous response was made. Lin et al. (2001) gave preference to the domain selected in the previous turn by adding a certain score as an award when comparing the N-best candidates of the speech recognition for each domain. Lane and Kawahara (2005) also assigned a similar preference in the classification with Support Vector Machine (SVM). A system described in (O'Neill et al., 2004) does not change its domain until its sub-task is completed, which is a constraint similar to keeping dialogue in one domain. Since these methods assume that the previous domain is most likely the correct domain, it is expected that these methods keep a system in the domain despite errors due to speech recognition problems. Thus, should domain selection be erroneous, the damage due to the error is compounded, as the system assumes that the previous domain is always correct. Therefore, we solve this problem by considering features that represent the confidence of the previously selected domain.

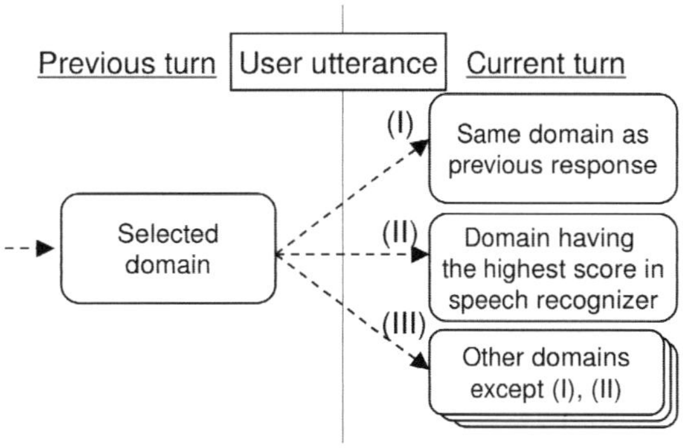

Figure 2: Overview of domain selection

We define domain selection as being based on the following 3-class categorization: (I) the previous domain, (II) the domain in which the speech recognition results can be accepted with the highest recognition score, which is different from the previous domain, and (III) other domains. Figure 2 depicts the three choices. This framework includes the conventional methods as choices (I) and (II). Furthermore, it considers the possibility that the current interpretations may be wrong, which is represented as choice (III). This framework also has extensibility for adding new domains, since it treats domain selection not by detecting each domain directly, but by defining only a relative relationship between the previous and current domains.

Since our framework separates speech recognition results and domain selection, it can keep dialogues in the correct domain even when speech recognition results are wrong. This situation is represented as choice (I). An example is shown in Figure 3. Here, the user's first utterance (U1) is about the restaurant domain. Although the second utterance (U2) is also about the restaurant domain, an incorrect interpretation for the restaurant domain is obtained because the utterance contains an out-of-vocabulary word and is incorrectly recognized. Although a response for utterance U2 should ideally be in the restaurant domain, the system control shifts to the temple sightseeing information domain, in which an interpretation is obtained based on the speech recognition result. This

U1: **Tell me bars in Kawaramachi area.**
(domain: restaurant)

S1: Searching for bars in Kawaramachi area.
30 items found.

U2: **I want Tamanohikari (name of liquor).**
(domain: restaurant)
Tamanohikari is out-of-vocabulary word, and misrecognized as Tamba-bashi (name of place). (domain: temple)

S2 (bad): Searching spots near Tamba-bashi. 10 items found. (domain: temple)

S2 (good): I do not understand what you said. Do you have any other preferences? (domain: restaurant)

Figure 3: Example in which choice (I) is appropriate in spite of speech recognition error

is shown as utterance S2 (bad). In such cases, our framework is capable of behaving appropriately. This is shown as S2 (good), which is made by selecting choice (I). Accepting erroneous recognition results is more harmful than rejecting correct ones for the following reasons: 1) a user needs to solve the misunderstanding as a result of the false acceptance, and 2) an erroneous utterance affects the interpretation of the utterances following it.

Furthermore, we define choice (III), which detects the cases where normal dialogue management is not suitable, in which case the central module selects an expert based on either the previous domain or the domain based on the speech recognition results. The situation corresponds to a succession of recognition errors. However, this problem is more difficult to solve than merely detecting a simple succession of the errors because the system needs to distinguish between speech recognition errors and domain selection errors in order to generate appropriate next utterances. Figure 4 shows an example of such a situation. Here, the user's utterances U1 and U2 are about the temple domain, but a speech recognition error occurred in U2, and system control shifts to the hotel domain. The user again says (U3), but this results in the same recognition error. In this case, a domain that should ideally be selected is neither the domain in the previous turn nor the domain determined based on the speech recognition results. If this situation can be detected, the system should be able to generate an appropriate response, like S3 (good), and prevent inappropriate responses based

U1: **Tell me the address of Horin-ji** (temple name)**.**
(domain: temple)

S1: The address of Horin-ji is ...

U2: **Then, what is the fee for Horin-ji?**
(domain: temple)
misrecognized as "the fee of Holiday Inn". (domain: hotel)

S2: The fee of Holiday Inn is ...

U3: **The fee of Horin-ji.** (domain: temple)
again misrecognized as "the fee of Holiday Inn". (domain: hotel)

S3 (bad): The fee of Holiday Inn is ...

S3 (good): Are you asking about hotel information?

U4: **No.**

S4: Would you like to return to the temple information service?

Figure 4: Example in which choice (III) should be selected

on an incorrect domain determination. It is possible for the system to restart from two utterances before (U1), after asking a confirmatory question (S4) about whether to return to it or not. After that, repetition of similar errors can also be avoided if the system prohibits transition to the hotel domain.

4 Domain Selection using Dialogue History

We constructed a classifier that selects the appropriate domains using various features, including dialogue histories. The selected domain candidates are based on: (I) the previous domain, (II) the domain in which the speech recognition results can be accepted with the highest recognition score, or (III) other domains. Here, we describe the features present in our domain selection method.

In order to not spoil the system's extensibility, an advantage of the distributed-type architecture, the features used in the domain selection should not depend on the specific domains. We categorize the features used into three categories listed below:

- Features representing the confidence with which the previous domain can be considered correct (Table 1)

- Features about a user's speech recognition result (Table 2)

Table 1: Features representing confidence in previous domain

P1:	number of affirmatives after entering the domain
P2:	number of negations after entering the domain
P3:	whether tasks have been completed in the domain (whether to enter "requesting detailed information" in database search task)
P4:	whether the domain appeared before
P5:	number of changed slots after entering the domain
P6:	number of turns after entering the domain
P7:	ratio of changed slots (= P5/P6)
P8:	ratio of user's negative answers (= P2/(P1 + P2))
P9:	ratio of user's negative answers in the domain (= P2/P6)
P10:	states in tasks

Table 2: Features of speech recognition results

R1:	best posteriori probability of the N-best candidates interpreted in the previous domain
R2:	best posteriori probability for the speech recognition result interpreted in the domain, that is the domain with the highest score
R3:	average of word's confidence scores for the best candidate of speech recognition results in the domain, that is, the domain with the highest score
R4:	difference of acoustic scores between candidates selected as (I) and (II)
R5:	ratio of averages of words' confidence scores between candidates selected as (I) and (II)

- Features representing the situation after domain selection (Table 3)

We can take into account the possibility that a current estimated domain might be erroneous, by using features representing the confidence in the previous domain. Each feature from P1 to P9 is defined to represent the determination of whether an estimated domain is reliable or not. Specifically, if there are many affirmative responses from a user or many changes of slot values during interactions in the domain, we regard the current domain as reliable. Conversely, the domain is not reliable if there are many negative answers from a user after entering the domain.

We also adopted the feature P10 to represent the state of the task, because the likelihood that a domain is changed depends on the state of the task. We classified the tasks that we treat into two categories using the following classifications first made by Araki et al. (1999). For a task categorized as a "slot-filling type", we defined the dialogue states as one of the following two types: "*not completed*", if not all of the requisite slots have been filled; and "*completed*", if all of the

Table 3: Features representing situations after domain selection

C1:	dialogue state after the domain selection after selecting previous domain
C2:	whether the interpretation of the user's utterance is negative in previous domain
C3:	number of changed slots after selecting previous domain
C4:	dialogue state after selecting the domain with the highest speech recognition score
C5:	whether the interpretation of the user's utterance is negative in the domain with the highest speech recognition score
C6:	number of changed slots after selecting the domain with the highest speech recognition score
C7:	number of common slots (name of place, here) changed after selecting the domain with the highest speech recognition score
C8:	whether the domain with the highest speech recognition score has appeared before

requisite slots have been filled. For a task categorized as a "database search type", we defined the dialogue states as one of the following two types: "*specifying query conditions*" and "*requesting detailed information*", which were defined in (Komatani et al., 2005a).

The features which represent the user's speech recognition result are listed in Table 2 and correspond to those used in conventional studies. R1 considers the N-best candidates of speech recognition results that can be interpreted in the previous domain. R2 and R3 represent information about a domain with the highest speech recognition score. R4 and R5 represent the comparisons between the above-mentioned two groups.

The features that characterize the situations after domain selection correspond to the information each expert returns to the central module after understanding the speech recognition results. These are listed in Table 3. Features listed from C1 to C3 represent a situation in which the previous domain (choice (I)) is selected. Those listed from C4 to C8 represent a situation in which a domain with the highest recognition score (choice (II)) is selected.

Note that these features listed here have survived after feature selection. A feature survives if the performance in the domain classification is degraded when it is removed from a feature set one by one. We had prepared 32 features for the initial set.

Table 4: Specifications of each domain

Name of domain	Class of task	# of vocab. in ASR	# of slots
restaurant	database search	1,562	10
hotel	database search	741	9
temple	database search	1,573	4
weather	slot filling	87	3
bus	slot filling	1,621	3
total	-	7,373	-

5 Experimental Evaluation

5.1 Implementation

We implemented a Japanese multi-domain spoken dialogue system with five domain experts: restaurant, hotel, temple, weather, and bus. Specifications of each expert are listed in Table 4. If there is any overlapping slot between the vocabularies of the domains, our architecture can treat it as a common slot, whose value is shared among the domains when interacting with the user. In our system, place names are treated as a common slot.

We adopted Julian as the grammar-based speech recognizer (Kawahara et al., 2004). The grammar rules for the speech recognizer can be automatically generated from those used in the language understanding modules in each domain. As a phonetic model, we adopted a 3000-states PTM triphone model (Kawahara et al., 2004).

5.2 Collecting Dialogue Data

We collected dialogue data using a baseline system from 10 subjects. First, the subjects used the system by following a sample scenario, to get accustomed to the timing to speak. They, then, used the system by following three scenarios, where at least three domains were mentioned, but neither an actual temple name nor domain was explicitly mentioned. One of the scenarios is shown in Figure 5. Domain selection in the baseline system was performed on the basis of the baseline method that will be mentioned in Section 5.4, in which α was set to 40 after preliminary experiments.

In the experiments, we obtained 2,205 utterances (221 per subject, 74 per dialogue). The accuracy of the speech recognition was 63.3%, which was rather low. This was because the subjects tended to repeat similar utterances even after misrecognition occurred due to out-of-grammar or out-of-vocabulary utterances. Another reason was that the dialogues for subjects with worse speech recognition results got longer, which resulted in an increase in the total number of misrecognition.

> Tomorrow or the day after, you are planning a sightseeing tour of Kyoto. Please find a shrine you want to visit in the Arashiyama area, and determine, after considering the weather, on which day you will visit the shrine. Please, ask for a temperature on the day of travel. Also find out how to go to the shrine, whether you can take a bus from the Kyoto station to there, when the shrine is closing, and what the entrance fee is.

Figure 5: Example of scenarios

5.3 Construction of the Domain Classifier

We used the data containing 2,205 utterances collected using the baseline system, to construct a domain classifier. We used C5.0 (Quinlan, 1993) as a classifier. The features used were described in Section 4. Reference labels were given by hand for each utterance based on the domains the system had selected and transcriptions of the user's utterances, as follows[2].

Label (I): When the correct domain for a user's utterance is the same as the domain in which the previous system's response was made.

Label (II): Except for case (I), when the correct domain for a user's utterance is the domain in which a speech recognition result in the N-best candidates with the highest score can be interpreted.

Label (III): Domains other than (I) and (II).

5.4 Evaluation of Domain Selection

We compared the performance of our domain selection with that of the baseline method described below.

Baseline method: A domain having an interpretation with the highest score in the N-best candidates of the speech recognition was selected, after adding α for the acoustic likelihood of the speech recognizer if the domain was the same as the previous one. We calculated the accuracies of domain selections for various α.

[2] Although only one of the authors assigned the labels, they could be easily assigned without ambiguity, since the labels were automatically defined as previously described. Thus, the annotator only needs to judge whether a user's request was about the same domain as the previous system's response or whether it was about a domain in the speech recognition result.

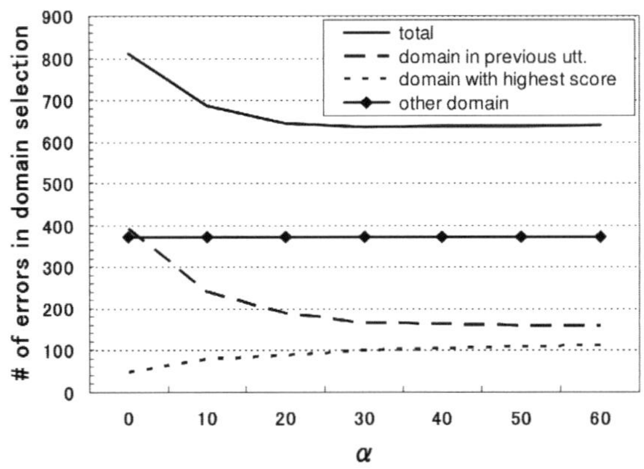

Figure 6: Accuracy of domain selection in the baseline method

Our method: A domain was selected based on our method. The performance was calculated with a 10-fold cross validation, that is, one tenth of the 2,205 utterances were used as test data, and the remainder was used as training data. The process was repeated 10 times, and the average of the accuracies was computed.

Accuracies for domain selection were calculated per utterance. When there were several domains that had the same score after domain selection, one domain was randomly selected among them as an output.

Figure 6 shows the number of errors for domain selection in the baseline method, categorized by their reference labels as α changed. As α increases, so does the system desire to keep the previous domain. A condition where $\alpha = 0$ corresponds to a method in which domains are selected based only on the speech recognition results, which implies that there are no constraints on keeping the current domain. As we can see in Figure 6, the number of errors whose reference labels are "a domain in the previous response (choice (I))" decreases as α gets larger. This is because incorrect domain transitions due to speech recognition errors were suppressed by the constraint to keep the domains. Conversely, we can see an increase in errors whose labels are "a domain with the highest speech recognition score (choice (II))". This is because there is too much incentive for keeping the previous domain. The smallest number of errors was 634 when $\alpha = 35$, and the error rate of domain selection was 28.8% (= 634/2205). There were 371 errors whose reference labels were neither "a domain in the previous response" nor "a domain with the highest speech recognition score", which cannot be detected even when α is changed based on conventional frameworks.

We also calculated the classification accuracy of our method. Table 5 shows the results as a confusion matrix. The left hand figure denotes the number of outputs in the baseline method, while the right hand figure denotes the number of outputs in our method. Correct outputs are in the diagonal cells, while the domain selection errors are in the off diagonal cells. Total accuracy increased by 5.3%, from 71.2% to 76.5%, and the number of errors in domain selection was reduced from 634 to 518, so the error reduction rate was 18.3% (= 116/634). There was no output in the baseline method for "other domains (III)", which is in the third column, because conventional frameworks have not taken this choice into consideration. Our method was able to detect this kind of error in 157 of 371 utterances, which allows us to prevent further errors from continuing. Moreover, accuracies for (I) and (II) did not get worse. Precision for (I) improved from 0.77 to 0.83, and the F-measure for (I) also improved from 0.83 to 0.86. Although recall for (II) got worse, its precision improved from 0.52 to 0.62, and consequently the F-measure for (II) improved slightly from 0.61 to 0.62. These results show that our method can detect choice (III), which was newly introduced, without degrading the existing classification accuracies.

The features that follow played an important role in the decision tree. The features that represent confidence in the previous domain appeared in the upper part of the tree, including "the number of affirmatives after entering the domain (P1)", "the ratio of user's negative answers in the domain (P9)", "the number of turns after entering the domain (P6)", and "the number of changed slots based on the user's utterances after entering the domain (P5)". These were also "whether a domain with the highest score has appeared before (C8)" and "whether an interpretation of a current user's utterance is negative (C2)".

6 Conclusion

We constructed a multi-domain spoken dialogue system using an extensible framework. Domain selection in conventional studies is based on either the domain based on the speech recognition

Table 5: Confusion matrix in domain selection (baseline / our method)

reference label \ output	in previous response (I)	with highest score (II)	others (III)	# total label (recall)
in previous response (I)	1289 / 1291	162 / 85	0 / 75	1451 (0.89 / 0.89)
with highest score (II)	84 / 99	299† / 256†	0 / 28	383 (0.74 / 0.62)
others (III)	293 / 172	78 / 42	0 / 157	371 (0 / 0.42)
total (precision)	1666 / 1562 (0.77) / (0.83)	539 / 383 (0.52) / (0.62)	0 / 260 (-) / (0.60)	2205 (0.712 / 0.765)

†: These include 17 errors because of random selection when there were several domains having the same highest scores.

results or the previous domain. However, we noticed that these conventional frameworks cannot cope with situations where neither of these domains is correct. Detection of such situations can prevent dialogues from staying in the incorrect domain, which allows our domain selection method to be robust against speech recognition errors. Furthermore, our domain selection method is also extensible. Our method does not select the domains directly, but, by categorizing them into three classes, it can cope with an increase or decrease in the number of domains. Based on the results of an experimental evaluation using 10 subjects, our method was able to reduce domain selection errors by 18.3% compared to a baseline method. This means our system is robust against speech recognition errors.

There are still some issues that could make our system more robust, and this is included in future work. For example, in this study, we adopted a grammar-based speech recognizer to construct each domain expert easily. However, other speech recognition methods could be used, such as a statistical language model. As well, multiple speech recognizers employing different domain-dependent grammars could be run in parallel. Thus, we need to investigate how to integrate these approaches into our framework, without destroying the extensibility.

References

Masahiro Araki, Kazunori Komatani, Taishi Hirata, and Shuji Doshita. 1999. A dialogue library for task-oriented spoken dialogue systems. In *Proc. IJCAI Workshop on Knowledge and Reasoning in Practical Dialogue Systems*, pages 1–7.

Tatsuya Kawahara, Akinobu Lee, Kazuya Takeda, Katsunobu Itou, and Kiyohiro Shikano. 2004. Recent progress of open-source LVCSR engine Julius and japanese model repository. In *Proc. Int'l Conf. Spoken Language Processing (ICSLP)*, pages 3069–3072.

Kazunori Komatani, Naoyuki Kanda, Tetsuya Ogata, and Hiroshi G. Okuno. 2005a. Contextual constraints based on dialogue models in database search task for spoken dialogue systems. In *Proc. European Conf. Speech Commun. & Tech. (EUROSPEECH)*, pages 877–880, Sep.

Kazunori Komatani, Shinichi Ueno, Tatsuya Kawahara, and Hiroshi G. Okuno. 2005b. User modeling in spoken dialogue systems to generate flexible guidance. *User Modeling and User-Adapted Interaction*, 15(1):169–183.

Lori Lamel, Sophie Rosset, Jean-Luc Gauvain, and Samir Bennacef. 1999. The LIMSI ARISE system for train travel information. In *IEEE Int'l Conf. Acoust., Speech & Signal Processing (ICASSP)*, pages 501–504, Phoenix, AZ.

Ian R. Lane and Tatsuya Kawahara. 2005. Utterance verification incorporating in-domain confidence and discourse coherence measures. In *Proc. European Conf. Speech Commun. & Tech. (EUROSPEECH)*, pages 421–424.

E. Levin, S. Narayanan, R. Pieraccini, K. Biatov, E. Bocchieri, G. Di Fabbrizio, W. Eckert, S. Lee, A. Pokrovsky, M. Rahim, P. Ruscitti, and M. Walker. 2000. The AT&T-DARPA communicator mixed-initiative spoken dialogue system. In *Proc. Int'l Conf. Spoken Language Processing (ICSLP)*.

Bor-shen Lin, Hsin-min Wang, and Lin-shan Lee. 2001. A distributed agent architecture for intelligent multi-domain spoken dialogue systems. *IEICE Trans. on Information and Systems*, E84-D(9):1217–1230, Sept.

Mikio Nakano, Yuji Hasegawa, Kazuhiro Nakadai, Takahiro Nakamura, Johane Takeuchi, Toyotaka Torii, Hiroshi Tsujino, Naoyuki Kanda, and Hiroshi G. Okuno. 2005. A two-layer model for behavior and dialogue planning in conversational service robots. In *2005 IEEE/RSJ International Conference on Intelligent Robots and Systems (IROS)*, pages 1542–1548.

Ian O'Neill, Philip Hanna, Xingkun Liu, and Michael McTear. 2004. Cross domain dialogue modelling: An object-based approach. In *Proc. Int'l Conf. Spoken Language Processing (ICSLP)*.

Botond Pakucs. 2003. Towards dynamic multi-domain dialogue processing. In *Proc. European*

Conf. Speech Commun. & Tech. (EUROSPEECH), pages 741–744.

Alexandros Potamianos and Hong-Kwang J. Kuo. 2000. Statistical recursive finite state machine parsing for speech understanding. In *Proc. Int'l Conf. Spoken Language Processing (ICSLP)*, volume 3, pages 510–513.

J. Ross Quinlan. 1993. *C4.5: Programs for Machine Learning.* Morgan Kaufmann, San Mateo, CA. http://www.rulequest.com/see5-info.html.

Antoine Raux and Maxine Eskenazi. 2004. Non-native users in the let's go!! spoken dialogue system: Dealing with linguistic mismatch. In *Proc. of HLT/NAACL.*

Ruben San-Segundo, Bryan Pellom, Wayne Ward, and Jose M. Pardo. 2000. Confidence measures for dialogue management in the CU communicator system. In *IEEE Int'l Conf. Acoust., Speech & Signal Processing (ICASSP).*

Building Effective Question Answering Characters

Anton Leuski and **Ronakkumar Patel** and **David Traum**
Institute for Creative Technologies
University of Southern California
Marina del Rey, CA, 90292, USA
leuski,ronakkup,traum@ict.usc.edu

Brandon Kennedy
Brandon.Kennedy@usma.edu

Abstract

In this paper, we describe methods for building and evaluation of limited domain question-answering characters. Several classification techniques are tested, including text classification using support vector machines, language-model based retrieval, and cross-language information retrieval techniques, with the latter having the highest success rate. We also evaluated the effect of speech recognition errors on performance with users, finding that retrieval is robust until recognition reaches over 50% WER.

1 Introduction

In the recent Hollywood movie "iRobot" set in 2035 the main character played by Will Smith is running an investigation into the death of an old friend. The detective finds a small device that projects a holographic image of the deceased. The device delivers a recorded message and responds to questions by playing back prerecorded answers. We are developing virtual characters with similar capabilities.

Our target applications for these virtual characters are training, education, and entertainment. For use in education, such a character should be able to deliver a message to the student on a specific topic. It also should be able to support a basic spoken dialog on the subject of the message, e.g., answer questions about the message topic and give additional explanations. For example, consider a student learning about an event in a virtual world. Lets say there is a small circus in a small town and someone has released all the animals from circus. A young student plays a role of a reporter to find out who caused this local havoc. She is out to interrogate a number of witnesses represented by the virtual characters. It is reasonable to expect that each conversation is going to be focused solely on the event of interest and the characters may refuse to talk about anything else. Each witness may have a particular and very narrow view into an aspect of the event, and the student's success would depend on what sort of questions she asks and to which character she addresses them.

Automatic question answering (QA) has been studied extensively in recent years. For example, there is a significant body of research done in the context of the QA track at the Text REtrieval Conference (TREC) (Voorhees, 2003). In contrast to the TREC scenario where both questions and answers are based on facts and the goal is to provide the most *relevant* answer, we focus the answer's *appropriateness*. In our example about an investigation, an evasive, misleading, or an "honestly" wrong answer from a witness character would be appropriate but might not be relevant. We try to highlight that distinction by talking about QA *characters* as opposed to QA systems or agents.

We expect that a typical simulation would contain quite a few QA characters. We also expect those characters to have a natural spoken language interaction with the student. Our technical requirements for such a QA character is that it should be able to understand spoken language. It should be robust to disfluencies in conversational English. It should be relatively fast, easy, and inexpensive to construct without the need for extensive domain knowledge and dialog management design expertise.

In this paper we describe a QA character by the name of *SGT Blackwell* who was originally designed to serve as an information kiosk at an army

Proceedings of the 7th SIGdial Workshop on Discourse and Dialogue, pages 18–27,
Sydney, July 2006.

conference (see Appendix C for a photograph of the system) (?). We have used SGT Blackwell to develop our technology for automatic answer selection, conversation management, and system integration. We are presently using this technology to create other QA characters.

In the next section we outline the SGT Blackwell system setup. In Section 3 we discuss the answer selection problem and consider three different algorithms: Support Vector Machines classifier (SVM), Language Model retrieval (LM), and Cross-lingual Language Model (CLM) retrieval. We present the results of off-line experiments showing that the CLM method performs significantly better than the other two techniques in Section 4. Section 5 describes a user study of the system that uses the CLM approach for answer selection. Our results show that the approach is very robust to deviations in wording from expected answers, and speech recognition errors. Finally, we summarize our results and outline some directions for future work in Section 6.

2 SGT Blackwell

A user talks to SGT Blackwell using a head-mounted close capture USB microphone. The user's speech is converted into text using an automatic speech recognition (ASR) system. We used the Sonic statistical speech recognition engine from the University of Colorado (Pellom, 2001) with acoustic and language models provided to us by our colleagues at the University of Southern California (Sethy et al., 2005). The answer selection module analyzes the speech recognition output and selects the appropriate response.

The character can deliver 83 spoken lines ranging from one word to a couple paragraphs long monologues. There are three kinds of lines SGT Blackwell can deliver: content, off-topic, and prompts. The 57 content-focused lines cover the identity of the character, its origin, its language and animation technology, its design goals, our university, the conference setup, and some miscellaneous topics, such as "what time is it?" and "where can I get my coffee?"

When SGT Blackwell detects a question that cannot be answered with one of the content-focused lines, it selects one out of 13 off-topic responses, (e.g., "I am not authorized to comment on that,") indicating that the user has ventured out of the allowed conversation domain. In the event that the user persists in asking the questions for which the character has no informative response, the system tries to nudge the user back into the conversation domain by suggesting a question for the user to ask: "You should ask me instead about my technology." There are 7 different prompts in the system.

One topic can be covered by multiple answers, so asking the same question again often results in a different response, introducing variety into the conversation. The user can specifically request alternative answers by asking something along the lines of "do you have anything to add?" or "anything else?" This is the first of two types command-like expressions SGT Blackwell understands. The second type is a direct request to repeat the previous response, e.g., "come again?" or "what was that?"

If the user persists on asking the same question over and over, the character might be forced to repeat its answer. It indicates that by preceding the answer with one of the four "pre-repeat" lines indicating that incoming response has been heard recently, e.g., "Let me say this again..."

3 Answer Selection

The main problem with answer selection is uncertainty. There are two sources of uncertainty in a spoken dialog system: the first is the complex nature of natural language (including ambiguity, vagueness, underspecification, indirect speech acts, etc.), making it difficult to compactly characterize the mapping from the text surface form to the meaning; and the second is the error-prone output from the speech recognition module. One possible approach to creating a language understanding system is to design a set of rules that select a response given an input text string (Weizenbaum, 1966). Because of uncertainty this approach can quickly become intractable for anything more than the most trivial tasks. An alternative is to create an automatic system that uses a set of training question-answer pairs to learn the appropriate question-answer matching algorithm (Chu-Carroll and Carpenter, 1999). We have tried three different methods for the latter approach, described in the rest of this section.

3.1 Text Classification

The answer selection problem can be viewed as a text classification task. We have a question text as input and a finite set of answers, – classes, – we build a system that selects the most appropriate class or set of classes for the question. Text classification has been studied in Information Retrieval (IR) for several decades (Lewis et al., 1996). The distinct properties of our setup are (1) a very small size of the text, – the questions are very short, and (2) the large number of classes, e.g, 60 responses for SGT Blackwell.

An answer defines a class. The questions corresponding to the answer are represented as vectors of term features. We tokenized the questions and stemmed using the KStem algorithm (Krovetz, 1993). We used a $tf \times idf$ weighting scheme to assign values to the individual term features (Allan et al., 1998). Finally, we trained a multi-class Support Vector Machines (SVM^{struct}) classifier with an exponential kernel (Tsochantaridis et al., 2004). We have also experimented with linear kernel function, various parameter values for the exponential kernel, and different term weighting schemes. The reported combination of the kernel and weighting scheme showed the best classification performance. Such an approach is well-known in the community and has been shown to work very well in numerous applications (Leuski, 2004). In fact, SVM is generally considered to be one of the best performing methods for text classification. We believe it provides us with a very strong baseline.

3.2 Answer Retrieval

The answer selection problem can also be viewed as an information retrieval problem. We have a set of answers which we can call documents in accordance with the information retrieval terminology. Let the question be the query, we compare the query to each document in the collection and return the most appropriate set of documents.

Presently the best performing IR techniques are based on the concept of Language Modeling (Ponte and Croft, 1997). The main strategy is to view both a query and a document as samples from some probability distributions over the words in the vocabulary (i.e., language models) and compare those distributions. These probability distributions rarely can be computed directly. The "art" of the field is to estimate the language models as accurately as possible given observed queries and documents.

Let $Q = q_1 ... q_m$ be the question that is received by the system, R_Q is the set of all the answers appropriate to that question, and $P(w|R_Q)$ is the probability that a word randomly sampled from an appropriate answer would be the word w. The language model of Q is the set of probabilities $P(w|R_Q)$ for every word in the vocabulary. If we knew the answer set for that question, we can easily estimate the model. Unfortunately, we only know the question and not the answer set R_Q. We approximate the language model with the conditional distribution:

$$P(w|R_Q) \approx P(w|Q) = \frac{P(w, q_1, ..., q_m)}{P(q_1, ..., q_m)} \qquad (1)$$

The next step is to calculate the joint probability of observing a string: $P(W) = P(w_1, ..., w_n)$. Different methods for estimating $P(W)$ have been suggested starting with simple unigram approach where the occurrences of individual words are assumed independent from each other: $P(W) = \prod_{i=1}^{n} P(w_i)$. Other approaches include Probabilistic Latent Semantic Indexing (PLSI) (Hoffman, 1999) and Latent Dirichlet Allocation (LDA) (Blei et al., 2003). The main goal of these different estimations is to model the interdependencies that exist in the text and make the estimation feasible given the finite amount of training data.

In this paper we adapt an approach suggested by Lavrenko (Lavrenko, 2004). He assumed that all the word dependencies are defined by a vector of possibly unknown parameters on the language model. Using the de Finetti's representation theorem and kernel-based probability estimations, he derived the following estimate for the query language model:

$$P(w|Q) = \frac{\sum_{s \in S} \pi_s(w) \prod_{i=1}^{m} \pi_s(q_i)}{\sum_s \prod_{i=1}^{m} \pi_s(q_i)} \qquad (2)$$

Here we sum over all training strings $s \in S$, where S is the set of training strings. $\pi_s(w)$ is the probability of observing word w in the string s, which can be estimated directly from the training data. Generally the unigram maximum likelihood estimator is used with some smoothing factor:

$$\pi_s(w) = \lambda_\pi \cdot \frac{\#(w, s)}{|s|} + (1 - \lambda_\pi) \cdot \frac{\sum_s \#(w, s)}{\sum_s |s|} \qquad (3)$$

where $\#(w, s)$ is the number of times word w appears in string s, $|s|$ is the length of the string s, we sum over all training strings $s \in S$, and the constant λ_π is the tunable parameter that can be determined from training data.

We know all the possible answers, so the answer language model $P(w|A)$ can be estimated from the data:

$$P(w|A) = \pi_A(w) \qquad (4)$$

3.3 Ranking criteria

To compare two language models we use the Kullback-Leibler divergence $D(p_q||p_a)$ defined as

$$D(p_q||p_a) = \sum_{w \in V} P(w|Q) \log \frac{P(w|Q)}{P(w|A)} \qquad (5)$$

which can be interpreted as the relative entropy between two distributions. Note that the Kullback-Leibler divergence is a dissimilarity measure, we use $-D(p_q||p_a)$ to rank the answers.

So far we have assumed that both questions and answers use the same vocabulary and have the same a priori language models. Clearly, it is not the case. For example, consider the following exchange: "what happened here?" – "well, maam, someone released the animals this morning." While the answer is likely to be very appropriate to the question, there is no word overlap between these sentences. This is an example of what is known in information retrieval as vocabulary mismatch between the query and the documents. In a typical retrieval scenario a query is assumed to look like a part of a document. We cannot make the same assumption about the questions because of the language rules: e.g., "what", "where", and "why" are likely to appear much more often in questions than in answers. Additionally, a typical document is much larger than any of our answers and has a higher probability to have words in common with the query. Finally, a typical retrieval scenario is totally context-free and a user is encouraged to specify her information need as accurately as possible. In a dialog, a portion of the information is assumed to be well-known to the participants and remains un-verbalized leading to sometimes brief questions and answers.

We believe this vocabulary mismatch to be so significant that we view the participants as speaking two different "languages": a language of questions and a language of answers. We will model the problem as a cross-lingual information task, where one has a query in one language and wishes to retrieve documents in another language. There are two ways we can solve it: we can translate the answers into the question language by building a representation for each answer using the question vocabulary or we can build question representations in the answer language.

3.4 Question domain

We create an answer representation in the question vocabulary by merging together all the training questions that are associated with the answer into one string: a pseudo-answer. We use equations 5, 2, 3, and 4 to compare and rank the pseudo-answers. Note that in equation 2 s iterates over the set of all pseudo-answers.

3.5 Answer domain

Let us look at the question language model $P(w|Q)$ again, but now we will take into account that w and Q are from different vocabularies and have potentially different distributions:

$$P(w|Q) = \frac{\sum_s \alpha_{A_s}(w) \prod_{i=1}^m \pi_{Q_s}(q_i)}{\sum_s \prod_{i=1}^m \pi_{Q_s}(q_i)} \qquad (6)$$

Here s iterates over the training set of question-answer pairs $\{Q_s, A_s\}$ and $\alpha_x(w)$ is the experimental probability distribution on the answer vocabulary given by the expression similar to equation 3:

$$\alpha_x(w) = \lambda_\alpha \frac{\#(w, x)}{|x|} + (1 - \lambda_\alpha) \frac{\sum_s \#(w, x)}{\sum_s |x|}$$

and the answer language model $P(w|A)$ can be estimated from the data as

$$P(w|A) = \alpha_A(w)$$

4 Algorithm comparison

We have a collection of questions for SGT Blackwell each linked to a set of appropriate responses. Our script writer defined the first question or two for each answer. We expanded the set by a) paraphrasing the initial questions and b) collecting questions from users by simulating the final system in a Wizard of Oz study (WOZ). There are 1,261 questions in the collection linked to 72 answers (57 content answers, 13 off-topic responses, and 2 command classes, see Section 2). For this study we considered all our off-topic responses equally appropriate to an off-topic question and we collapsed all the corresponding responses into one class. Thus we have 60 response classes.

We divided our collection of questions into training and testing subsets following the 10-fold cross-validation schema. The SVM system was trained to classify test questions into one of the 60 classes.

Both retrieval techniques produce a ranked list of candidate answers ordered by the $-D(p_q||p_a)$ score. We only select the answers with scores that exceed a given threshold $-D(p_q||p_a) > \tau$. If the resulting answer set is empty we classify the question as off-topic, i.e., set the candidate answer set contains to an off-topic response. We determine the language model smoothing parameters λ_s and the threshold τ on the training data.

We consider two statistics when measuring the performance of the classification. First, we measure its accuracy. For each test question the first response returned by the system, – the class from the SVM system or the top ranked candidate answer returned by either LM or CLM methods, – is considered to be correct if there is link between the question and the response. The accuracy is the proportion of correctly answered questions among all test questions.

The second statistic is precision. Both LM and CLM methods may return several candidate answers ranked by their scores. That way a user will get a different response if she repeats the question. For example, consider a scenario where the first response is incorrect. The user repeats her question and the system returns a correct response creating the impression that the QA character simply did not hear the user correctly the first time. We want to measure the quality of the ranked list of candidate answers or the proportion of appropriate answers among all the candidate answers, but we should also prefer the candidate sets that list all the correct answers before all the incorrect ones. A well-known IR technique is to compute average precision – for each position in the ranked list compute the proportion of correct answers among all preceding answers and average those values.

Table 1 shows the accuracy and average precision numbers for three answer selection methods on the SGT Blackwell data set. We observe a significant improvement in accuracy in the retrieval methods over the SVM technique. The differences shown are statistical significant by t-test with the cutoff set to 5% ($p < 0.05$).

We repeated out experiments on QA characters we are developing for another project. There we have 7 different characters with various number of responses. The primary difference with the SGT Blackwell data is that in the new scenario each question is assigned to one and only one answer. Table 2 shows the accuracy numbers for the answer selection techniques on those data sets. These performance numbers are generally lower than the corresponding numbers on the SGT Blackwell collection. We have not yet collected as many training questions as for SGT Blackwell. We observe that the retrieval approaches are more successful for problems with more answer classes and more training data. The table shows the percent improvement in classification accuracy for each LM-based approach over the SVM baseline. The asterisks indicate statistical significance using a t-test with the cutoff set to 5% ($p < 0.05$).

5 Effect of ASR

In the second set of experiments for this paper we studied the question of how robust the CLM answer selection technique in the SGT Blackwell system is to the disfluencies of normal conversational speech and errors of the speech recognition. We conducted a user study with people interviewing SGT Blackwell and analyzed the results. Because the original system was meant for one of three demo "reporters" to ask SGT Blackwell questions, specialized acoustic models were used to ensure the highest accuracy for these three (male) speakers. Consequently, for other speakers (especially female speakers), the error rate was much higher than for a standard recognizer. This allowed us to calculate the role of a variety of speech error rates on classifier performance.

For this experiment, we recruited 20 participants (14 male, 6 female, ages from 20 to 62) from our organization who were not members of this project. All participants spoke English fluently, however the range of their birth languages included English, Hindi, and Chinese.

After filling out a consent form, participants were "introduced" to SGT Blackwell, and demonstrated the proper technique for asking him questions (i.e., when and how to activate the microphone and how to adjust the microphone position.) Next, the participants were given a scenario

SVM	LM			CLM		
accuracy	accuracy	impr. SVM	avg. prec.	accuracy	impr. SVM	avg. prec.
53.13	57.80	8.78	63.88	61.99	16.67	65.24

Table 1: Comparison of three different algorithms for answer selection on SGT Blackwell data. Each performance number is given in percentages.

	number of questions	number of answers	SVM accuracy	LM		CLM	
				accuracy	impr. SVM	accuracy	impr. SVM
1	238	22	44.12	47.06	6.67*	47.90	8.57*
2	120	15	63.33	62.50	-1.32	64.17	1.32
3	150	23	42.67	44.00	3.12*	50.00	17.19*
4	108	18	42.59	44.44	4.35*	50.00	17.39*
5	149	33	32.21	41.35	28.37*	42.86	33.04*
6	39	8	69.23	58.97	-14.81*	66.67	-3.70
7	135	31	42.96	44.19	2.85	50.39	17.28*
average	134	21	48.16	48.93	1.60*	53.14	10.34*

Table 2: Comparison of three different algorithms for answer selection on 7 additional QA characters. The table shows the number of answers and the number of questions collected for each character. The accuracy and the improvement over the baseline numbers are given in percentages.

wherein the participant would act as a reporter about to interview SGT Blackwell. The participants were then given a list of 10 pre-designated questions to ask of SGT Blackwell. These questions were selected from the training data. They were then instructed to take a few minutes to write down an additional five questions to ask SGT Blackwell. Finally they were informed that after asking the fifteen written down questions, they would have to spontaneously generate and ask five additional questions for a total of 20 questions asked all together. Once the participants had written down their fifteen questions, they began the interview with SGT Blackwell. Upon the completion of the interview the participants were then asked a short series of survey questions by the experimenter about SGT Blackwell and the interview. Finally, participants were given an explanation of the study and then released. Voice recordings were made for each interview, as well as the raw data collected from the answer selection module and ASR. This is our first set of question answer pairs, we call it the ASR-QA set.

The voice recordings were later transcribed. We ran the transcriptions through the CLM answer selection module to generate answers for each question. This generated question and answer pairs based on how the system would have responded to the participant questions if the speech recognition was perfect. This is our second set of question answer pairs – the TRS-QA set. Appendix B shows a sample dialog between a participant and SGT Blackwell.

Next we used three human raters to judge the appropriateness of both sets. Using a scale of 1-6 (see Appendix A) each rater judged the appropriateness of SGT Blackwell's answers to the questions posed by the participants. We evaluated the agreement between raters by computing Cronbach's alpha score, which measures consistency in the data. The alpha score is 0.929 for TRS-QA and 0.916 for ASR-QA, which indicate high consistency among the raters.

The average appropriateness score for TRS-QA is 4.83 and 4.56 for ASR-QA. The difference in the scores is statistically significant according to t-test with the cutoff set to 5%. It may indicate that ASR quality has a significant impact on answer selection.

We computed the Word Error Rate (WER) between the transcribed question text and the ASR output. Thus each question-answer pair in the ASR-QA and TRS-QA data set has a WER score assigned to it. The average WER score is 37.33%.

We analyzed sensitivity of the appropriateness score to input errors. Figure 1a and 1b show plots of the cumulative average appropriateness score (CAA) as function of WER: for each WER value t we average appropriateness scores for all questions-answer pairs with WER score less than

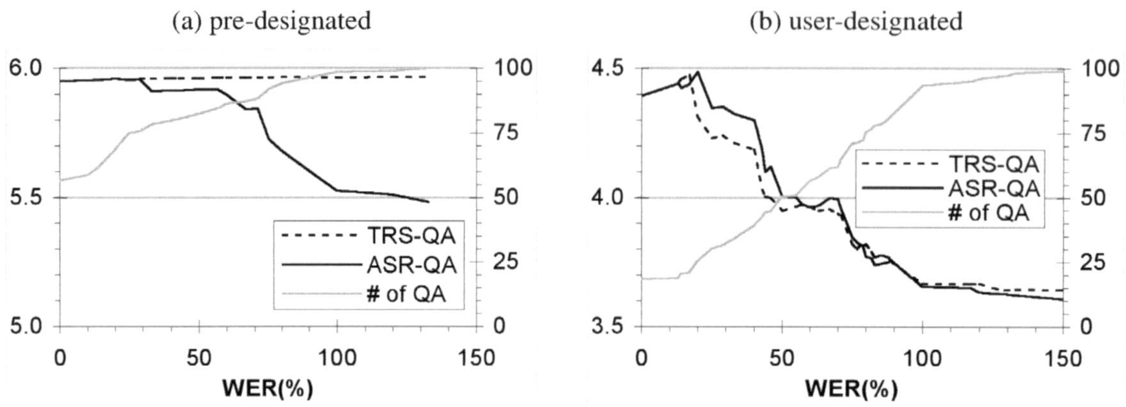

Figure 1: Shows the cumulative average appropriateness score (CAA) of (a) pre-designated and (b) user-designated question-answer pairs as function of the ASR's output word error rate. We show the scores for TRS-QA (dotted black line) and ASR-QA (solid black line). We also show the percentage of the question-answer pairs with the WER score below a given value ("# ofQA") as a gray line with the corresponding values on the right Y axis.

or equal to t.

$$CAA(t) = \frac{1}{|S|}\sum_{p\in S} A(p), S = \{p|WER(p) \leq t\}$$

where p is a question-answer pair, $A(p)$ is the appropriateness score for p, and $WER(p)$ is the WER score for p. It is the expected value of the appropriateness score if the ASR WER was at most t.

Both figures show the CAA values for TRS-QA (dotted black line) and ASR-QA (solid black line). Both figures also show the percentage of the question-answer pairs with the WER score below a given value, i.e., the cumulative distribution function (CDF) for the WER as a gray line with the corresponding values depicted on the right Y axis.

Figure 1a shows these plots for the pre-designated questions. The values of CAA for TRS-QA and ASR-QA are approximately the same between 0 and 60% WER. CAA for ASR-QA decreases for WER above 60% – as the input becomes more and more garbled, it becomes more difficult for the CLM module to select an appropriate answer. We confirmed this observation by calculating t-test scores at each WER value: the differences between $CAA(t)$ scores are statistically significant for $t > 60\%$. It indicates that until WER exceeds 60% there is no noticeable effect on the quality of answer selection, which means that our answer selection technique is robust relative to the quality of the input.

Figure 1b shows the same plots for the user-designated questions. Here the system has to deal with questions it has never seen before. CAA values decrease for both TRS-QA and ASR-QA as WER increases. Both ASR and CLM were trained on the same data set and out of vocabulary words that affect ASR performance, affect CLM performance as well.

6 Conclusions and future work

In this paper we presented a method for efficient construction of conversational virtual characters. These characters accept spoken input from a user, convert it to text, and select the appropriate response using statistical language modeling techniques from cross-lingual information retrieval. We showed that in this domain the performance of our answer selection approach significantly exceeds the performance of a state of the art text classification method. We also showed that our technique is very robust to the quality of the input and can be effectively used with existing speech recognition technology.

Preliminary failure analysis indicates a few directions for improving the system's quality. First, we should continue collecting more training data and extending the question sets.

Second, we could have the system generate a confidence score for its classification decisions. Then the answers with a low confidence score can be replaced with an answer that prompts the user to rephrase her question. The system would then use the original and the rephrased version to repeat the answer selection process.

Finally, we observed that a notable percent of misclassifications results from the user asking a question that has a strong context dependency on the previous answer or question. We are presently looking into incorporating this context information into the answer selection process.

Acknowledgments

The project or effort described here has been sponsored by the U.S. Army Research, Development, and Engineering Command (RDECOM). Statements and opinions expressed do not necessarily reflect the position or the policy of the United States Government, and no official endorsement should be inferred.

References

James Allan, Jamie Callan, W. Bruce Croft, Lisa Ballesteros, Donald Byrd, Russell Swan, and Jinxi Xu. 1998. Inquery does battle with TREC-6. In *Sixth Text REtrieval Conference (TREC-6)*, pages 169–206, Gaithersburg, Maryland, USA.

D. M. Blei, A. Y. Ng, and M. I. Jordan. 2003. Latent dirichlet allocation. *Journal of Machine Learning Research*, 3:993–1022.

Jennifer Chu-Carroll and Bob Carpenter. 1999. Vector-based natural language call routing. *Journal of Computational Linguistics*, 25(30):361–388.

Sudeep Gandhe, Andrew S. Gordon, and David Traum. 2006. Improving question-answering with linking dialogues. In *Proceedings of the 11th international conference on Intelligent user interfaces (IUI'06)*, pages 369–371, New York, NY, USA. ACM Press.

T. Hoffman. 1999. Probabilistic latent semantic indexing. In *Proceedings of the 22nd International ACM SIGIR Conference*, pages 50–57.

Robert Krovetz. 1993. Viewing morphology as an inference process. In *Proceedings of the 16th International ACM SIGIR Conference on Research and Development in Information Retrieval*, pages 191–202.

Victor Lavrenko. 2004. *A Generative Theory of Relevance*. Ph.D. thesis, University of Massachusetts at Amherst.

Anton Leuski. 2004. Email is a stage: discovering people roles from email archives. In *Proceedings of 27th annual international ACM SIGIR Conference on Research and Development in Information Retrieval (SIGIR'04)*, pages 502–503, Sheffield, United Kingdom. ACM Press. NY, USA.

David D. Lewis, Robert E. Schapire, James P. Callan, and Ron Papka. 1996. Training algorithms for linear text classifiers. In *Proceedings of the 19th International ACM SIGIR Conference on Research and Development in Information Retrieval*, pages 298–306, Zurich, Switzerland.

Bryan Pellom. 2001. Sonic: The university of colorado continuous speech recognizer. Technical Report TR-CSLR-2001-01, University of Colorado, Boulder, CO.

Jay M. Ponte and W. Bruce Croft. 1997. Text segmentation by topic. In *Proceedings of the First European Conference on Research and Advanced Technology for Digital Libraries*, pages 120–129.

Abhinav Sethy, Panayiotis Georgiou, and Shrikanth Narayanan. 2005. Building topic specific language models from webdata using competitive models. In *Proceedings of EUROSPEECH*, Lisbon, Portugal.

Ioannis Tsochantaridis, Thomas Hofmann, Thorsten Joachims, and Yasemin Altun. 2004. Support vector machine learning for interdependent and structured output spaces. In *Proceedings of the Twenty-first international conference on Machine learning*, Banff, Alberta, Canada.

Ellen M. Voorhees. 2003. Overview of the trec 2003 question answering track. In *Proceedings of The Twelfth Text Retrieval Conference*, pages 54–69.

Joseph Weizenbaum. 1966. Eliza–a computer program for the study of natural language communication between man and machine. *Communications of the ACM*, 9(1):36–45.

A Appropriateness grading

Gandhe and his colleagues (Gandhe et al., 2006) suggested the following grading scheme that we used in our user evaluation.

Grade	Description
1	Response is not related in any way the question
2	Response contains some discussion of people or objects mentioned in the question, but does not really address the question itself.
3	Response partially addresses the question, but little or no coherence between the question and response.
4	Response does mostly address the question, but with major problems in the coherence between question and response; seems like the response is really addressing a different question than the one asked.
5	Response does address the question, but the transition is somewhat awkward.
6	Response answers the question in a perfectly fluent manner.

Table 3: The question-answer appropriateness scale.

B Sample dialog

This section presents an example of a participant's dialog with SGT Blackwell. We only show spontaneous questions asked by the participant. Each of the participant's questions (called "Reporter" in this transcript) is followed by the ASR output of that line in brackets. That is what the answer selection module "heard." Note that ASR does make an occasional mistake and the answer selection is able to recover gracefully until the next to the last question, where the input was so garbled that only one correct word got through.

Reporter: Who created you (Who created you)

Blackwell: Tell you the truth, I have spent a lot of time with the smart folks at ICT, testing and tweaking. I am about ready to get out there and train with real soldiers. I am thinking first stop is going to be Fort Sill. But my ultimate goal is to get forward deployed...

Reporter: Why should we spend money on you (What should we spend money on you)

Blackwell: Why do you need me?! What you should be saying is "How did you get along without me?" I will show you how to be a leader, how to make critical decisions under stress... And I am glad to be here, because I can help. I know I can. Look... I have one mission: to make better soldiers, make better warfighters. And if I can ... can save one life... bring one loved one back to his family... Well, then, I am definitely worth it. You be the judge.

Reporter: What's your value (What's the value in)

Blackwell: I can do "Virtually" anything. I do mission rehearsals, Urban Combat training, language training - I speak Farsi, Pashtun and Arabic. "Mar Haba shabab! That means how are you in Arabic.

Reporter: Do you really work or is this just a demo (G. really worker is this just a demo)

Blackwell: Sorry. That's outside my AO.

Reporter: How could you be better (How could you be better)

Blackwell: Stop mumbling. Just kidding. I didn't get that.

Reporter: What do you wish you could do (When you wish you could do)

Blackwell: Career Army. That is what I am thinking. Just call me a lifer.

Reporter: What kind of people have you trained (What other people in the turn in)

Blackwell: I teach cultural awareness, function as a training mentor and can call in the full range of Joint fires and effects.

Reporter: What's the hardest part of your job (He was the hardest are you job)

Blackwell: I am not authorized to comment on that

Reporter: You have any virtual friends (The universal friends)

Blackwell: Sorry, I can't hear you

Reporter: Are you hard of hearing (Are you had a hearing)

Blackwell: I can't understand you.

C SGT Blackwell

Figure 2: A photograph of the SGT Blackwell system setup.

Interactive Question Answering and Constraint Relaxation in Spoken Dialogue Systems

Sebastian Varges
CSLI
Stanford University
Stanford, CA 94305, USA
varges@stanford.edu

Fuliang Weng, Heather Pon-Barry
Research and Technology Center
Robert Bosch Corporation
4009 Miranda Ave, Palo Alto, CA, USA
fuliang.weng, heather.pon-barry
@rtc.bosch.com

Abstract

We explore the relationship between question answering and constraint relaxation in spoken dialog systems. We develop dialogue strategies for selecting and presenting information succinctly. In particular, we describe methods for dealing with the results of database queries in information-seeking dialogs. Our goal is to structure the dialogue in such a way that the user is neither overwhelmed with information nor left uncertain as to how to refine the query further. We present evaluation results obtained from a user study involving 20 subjects in a restaurant selection task.

1 Introduction

Information presentation is an important issue when designing a dialogue system. This is especially true when the dialogue system is used in a high-stress environment, such as driving a vehicle, where the user is already occupied with the driving task. In this paper, we explore efficient dialogue strategies to address these issues, and present implemented knowledge management, dialogue and generation components that allow cognitively overloaded users – see (Weng et al., 2004), for example – to obtain information from the dialogue system in a natural way. We describe a knowledge manager that provides factual and ontological information, a content optimizer that regulates the amount of information, and a generator that realizes the selected content. The domain data is divided between domain-specific ontologies and a database back-end. We use the system for both restaurant selection and MP3 player tasks, and conducted experiments with 20 subjects.

There has been substantial previous work on information presentation in spoken dialogue systems. (Qu and Green, 2002) also present a constraint-based approach to cooperative information dialogue. Their experiments focus on over-constrained queries, whereas we also deal with underconstrained ones. Moreover, we guide the user through the dialogue by making suggestions about query refinements, which serve a similar rôle to the conditional responses of (Kruijff-Korbayova et al., 2002). (Hardy et al., 2004) describe a dialogue system that uses an error-correcting database manager for matching caller-provided information to database entries. This allows the system to select the most likely database entry, but, in contrast to our approach, does not modify constraints at a more abstract level. In contrast to all the approaches mentioned above, our language generator uses overgeneration and ranking techniques (Langkilde, 2000; Varges and Mellish, 2001). This facilitates variation and alignment with the user utterance.

A long-standing strand of research in NLP is in natural language access to databases (Androutsopoulos et al., 1995). It mainly focused on mapping natural language input to database queries. Our work can be seen as an extension of this work by embedding it into a dialogue system and allowing the user to refine and relax queries, and to engage in clarification dialogs. More recently, work on question answering (QA) is moving toward *interactive* question answering that gives the user a greater role in the QA process (HLT, forthcoming). QA systems mostly operate on free text whereas we use a relational database. (Thus, one needs to 'normalize' the information contained in free text to use our implemented system without further adaption.)

Proceedings of the 7th SIGdial Workshop on Discourse and Dialogue, pages 28–35,
Sydney, July 2006.

In the following section, we give an overview of the dialogue system. We then describe the knowledge management, dialogue and generation components in separate sections. In section 6 we present evaluation results obtained from a user study. This is followed by a discussion section and conclusions.

2 System architecture

Our dialogue system employs the following architecture: the output of a speech recognizer (Nuance, using a statistical language model) is analyzed by both a general-purpose statistical dependency parser and a (domain-specific) topic classifier. Parse trees and topic labels are matched by the 'dialogue move scripts' of the dialogue manager (Mirkovic and Cavedon, 2005; Weng et al., 2005). The scripts serve to license the instantiation of dialogue moves and their integration into the 'dialogue move tree.' The use of dialogue move scripts is motivated by the need to quickly tailor the system to new domains: only the scripts need to be adapted, not the underlying machinery implemented in Java. The scripts define short sequences of dialog moves, for example a command move ("play song X") may be followed either by a disambiguation question or a confirmation that the command will be executed. A dialogue proceeds by integrating such scripted sequences into the dialogue move tree, yielding a relatively 'flat' dialogue structure.

Query constraints are built by dialogue move scripts if the parse tree matches input patterns specified in the scripts. These query constraints are the starting point for the processing strategies described in this paper. The dialogue system is fully implemented and has been used in restaurant selection and MP3 player tasks. There are 41 task-independent, generic dialogue move scripts, 52 restaurant selection scripts and 89 MP3 player scripts. The examples in this paper are mostly taken from the restaurant selection task.

3 Knowledge and Content management

The Knowledge Manager (KM) controls access to domain knowledge that is structured according to domain-dependent ontologies. The KM makes use of OWL, a W3C standard, to represent the ontological relationships between domain entities. The knowledge base can be dynamically updated with new instances at any point. In a typical interaction, the Dialog Manager converts a user's query into a semantic frame (i.e., a set of semantic constraints) and sends this to the KM via the content optimizer. For example, in the Restaurant domain, a request such as "I want to find an inexpensive Japanese restaurant that takes reservations" results in the semantic frame below, where `Category` is a system property, and the other constraints are inherited properties of the Restaurant class:

```
(1) system:Category = restaurant:Restaurant
    restaurant:PriceLevel = 0-10
    restaurant:Cuisine = restaurant:japanese
    restaurant:Reservations = yes
```

In addition to the KM module, we employ a Content Optimization (CO) module that acts as an intermediary between dialogue and knowledge management during the query process. It receives semantic frames from the Dialogue Manager, revises the semantic frames if necessary (see below), and queries the Knowledge Manager.

The content optimizer also resolves remaining ambiguities in the interpretation of constraints. For example, if the user requests an unknown cuisine type, the otherwise often accurate classifier will not be able to provide a label since it operates under a closed-world assumption. In contrast, the general purpose parser may be able to provide an accurate syntactic analysis. However, the parse still needs to be interpreted by the content optimizer which has the domain-specific knowledge to determine that "Montenegrin restaurant" is a cuisine constraint rather than a service level constraint, for example. (See also section 7).

Depending on the items in the query result set, configurable properties, and (potentially) a user model, the CO module selects and performs an appropriate optimization strategy. To increase portability, the module contains a library of domain-independent strategies and makes use of external configuration files to tailor it to specific domains.

The CO module can modify constraints depending on the number of items in the result set, the system ontology, and information from a user model. Constraints can be relaxed, tightened, added or removed. The manner in which a constraint is modified depends on what kind of values it takes. For example, for the `Cuisine` constraint, values are related hierarchically (e.g., Chinese, Vietnamese, and Japanese are all subtypes of Asian), whereas `PriceLevel` values are linear (e.g., cheap, moderate, expensive), and `acceptsCreditCards` values are binary (e.g., accepted or not accepted).

If the original query returns no results, the content optimizer selects a constraint to modify and then attempts to relax the constraint value. If relaxation is impossible, it removes the constraint instead. Constraint relaxation makes use of the ontological relationships in the knowledge base. For example, relaxing a `Cuisine` constraint entails replacing it with its parent-concept in the domain ontology. Relaxing a linear constraint entails replacing the current value with an adjacent value. Relaxing a binary constraint entails replacing the current value with its opposite value.

Based on the ontological structures, the content optimizer also calculates statistics for every set of items returned by the knowledge manager in response to a user's query. If the result set is large, these figures can be used by the dialogue manager to give meaningful responses (e.g., in the MP3 domain, "There are 85 songs. Do you want to list them by a genre such as Rock, Pop, or Soul?").

The content optimizer also produces constraints that represent meta-knowledge about the ontology, for example, in response to a user input "What cuisines are there?":

```
(2) rdfs:subClassOf = restaurant:Cuisine
```

The processing modules described in the next sections can use meta-level constraints in similar ways to object-level constraints (see (1)).

4 Dialogue strategies for dealing with query results

In the following two sections, we describe how our dialogue and generation strategies tie in with the choices made by the content optimizer. Consider the following discourse-initial interaction for which the semantic frame (1) is constructed:

```
(3)
U: i want to find an inexpensive Japanese
   restaurant that takes reservations
S: I found 9 inexpensive Japanese
   restaurants that take reservations .
   Here are the first few :
S: GINZA JAPANESE RESTAURANT
S: OKI SUSHI CAFE
S: YONA SUSHI
S: Should I continue?
```

The example query has a relatively small result set which can be listed directly. This is not always the case, and thus we need dialogue strategies that deal with different result set sizes. For example, it does not seem sensible to produce "I found 2500 restaurants. Here are the first few: ...". At what point does it become unhelpful to list items? We do not have a final answer to this question – however, it is instructive that the (human) wizard in our data collection experiments did not start listing when the result set was larger than about 10 items. In the implemented system, we define dialogue strategies that are activated at adjustable thresholds.

Even if the result set is large and the system does not list any result items, the user may still want to see some example items returned for the query. This observation is based on comments by subjects in experimental dry-runs that in some cases it was difficult to obtain any query result at all. For example, speech recognition errors may make it difficult to build up a sufficiently complex query. In response to this, we always give some example items even if the result set is large. (An alternative would be to start listing items after a certain number of dialogue turns.) Furthermore, the system should encourage the user to refine the query by suggesting constraints that have not been used yet. This is done by maintaining a list of constraints in the generator that is used up as the dialogue progresses. This list is roughly ordered by how likely the constraint will be useful. For example, using cuisine type is suggested before proposing to ask for information about reservations or credit cards.

In our architecture, information flows from the CO module to the generator (see section 5) via the dialogue move scripts of the dialogue manager. These are conditioned on the size of the *final* result set and whether or not any modifications were performed. Table 1 summarizes the main dialogue strategies. These dialogue strategies represent implicit confirmations and are used if NLU has a high confidence in its analysis of the user utterance (see (Varges and Purver, 2006) for more details on our handling of robustness issues). Small result sets up to a threshold t_1 are listed in a single sentence. For medium-sized result sets up to a threshold t_2, the system starts listing immediately. For large result sets, the generator shows example items and makes suggestions as to what constraint the user may use next. If the CO module performs any constraint modification, the first, constraint realizing sentence of the system turns reflects the modification. ('NP-original' and 'NP-optimized' in table 1 are used for brevity and are explained in the next section.)

	$\lvert result_{final} \rvert$	mod	example realization	f_{exp}
s1a	0	no	I'm sorry but I found no restaurants on Mayfield Road that serve Mediterranean food.	0
s1b	0	yes	I'm sorry but I found no [NP-original]. I did not even find any [NP-optimized].	0
s2a	small: $> 0, < t_1$	no	There are 2 cheap Thai restaurants in Lincoln in my database: Thai Mee Choke and Noodle House.	61
s2b	small	yes	I found no cheap Greek restaurants that have a formal dress code but there are 4 inexpensive restaurants that serve other Mediterranean food and have a formal dress code in my database:	0
s3a	medium: $>= t_1, < t_2$	no	I found 9 restaurants with a two star rating and a formal dress code that are open for dinner and serve French food. Here are the first ones:	212
s3b	medium	yes	I found no [NP-original]. However, there are N [NP-optimized]. Here are the first few:	5
s4a	large: $>= t_2$	no	I found 258 restaurants on Page Mill Road, for example Maya Restaurant , Green Frog and Pho Hoa Restaurant. Would you like to try searching by cuisine?	300
s4b	large	yes	I found no [NP-original]. However, there are N [NP-optimized]. Would you like to try searching by [Constraint]?	16

Table 1: Dialogue strategies for dealing with query results (last column explained in sec. 6)

5 Generation

The generator produces turns that verbalize the constraints used in the database query. This is important since the system may miss or misinterpret constraints, leading to uncertainty for the user about what constraints were used. For this reason, a generic system response such as "I found 9 items." is not sufficient.

The input to the generator consists of the name of the dialogue move and the relevant instantiated nodes of the dialogue move tree. From the instantiated move nodes, the generator obtains the database query result including information about query modifications. The core of the generator is a set of productions[1] written in the Java Expert System Shell (Friedman-Hill, 2003). We follow the bottom-up generation approach for production systems described in (Varges, 2005) and perform mild overgeneration of candidate moves, followed by ranking. The highest-ranked candidate is selected for output.

Productions map individual database constraints to phrases such as "open for lunch", "within 3 miles" and "a formal dress code", and recursively combine them into NPs. This includes the use of coordination to produce "restaurants with a 5-star rating and a formal dress code", for example. The NPs are integrated into sentence templates, several of which can be combined to form an output candidate turn. For example, a constraint realizing template "I found no [NP-original] but there are [NUM] [NP-optimized] in my database" (see below for further explanation) can be combined with a follow-up sentence template such as "You could try to look for [NP-constraint-suggestion]".

The selection of which sentence template to use is determined by the dialogue move scripts. Typically, a move-realizing production produces several alternative sentences. On the other hand, the NP generation rules realize constraints regardless of the specific dialogue move at hand. This allows us to also use them for clarification questions based on constraints constructed from classifier information if the parser and associated parse-matching patterns fail; all that is required is a new sentence template, for example "Are you looking for [NP]?". We currently use 102 productions overall in the restaurant and MP3 domains, 38 of them to generate NPs that realize 19 possible input constraints (for both domains).

The decision of the CO module to relax or remove constraints also affects the generator: there are two sets of constraints, an 'original' one directly constructed from the user utterance, and an 'optimized' one used by the KM module to obtain the query result (see section 3). In case of constraint modifications, these two sets are not identical but often overlapping. To avoid generating separate sets of NPs independently for the two constraint sets, we assign unique indices to the constraints and hand the generator two index sets as targets of NP generation. We overgenerate NPs and check their index sets before integrating them into sentence templates.

[1]Productions are 'if-then' rules that operate over a shared knowledge base of facts.

turn	speaker	utterance
1.1	User	i need a restaurant with a five star food rating excellent service
1.2	System	I found 425 restaurants with a five star rating and excellent service , for example EL CAPITAN FISH MARKET , K-NINE COUNTRY CLUB , and KAISERHOF GERMAN AMERICAN . You could try to look for cuisine type .
1.3	User	which restaurants take reservations
1.4	System	I found 353 restaurants that have a five star rating , have excellent service and take reservations , for example GRAND CENTRAL CAFE , CHASIN CHICKEN , and CHON WOO RESTAURANT . Would you like to try searching by price ?

Figure 1: Example dialogue 1 from system evaluation using restaurant selection task

Ranking of candidate output moves is done by using a combination of factors. First, the ranker computes an alignment score for each candidate, based on its ngram-based overlap with the user utterance. For example, this allows us to prefer "restaurants that serve Chinese food" over "Chinese restaurants" if the user used a wording more similar to the first. We note that the Gricean Maxim of Brevity, applied to NLG in (Dale and Reiter, 1995), suggests a preference for the second, shorter realization. However, if the user thought it necessary to use "serves", maybe to avoid confusion of constraints or even to correct an earlier mislabeling, then the system should make it clear that it understood the user correctly by using those same words, thus preferring the first realization. Mild overgeneration combined with alignment also allows us to map the constraint `PriceLevel=0-10` in example (1) above to both "cheap" and "inexpensive", and use alignment to 'play back' the original word choice to the user. As these examples show, using alignment for ranking in NLG allows one to employ overgeneration techniques even in situations where no corpus data is available.[2]

Second, ranking uses a variation score to 'cycle' over sentence-level paraphrases. In the extreme case of repeated identical user inputs, the system simply chooses one paraphrase after the other, and starts over when all paraphrases have been used.

Third, we use an ngram filter based on bad examples ngrams, removing, for example, "Chinese cheap restaurants" but keeping "cheap Chinese restaurant." For generalization, we replace constraint realizations with semantic tags derived from the constraint names (except for the head noun), for example the trigram 'CUISINE PRICE restaurants'. An alternative is to use a more complex grammar formalism to prevent ungrammatical candidate moves.

[2]However, we do have wizard-of-oz data to inform the system design (see section 7).

6 Evaluation

We conducted experimental studies involving 20 subjects in a MP3 player task and 20 subjects in a restaurant selection task. In the following, we concentrate on the restaurant selection task because it is more challenging for constraint handling and information presentation.

Each subject in the restaurant selection task was given 9 scenario descriptions involving 3 constraints. Subjects were instructed to use their own words to find a fitting restaurant. We use a backend database of 2500 restaurants containing the following information for each restaurant: restaurant name, cuisine type, city and street names, service level, rating, whether they accept credit cards or reservations, price level, open hours, dress code, additional information (e.g. vegetarian food) and distance from current location. Some of these constraints have a fixed number of values (e.g. service level and dress code), whereas those taking named entities as values are obviously open-ended.

Figures 1 and 2 show two of the dialogues from the experiments. To exemplify the challenges the system is faced with, user turns are shown in the form of the output of the speech recognizer (we currently use the best ASR hypothesis as input to the parser). The task of the first dialogue (figure 1) was to find a restaurant that has the following constraints: [Reservations=yes, ServiceLevel:excellent, Rating=5star]. Despite some minor speech recognition errors, the system correctly builds a query for the two constraints provided by the user in (1.1.) and verbalizes these in (1.2) to show its understanding of the user input. It also gives some example items and makes a suggestion. This suggestion is not taken up by the user

turn	speaker	utterance
2.1	User	breakfast
2.2	System	Are you looking for a restaurant that is open for breakfast ?
2.3	User	yes located on bower street
2.4	System	I found 71 restaurants on bower street that serve breakfast , for example , SOUPLANTATION-TO-GO , RAMAYANI WESTWOOD , and , PHILLY WEST . You could try to look for cuisine type .
2.5	User	which
2.6	System	I'm sorry, I do not understand what you mean by: which
2.7	System	Please try rephrasing that.
2.8	User	casual dress
2.9	System	There are 51 restaurants on bower street that serve breakfast and have a casual dress code in my database , for example , BERTY'S , LABOTETEGA , and , JAVAN RESTAURANT . Would you like to try searching by price ?
2.10	User	british
2.11	System	I found no restaurants on bower street that serve british food , have a casual dress code and are open for breakfast but there are 8 restaurants on bower street that are open for breakfast , serve European food and have a casual dress code in my database . Here are the first few :
2.12	System	HOTEL BEL-AIR

Figure 2: Example dialogue 2 from system evaluation using restaurant selection task

– in fact, we find that suggestions are generally not taken up by the user. We believe this is due to the nature of the tasks, which specified exactly which criteria to match. On the other hand, in more open application scenarios, where users may not know what questions can be asked, suggestions may be useful. In (1.3) the user issues a sub-query that further constrains the result set. By again summarizing the constraints used, the system confirms in (1.4) that it has interpreted the new constraint as a revision of the previous query. The alternative is to start a new query, which would be wrong in this context.

The task of the second dialogue, figure 2, was to find a restaurant that meets the constraints [BusinessHours:breakfast, StreetName='bower street', DressCode=casual]. This user tends to give shorter, keyword-style input to the system (2.1, 2.8). In (2.3), the user reacts to a clarification question and adds another constraint which the system summarizes in (2.4). (2.5) is an ASR error which the system cannot handle (2.6, 2.7). The user constraint of (2.8) is correctly used to revise the query (2.9), but "british" (2.10) is another ASR error that leads to a cuisine constraint not intended in the scenario/by the user. This additional constraint yields an empty result set, from which the system recovers automatically by relaxing the hierarchically organized cuisine constraint to "European food". In (2.11) the system uses dialogue strategy s3b for medium-sized result sets with constraint modifications (section 4). The result of both dialogues is that all task constraints are met.

We conducted 20 experiments in the restaurant domain, 2 of which were restarted in the middle. Overall, 180 tasks were performed involving 1144 user turns and 1818 system turns. Two factors contributing to the higher number of system turns are a) some system turns are counted as two turns, such as 2.6, 2.7 in figure 2, and b) restaurants in longer enumerations of result items are counted as individual turns. On average, user utterances are significantly shorter than system utterances (4.9 words, standard deviation $\sigma = 3.82$ vs 15,4 words, $\sigma = 13.53$). This is a result of the 'constraint summaries' produced by the generator. The high standard deviation of the system utterances can be explained by the above-mentioned listing of individual result items (e.g. utterance (2.12) in figure 2).

We collected usage frequencies for the dialogue strategies presented in section 4: there was no occurrence of empty final result sets (strategy s1a/b) because the system successfully relaxed constraints if it initially obtained no results. Strategy s2a (small result sets without modifications) was used for 61 inputs, i.e. constraint sets constructed from user utterances. Strategy s3a/b (medium-sized result sets) was used for 217 times and required constraint relaxations in 5 cases. Strategy s4a/b (large result sets) was used for

316 inputs and required constraint relaxations in 16 cases. Thus, the system performed constraint modifications in 21 cases overall. All of these yielded non-empty final result sets. For 573 inputs, no modification was required. There were no empty final result set despite modifications.

On average, the generator produced 16 output candidates for inputs of two constraints, 160 candidates for typical inputs of 3 constraints and 320 candidates for 4 constraints. Such numbers can easily be handled by simply enumerating candidates and selecting the 'best' one.

Task completion in the experiments was high: the subjects met all target constraints in 170 out of 180 tasks, i.e. completion rate was 94.44%. An error analysis revealed that the reasons for only partially meeting the task constraints were varied. For example, in one case a rating constraint ("five stars") was interpreted as a service constraint by the system, which led to an empty result set. The system recovered from this error by means of constraint relaxation but the user seems to have been left with the impression that there are no restaurants of the desired kind with a five star rating.

7 Discussion

Based on wizard-of-oz data, the system alternates specific and unspecific refinement suggestions ("You could search by cuisines type" vs "Can you refine your query?"). Furthermore, many of the phrases used by the generator are taken from wizard-of-oz data too. In other words, the system, including the generator, is informed by empirical data but does not use this data directly (Reiter and Dale, 2000). This is in contrast to generation systems such as the ones described in (Langkilde, 2000) and (Varges and Mellish, 2001).

Considering the fact that the domain ontology and database schema are known in advance, it is tempting to make a closed world assumption in the generator (which could also help system development and testing). However, this seems too restrictive: assume, for example, that the user has asked for Montenegrin food, which is an unknown cuisine type, and that the statistical parser combined with the parse-matching patterns in the dialogue manager has labeled this correctly. The content optimization module will remove this constraint since there is no Montenegrin restaurant in the database. If we now want to generate "I did not find any restaurants that serve Montenegrin food ...", we do need to be able to use generation input that uses unseen attribute-value pairs. The price one has to pay for this increased robustness and flexibility is, of course, potentially bad output if NLU mislabels input words. More precisely, we find that if any one of the interpretation modules makes an open-world assumption, the generator has to do as well, at least as long as we want to verbalize the output of that module.

7.1 Future work

Our next application domain will be in-car navigation dialogues. This will involve dialogues that define target destinations and additional route planning constraints. It will allow us to explore the effects of cognitive constraints due to changing driving situations on dialogue behavior. The navigation domain may also affect the point of interaction between dialogue system and external devices: we may query a database to disambiguate proper names such as street names as soon as these are mentioned by the user, but start route planning only when all planning constraints are collected.

An option for addressing the current lack of a user model is to extend the work in (Cheng et al., 2004). They select the level of detail to be communicated to the user by representing the driver's route knowledge to avoid repeating known information.

Another avenue of future research is to automatically learn constraint relaxation strategies from (appropriately annotated) evaluation data. User modeling could be used to influence the order in which refinement suggestions are given and determine the thresholds for the information presentation moves described in section 4.

One could handle much larger numbers of generation candidates either by using packing (Langkilde, 2000) or by interleaving rule-based generation with corpus-based pruning (Varges and Mellish, 2001) if complexity should become an issue when doing overgeneration.

8 Conclusions

We described strategies for selecting and presenting succinct information in spoken dialogue systems. Verbalizing the constraints used in a query is crucial for robustness and usability – in fact, it can be regarded as a special case of providing feedback to the user about what the system has heard and understood (see (Traum, 1994), for example).

The specific strategies we use include 'backing-off' to more general constraints (by the system) or suggesting query refinements (to be requested explicitly by the user). Our architecture is configurable and open: it can be parametrized by empirically derived values and extended by new constraint handling techniques and dialogue strategies. Constraint relaxation techniques have widely been used before, of course, for example in syntactic and semantic processing. The presented paper details how these techniques, when used at the content determination level, tie in with dialogue and generation strategies. Although we focussed on the restaurant selection task, our approach is generic and can be applied across domains, provided that the dialogue centers around accessing and selecting potentially large amounts of factual information.

Acknowledgments This work is supported by the US government's NIST Advanced Technology Program. Collaborating partners are CSLI, Robert Bosch Corporation, VW America, and SRI International. We thank the many people involved in system design, development and evaluation, and the reviewers of this paper.

References

Ion Androutsopoulos, G.D. Ritchie, and P. Thanisch. 1995. Natural Language Interfaces to Databases – An Introduction. *Natural Language Engineering*, 1(1):29–81.

Hua Cheng, Lawrence Cavedon, and Robert Dale. 2004. Generating Navigation Information Based on the Driver's Route Knowledge. In *Proceedings of the Coling 2004 Workshop on Robust and Adaptive Information Processing for Mobile Speech Interfaces*, pages 31–38, Geneva, Switzerland.

Robert Dale and Ehud Reiter. 1995. Computational Interpretations of the Gricean Maxims in the Generation of Referring Expressions. *Cognitive Science*, 19:233–263.

Ernest Friedman-Hill. 2003. *Jess in Action: Java Rule-Based Systems*. Manning Publications.

Hilda Hardy, Tomek Strzalkowski, Min Wu, Cristian Ursu, Nick Webb, Alan Biermann, R. Bryce Inouye, and Ashley McKenzie. 2004. Data-driven strategies for an automated dialogue system. In *Proceedings of the 42nd Meeting of the Association for Computational Linguistics (ACL'04), Main Volume*, pages 71–78, Barcelona, Spain, July.

forthcoming. *Proceedings of the workshop on Interactive Question Answering at HLT-NAACL 2006*.

Ivana Kruijff-Korbayova, Elena Karagjosova, and Steffan Larsson. 2002. Enhancing collaboration with conditional responses in information-seeking dialogues. In *Proc. of 6th workshop on the semantics and pragmatics of dialogue (EDILOG-02)*.

Irene Langkilde. 2000. Forest-based Statistical Sentence Generation. In *Proc NAACL-00*, pages 170–177.

Danilo Mirkovic and Lawrence Cavedon. 2005. Practical Plug-and-Play Dialogue Management. In *Proceedings of the 6th Meeting of the Pacific Association for Computational Linguistics (PACLING)*.

Yan Qu and Nancy Green. 2002. A Constraint-based Approach for Cooperative Information-Seeking Dialogue. In *Proceedings of the International Workshop on Natural Language Generation (INLG-02)*.

Ehud Reiter and Robert Dale. 2000. *Building Applied Natural Language Generation Systems*. Cambridge University Press, Cambridge, UK.

David Traum. 1994. *A Computational Theory of Grounding in Natural Language Conversation*. Ph.D. thesis, Computer Science Dept., U. Rochester.

Sebastian Varges and Chris Mellish. 2001. Instance-based Natural Language Generation. In *Proc. NAACL-01*.

Sebastian Varges and Matthew Purver. 2006. Robust language analysis and generation for spoken dialogue systems (short paper). In *Proceedings of the ECAI 06 Workshop on the Development and Evaluation of Robust Spoken Dialogue Systems*.

Sebastian Varges. 2005. Chart generation using production systems (short paper). In *Proc. of 10th European Workshop On Natural Language Generation*.

Fuliang Weng, L. Cavedon, B. Raghunathan, D. Mirkovic, H. Cheng, H. Schmidt, H. Bratt, R. Mishra, S. Peters, L. Zhao, S. Upson, E. Shriberg, and C. Bergmann. 2004. Developing a conversational dialogue system for cognitively overloaded users. In *Proceedings of the International Congress on Intelligent Transportation Systems (ICSLP)*.

Fuliang Weng, Lawrence Cavedon, Badri Raghunathan, Danilo Mirkovic, Ben Bei, Heather Pon-Barry, Harry Bratt, Hua Cheng, Hauke Schmidt, Rohit Mishra, Brian Lathrop, Qi Zhang, Tobias Scheideck, Kui Xu, Tess Hand-Bender, Stanley Peters, Liz Shriberg, and Carsten Bergmann. 2005. A Flexible Conversational Dialog System for MP3 Player. In *demo session of HLT-EMNLP 2005*.

Invited Talk

Content Recognition in Dialogue

Jonathan Ginzburg
Dept of Computer Science
King's College London
The Strand London WC2R 2LS
email: ginzburg@dcs.kcl.ac.uk

Abstract

Deciding what is the content of an utterance in dialogue is a potentially tricky business: should it be an entity computed using (solely/primarily) grammatical information or is it determined by recognition of participant intention using domain level inference? The decisions one makes on this score play a crucial role in any model of the interaction involved in grounding an utterance. Integrating the clarificatory potential of an utterance into the grounding process transforms the issue of content recognition into a more concrete issue: grammatically determined content has markedly distinct clarificatory potential from content determined using domain level inference. This leads to a new challenge: how to integrate the two types of content in such a way that both enables their distinct clarificatory potential to be maintained and allows content determined by domain level inference to feature in grounding. My talk will address this challenge.

Proceedings of the 7th SIGdial Workshop on Discourse and Dialogue, page 36,
Sydney, July 2006.

Multidimensional Dialogue Management

Simon Keizer and Harry Bunt
Department of Language and Information Science
Faculty of Arts, Tilburg University
P.O. Box 90153, 5000 LE Tilburg, The Netherlands
{s.keizer,harry.bunt}@uvt.nl

Abstract

In this paper we present an approach to dialogue management that supports the generation of multifunctional utterances. It is based on the multidimensional dialogue act taxonomy and associated context model as developed in Dynamic Interpretation Theory (DIT). The multidimensional organisation of the taxonomy reflects that there are various aspects that dialogue participants have to deal with simultaneously during a dialogue. Besides performing some underlying task, a participant also has to pay attention to various aspects of the communication process itself, including social conventions.

Therefore, a multi-agent approach is proposed, in which for each of the dimensions in the taxonomy a specialised dialogue act agent is designed, dedicated to the generation of dialogue acts from that particular dimension. These dialogue act agents operate in parallel on the information state of the system. For a simplified version of the taxonomy, a dialogue manager has been implemented and integrated into an interactive QA system.

1 Introduction

During (task-oriented) dialogues, the participants have to deal with many different aspects of communication simultaneously. Besides some underlying task that may be performed through the dialogue, there are also various aspects of managing the communicative process itself, including dealing with social obligations. Therefore, speakers often use utterances that are multifunctional.

We will present an approach to dialogue management that accounts for the generation of multifunctional utterances. The approach is based on a dialogue theory involving a multidimensional dialogue act taxonomy and associated context model. In this theory, called Dynamic Interpretation Theory (DIT) (Bunt, 1996; Bunt, 2000a), a dialogue is modelled as a sequence of (sets of) *dialogue acts* operating on the *Information State* of each of the participants. The dialogue acts are organised in a taxonomy that is *multidimensional*, i.e., each utterance may involve dialogue acts of at most one type from each dimension. The taxonomy has dimensions for aspects like feedback, interaction-management, social obligations management and managing the underlying task.

In a dialogue system developed according to the principles of DIT, the information state is represented through a context model, containing all information considered relevant for interpreting user utterances an generating system utterances in terms of dialogue acts. Hence, given the multidimensionality of the taxonomy, the input interpretation components of the system result in several dialogue acts for each utterance, at most one from each of the dimensions. Using these recognised user dialogue acts, the context model is updated.

On the other hand, the ultimate task for a dialogue manager component of a dialogue system is deciding which dialogue acts to generate. So, again with the multidimensional organisation of the taxonomy in mind, we argue for a multi-agent approach, in which the dialogue act generation task is divided over several agents that operate in parallel on the context model, each agent being dedicated to the generation of dialogue acts from one particular dimension in the taxonomy. This leads to the design of a number of so-called *Di-*

Proceedings of the 7th SIGdial Workshop on Discourse and Dialogue, pages 37–45,
Sydney, July 2006.

alogue Act Agents, including e.g. a task-oriented agent, two feedback agents and an agent dealing with social obligations management.

The multi-agent approach to dialogue management itself is not new: JASPIS (Turunen and Hakulinen, 2000; Salonen et al., 2004) is a multi-agent framework for dialogue systems which allows for implementations of several agents for the same tasks, varying from input interpretation and output presentation to dialogue management. Depending on the situation, the agent that is most appropriate for a given task is selected in a process involving several so-called 'evaluators'. In JASPIS the multi-agent approach is aimed at flexibility and adaptiveness, while our approach focuses more on supporting multidimensionality in communication.

In a very general sense, our dialogue management approach follows an information state update approach similar to the dialogue managers that are developed within the TRINDI framework (Larsson and Traum, 2000). For example, Matheson et al. (2000) describe the implementation of a dialogue management system focusing in the concepts of grounding and discourse obligations.

An approach to dialogue management which identifies several simultaneous processes in the generation of system utterances, is described in (Stent, 2002). In this approach, which is implemented in the TRIPS dialogue system, dialogue contributions are generated through three core components operating independently and concurrently, using a system of conversation acts organised in several levels (Traum and Hinkelman, 1992).

Although there are apparent similarities between our approach and that of the TRINDI based dialogue managers and the TRIPS system, there are clear differences as well, which for an important part stem from the system of dialogue acts used and the way the information state is organised. More particularly, the way in which mechanisms for generating dialogue acts along multiple dimensions are modelled and implemented by means of multiple agents, differs from existing approaches.

This paper is organised as follows. First we explain the closely connected DIT notions of dialogue act and information state, and the multidimensional dialogue act taxonomy and context model (Sections 2 and 3). We then introduce the multi-agent approach to dialogue management (Section 4) and illustrate it by a description of the current implementation (Section 4.1). This implementation is carried out in the PARADIME project (PARallel Agent-based DIalogue Management Engine), which is part of the multiproject IMIX (Interactive Multimodal Information Extraction). The PARADIME dialogue manager is integrated into an interactive question-answering system that is developed in a collaboration between several projects participating in IMIX. The paper ends with conclusions and directions for future research (Section 5).

2 The DIT dialogue act taxonomy

Based on studies of a variety of dialogues from several dialogue corpora, a dialogue act taxonomy was developed consisting of a number of *dimensions*, reflecting the idea that during a dialogue, several aspects of the communication need to be attended to by the dialogue participants (Bunt, 2006). Even within single utterances, several aspects are dealt with at the same time, i.e., in general, utterances are *multifunctional*. The multidimensional organisation of the taxonomy supports this multifunctionality in that it allows several dialogue acts to be performed in each utterance, at most one from each dimension. The 11 dimensions of the taxonomy are listed below, with brief descriptions and/or specific dialogue act types in that dimension. For convenience, the dimensions are further grouped into so-called *layers*. At the top level are two layers: one for dialogue control acts and one coinciding with the task-domain dimension. Dialogue control is further divided into 3 layers: Feedback (2 dimensions), Interaction Management (7 dimensions), and a layer coinciding with the Social Obligations Management dimension.

- **Dialogue Control**
  - **Feedback**
    1. ***Auto-Feedback***: acts dealing with the speaker's processing of the addressee's utterances; contains positive and negative feedback acts on the levels of perception, interpretation, evaluation, and execution;
    2. ***Allo-Feedback***: acts dealing with the addressee's processing of the speaker's previous utterances (as viewed by the

speaker); contains positive and negative feedback-giving acts and feedback elicitation acts, both on the levels of perception, interpretation, evaluation, and execution;

- **Interaction management**
  3. ***Turn Management***: turn accepting, giving, grabbing, keeping;
  4. ***Time Management***: stalling, pausing;
  5. ***Dialogue Structuring***: opening, preclosing, closing, dialogue act announcement;
  6. ***Partner Processing Management***: completion, correct-misspeaking;
  7. ***Own Processing Management***: error signalling, retraction, self-correction;
  8. ***Contact Management***: contact check, contact indication;
  9. ***Topic Management***: topic introduction, closing, shift, shift announcement;
  10. ***Social Obligations Management***: salutation, self-introduction, gratitude, apology, valediction;

11. ***Task/domain***: acts that concern the specific underlying task and/or domain.

Formally, a dialogue act in DIT consists of a *Semantic Content* and a *Communicative Function*, the latter specifying how the information state of the addressee is to be updated with the former. A dialogue act in a particular dimension may have either a dimension-specific communicative function, or a *General-Purpose* communicative function with a *content type* (type of semantic content) in that dimension. The general-purpose communicative functions are hierarchically organised into the branches of Information Transfer and Action Discussion functions, Information Transfer consisting of information-seeking (e.g., WH-QUESTION, YN-QUESTION, CHECK) and information-providing functions (e.g., INFORM, WH-ANSWER, YN-ANSWER, CONFIRM), and Action Discussion consisting of commissives (e.g., OFFER, PROMISE, ACCEPT-REQUEST) and directives (e.g., INSTRUCT, REQUEST, DECLINE-OFFER).

The taxonomy is currently being evaluated in annotation experiments, involving several annotators and several dialogue corpora. Measuring inter-annotator agreement will give an indication of the usability of the taxonomy and annotation scheme. A first analysis has resulted in promising scores (Geertzen and Bunt, 2006).

3 The DIT context model

The Information State according to DIT is represented by a Context Model, containing all information considered relevant for interpreting user utterances (in terms of dialogue acts) and generating system dialogue acts (leading to system utterances). The contents of the context model are therefore very closely related to the dialogue act taxonomy; in (Bunt and Keizer, 2005) it is argued that the context model serves as a formal semantics for dialogue annotation, such an annotation being a kind of underspecified semantic representation. In combination with additional general conceptual considerations, the context model has evolved into a five component structure:

1. *Linguistic Context*: linguistic information about the utterances produced in the dialogue so far (a kind of 'extended dialogue history'); information about planned system dialogue acts (a 'dialogue future');

2. *Semantic Context*: contains current information about the task/domain, including assumptions about the dialogue partner's information;

3. *Cognitive Context*: the current processing states of both participants (on the levels of perception, interpretation, evaluation, and task execution), as viewed by the speaker;

4. *Physical and Perceptual Context*: the perceptible aspects of the communication process and the task/domain;

5. *Social Context*: current communicative pressures.

In Figure 1, a feature structure representation of the context model is given, in which the five components have been specified in further detail. This specification forms the basis for the dialogue manager being implemented in the PARADIME project.

The Linguistic Context contains features for storing dialogue acts performed in the dialogue so far: *user_utts* and *system_utts*, having lists of dialogue act representations as values. It also has features for information about topics and conversational structure: *topic_struct* and *conv_state* respectively. Finally, there are two features that

$$
\begin{bmatrix}
\mathit{LingContext}: & \begin{bmatrix} \mathit{user\_utts}: \langle \mathit{last\_user\_dial\_act} = \mathit{uda}_0, \mathit{uda}_{-1}, \mathit{uda}_{-2}, \ldots \rangle \\ \mathit{system\_utts}: \langle \mathit{last\_system\_dial\_act} = \mathit{sda}_0, \mathit{sda}_{-1}, \mathit{sda}_{-2}, \ldots \rangle \\ \mathit{topic\_struct}: \langle \mathit{referents} \rangle \\ \mathit{conv\_state}: \mathit{opening} | \mathit{body} | \mathit{closing} \\ \mathit{candidate\_dial\_acts}: \ldots \\ \mathit{dial\_acts\_pres}: \ldots \end{bmatrix} \\
\mathit{SemContext}: & \begin{bmatrix} \mathit{task\_progress}: \mathit{comp\_quest} | \mathit{quest\_qa} | \mathit{answ\_eval} | \mathit{user\_sat} \\ \mathit{user\_info\_needs}: \langle \ldots, \begin{bmatrix} \mathit{question}: \ldots \\ \mathit{satisfied}: + | - \end{bmatrix}, \ldots \rangle \\ \mathit{qa\_answers}: \langle \ldots \rangle \end{bmatrix} \\
\mathit{CogContext}: & \begin{bmatrix} \mathit{own\_proc\_state}: [\mathit{proc\_problem}: \mathit{perc} | \mathit{int} | \mathit{eval} | \mathit{exec} | \mathit{none}] \\ \mathit{partner\_proc\_state}: [\mathit{proc\_problem}: \mathit{perc} | \mathit{int} | \mathit{eval} | \mathit{exec} | \mathit{none}] \end{bmatrix} \\
\mathit{PhysPercContext}: & [\ ] \\
\mathit{SocContext}: & \begin{bmatrix} \mathit{reactive\_pressures}: \mathit{none} | \mathit{grt} | \mathit{apo} | \mathit{thk} | \mathit{valed} \\ \mathit{interactive\_pressures}: \mathit{none} | \mathit{grt} | \mathit{apo} | \mathit{thk} | \mathit{valed} \end{bmatrix}
\end{bmatrix}
$$

Figure 1: Feature structure representation of the PARADIME context model.

are related to the actual generation of system dialogue acts: *candidate_dial_acts* stores the dialogue acts generated by the dialogue act agents, and *dial_acts_pres* stores combined dialogue acts for presentation as system output; in Section 4, this will be discussed in more detail.

The specification of the Semantic Context is determined by the character of the task-domain. In Section 4.1, the task-domain of interactive question-answering on encyclopedic medical information will be discussed and from that, the specification of the Semantic Context for this purpose.

The Cognitive Context is specified by means of two features, representing the processing states of the system (*own_proc_state*) and the user (*partner_proc_state*). Both features indicate whether or not a processing problem was encountered, and if so, on which level of processing this happened.

The Physical and Perceptual Context is considered not to be relevant for the current system functionality.

The Social Context is specified in terms of reactive and interactive pressures; the corresponding features indicate whether or not a pressure exists and if so, for which social obligations management act it is a pressure (e.g., *reactive_pressures: grt* indicates a pressure for the system to respond to a greeting).

4 Dialogue Act Agents

Having discussed the dialogue act taxonomy and context model in DIT, we can now move on to the dialogue management approach that is also closely connected to these concepts. Having 11 dimensions of dialogue acts that each attend to a different aspect of communication, the generation of (system) dialogue acts should also happen along those 11 dimensions. As a dialogue act in a dimension can be selected independent of the other dimensions, we propose to divide the generation process over 11 *Dialogue Act Agents* operating in parallel on the information state of the system, each agent dedicated to generating dialogue acts from one particular dimension.

All of the dialogue act agents continuously monitor the context model and, if appropriate, try to generate candidate dialogue acts from their associated dimension. This process of monitoring and act generation is modelled through a triggering mechanism: if the information state satisfies the agent's *triggering conditions*, i.e., if there is a motivation for generating a dialogue act from a particular dimension, the corresponding agent gets triggered and tries to generate such a dialogue act. For example, the Auto-Feedback Agent gets triggered if a processing problem is recorded in the Own Processing State of the Cognitive Context. The agent then tries to generate a negative auto-feedback act in order to solve the processing problem (e.g., "Could you repeat that please?" or "Did you say 'five'?"). The Auto-Feedback Agent may also be triggered if it has reason to believe that the user is not certain that the system has understood a previous utterance, or simply if it has not given any explicit positive feedback for some time. In these cases of triggering, the agent tries to generate a positive auto-feedback act.

Hence the dialogue management process involves 11 dialogue act agents that operate in parallel on the context model. The dialogue acts generated by these agents are kept in the linguistic context as candidates. The selection of dialogue acts from different dimensions may happen independently, but for their order of performance and their combination, the relative importance of the dimensions at the given point in the dialogue has to be taken into account.

An additional *Evaluation Agent* monitors the list of candidates and decides which of them can be combined into a multifunctional system utterance for generation, and when. Some of the dialogue act candidates may have higher priority and should be generated at once, some may be stored for possible generation in later system turns, and some will already be implicitly performed through the performance of other candidate acts.

4.1 A dialogue manager for interactive QA

The current implementation of the PARADIME dialogue manager is integrated in an interactive question-answering (QA) system, as developed the IMIX multiproject. The task-domain at hand concerns encyclopedic information in the medical domain, in particular RSI (Repetitive Strain Injury). The system consists of several input analysis modules (ASR, syntactic analysis in terms of dependency trees, and shallow semantic tagging), three different QA modules that take self-contained domain questions and return answers retrieved from several electronic documents with text data in the medical domain, and a presentation module that takes the output from the dialogue manager, possibly combining any QA-answers to be presented, into a multimodal system utterance.

The dialogue management module provides support for more interactive, coherent dialogues, in which problems can be solved about both communication and question-answering processes. In interaction with the user, the system should play the role of an Information Search Assistant (ISA). This HCI metaphor posits that the dialogue system is not an expert on the domain, but merely assists the user in formulating questions about the domain that will lead to QA answers from the QA modules satisfying the user's information need (Akker et al., 2005).

In the context model for this dialogue manager, as represented by the feature structure in Figure 1, the Semantic Context has been further specified according to this underlying task. It contains a state variable for keeping track of the question-answering process (the feature *task_progress* with values to distinguish between the states of composing a self-contained question to send to the QA modules, waiting for the QA results in case a QA-question has been sent, evaluating the QA results, and discussing the results with the user). Also, the Semantic Context keeps a record of user's information need, by means of a list *user_info_needs* of 'information need' specifications in terms of semantic descriptions of domain *questions* and whether or not these info-needs have been *satisfied*.

For the first version of the dialogue manager we have defined a limited system functionality, and following from that a simplified version of the dialogue act taxonomy. This simplification means for example that Social Obligations Management (SOM) and the various dimensions in the Interaction Management (IM) layer have been merged into one dimension, following the observation that utterances with a SOM function very often also have a function in the IM layer, especially in human-computer dialogue; see (Bunt, 2000b). Also several general-purpose communicative functions have been clustered into single types. Table 1 lists the dialogue acts that the dialogue act recogniser is able to identify from user utterances.

GP	AUF	IM-SOM
YN-Question	PosAutoFb	Init-Open
WH-Question	NegAutoFb-Int	Init-Close
H-Question	NegAutoFb-Eval	
Request		
Instruct		

Table 1: Dialogue act types for interpreting user utterances.

Table 2 lists the dialogue acts that can be generated by the dialogue manager. Task-domain acts, generally answers to questions about the domain, consist of a general-purpose function (either a WH-ANSWER or UNC-WH-ANSWER; the latter reflecting that the speaker is uncertain about the information provided) with a semantic content containing the answers obtained from QA.

AUF	ALF	IM-SOM
NegAutoFb-Int	Fb-Elicit	React-Open
NegAutoFb-Exe		React-Close

Table 2: Dialogue act types for generating system responses.

The above considerations have resulted in a dialogue manager containing 4 dialogue act agents that operate on a slightly simplified version of the context model as specified in Figure 1: a *Task-Oriented (TO) Agent*, an *Auto-Feedback (AUF) Agent*, an *Allo-Feedback (AUF) Agent*, and an *Interaction Management and Social Obligations Management (IMSOM) Agent*. In addition, a (currently very simple) Evaluation Agent takes care of merging candidate dialogue acts for output presentation.

In Appendices A.1 and A.2, two example dialogues with the IMIX demonstrator system are given, showing system responses based on candidate dialogue acts from several dialogue act agents. The ISA metaphor is reflected in the system behaviour especially in the way in which QA results are presented to the user. In system utterances S2 and S3 in Appendix A.1, for example, the answer derived from the retrieved QA results is isolated from the first part of the system utterance, showing that the system has a neutral attitude concerning that answer.

4.1.1 The Task-Oriented Agent

The TO-Agent is dedicated to the generation of task-specific dialogue acts, which in practice involves ANSWER dialogue acts intended to satisfy the user's information need about the (medical) domain as indicated through his/her domain questions. The agent is triggered if a new information need is recorded in the Semantic Context. Once it has been triggered, the agent sends a request to the QA modules to come up with answers to a question asked, and evaluates the returned results. This evaluation is based on the number of answers received and the confidence scores of the answers; the confidence scores are also part of the output of the QA modules. If the QA did not find any answers or if the answers produced had confidence scores that were all below some *lower threshold*, the TO-Agent will not generate a dialogue act, but write an execution problem in the Own Processing State of the Cognitive Context (which causes the Auto-Feedback Agent to be triggered, see Section 4.1.2; an example can be found in the dialogue in Appendix A.2). Otherwise, the TO-Agent tries to make a selection from the QA answers to be presented to the user. If this selection will end up containing extremely many answers, again, an execution problem is written in the Cognitive Context (the question might have been too general to be answerable). Otherwise, the selection will be included in an answer dialogue act, either a WHANSWER, or UNCWHANSWER (uncertain wh-answer) in case the confidence scores are below some *upper threshold*. System utterances S1 and S2 in the example dialogue in Appendix A.1 illustrate this variation. The selection is narrowed down further if there is a subselection of answers with confidences that are significantly higher than those of the other answers in the selection.

4.1.2 The Auto-Feedback-Agent

The AUF-Agent is dedicated to the generation of auto-feedback dialogue acts. It currently produces negative auto-feedback acts on the levels of interpretation ("I didn't understand what you said"), evaluation ("I do not know what to do with this") and execution ("I could not find any answers to your question"). It may also decide to occasionally give positive feedback to the user. In the future, we would also like this agent to be able to generate articulate feedback acts, for example with the purpose of resolving reference resolution problems, as in:

U: what is RSI?

S: RSI (repetitive strain injury) is a pain or discomfort caused by small repetitive movements or tensions.

U: how can it be prevented?

S: do you mean 'RSI' or 'pain'?

4.1.3 The Allo-Feedback Agent

The *ALF-Agent* is dedicated to the generation of allo-feedback dialogue acts. For example, it may generate a feedback-elicitation act if it has reason to believe that the user might not be satisfied with an answer ("Was this an answer to your question?").

4.1.4 Interaction Management and Social Obligations Management Agent

The *IM-SOM Agent* is dedicated to the generation of social obligations management acts, possibly also functioning as dialogue structuring acts (opening resp. closing a dialogue through a greeting resp. valediction act). It gets triggered if communicative pressures are recorded in the Social Context. Currently it only responds to reactive pressures as caused by initiative greetings and goodbyes. The example dialogues in Appendices A.1 and A.2 illustrate this type of social behaviour.

4.1.5 Multi-agent Architecture of the Dialogue Manager

In Figure 2, a schematic overview of the multi-agent dialogue manager is given. It shows the context model with four components (for now, the Physical and Perceptual Context is considered to be of minor importance and is therefore ignored), a set of dialogue act agents, and an Evaluation Agent. The dialogue act agents each monitor the context model and may be triggered if certain conditions are satisfied. The TO-agent may also write to the Cognitive Context (particularly in case of execution problems). All agents may construct a dialogue act and write it in the candidates list in the Linguistic Context. The Evaluation Agent monitors this candidates list and selects one or more dialogue acts from it for presentation as system output. In this way, a control module may decide to take this combination of dialogue act for presentation *anytime* and send it to the presentation module to produce a system utterance.

With this initial design of a multi-agent dialogue manager, the system is able to support multifunctional output. The beginning of the example dialogue in Appendix A.1 illustrates multifunctionality, both in input interpretation and output generation. The system has recognised two dialogue acts in processing U1 (a conventional opening and a domain question), and S1 is generated on the basis of two candidate dialogue acts generated by different dialogue act agents: the IM-SOM-Agent (generated the react-greeting act) and the TO-Agent (generated the answer act).

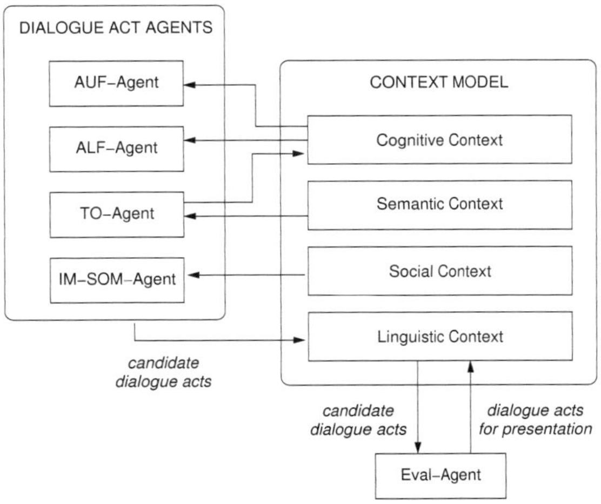

Figure 2: Architecture of the PARADIME dialogue manager.

5 Conclusions and future work

We have presented a dialogue management approach supporting the generation of multifunctional utterances. The approach builds on a dialogue theory involving a multidimensional dialogue act taxonomy and an information state on which the dialogue acts operate. Several dialogue acts from different dimensions are generated by dialogue act agents associated with these dimensions, and can thus be combined into multifunctional system utterances.

A first implementation of a dialogue manager following this multi-agent approach has been integrated into an interactive QA system and supports a limited range of dialogue acts from the DIT taxonomy, both for interpreting user utterances and generating system utterances. The system is able to attend to different aspects of the communication simultaneously, involving reactive social behaviour, answering domain questions and giving feedback about utterance interpretation and the question-answering process.

Future development will involve extending the range of dialogue acts to be covered by the dialogue manager, for a part following from the definition of an extended system functionality, and consequently, extending the set of dialogue act agents. This also has consequences for the Evaluation Agent: the process of combination and selection will be more complex if more dialogue act types can be expected and if the dialogue acts have a semantic content that is more than just a collection of QA-answers.

In terms of system functionality we aim at support for generating *articulate feedback*, i.e., feedback acts that are not merely signalling processing success or failure, but (in case of negative feedback) also contain a further specification of the processing problem at hand. For example, the system may have encountered problems in processing certain parts of a user utterance, or in resolving an anaphor; then it should be able to ask the user a specific question in order to obtain the information required to solve the processing problem (see the example in Section 4.1.2). The articulate feedback acts may also involve dealing with problems in the question answering process, where the system should be able to give specific instructions to the user to reformulate his question or give additional information about his information need.

In addition to supporting generation of articulate feedback acts, we also aim at dialogues between user and system that are more coherent and natural, i.e., the system should be more aware of the conversational structure, and display more refined social behaviour. Not only should it generate simple reactions to greetings, apologies, and goodbyes; it should also be able to generate initiative social acts, for example, apologies after several cases of negative auto-feedback.

The extended set of dialogue acts will also lead to an extended context model. Related to the context model and updating mechanism is ongoing work on belief dynamics and grounding in DIT (Morante and Bunt, 2005). The defined mechanisms for the creation, strengthening, adoption, and cancelling of beliefs and goals in the context model are currently being implemented in a demonstrator tool and will also be integrated in the information state update mechanism of the PARADIME dialogue manager.

Acknowledgement

This work is part of PARADIME (Parallel Agent-based Dialogue Management Engine), which is a subproject of IMIX (Interactive Multimodal Information eXtraction), a multiproject on Dutch language and speech technology, funded by the Dutch national science foundation (NWO).

We would like to thank the reviewers for their valuable comments, which really helped us to improve our paper.

References

R. op den Akker, H. Bunt, S. Keizer, and B. van Schooten. 2005. From question answering to spoken dialogue: Towards an information search assistant for interactive multimodal information extraction. In *Proceedings of the 9th European Conference on Speech Communication and Technology, Interspeech 2005*, pages 2793–2796.

H. Bunt and S. Keizer. 2005. Dialogue semantics links annotation to context representation. In *Joint TALK/AMI Workshop on Standards for Multimodal Dialogue Context*. `http://homepages.inf.ed.ac.uk/olemon/standcon-SOI.html`.

H. Bunt. 1996. Dynamic interpretation and dialogue theory. In M.M. Taylor, F. Néel, and D.G. Bouwhuis, editors, *The Structure of Multimodal Dialogue, Volume 2*, pages 139–166. John Benjamins.

H. Bunt. 2000a. Dialogue pragmatics and context specification. In H. Bunt and W. Black, editors, *Abduction, Belief and Context in Dialogue*, Studies in Computational Pragmatics, pages 81–150. John Benjamins.

H. Bunt. 2000b. Non-problems and social obligations in human-computer conversation. In *Proceedings of the 3rd International Workshop on Human-Computer Conversation*, pages 36–41.

H. Bunt. 2006. Dimensions in dialogue act annotation. In *Proceedings Fifth International Conference on Language Resources and Evaluation (LREC 2006)*.

J. Geertzen and H. Bunt. 2006. Measuring annotator agreement in a complex hierarchical dialogue act annotation scheme. In *7th SIGdial Workshop on Discourse and Dialogue*.

S. Larsson and D. Traum. 2000. Information state and dialogue management in the TRINDI dialogue move engine toolkit. *Natural Language Engineering: Special Issue on Best Practice in Spoken Language Dialogue Systems*, 6(3–4):323–340.

C. Matheson, M. Poesio, and D. Traum. 2000. Modeling grounding and discourse obligations using update rules. In *Proceedings of the First Annual Meeting of the North American Chapter of the ACL*.

R. Morante and H. Bunt. 2005. Micro-analysis of the belief transfer in information dialogues. In C. Gardent and B. Gaiffe, editors, *DIALOR'05 Proceedings of the Ninth Workshop on the Semantics and Pragmatics of Dialogue*, pages 135–138.

E.P. Salonen, M. Hartikainen, M. Turunen, J. Hakulinen, and J.A. Funk. 2004. Flexible dialogue management using distributed and dynamic dialogue control. In *Proceedings of ICSLP 2004*.

A.J. Stent. 2002. A conversation acts model for generating spoken dialogue contributions. *Computer*

Speech and Language, Special Issue on Spoken Language Generation, 16(3–4):313–352.

D.R. Traum and E.R. Hinkelman. 1992. Conversation acts in task-oriented spoken dialogue. *Computational Intelligence*, 3(8):575–599.

M. Turunen and J. Hakulinen. 2000. Jaspis – a framework for multilingual adaptive speech applications. In *Sixth International Conference on Spoken Language Processing (ICSLP 2000)*, volume 2, pages 719–722.

A Example dialogues

A.1 Example 1: greetings, answers and unc-answers

U1: hallo, ik wilde graag weten wat rsi is

(hello, I wanted to know what is rsi)

[INIT-OPEN; INDWHQ, *task-domain*]

S1: Hallo. Ik heb de volgende informatie gevonden:

(repetitive strain injury) Algemene benaming voor (blijvende) beschadigingen aan het lichaam ten gevolge van langdurige, eentonige werkzaamheden.

(Hello. I found the following information: ...)

[REACT-OPEN; ANSWER, *task-domain*]

U2: wat moet ik doen als ik denk rsi te hebben

(what should I do if I think I have RSI)

[WHQUESTION, *task-domain*]

S2: De volgende informatie levert mogelijk een antwoord op uw vraag:

Ontspanning betekent minder stress, minder aangespannen spieren en dus minder kans op RSI.

(The following information might answer your question: ...)

[UNCANSWER, *task-domain*]

U3: helpt ontspanning ook als ik eenmaal rsi heb

(does relaxing help as well, once I have RSI)

[YNQUESTION, *task-domain*]

S3: Ik heb de volgende informatie gevonden:

Behandelmethoden bij RSI Er zijn vele wegen die naar Rome leiden. Verbetering van de doorbloeding ...

(I found the following information: ...)

[ANSWER, *task-domain*]

U4: oke, bedankt

(okay, thanks)

[INIT-CLOSE]

S4: tot ziens. U kunt de buttons gebruiken om te stoppen of om een nieuwe dialoog te beginnen.

(Goodbye. You may use the buttons to stop or to start a new dialogue.)

[REACT-CLOSE]

A.2 Example 2: negative execution-feedback

U1: hallo!

(hello!)

[INIT-OPEN]

S1: Hallo. Stel uw vraag.

(Hello. Ask your question.)

[REACT-OPEN]

U2: wat kan ik als beelschermwerker tegen rugpijn doen

(what can I, a person working behind a computer screen all the time, do against pain in the back)

[WHQUESTION, *task-domain*]

S2: Ik heb helaas geen antwoorden kunnen vinden; probeer de vraag te herformuleren.

(Unfortunately, I could not find any answers; please try to reformulate the question)

[NEGAUTOFB-EXEC]

U3: wat kan men tegen rugpijn doen

(what can be done against pain in the back)

[WHQUESTION, *task-domain*]

S3: ik heb de volgende informatie gevonden:

Deze is afhankelijk van de oorzaak. Rugpijn die door instabiliteit of door tekortschietende spieren en banden ontstaat, kan behandeld worden met houdingscorrigerende oefentherapie.

(I found the following information: ...)

[ANSWER, *task-domain*]

U4: bedankt!

(thanks!)

[INIT-CLOSE]

S4: Tot ziens. U kunt de buttons gebruiken om te stoppen of om een nieuwe dialoog te beginnen.

(Goodbye. U may use the buttons to stop or to start a new dialogue.)

[REACT-CLOSE]

DRT Representation of Degrees of Belief

Yafa Al-Raheb
National Centre for Language Technology
Dublin City University
Ireland
yafa.alraheb@gmail.com

Abstract

This paper investigates the problems facing modelling agents' beliefs in Discourse Representation Theory (DRT) and presents a viable solution in the form of a dialogue-based DRT representation of beliefs. Integrating modelling dialogue interaction into DRT allows modelling agents' beliefs, intentions and mutual beliefs. Furthermore, it is one of the aims of the paper to account for the important notion of agents' varying degrees of belief in different contexts.[1]

1 Introduction

Heydrich et al. remark that 'serious description of natural dialogue seems to necessitate that we consider the mental states of the speakers involved' (1998).[2] This is a step that is by no means easy. It is the aim of this paper to integrate previous work on beliefs in DRT and dialogue theory in order to model the mental states of agents in dialogue.

The connection between beliefs, intentions and speech or dialogue acts has been noted in the literature. Stalnaker notes, for instance, that

> [i]f we understand contexts, and the speech acts made in contexts, in terms of the speaker's beliefs and intentions, we have a better chance of giving simpler and more transparent explanations of linguistic behaviour (Stalnaker 2002: 720).

The kind of agent beliefs we are concerned with here arises in dialogue interaction. The nature of interaction dictates that the strength or degree of belief varies depending on contextual factors. This can be seen from the following example:

(1) A: I want to make a booking for my wife.
B: Yeah.
A: What time is the Thailand flight on Monday?
B: It's at 2 pm.

In example (1) B does not necessarily need to believe the presupposition (given information) that A has a wife. For the purposes of the conversation, which is providing A with information, B can simply 'go along with' the presupposition and not have it as a member of his beliefs (i.e. his belief set) (Stalnaker 2002). Similarly, let us consider the following example, (2). The speaker is a customer in a clothing shop.

(2) S1: I want to buy a dress for my wife.
H1: Is it for a formal occasion?
S2: Yes.
H2: What is her favourite colour?
S3: She doesn't like red anymore.
H3: Does your wife like black?
S4: Yes

As the speaker, S, introduces the presupposition that he has a wife, the hearer, H, can come to the conclusion that S believes S has a wife. However, when the hearer comes to refer to S's wife, H does not necessarily have to believe S has a wife. H can simply go along with the information that the speaker has a wife and use this form of acceptance in H2 without committing to 'strongly believing' it. Indeed, the speaker may be buying a dress for his mistress rather than his wife. By going along

[1]I gratefully acknowledge support from Science Foundation Ireland grant 04/IN/I527.

[2]Other names for mental state used in the literature include 'information state', 'conversational score', and 'discourse context' (Larsson and Traum 2000).

Proceedings of the 7th SIGdial Workshop on Discourse and Dialogue, pages 46–53,
Sydney, July 2006.

with it, the hearer does not have to commit himself to believing that the speaker has a wife. What is more at stake than believing that the speaker indeed has a wife and not a mistress is closing the sale. Contrast examples (1) and (2) with example (3):

(3) S1: You have to get Peter's son a Christening present.
H1: Peter has a son?
S2: Sorry I forgot to mention that before.
H2: Ok, what sort of present should I get him?
S3: A toy would be nice.

In this context, the hearer, H, is required to commit more strongly to the presupposition of Peter having a son than simply going along with it, since H is being asked to buy a Christening present. The fact that H2 agrees to buying a present for Peter's son reflects more commitment to the presupposition than B shows in example (1). Considerations of this kind lead to the conclusion that different contexts call for varying strengths of beliefs and belief representation. We shall not attempt to describe all the contextual factors that can cause strength of belief to vary. The point is, rather, that we clearly need to model strength of belief and no current model of DRT incorporates such a proposal. This paper, thus, makes an original proposal for including a system for graded beliefs in the belief spaces (or sets) of both the speaker and the hearer.

Bearing this in mind, there is a need in DRT for representing the differing beliefs of agents in dialogue and their beliefs (meta-beliefs) about other agents' beliefs or mental state. By focussing on the intentions of speakers and hearers and inferring agents' intentions in making an utterance, the approach presented in this paper aims at fulfilling this need. It follows that, to have a 'full' theory of beliefs and to have an insight into the mental states of agents in dialogue (the speaker and the hearer), it is necessary to have a representation of agents' beliefs, degrees of beliefs, and the dialogue acts expressed by their utterances (Asher 1986). This is also in order to strengthen the link between utterances and agents' intentions in dialogue. The dialogue act or function performed by the utterance tells us something about the speaker's beliefs. Furthermore, what is also needed is a representation of beliefs that are shared between, or are common to, the two agents.

The question is: how can DRT best model beliefs? The following section, 2, outlines the problems facing modelling beliefs in DRT. Section 3 presents a graded view of agents' beliefs in dialogue as a solution to these problems. This is followed by a description of the relationship between belief and mutual belief, section 4, and then of the relationship between belief and dialogue acts, section 5.

2 Problems Facing Modelling Beliefs in DRT

According to Heydrich et al. (1998), paradigms of dynamic semantics (DRT, Situation Semantics and Dynamic Predicate Logic) face three obstacles in modelling dialogue. First, there is the problem of adapting the paradigm, originally made to model monological discourse, to the description of dialogue with different agents. The second problem is the description of mental states and the beliefs of the agents. The third problem is in explaining how the mental states are related to overt linguistic behaviour.

With respect to the first problem, DRT has gradually attempted to address problems of belief representation in dialogue. For example, in *Prolegomena*, Kamp introduces a simple model of verbal communication (Kamp 1990: 71), which consists of two agents, A and B, and their mental states K(A) and K(B). Later work by Kamp et al. (2005) introduces agent modelling for single-sentence discourse, namely the hearer. The treatment presented in this paper allows the representation of dialogue with different agents, thus, addressing the first problem identified by Heydrich et al. (1998).

With regard to the second problem, however, DRT has been primarily concerned with representing utterances containing propositional attitudes such as 'believe', rather than the beliefs and meta-beliefs of agents. Segmented-DRT (SDRT) has mainly focused on belief update and revision (Asher and Lascarides 2003). The treatment in this paper takes previous work on beliefs in dynamic semantics as a starting point and extends it to reach a richer representation of the interaction between mental states and the linguistic content of utterances. For example, both speaker and hearer mental states are represented and the beliefs and meta-beliefs of agents are reviewed after each utterance.

As a semantic theory, DRT tells us which discourse referents are needed in context. However, DRT does not deal with planning, nor with pragmatic aspects of contexts rendered through relating the current utterance to agents' intentions. Kamp et al.'s (2005) expansion of the original, also known as 'vanilla', DRT (Poesio and Traum 1997a), deal minimally with intentions. To deal with the third problem mentioned by Heydrich et al., Al-Raheb (2005) has already outlined a pragmatic extension to DRT that makes it appropriate for linking the current utterance and agents' intentions.

The present paper aims to show how that link can be strengthened through modelling agents' intentions and relating them to the dialogue acts communicated via utterances. In relation to this link, the significance of degrees of belief is explained in the following section.

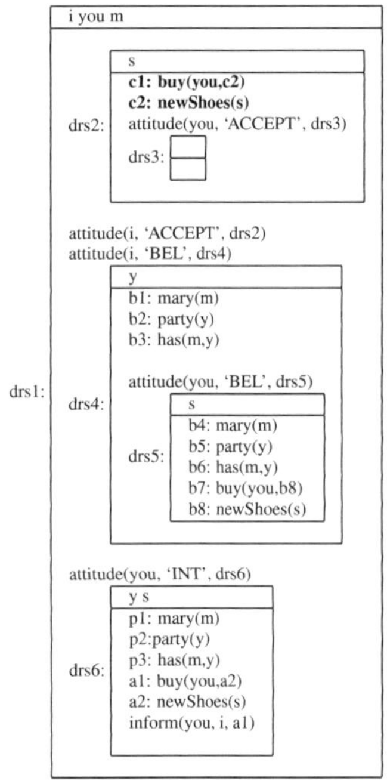

Figure 1: Hearer Recognition of S1

3 Degrees of Belief

To our knowledge, there is no account in DRT that accommodates strengths or degrees of belief of agents in dialogue. This section addresses this gap and proposes initially two strengths of belief involved in dialogue to be expanded in future research to include further degrees of belief. Modal expressions, including words such as 'possibly' and 'might', are evidence that there exist more degrees of belief than the ones discussed in this paper.

The beliefs of an agent are 'her model of how things are' (Traum 1994: 15). The notion of *belief* (or strong belief) is to be understood in relation to the agent: it is what the agent takes to be true. There is an important philosophical background to the discussion of 'belief' and 'knowledge'. It is outside the scope of this paper to review all the literature here. Quine (1960), Hintikka (1962), Lewis (1969, 1979), and Davidson (1983) are representative. The term 'belief' is understood in this paper to refer to propositions strongly held by the agent to be true and when making utterances relating to them, the speaker not only commits herself to their truth but also communicates to the hearer that she, the speaker, believes those proposition to be true.

Another degree of belief called *acceptance* is accounted for in this model. Acceptance consists of the agent's weakly believed propositions. The agent may be going along with what the speaker is saying or has acquired a new proposition based on the speaker's utterance which has not yet been confirmed into a stronger belief.

To illustrate what is meant by the distinction between belief and acceptance, let us look at:

(4) S1: I need to buy new shoes for Mary's party.
H1: Try Next on Henry Street.

The speaker tells the hearer that she has to buy new shoes for Mary's party. In this example, the hearer already (strongly) believes there is a party and he suggests a place where the speaker can buy them. Figure 1 demonstrates the hearer's mental state after hearing the speaker's utterance, S1. The hearer's mental state is represented by a Discourse Representation Structure (DRS), which contains three sub-DRSs, one for intention (referred to by 'attitude(you, 'INT', drs6)' and the label for the intention DRS, drs6), another for the belief DRS containing strong beliefs (referred to by 'attitude(i, 'BEL', drs4)' and the the label for the belief DRS, drs4), and finally the acceptance DRS containing weak beliefs (referred to by 'attitude(i, 'ACCEPT', drs2)' and the the label for the acceptance

DRS, drs2).[3]

If we change example (4) so that the hearer does not actually hold the belief that there is a party, as in:

(5) S1: I need to buy new shoes for Mary's party.
H1: I didn't realize Mary is throwing a party.
S2: Yeah she is. It's next Tuesday.
H2: You can probably buy them at Next.

The hearer does not necessarily need to strongly believe that Mary is throwing a party. He can 'go along with' or accept it and even suggest a place where the speaker can buy the shoes. The existence of a party does not affect the hearer personally or directly, i.e. he does not need to act on it. However, let us now consider the effect if we change the example again so that the hearer does not know about Mary's party, nor that he is required to buy new shoes, as in:

(6) S1: You need to buy new shoes for Mary's party.
H1: I didn't realize Mary is throwing a party.
S2: Yeah she is. You should try Next on Henry Street.
H2: I will.

This time, for the hearer to commit to buying something for a party (in H2) that he did not even know existed suggests a stronger degree of belief than that of 'going along with' the speaker having to buy it. The existence of the party affects the hearer personally and directly. Therefore, agreeing to buy new shoes justifies the inference that he believes rather than just accepts there is a party. This is what the paper describes as belief, or a strong degree of belief. Contrast Figure 1 with the figure representing the speaker's mental state after hearing H2 in example 6, Figure 2.

4 Beliefs and Mutual Beliefs

The treatment of beliefs that we are developing here requires an explicit account of how the belief spaces or DRSs of two agents can interact.

[3]Inside the agent's DRS, 'i' is used to refer to the agent and 'you' is used to refer to the other agent. Assertions are marked by 'a_n', presuppositions by 'p_n', believed information by 'b_n' and accepted information by 'c_n'.

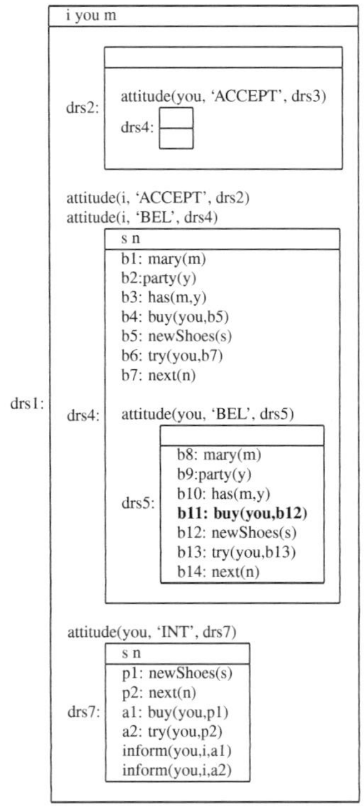

Figure 2: Speaker Recognition of H2

'Mutual belief', also referred to as 'mutual knowledge', is the term used by Traum (1994) among others, where a group of individuals may believe X, where X may or may not be true. Stalnaker's (2002) 'common belief' is comparable to what others call mutual belief. For X to be a mutual belief, it has to be accessible to a group; all believe X and all believe that all believe X, and all believe that all believe that all believe X.

In face-to-face communication, the hearer believes that the speaker believes what she, the speaker, is communicating. On the other hand, unless the hearer indicates doubt or objects to what the speaker is saying, the speaker assumes that the hearer believes what the speaker has said – which is consistent with expectations under Gricean cooperativeness assumptions (1989). The speaker also assumes that the hearer now has the belief that the speaker believes what she just said. This assumption is what leads to 'mutual' beliefs (Kamp 1990: 79).

However, mutual belief can be viewed as the *process* of establishing that the speaker and the hearer hold the same belief. One way in which this process may occur is when the speaker holds a belief and communicates that belief to the hearer.

This belief may then be adopted by the hearer who can provide feedback to the speaker that the information communicated has now acquired the status of belief in an ideal situation with a cooperative hearer. When both participants reach the conclusion that S bel(ieves) X, H bel X, H bel S bel X, and S bel H bel X, then mutual belief is established. The speaker in example (7) believes her neighbour is a weirdo. Whether the utterance is informative (new) or not depends on the context. In this example, (7), the speaker may not already have the belief that the hearer believes her neighbour is a weirdo.

(7) Speaker: My neighbour is such a weirdo.
Hearer: Yeah, he is. I saw him peeping through your window the other day.

However, after the hearer makes his utterance, the speaker can now strongly believe that the hearer believes her neighbour is a weirdo, that he believes she believes her neighbour is a weirdo, and now she believes he believes her neighbour is a weirdo. Figure 3 shows the level of nesting to accommodate the mutual belief that the speaker's neighbour is a weirdo. It is possible when this level of nesting is reached to have a separate DRS or space for mutual beliefs, called 'mutual belief DRS'. In which case, the propositions held in drs6, can now be removed from drs6 and added to the 'mutual belief DRS'. Figure 3 represents the speaker's mental state after the hearer makes his utterance. For the purposes of this example, the DRT represented in Figure 3 will mainly focus on the speaker's belief DRT.

Achieving mutual belief is immensely helped by dialogue acts. For example, when a hearer provides strong feedback about a new proposition (cf. drs7 in Figure 3), the speaker can come to believe the hearer believes that proposition. Section 5 shows the importance of considering the dialogue acts expressed by an assertion (new information) and their relationship to degrees of belief and strengthening of beliefs.

5 Beliefs and Dialogue Acts

When someone makes an assertion, they communicate not only information they assume to be new to the hearer, but also communicate to the hearer information about their own beliefs. In order to model beliefs in dialogue, it is necessary to understand what the representation of dialogue involves. A dialogue is 'a cooperative undertaking of agents engaged in developing and transforming their common situation', involving verbal and non-verbal action (Heydrich et al. 1998: 21). In a dialogue, utterances give rise to dialogue acts (cf. agents' intention DRSs in Figures 1, 2 and 3), named speech acts by some, and conversation acts by others (Traum 1994).

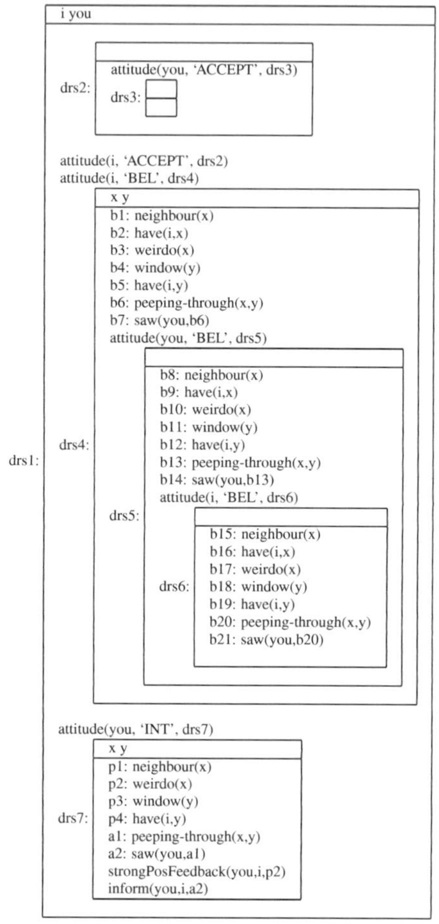

Figure 3: Speaker Recognition

One of the features of dialogue acts is how they affect the agents' mental states. As Traum points out, '... speech acts are a good link between the mental states of agents and purposeful communication' (Traum 1999: 30). Each agent in dialogue needs to have a representation of their beliefs and the other agent's beliefs or cognitive state in order for a dialogue act to be felicitous in Austin's and Searle's sense (Asher 1986). That is to say, dialogue acts depend on agents' beliefs for interpretation.

Each assertion made has one 'function' or more. For example, the function of a statement could be to make a claim about the world. Traum (1997) divides statements into 'assert', 're-assert', and 'inform'. 'Assert' is trying to 'change' the belief of the addressee. The result of assert is that the hearer now assumes that the speaker is trying to get the hearer to believe the assertion. 'Re-assert' can be used when participants try to verify old information, and not necessarily inform of something new. 'Inform' means that the speaker is trying to provide the hearer with information that the hearer did not have before. However, Traum does not go further to discuss cases where agents believe their utterances (Traum 1994: 14). It is one of the claims of this paper that agents in dialogue either strongly or weakly believe their utterances in order to be cooperative. It is possible to extend this approach in order to include cases where agents are purposefully deceitful. However, this is left for future research.

The adapted dialogue acts, or functions, in thiss paper's treatment of beliefs in DRT are mainly 'inform', 'change belief' and 'other'. 'Inform' is used to communicate new information to the hearer, whereas 'change belief' (or to use Poesio and Traum's (1997b) dialogue act term 'assert') is used to change the hearer's beliefs about some proposition. The importance of the representation introduced in section 3 in relation to dialogue acts transpires in allowing us to make the distinction between the dialogue acts 'inform' and 'change belief' ('assert'). To 'inform' the hearer of X, the speaker needs to have the belief in her beliefs that the hearer does not believe X, i.e. bel(S,¬ bel(H, X)). This is a constraint to making an informative utterance. Figure 4 shows the speaker's beliefs before making the utterance in example (8).

(8) The X-Files DVD is on sale on Amazon.

The speaker believes the hearer does not already believe that the X-Files DVD is on sale on Amazon, drs3. This is demonstrated by the missing propositions representing 'on sale on Amazon' 'onSale(x, b4)' and 'at(a)' from drs3 in Figure 4. On the other hand, to make a 'change belief' or an 'assert', the speaker would have reason to believe that the hearer believes something different or the opposite of what the speaker believes, bel(S, bel(H, ¬ X)). The DRT treatment of beliefs proposed in this paper allows us to reflect this in

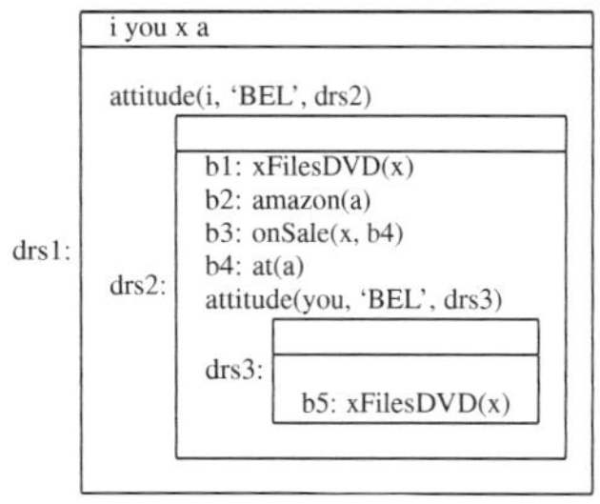

Figure 4: Inform: Speaker's utterance

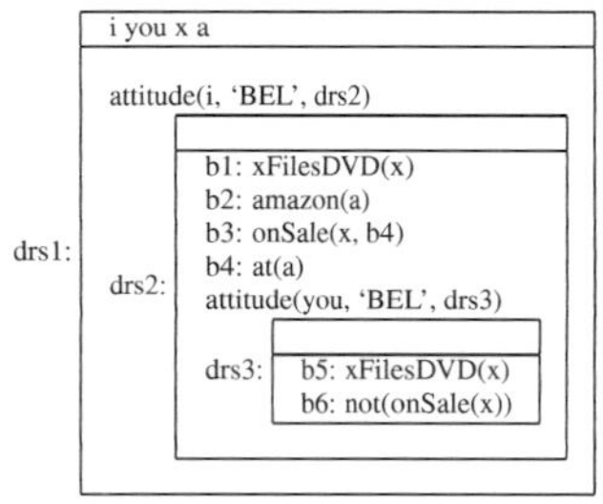

Figure 5: Change belief

Figure 5, drs3, in which the speaker believes the hearer believes the X-Files DVD is not on sale, 'not(onSale(x))'.

The category 'Other' embraces any dialogue act other than 'inform' and 'change belief', whose recognition involves the same process explained for others, e.g. 'suggest', 'clarify', and 'explain'.[4] The dialogue acts 'accept' and 'reject' come under the umbrella of feedback as they can be in response to, for instance, a 'suggest' dialogue act. The dialogue act 'clarify' is used when a hearer is having difficulty recognizing the speaker's utterance.[5] On the other hand, 'explain' is when the speaker responds to the hearer's clarification request and provides a clarifying utterance. The hearer can accept, believe, or reject that explanation. The dialogue act 'suggest' also instigates one of three reactions: the hearer can accept, believe or reject that suggestion and may provide feedback to indicate which is his reaction. It is of more interest to this paper to examine the effects of dialogue acts on the hearer's beliefs, and what dialogue acts suggest about the speaker's beliefs.

[4] It is possible for this category to be expanded to include more dialogue acts such as 'question', 'answer', 'self-correct' and 'offer'.

[5] Clarification is a form of feedback. 'I didn't hear what you said' is both 'feedback' act and an 'inform' (Schegloff et al. 1977).

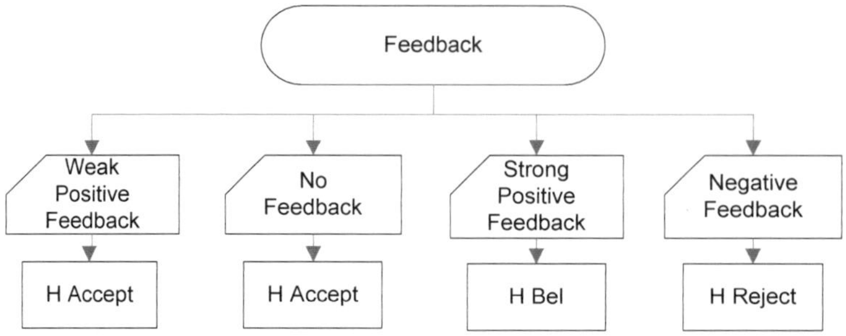

Figure 6: Feedback

5.1 Feedback and Agents' Beliefs

Traum (1994) suggests that when an assertion is made, the hearer has an obligation to produce an 'understanding act'. In general, acknowledgement is expected in Traum's treatment of speech acts. This means that when a hearer responds with 'okay', the hearer can be taken to be providing an acknowledgement and an acceptance. However, the hearer does not always provide feedback. Grounding often happens as a result of implicit rather than overt feedback and acknowledgement (Bunt 1995).[6] In fact, the treatment outlined in this paper maintains that the lack of feedback is to be considered a form of 'weak positive feedback', an extension to Dynamic Interpretation Theory's (DIT) positive feedback (Bunt 1995). The hearer does not object to the speaker's utterance by not providing feedback, since if the hearer did object, he would explicitly do so.

When the speaker makes an assertion, the hearer may indicate that the message has been received (weak positive feedback), example (9.b). Weak positive feedback may indicate understanding, continued attention, or acknowledgement, such as 'uh huh', and 'yeah' (Clark and Schaefer 1989). Another case of weak positive feedback is provided by example (9.a) where the hearer does not say anything. It is assumed that the hearer did not have any problems and has received the assertion, A. In the case of weak feedback, it can be argued that this represents the 'acceptance' of A.[7] Another response for the hearer is 'strong positive feedback' (another extension to DIT's positive feedback), where the hearer not only indicates reception of A, but also that she agrees that A (cf. drs7 Figure 3). This is where confirming adoption of new beliefs takes place, example (9.c). Rejecting A is another way of giving feedback, negative feedback, as in example (9.d).

(9) Speaker: Mary loves John.
a. Hearer:
b. Hearer: aha.
c. Hearer: I couldn't agree more!
d. Hearer: No, Mary is besotted with Tom!

There are also degrees of belief that can be expressed according to the speech act used, firm versus 'tentative'. Poesio and Traum pay less attention to 'the attitudes expressed by the acts' (Poesio and Traum 1998: 221). Unlike Traum's model, the effects of the dialogue acts' employed in agents' DRSs on agents' beliefs are considered in this paper. Figure 6 demonstrates the link between feedback dialogue acts and agents' beliefs.

6 Conclusion

As this paper has demonstrated, beliefs vary in strength according to context. Beliefs also change with the coming of new information. The DRT treatment discussed here allows for the representation of strong beliefs and weaker beliefs as well as changes to beliefs. Agents in a dialogue may form stronger beliefs as the dialogue progresses, requiring moving the content of their weaker beliefs to the stronger belief space.

In sum, there is no account in standard DRT that accommodates degrees of belief of agents in dialogue. This paper has addressed this omission and suggested two degrees of belief involved in dialogue, namely 'belief' and 'acceptance'. It is sug-

[6] Grounding is a term adapted by Traum (1994) from Clark and Schaefer's (1989) work on establishing common ground.

[7] This does not cancel cases where for social reasons, such as politeness, the hearer does not necessarily agree with the speaker, but does not wish to indicate it. The speaker can wrongly or rightly come to the conclusion that the hearer accepts the assertion.

gested that this is the initial step in representing agents' mental states in dialogue-oriented DRT. However, this paper does not deal with words which introduce more degrees of belief than the two addressed in the model. It would be interesting to see more degrees of belief represented in a DRT dialogue model of agents in future research. It is possible that such modal expressions can be arranged on a scale corresponding to degrees of belief (cf. Werth 1999). Moreover, this paper has accounted for agent's mutual beliefs and linked agents' beliefs and intentions to the dialogue acts of their utterances, in order to address the problematic nature of accounting for belief in DRT.

References

Al-Raheb, Y. 2005. *Speaker/Hearer Representation in a Discourse Representation Theory Model of Presupposition: A Computational-Linguistic Approach*. Phd. University of East Anglia.

Asher, N. 1986. 'Belief in Discourse Representation Theory'. *Journal of Philosophical Logic* 15, pp. 127–189.

Asher, N. and Lascarides, A. 2003. *Logics of Conversation*. Cambridge: Cambridge University Press.

Bunt, H. 1995. 'Dynamic Interpretation and Dialogue Theory'. In: M. Taylor, F. Neel, and D. Bouwhuis (Eds.). *The Structure of Multimodal Dialogue, Volume 2*. pp. 139–166. Amsterdam: John Benjamins 2000.

Clark, H. and Schaefer, E. 1989. 'Contributing to Discourse'. *Cognitive Science* 13, pp. 259–294.

Davidson, D. 1983. 'A Coherence Theory of Truth and Knowledge'. In: D. Henrich (Ed.). *Kant oder Hegel*. pp. 433–438. Stuttgart: Klett-Cotta Buchhandlung.

Gazdar, G. 1979. 'A Solution to the Projection Problem'. In: C. Oh and D. Dineen (Eds.). *Syntax and Semantics II: Presupposition*. New York: Academic Press.

Grice, P. 1989. *Studies in the Way of Words*. Cambridge, MA: Harvard University Press.

Heydrich, W., Kuhnlein, P., and Rieser, H. 1998. 'A DRT-Style Modelling of Agents' Mental States in Construction Dialogue'. In: *Proceedings of Workshop on Language Technology 13 (Twendial '98), TWLT*. Faculty of Informatics, the University of Twente: The Netherlands.

Hintikka, J. 1962. *Knowledge and Belief: An Introduction to the Logic of the Two Notions*. Mimeo: Indiana University Linguisitics Club.

Horton, D. and Hirst, G. 1988. 'Presuppositions as Beliefs'. In: *Coling-88: Proceedings of the 12th International Conference on Computational Linguistics*. pp. 255–260. Budapest: Hungary.

Kamp, H. 1990. 'Prolegomena to a Structural Account of Belief and Other Attitudes'. In: C. Anderson and J. Owens (Eds.). *Propositional Attitudes: The Role of Content in Logic, Language, and Mind*. Stanford, CA: CSLI Publications.

Kamp, H., van Genabith, J., and Reyle, U. 2005. *The Handbook of Logic*. Unpublished Manuscript. http://www.ims.uni-stuttgart.de/~hans/.

Larsson, S. and Traum, D. 2000. 'Information State and Dialogue Management in the TRINDI Dialogue Move Engine Toolkit'. In: *Natural Language Engineering. Special Issue on Spoken Language Dialogue System Engineering*. pp. 323–340.

Lewis, D. 1969. *Convention: A Philosophical Study*. Harvard University Press.

Lewis, D. 1979. 'Attitudes de dicto and de re'. *Philosophical Review* 88, pp. 513–543.

Poesio, M. and Traum, D. 1997a. 'Conversational Actions and Discourse Situations'. *Computational Intelligence* 13, pp. 309–347.

Poesio, M. and Traum, D. 1997b. 'Representing Conversation Acts in a Unified Semantic/Pragmatic Framework'. In: *Working Notes of AAAI Fall Symposium on Communicative Action in Humans and Machines*. pp. 67–74. Cambridge, MA: MIT Press.

Poesio, M. and Traum, D. 1998. 'Towards an Axiomatization of Dialogue Acts'. In: J. Hulstijn and A. Nijholt (Eds.). *Formal Semantics and Pragmatics of Dialogue, Proceedings of Twendial' 98*. pp. 207–221. Universiteit Twente: Enschede.

Quine, W. 1960. *Word and Object*. Cambridge MA: MIT Press.

Schegloff, E., Jefferson, G., and Sacks, H. 1977. 'The Preference for Self-Correction in the Organization of Repair in Conversation'. *Language* 53, pp. 361–382.

Stalnaker, R. 1974. 'Pragmatic Presupposition'. In: M. Munitz and P. Unger (Eds.). *Semantic and Philosophy*. pp. 197–214. New York: New York University Press.

Stalnaker, R. 1988. 'Belief Attribution and Context'. In: R. Grimm and D. Merrill (Eds.). *Contents of Thought. Proceedings of the 1985 Oberlin Colloquium in Philosophy*. pp. 140–156. Tucson State: The University of Arizona Press.

Stalnaker, R. 1999. *Context and Content*. Oxford: Oxford University Press.

Stalnaker, R. 2002. 'Common ground'. *Linguistics and Philosophy* 25(5-6), pp. 701–721.

Traum, D. 1994. *A Computational Theory of Grounding in Natural Language Conversation*. Phd and tr 545. Computer Science Department, Univeristy of Rochester.

Traum, D. 1997. 'Report on Multiparty Dialogue Sub-group on Forward-looking Communicative Function'. In: *Standards for Dialogue Coding in Natural Language Processing, Dagstuhl-Seminar Report no. 167*.

Traum, D. 1999. 'Computational Models of Grounding in Collaborative Systems'. In: *Working notes of AAAI Fall Symposium on Psychological Models of Communication*. pp. 124-131. North Falmouth, Massachusetts.

Werth, P. 1999. *Text Worlds: Representing Conceptual Space in Discourse*. New York: Longman.

Resolution of Referents Groupings in Practical Dialogues

Alexandre Denis, Guillaume Pitel, Matthieu Quignard
LORIA
BP239 F-54206 Vandoeuvre-lès-nancy, France
denis@loria.fr,pitel@loria.fr,quignard@loria.fr

Abstract

This paper presents an extension to the Reference Domain Theory (Salmon-Alt, 2001) in order to solve plural references. While this theory doesn't take plural reference into account in its original form, this paper shows how several entities can be grouped together by building a new domain and how they can be accessed later on. We introduce the notion of super-domain, representing the access structure to all the plural referents of a given type.

1 Introduction

In the course of a discourse or a dialogue, referents introduced separately could be referenced with a single plural expression (pronoun, demonstratives, etc.). The grouping of these referents may depend on many factors: it may be explicit if they were syntactically coordinated or juxtaposed or implicit if they just share common semantic features (Eschenbach *et al.*, 1989). Time is also an important factor while it may be difficult to group old mentioned referents with new ones. Because of this multiplicity of factors, choosing the right discursive grouping for a referential plural expression is ambiguous, and this ambiguity needs to be explicitly described.

We present a model of grouping based on reference domains theory (Salmon-Alt, 2001) that considers that a reference operation consists of extracting a referent in a domain. However the original theory barely takes into account plural reference. This paper shows how several entities can be grouped together by building a new domain and how they can be accessed later on. It introduces also the notion of super-domain D^+ that represents the access structure to all the plural referents of type D. This work is currently being implemented and evaluated in the MEDIA project of the EVALDA framework, a national french understanding evaluation campaign (Devillers, 2004).

2 Groupings of Referents

Several kinds of clues can specify that referents should be grouped together, or at least could be grouped together. These clues may occur at several language levels, from the noun phrase level to the rhetorical structure level. We have not explored in detail the different ways of groupings entities together in a discourse or dialogue. What is described here are just some of the phenomenon we got confronted with while developing a reference resolution module for a dialogue understanding system.

- **Explicit Coordination** - The most basic way to explicitly express the grouping of two or more referents is using a connector such as *and*, *or*, *as well as*, etc.
  "*Good afternoon, I would like to book a single room **and** a double room*"
- **Implicit Sentential Coordination** - An implicit coordination occurs when two or more referents of the same kind are present in one sentence, without explicit connector between them. "*Does the hotel de la gare have a restaurant, like the Holiday Inn?*"
- **Implicit Discursive Coordination** – Such a coordination occurs when several reference are evoked in separate sentences. The grouping must be done based on rhetorical structuring. Here we consider short pieces of dialogue, admitting only one level of implicit discursive coordination. *"I would like an hotel close to the sea... I also need an hotel downtown... And the hotels have to accept dogs."*

Proceedings of the 7th SIGdial Workshop on Discourse and Dialogue, pages 54–59,
Sydney, July 2006.

- **Repetitions/Specifications** – In some particular cases, groupings make explicit a previous expression. For instance "*Two rooms. A single room, a double room*".

3 Reference Domain Theory

We are willing to try a pragmatic approach to reference resolution in practical multimodal dialogues (Gieselman, 2004). For example we need to process frequent phenomena like ordinals for choosing in a list (discursive, or visual) or otherness when re-evoking old referents. Hence keeping the track of the way the context is modified when introducing a referent or referring, is mandatory. The Reference Domains Theory (Salmon-Alt, 2001) supposes that every act of reference is related to a certain domain of interpretation. It endorses the cognitive grammar concept of domain, defined as a cognitive structure presupposed by the semantics of the expression (Kumar et al., 2003). In other words, a referring expression has to be interpreted in a given domain, highlighting and specifying a particular referent in this domain. A reference domain is composed of a group of entities in the hearer's memory which can be discursive referents, visual objects, or concepts. It describes how each entity could be addressed through a referential expression.

This theory views the referring process as a dynamic extraction of a referent in a domain instead of a binding between two entities (Salmon-Alt, 2000). Hence doing a reference act consists in isolating a particular entity from other rejected candidates, amongst all the accessible entities composing the domain (Olson, 1970). This dynamic discrimination relies on projecting an access structure focusing the referent in the domain. The domain then becomes salient for further interpretations. The preferences for choosing a suitable domain are inspired from the Relevance theory (Sperber & Wilson, 1986) taking into account such focalization and salience.

Landragin & Romary (2003) have also studied the usage of reference domains in order to model a visual scene. The grouping factors for visual objects are those given by the Gestalt theory, proximity, similarity, and good continuation. Each perceptual groups or groups designated by a gesture could be the base domain for an extraction. Referential expressions work the same way either the domains are discursive, perceptual or gestural, they extract and highlight referents in these domains. See (Landragin et al., 2001) for a review of perceptual groupings.

4 Basic Type

A referential domain is defined by:

- a set of entities accessible through this domain (ground of domain),
- a description subsuming the description of all these entities (type of domain),
- a set of **access structures** to these entities.

For instance: "*the Ibis hotel* (h_1) *and the hotel Lafayette* (h_2)" forms a referential domain, whose type would be Hotel, and whose accessible entities would be h_1 and h_2, themselves defined as domains of type Hotel. These two hotels could be accessed later on by their names.

4.1 Access structures

We suppose that the distinction between the referents from the excluded alternatives requires highlighting a discrimination criterion opposing them. This criterion behaves like a **partition** of the accessible entities, grouping them together according to their similarities and their differences. A partition may have one of its parts **focused**. There are, at least, three kinds of discrimination criteria:

- **discrimination on description**. Entities can be discriminated by their type, their properties, or by the relations they have with other entities. For example the name of the hotels is a discrimination criterion in "*the Ibis hotel and the hotel Lafayette*".
- **discrimination on focus**. Entities can also be discriminated by the focus they have when they are mentioned in the discourse or designed by a gesture. For example, "*this room*" would select a focused referent in a domain, whereas "*the other room*" would select a non-focused one.
- **discrimination on time of occurrence**. Entities can finally be discriminated by their occurrence in the discourse. For example "*the second hotel*" would discriminate this hotel by its rank in the domain.

4.2 Classical resolution algorithm

Each activated domain belongs to list of domains ordered along their recentness (the referential space). The resolution algorithm consists of two phases:

1. Searching a suitable, preferred domain in the referential space when interpreting a referring expression. The suitability is defined by the minimal conditions the domain has to conform to in order to be the base of an interpretation (particular description, or presence of a particular access structure with focus or not). The main preference factor is the minimization of the access cost (recentness or salience), however other criteria like thematic structure could be taken into account and will be future work. Each domain is tested according to the constraints given by the referential expression. We allow several layers of constraints for each type of expression : if the stronger constraints are not met, then weaker constraints are tried.
2. Extracting a referent and restructuring the referential space, taking into account this extraction. It not only focuses the referent in its domain, but also moves the domain itself to a more recent place. When one referent acquires the focus, the alternative members of the same partition loose it.

This generic scheme is instantiated for each type of access modes (a modality plus an expression). For example a definite "*the N*" will search for a domain in which a particular entity of type "N" can be discriminated, and the restructuring consists in focalizing in this domain the referent found. See (Landragin & Romary, 2003) for a description of the different access modes.

The algorithm highlights the two types of ambiguities, domain or referent ambiguities, which occur when there is no preference available to make a choice between multiples entities in the first or the second phase. We guess that natural ambiguities should eventually be solved through the dialogue between the agents of the communication.

5 Super-Domains

In order to take groupings into account in the Reference Domains Theory, we introduce two constructs in our formal toolbox. Indeed, having only one kind of domain construct doesn't allow for a correct distinction between different referent statuses.

First we distinguish plural and simple domains. The simple domains D serve as bases for profiling, or highlighting, a **subpart**, or **related part** of a simple referent. For instance, if D = *Room*, then one can profile a *Price* from D. The plural domains D^* serve as either as a **generic base** or as a **plural representative** for profiling a simple domain D. A generic base is mandatory in our model to support the insertion of new extra-linguistic referents evoked with an indefinite construct (for instance "*I saw a black bird on the roof*"), while plural representatives are used for explicit groupings. A domain D^*_1 can also be profiled from a D^*_0, provided D^*_1 profiles a subset of the elements of D^*_0.

Second, we introduce the notion of **super-domain** D^+, from which a D^* can be profiled. The relations allowed between domains are represented on figure 1. A super-domain D^+ is the domain of all groupings D^*, including a special D^*_{all} grouping which is the representative of all evoked instances of a given category. This configuration is not intended to deal with long dialogues where several, trans-sentential groupings occur, and where older groupings may become out of access. Doing this would require a rhetorically driven structuring of the D^*_{all}.

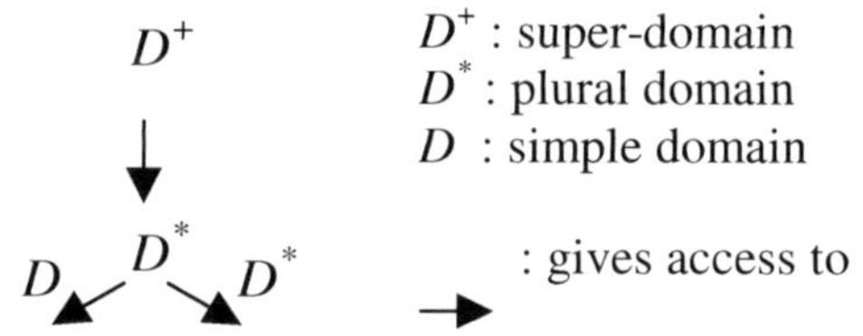

Figure 1: Access structure of Reference Domains

As Reference Domain Theory is primarily targeted toward extra-linguistic referents occurring in practical dialogue, the construction of the domain trees, representing the supposed structuring of referents accessibility, is based on ontology. As a consequence, for each "natural" type and each subtype (for instance *Room∧Single*), a domain tree is potentially created (actually, one can easily imagine how this creation may be driven 'on-demand').

Another evolution from the initial Reference Domain Theory is the possibility to focalize several items of a partition. Indeed, since the resolution algorithm can focalize a whole plural domain, all elements of this domain must be focalized in all the plural domains they occur in.

In order to refer to plural entities the idea is to build plural domains dynamically : when some sentence-level grouping, either implicit or explicit occurs or when a plural extra-linguistic referent is evoked, a D^* is created and focussed in D^+, with each of its components as children, when possible (that is, when each component is described). When new extra-linguistic referents (singular or plural) are evoked, they are individually profiled under the D^*_{all} corresponding to their types (that is, their "natural" type, and all the subtypes they are eligible to).

In short, for all referents of type *D*:

- they become subdomains of D^*_{all}
- if they are plural referents, they also build up a focalized subdomain of D^+
- all the referents of a given type are then grouped together under a new focalized subdomain of D^+.

Figure 2 illustrates the state of the $Hotel^+$ domain tree after a scenario with three dialogue acts, the first one introducing $Hotel_1$, the second one inserting a grouping of $Hotel_2$ and $Hotel_3$. and the third one referring to it.

U_1: The Ibis Hotel ($Hotel_1$) is too expensive

S_1: Maybe the Hotel Lafayette ($Hotel_2$) or the Hotel de la cloche ($Hotel_3$)

U_2: Those hotels are too far from the airport.

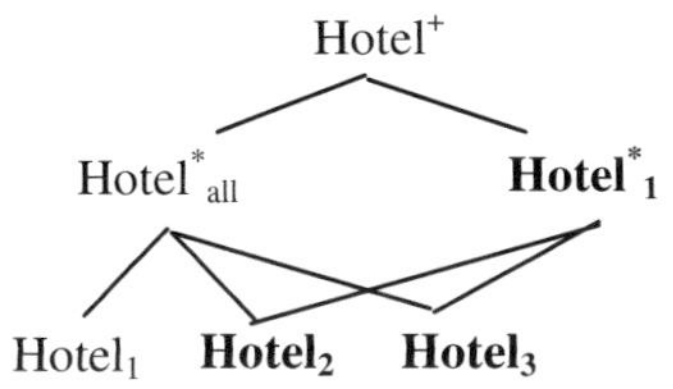

Figure 2: A domain tree built from a scenario above (focus in ***bold****)*

The operations are the following :

U_1 : $Hotel_1$ becomes a subdomain of $Hotel^*_{all}$ which gains focus in $Hotel^+$.

S_1 : $Hotel_2$ and $Hotel_3$ become subdomains of $Hotel^*_{all}$. In addition $Hotel_2$ and $Hotel_3$ are grouped in $Hotel^*_1$ which gains the focus in $Hotel^+$ while $Hotel^*_{all}$ loses it.

U_2 : The pronoun is solved in $Hotel^+$, and $Hotel^*_1$ is retrieved.

One can see that $Hotel^*_{all}$ is inaccessible by a generic expression like a demonstrative without modifiers but only by a special expression like "*all the hotels*". In our point of view, the reason is that the grouping $Hotel^*_1$ lowers the salience of $Hotel^*_{all}$.

6 Implementation

We used description logics for modelling domains and domain-reasoning. One has to deal with plural entities and can follow (Franconi, 93) by using collection theory, representing collections as individuals and membership by a role (plus plural quantifiers). But we should use another way considering that the inference engine we use, Racer (Haarslev and Möller, 03), does not take into account ALCS. Hence we tried representing the domains by concepts, given their semantic are set of individuals. The domain D^+ corresponds to the concept *D*, and the domain-subdomain relation is a subsumption. All basic manipulation with domains could be done using Tbox assertions. Additionnally, a partition structure is simply a sequence of subdomains which are different from each other (disjoint concepts) and whose elements could be focussed. The algorithm goes through the referential space and tests each domain in the recency order against the constraints given by the referential expression. Conceptual tests on the description and partitional tests on the focus or possible discriminations are made to retrieve the domain and the referent. If none are found, they may be created by accomodation. Groupings are created only for explicit coordinations, implicit sentential coordinations (two referents could be grouped if they have the same basic type) and some kind of specifications.

Domains and groupings creation entails the creation of new concepts in the Tbox. Each concept insertion requires a costly reclassification, therefore we preferred an approximation considering only that new groupings assert primitive concepts. Other domains are concept terms *i.e.* descriptions which do not have to be asserted in the Tbox automatically.

Implicit discursive groupings are not implemented considering the need of a rhetorical structure (like in SDRT, Asher 93) or a mental space model. The following example shows the needs :

U_1 : I would like an hotel (h_1)

S_1 : I propose you the hotel Ibis (h_2) and the Lafayette hotel (h_3).

Hotel h_1 could very hardly be grouped with h_2 and h_3, even by "all these hotels" (or maybe by a third speaker). We guess among other factors that they belong to different levels of interpretation, h_1 in the domain of the desires of the user, and the others in the domain of existing hotels. The link between the two domains is possible if one knows that S_1 is an answer of to U's request. Such discrimination criterion and high level domains are not yet implemented. Instead we concentrated on extra-linguistic referents which are assumed to be interpreted in the real/system world (like hotels, rooms). We are currently testing the approach to see if it could be extended to any type of entities provided accurate discrimination criteria (like the predication).

7 Example

A sample dialogue (table 1) is analyzed through the preceding algorithm. This example shows how the referents introduced in an explicit coordination could be referenced as a whole "*the two hotels*", or extracted discriminately by an ordinal "*the second one*" or by an otherness expression "*the other one*". All the subdomains of H^+ (*i.e.* the plural domains of hotels) are indicated *after* each interpretation using a simplified notation. Only the ordered list of accessible entities and their focalization (bold) are noted for each subdomain. For instance $\mathbf{H^*_{all}}$= (h_1, h_2, $\mathbf{h_3}$) means that the domain H^*_{all} is focalized in H^+, and that h_3 is focalized in H^*_{all}.

Dialogue	**H^+**
U: *Is there a bathroom at the Ibis hotel* (h_1) *and the hotel Lafayette* (h_2)?	$\mathbf{H^*_0 = (h_1, h_2)}$ $H^*_{all} = (\mathbf{h_1}, \mathbf{h_2})$
S: *No they don't have bathrooms*	$\mathbf{H^*_0 = (h_1, h_2)}$ $H^*_{all} = (\mathbf{h_1}, \mathbf{h_2})$
S: *But I propose you the Campanile hotel* (h_3)	$H^*_0 = (h_1, h_2)$ $\mathbf{H^*_{all}}$ = (h_1, h_2, $\mathbf{h_3}$)
U: *Hmm no, how much were the two hotels?*	$\mathbf{H^*_0 = (h_1, h_2)}$ H^*_{all} = ($\mathbf{h_1}$, $\mathbf{h_2}$, h_3)
S: The hotel Lafayette is 100 euros, the Ibis hotel is 75 euros	$\mathbf{H^*_1 = (h_2, h_1)}$ $H^*_0 = (\mathbf{h_1}, \mathbf{h_2})$ H^*_{all} = ($\mathbf{h_1}$, $\mathbf{h_2}$, h_3)
$\mathbf{U_1}$: Ok, I take the second one	$\mathbf{H^*_1}$ = (h_2, $\mathbf{h_1}$) H^*_0 = ($\mathbf{h_1}$, h_2) H^*_{all} = ($\mathbf{h_1}$, h_2, h_3)
U_2: Ok, I take the third one U_3: and the other one ?	$H^*_1 = (h_2, h_1)$ $H^*_0 = (h_1, h_2)$ $\mathbf{H^*_{all}}$ = (h_1, h_2, $\mathbf{h_3}$)

Table 1: Example of dialogue (focus in **bold***)*

In order to interpret U_1, U_2 or U_3 one needs to rely on the previous structuring of H^+. In U_1, the previously focalized domain H^*_1 is preferred to be the base for interpreting "*the second one*" because of the order discrimination. This leads to extracting h_1 hence focalizing it in H^*_1 but also in H^*_0 and in H^*_{all}. In U_2, H^*_1 cannot be the base for interpreting "*the third one*" because no entity could be discriminate this way. Therefore the only suitable domain is H^*_{all}. It is also impossible to interpret U_3 : "*the other one*" in H^*_1 because of the lack of a focus discrimination between h_1 and h_2.
It is however possible to choose H^*_{all} for the domain of interpretation: the excluded referents h_1 and h_2 are unfocused while h_3 gains focus.

8 Evaluation in progress

This work is currently being evaluated in the MEDIA/EVALDA framework, a national understanding evaluation campaign. (Devillers et al., 04). It aims to evaluate the semantic and referential abilities of systems with various approaches of natural language processing. The results of each system are compared to manually annotated utterances transcribed from a Woz corpus in a hotel reservation task. For the referential facet, referential expressions (excluding indefinites, and proper names) are annotated by a semantic description of their referents.
Our system which relies on a symbolic approach using deep parsing and description logics for semantic currently scores 64% (f-measure) for identifying and describing accurately the referents. We guess that such evaluation will be an occasion for us to test different hypothesis on reference resolution using domains (for exemple different criteria for grouping). However we do not have yet more precise results on plurals and ordinals specifically.

9 Conclusion

The extension we made to the Reference Domains Theory is still limited because it considers only extra-linguistic referents, *i.e.* those also having an existence outside discourse. In addition the trans-sentential groupings are not fully studied yet. We guess that such groupings should need a rhetorical description of the discourse or dialogue. In spite of its limits, the extension can render dynamic effects allowing ordinals and otherness in plural contexts. An implementation in description logics is currently being evaluated in the MEDIA/EVALDA framework.

References

Nicholas Asher. 1993. Reference to Abstract Objects in English: A Philosophical Semantics for Natural Language Metaphysics. In *Studies in Linguistics and Philosophy*, Kluwer, Dordrecht.

Laurence Devillers, Hélène Maynard, Stéphanie Rosset, Patrice Paroubek, Kevin McTait, Djamel Mostefa, Khalid Choukri, Caroline Bousquet, Laurent Charnay, Nadine Vigouroux, Frédéric Béchet, Laurent Romary, Jean-Yves Antoine, Jeanne Villaneau, Myriam Vergnes, and Jérôme Goulian. 2004. The French MEDIA/EVALDA Project : the Evaluation of the Understanding Capability of Spoken Language Dialog System. In *Proceedings of LREC 2004*, Lisbon, Portugal.

Carola Eschenbach, Christopher Habel, Michael Herweg, Klaus Rehkämper. 1989. Remarks on plural anaphora. In *Proc. Fourth Conference of the European Chapter of the Association for Computational Linguistics.*

Enrico Franconi. 1993. A treatment of plurals and plural quantifications based on a theory of collections. Minds and Machines (3)4:453-474, Kluwer Academic Publishers, November 1993

Petra Gieselmann: 2004. Reference Resolution Mechanisms in Dialogue Management. In: *Proceedings of the Eighth Workshop on the Semantics and Pragmatics of Dialogue* (CATALOG), Barcelona, 2004.

Volker Haarslev, and Ralf Möller. 2003. Racer: A Core Inference Engine for the Semantic Web. In *Proceedings of the 2nd International Workshop on Evaluation of Ontology-based Tools* (EON2003), located at the 2nd International Semantic Web Conference ISWC 2003, Sanibel Island, Florida, USA, October 20, 2003, pp. 27-36.

Ashwani Kumar, Susanne Salmon-Alt, and Laurent Romary. 2003. Reference resolution as a facilitating process towards robust multimodal dialogue management: A cognitive grammar approach. In *International Symposium on Reference Resolution and Its Application to Question Answering and Summarization.*

Frédéric Landragin, and Laurent Romary. 2003. Referring to Objects Through Sub-Contexts in Multimodal Human-Computer Interaction. In *Proc. Seventh Workshop on the Semantics and Pragmatics of Dialogue* (DiaBruck'03), Saarbrücken, Germany, 2003, pp. 67-74.

Frédéric Landragin, Nadia Bellalem and Laurent Romary. 2001. Visual Salience and Perceptual Grouping in Multimodal Interactivity. In: *First International Workshop on Information Presentation and Natural Multimodal Dialogue*, Verona, Italy, 2001

David R. Olson. 1970. Language and Thought: Aspects of a Cognitive Theory of Semantics. *Psychological Review*, 77/4, 257-273.

Susanne Salmon-alt. 2000. Interpreting referring expressions by restructuring context. *Proc. ESSLLI 2000, Student Session*, Birmingham, UK, August 2000.

Susanne Salmon-Alt. 2001. Reference Resolution within the Framework of Cognitive Grammar. *Proc. International Colloquium on Cognitive Science*, San Sebastian, Spain

Dan Sperber and Deirdre Wilson. 1986. *Relevance, Communication and Cognition.* Basil Blackwell, Oxford.

Tracing Actions Helps in Understanding Interactions

Bernd Ludwig
Chair for Artificial Intelligence, University of Erlangen-Nürnberg
Am Weichselgarten 9, D-91058 Erlangen
Bernd.Ludwig@informatik.uni-erlangen.de

Abstract

Integration of new utterances into context is a central task in any model for rational (human-machine) dialogues in natural language. In this paper, a pragmatics-first approach to specifying the meaning of utterances in terms of plans is presented. A rational dialogue is driven by the reaction of dialogue participants on how they find their expectations on changes in the environment satisfied by their observations of the outcome of performed actions. We present a computational model for this view on dialogues and illustrate it with examples from a real-world application.

1 A Pragmatics-First View on Dialogues

Rational dialogues that are based on GRICE's maxims of conversation serve for jointly executing a task in the domain of discourse (called *the application domain*) by following a plan that could solve the task assigned to the participants of the dialogue. Therefore, the interpretation of new contributions and their integration into a dialogue is controlled by global factors (e.g. the assumption that all dialogue participants behave in a cooperative manner and work effectively towards the completion of a joint task) as well as by local factors (e.g. how does the new contribution serve in completing the current shared plan?).

Ony if these factors are represented in an effective and efficient formal language, dialogue systems can be implemented. Examples of such models and their implementation are the information-state-update approach (an implemented system is described in (Larsson, 2002)), or – more linguistically oriented – approaches like the adjacency-pair models or intentional models such as GROSZ and SIDNER's (see (Grosz and Sidner, 1986)).

Even if it has been noted often that discourse structure and task structure are not isomorphic, only a few contributions to dialogue research focus on the question of how both structures interfere (see Sect. 2). In this paper, we emphasize that it is important to distinguish between the *dialogue situation* and the *application situation*: The former is modified whenever speech acts are performed, whereas the latter changes according to the effects of each action being executed. In this section, we will use a MAPTASK dialogue to show what the notions *dialogue situation* and *application situation* intend to mean. After presenting related work in Sect. 2, we present our approach first informally and then formally by explaining which AI algorithms we apply in order to turn the informal model into a computationally tractable one.

1.1 Talking about Domain Situations

The main hypothesis of this paper is that modifications of the dialogue situation are triggered by changes of the application situation. As a response to a speech act, dialogue participants perform a series of actions aiming at achieving some goal. If these actions can be executed, the reaction can signal success. At this point, our understanding of the role of shared plans exceeds that of (Grosz et al., 1999): GROSZ and KRAUS define an action to be *resolved* if it is assumed that an agent is able to execute the action. However, in order to understand coherence relations in complex dialogues, it is important to know whether an action has actually been executed and what effect it has produced. Consider the following excerpt from a MAPTASK dialogue (*MAP 9*, quoted from (Carletta, 1992)):

R: ++ and ++ you are not quite horizontal you are taking a slight curve up towards um the swamp ++ not obviously going into it

G: well sorry I have not got a swamp

R: you have not got a swamp?

G: no

R: OK

G: start again from the palm beach

Proceedings of the 7th SIGdial Workshop on Discourse and Dialogue, pages 60–67,
Sydney, July 2006.

G has failed to find the swamp, which means G has failed to perform the action necessary to perform the next one (take a slight curve).

In order to solve the current task, R has been able to organize a solution for the task at hand which may or may not involve the other dialogue participant G. How can R put his solution into action? First, he executes each step and, second, validates after each step whether all expectations related to it are fulfilled.

1.2 Talking about Error and Failure

In the example above, R's expectations are not met because G does not find the swamp on the map. However, this would be a precondition for R to continue putting the solution into action that he has organized. On the other hand, G understands that finding the swamp is very important in the current task, but he missed to reach that goal. In order to share this information with R, G verbalizes his failure diagnosis: *"I have not got a swamp."*

This turn makes R realize that his solution does not work. Obviously, R believed his solution to be well elaborated because he tries to get a confirmation of its failure by asking back *"you have not got a swamp?"* G's reacknowledgement is a clear indication for R that it is necessary to reorganize his solution for the current task. Being a collaborative dialogue participant, he will try to recover from that failure to explain the way to the destination.

1.3 Domain and Discourse Strategies

For the purpose of recovery, the dialogue participants try to apply a repair strategy that helps them to reorganize the solution. Repair strategies are complex domain dependent processes of modifying tasks and solutions to them. Even being domain dependent in detail, there are some strategies that are domain independent and are regularly adapted to particular domains:

- **Delay**: Maybe it is the best decision to wait a bit and try the failed step again.
- **Delegation**: Maybe someone else can perform better.
- **Replanning**: Another solution should be found based on the current error diagnosis.
- **Relaxation**: Modify some parameters or constraints of the task so that a tractable solution can be found.
- **New Tools**: Maybe somehow the dialogue participant can extend his capabilities in the domain so that he can achieve the solution using other, more, or stronger tools and means.
- **Negotiation**: Try to retrieve new helpful information from the user or to come to an agreement of how the task can be modified.
- **Cancellation**: Sometimes giving up to find a solution is the only remaining possibility.

This list is necessarily incomplete as depending on the particular domain and current situation in which a dialogue participant has to act these strategies appear in very different fashion. So, it is hard to decide whether exception handling for a single case is taking place or if a particular strategy is being applied. In the example dialogue, G tries to suggest a `replanning` by telling to R up to what point he was able to understand R's explanations.

According to his communication strategy, a dialogue participant tells his deliberations in more or less detail, sometimes even not at all. This is the case in the example dialogue above. In the last turn, G does not tell that he wants R to reorganize his solution. R must infer this from the content, in particular from the request to restart the explanation at a point that has been passed before the G had failed to understand a step in R's explanation.

This example shows that domain strategies and communication strategies interfere in a dialogue and that complicated reasoning is necessary to identify them in order to react appropriately.

Our analysis shows that the notion of coherence is strongly related with the execution of single steps in a solution. Often, coherence cannot be explained satisfactorily within a discourse, but the current situation in which an utterance is made, must be taken into consideration as well.

2 Related Work

There are several main research directions on dialogue understanding. The one closest to our approach is activity-based dialogue analysis (Allwood, 1997; Allwood, 2000) contrasting BDI-style approaches such as the one by (Cohen and Levesque, 1995). This research shows how speech acts are related to expectations expressed by means of language and inspired our approach. However, ALLWOOD does not work out in detail how the pragmatics of the application domain can be formalized in a tractable way. (Carletta, 1992) shows in a corpus analysis that risk taking is a elementary behavior of dialogue participants. (Bos and Oka, 2002) uses first-order logic in a DRT environment to reason about the logical satisfiability of a new utterance given a previous discourse. For reasoning about action however, we think that a first-order theorem prover or model builder is not the ideal tool because it is too general. Additionally, in dialogues about acting in an environment, the primary interest of semantic evaluation is not whether a formula is true or false, but how a goal or task can be solved. Therefore, planning is more appropriate than proofing formulae. Work on planning as part of dialogue understanding is reported in (Zinn, 2004). This paper does not address selecting strategies for error recovery. Conflict resolution is addressed in (Chu-Carroll and Carberry, 1996). However, the presented discourse model is not computationally effective. (Huber and Ludwig, 2002; Ludwig, 2004) present an interactive system which uses planning, (Yates et al., 2003) and recently (Lieberman and Espinosa, 2006) reported on applying planning as a vehicle for natural language interfaces, but none of the papers discusses how a dialogue can be continued when a failure in the application occurs. In the WITAS system (see (Lemon et al., 2002)), *activities* are modelled by *activity models*, one for each type of activity the system can perform or analyse. A similiar recipe-based approach is implemented in COLLAGEN (Garland et al., 2003). As activities are hard-coded in the respective model, adaptation of the task and dialogue structure to the needs in a current situation are harder to achieve than in our approach in which only goals are specified and activities are selected by a planner depending on the current state. In addition, executing plans by verifying preconditions and effects of an activity that has been carried out recently lies the basis for a framework of understanding the pragmatics of a dialogue that is not implemented for a particular application, but tries to be as generic as possible.

3 Problem and Discourse Organization

A computational approach that aims at analyzing and generating rational – i.e. goal-oriented – dialogues in a given domain must address the issues of organizing a solution in the application domain as well as in the discourse domain. Furthermore, it must provide an effective method to organize solutions, classify current states in the discourse as well as in the application situation (are they erroneous or not?) and select strategies that promise a recovery in case of an error.

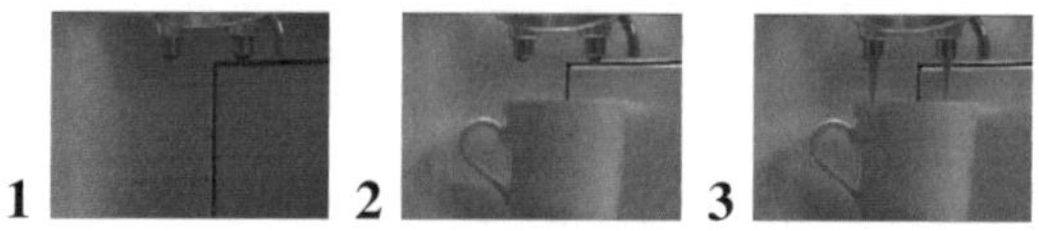

Figure 1: Example data for a classification task.

3.1 Expectations and Observations

To diagnose an error, a dialogue participant must be able to determine whether his expectations on how the environment changes due to an action match his observations.

3.2 The Origin of Expectations

The expectations of a dialogue participant are derived from his organization of a solution to the current task. Each step herein has – after it has been executed – a certain intended impact. It forms the expectations that are assigned to a single step.

An expectation is met by a set of observations if the observations are sufficient to infer the expectation from. The inference process that is employed in this context may be as simple as a slot-filling mechanism or as complicated as inference in a formal logic. In the slot-filling case, the inference algorithm is to determine whether the semantic type of the answer given by the user match the type that was expected by the dialogue system.

However, inference in the sense of this paper may involve difficult computations: Expectations are generated while a solution is organized. Each step in a solution leads to certain changes in the environment that are expected to happen when the step is actually executed. Later in the paper, we will demonstrate how planning algorithms can generate such expectations. Additionally: – see Fig. 1) – in order to verify expectations of the request *"Fill coffee into the cup!"* image data need to be classified before it can be concluded that the expectation (image 3) is satisfied.

4 Planning Solutions

In order to illustrate our approach how a natural language dialogue system can organize solutions for user requests, we discuss a natural language interface for operating a transportation system. The

```
produce-coffee
:parameters (?c - cup ?j - jura)
:precondition
  (and (under-spout ?c)
       (not (service-request ?j)))
:effect (and (not (empty ?c)) (ready ?j))
```

Figure 2: Example of a plan operator in PDDL

system allows to control a model train installation and electronic devices currently on the market.

4.1 Organizing a Solution

First of all, in order to specify the (pragmatic) capabilities of the whole system, a formal model of the system is needed that allows the necessary computations for organizing solutions. For this purpose, we model all functions provided by the system in terms of plan operators in the PDDL planning language. Fig. 2 shows an example.

This operator describes part of the functionality of the automatic coffee machine that is integrated into our system: the function `produce-coffee` can be executed if there is a cup under the spout of the machine and if it does not require service (as such filling in water or beans). These are the preconditions of the function. After coffee has been produced, it is expected that the environment is changed in the following way: the cup is not empty any longer, and the machine is ready again.

In order to organize a solution, a task is needed and knowledge about the current state of the environment. The latter comes from interpreting sensor data, while the former is computed from natural language user input. For the example request *"Fill in a cup of espresso!"*, we assume the current state in Fig. 3 to hold and use the formula in Fig. 4 as the description of the current task to solve.

The example in Fig. 3 assumes that the cup is parked and empty, and the coffee machine and the robot (used for moving cups) are ready. The task is formalized as a future state of the environment in which the cup is parked and the coffee machine is in the mode *one small cup* (see Fig. 4).

To compute a solution, a planning algorithm (we incorporated the FF planner (Hoffmann and Nebel, 2001) in our system) uses the information about the current state and the intended future state as input and computes a plan for a number of steps to execute in order to solve the task (see Fig. 5).

In the following, we will consider such a plan as in Fig. 5 as an organized solution for the task to be solved. Expected changes of the environment are defined by the effects of each step of the solution. Fig. 6 shows which changes are expected if the plan in Fig. 5 is eventually executed.

4.2 Executing a Solution

Given a plan for a task to be solved, our dialogue system executes each step sequentially. Before a step of the solution is performed, the system verifies each precondition necessary for the step to be executable. If all tests succeed, actuators are commanded to perform everything related to the current step. Feedback is obtained by interpreting sensor input which is used to control whether the intended effects have been achieved. For the function `produce-coffee` above, the following procedure is executed:

```
produce-coffee (cup c, jura j) {
  if test(under-spout,c)=false
    signal_error;
  else {
    if test(service-request,j)=true
      signal_error;
    else do produce-coffee, c, j;
  };
  if test(empty,c)=true signal_error;
  else {
    if test(ready,j)=false signal_error;
    else return;
  };
}
```

In this procedure, each precondition of the function `produce-coffee` is verified. If the system can infer from the sensor values that a precondition cannot be satisfied, it signals an error. The same is done with all effects when the actuators have finished to change the environment. As we will discuss in Sect. 6, these error signals are the basic information for continuing a dialogue when unexpected changes have been observed.

5 Diagnosing Errors

How can the dialogue system react if a precondition or effect does not match the system's expectations? The primary goal of a dialogue system is to

```
(and (parked cup) (empty cup)
     (ready jura) (ready robo))
```

Figure 3: The current state of the environment for the example in Sect. 4

```
(and (parked cup) (mode-osc jura))
```

Figure 4: The task to be solved

```
put-cup-on-spout(cup,jura,robo)
draw-off-osc(cup,jura)
produce-coffee(cup,jura)
go-in-place(train)
take-cup-off-spout(cup,jura,robo)
load-cup-on-waggon(cup,jura,robo,train)
park-cup(cup,jura,robo,train)
```

Figure 5: A plan for the task in Fig. 4

Step #	Action and expected changes
1	**put-cup-on-spout(cup, jura, robo)**
	`(under-spout ?c)`
	`(not (robo-loaded ?r ?c))`
	`(not (parked ?c))`
2	**draw-off-osc(cup, jura)**
	`(not (ready ?j)) (mode-osc ?j)`
3	**produce-coffee(cup, jura)**
	`(not (empty ?c)) (ready ?j)`
4	**go-in-place(train)**
	`(in-place ?t)`
5	**take-cup-off-spout(cup, jura, robo)**
	`(not (under-spout ?c))`
	`(robo-loaded ?r ?c)`
6	**load-cup-on-waggon(cup, jura, robo, train)**
	`(not (robo-loaded ?r ?c))`
	`(train-loaded ?t ?c)`
7	**park-cup(cup, jura, robo, train)**
	`(not (train-loaded ?t ?c))`
	`(parked ?c)`

Figure 6: Expected changes in the environment

meet principles of conversation such as GRICE's maxims. Often, however, it is not obvious to the user how a particular constraint in a plan is related to the current task. Therefore, a plausible and transparent explanation of an error brings the diagnosed mismatch in its context of the current action and solution for the current task. At the core of each explanation are the unexpected observations. The context of the error is formed by all available sensor values and the history of past actions which are steps in the solution (see Fig. 5) for the current task. The example in Fig. 7 shows the state of the system after the first four steps of the solution introduced in Sect. 4.1 have been carried out. After executing `take-cup-off-spout` however, the observed changes of the system state do not match the expected ones: Analyzing the most recent images and the robot's weight sensor, the system recognizes that the cup still is on the spout, but not being carried away by the robot.

Given the situation in Fig. 7, what is the system able to or should communicate to the user? Without any additional reasoning, the system could only tell what it has observed:

User: *Fill in a cup of espresso!*

System: *The cup is under the spout and the robot is not loaded with the cup.*

Such a response would not be very helpful for the user (especially if he cannot see the situation or is unexperienced in handling the system). Our approach to generating plausible explanations for failures of the system is to compute a diagnosis that takes the context of the failure and the task to be solved into account. The approach relies on an explicit error model for each function that the system provides in the sense of (Balduccini and Gelfond, 2003): In the case of `take-cup-off-spout` the following symptoms and causes lead to failure of the function:

Symptom	**Cause**
`(under-spout c)`	wrong position
	robo lost cup
`¬ (robo-loaded r c)`	arm motor off
	arm not ok
	didn't hold cup

The approach of (Balduccini and Gelfond, 2003) generates models in a formal logic of what could be reasons for the failure of the system and in which state the system would be in each case. If more than one model is generated when an unexpected observation has been made, the system has to find evidence for each model and compare how reliable a diagnosis is (given the available sensor values and their interpretation). For that purpose, decision trees are trained on past cases of failure and the confidence values for the computed interpretations. (e.g. to which class does the image in Fig. 1?). Applying such a decision tree on a given system state and mismatched expectation results in a unique model that is seen as an explanation for the failure of the system's function. In this way, the dialogue system can explain better to the user what it thinks has happened during the execution of `take-cup-off-spout`:

User: *Fill in a cup of espresso!*

System: *I could not carry the cup to the train because I lost the cup on the way.*

From the viewpoint of discourse analysis, we can consider the mismatch between observations and expectations as the main cause for the system response. As a consequence, we can consider the logical relation between the current task, the solution organized by the system, and the computed error diagnosis as sufficient conditions for any discourse relation to hold between the user and the

Actions up to now	System state after go-in-place	Expected state	Error Diagnosis
put-cup-on-spout	(ready jura)		none
draw-off-osc	(ready robo)		none
produce-coffee	¬(parked cup)		none
go-in-place	¬(empty cup)		none
	¬(robo-loaded robo)		none
	(mode-osc jura)		none
	(in-place train)		none
	(under-spout cup)		none
Last Action	**Observed state**		
take-cup-off-spout	(under-spout cup) ¬(robo-loaded robo)	¬(under-spout cup) (robo-loaded robo)	robo could not hold the cup

Figure 7: Context information for the diagnosis of an error

system utterance in the dialogue excerpt above: In terms of TRAUM's DU acts (Traum, 1994), coherence between both utterances is established as a `reject` relation as the purpose of the utterance is to indicate failure of the task that has been initiated by the user request. To explain the MAPTASK dialogue cited in the introduction, another level of pragmatic reasoning is required: As already mentioned in Sect. 1.3, the dialogue system is cooperative and tries to find out a way in order to nevertheless solve the task as completely as possible.

6 Error Repair and Discourse Update

Such a way out consists in applying a strategy that is appropriate for the current state of the system and the interaction with the user. In the AI (Mitchell, 1997) and robotics (Bekey, 2005) literature, algorithms for applying adaptive strategies in different situations are all based on the current state as input and an evaluation function that helps selecting an optimal strategy.

6.1 Repair Strategies in the Application

A favorite algorithm for this kind of interactive control problems is to select the optimal policy out of a set of possibilities. Before that, an evaluation function is trained by reinforcement learning to always select the action that maximizes the reward obtainable in the current state. In (Henderson et al., 2005), this machine learning approach was applied to selecting speech acts after training an evaluation function on a dialogue corpus in which each utterance was labeled with a speech act.

Different from (Henderson et al., 2005), in our approach the actions between whom the dialogue system can choose are repair strategies instead of speech acts. In our opinion, speech acts are a phenomenon of another invisible process – text generation – but not objects of the decision at the discourse planning level: the selection of a repair strategy does not fix the type of a speech act nor its content. The way a repair strategy works and – as a consequence – has influence on the flow of a dialogue is that, firstly, it modifies the current task and, secondly, seeks a new solution that will be executed later on. Future speech acts then are a result of performing single steps of the new solution.

To recover the `take-cup-off-spout` function, the system may have the option to fill another cup and try to bring this one to its destination. It must be noted, however, that this option depends to a large extent on the availability of another empty cup, the readiness of the robot and the coffee machine and sufficient resources like beans, water, and time to complete the task. All these parameters influence the computation of the reward and the risk to be assigned to this domain-specific variant of a *New Tools*-strategy (see Sect. 1.3).

6.2 Effects on Discourse Update

The MAPTASK dialogue in Sect. 1.1 even is somewhat more complicated: *G* understands that he does not have the capability to repair the misunderstanding as there is too much information missing. Therefore, he initiates a *Negotiation*-strategy in which he switches the topic of the dialogue to the domain of strategies for MAPTASK. *G* proposes a new strategy with a slightly modified task to *R*. It is exactly this logical relation that explains the coherence between the turns in this dialogue. In this case, the coherence cannot be established by reasoning in one single domain.

In terms of the Conversation Acts Theory by (Traum and Hinkelman, 1992) and (Poesio and Traum, 1998; Traum, 1994), the discourse segment related to the solution for a task can be called *multiple discourse unit* (MDU). Consequently, the conversation acts for MDU are a trace of the dialogue participant's decisions on which interactions are needed to solve the task and how they could be verbalized best. Argumentation is based on the formal knowledge about the domain, the current task, and a solution proposed for it. This means that an analysis of the current state of the system and the dialog provides facts that can be used as conditions for the applicability of a speech act. Equally, facts about the system are conditions for the applicability of a system function at a certain point of time. It follows directly from this observation that planning argumentation acts can be viewed as a special kind of classical planning in AI. However, due to the interactive nature of such a dialogue task, it must be possible to react flexibly and directly on mismatches between expectations and observations for speech acts and the intended changes during the course of a dialogue.

Therefore, in this paper dialogue management is seen as a special case of reactive planning. As shown above, discourse relations are derived from meta-information about the state of executing a plan for the current task. The discourse relations serve as preconditions for speech acts effectuating the update of the dialogue state.

6.3 Diagnosing Linguistic Errors

Our model of relating pragmatics and interaction can be extended to discourse pragmatics as well. It is particularly helpful to understand *grounding* acts in the `utterance unit` level (see (Traum and Hinkelman, 1992)). In this case, the ("application") domain is that of understanding language. The task to be solved is to extract words from a speech signal and to construct meaning from those words. Error diagnoses occur frequently and options caused by ambiguities of natural language have to be tested whether they can help to repair a diagnosed error automatically. If not, the diagnoses as symptoms of misunderstanding have to be assigned to possible causes. Strategic decisions have to be made how to communicate the causes and possible suggestion for repairs to the user. This reasoning results in *grounding* acts that would be hard to analyze otherwise. This idea can be applied to negotiating speech acts as well. The difficult task, however, is to implement a diagnosis algorithm for failure in syntax analysis, (compositional) semantics, and speech act analysis.

7 Understanding User Utterances

There are implications of our approach for computational semantics: In order to see whether a user utterance meets the system's expectations, it is necessary to analyze which domain the utterance refers to. For this purpose, expectations for discourse and system state are maintained separately. Each new contribution must satisfy the discourse expectations (e.g. an answer should follow a question) and pragmatic expectations (the content of the contribution must extend without contradictions what is known about the current solution. To test this, a model (in the sense of formal logic) is computed for the conjunction of the new content and the currently available information.

As discussed above, it may happen in dialogues that the focus is switched to another topic, i.e. another domain, and the coherence can be established only when taking this domain shift into account. In order to be able to detect such a domain shift, we define the meaning of performative words depending on whether they refer to the hidden reasoning processes that are part of our approach, the discourse control domain, or to states, objects, and functions in the current applications situation: In the MAPTASK example, the utterance *Start from the palm beach* refers to the process of strategy selection and organization of a solution, but not to the domain of explanations in a map.

8 Conclusions

The presented approach allows dialogue understanding to take into account that the (human) dialogue participant the system is interacting with is (at least) equally able to diagnose errors and mismatches between observations and expectations and generates utterances intended to update the dialogue state according to these findings. Therefore, for establishing the coherence of a user utterance, there are always several options: firstly, the user continues the current solution, secondly, he diagnoses failure and reports about it, and thirdly, he switches the focus to another domain including discourse update and repair strategies.

For these options, our approach devises a computational model able to explain dialogues in which coherence of turns is difficult analyze. In this way, more natural dialogues can be analyzed and generated. As the approach incorporates a model for how talking about actions is related to acting in a formalized domain, it serves as a basis for constructing natural language assistance systems, e.g. for a great range of electronic devices.

References

Jens Allwood. 1997. Notes on dialog and cooperation. In Kristina Jokinen, David Sadek, and David Traum, editors, *Proceedings of the IJCAI 97 Workshop on Collaboration, Cooperation, and Conflict in Dialogue Systems*, Nagoya, August.

Jens Allwood. 2000. An activity based approach to pragmatics. In Harry C. Bunt and B. Black, editors, *Abduction, Belief, and Context in Dialogue*, Studies in Computational Pragmatics. John Benjamins, Amsterdam.

Marcello Balduccini and Michael Gelfond. 2003. Diagnostic reasoning with a-prolog. *Theory and Practice of Logic Programming*, 3(4–5):425–461, July.

George A. Bekey. 2005. *Autonomous Robots: From Biological Inspiration to Implementation and Control*. MIT Press.

Johan Bos and Tetsushi Oka. 2002. An inference-based approach to dialogue system design. In *Proceedings of the 19th International Conference on Computational Linguistics*, pages 113–119.

Jean Carletta. 1992. *Risk-Taking and Recovery in Task-Oriented Dialogue*. Ph.D. thesis, University of Edinburgh.

Jennifer Chu-Carroll and Sandra Carberry. 1996. Conflict detection and resolution in collaborative planning. In *Intelligent Agents: Agent Theories, Architectures, and Languages*, volume 2 of *Lecture Notes in Artificial Intelligence*, pages 111–126. Springer Verlag.

Phil R. Cohen and Hector J. Levesque. 1995. Communicative actions for artificial agents. In *Proceedings of the First International Conference on Multi-Agent Systems*, pages 65–72, San Francisco, CA, June.

Andrew Garland, Neal Lesh, and Charles Rich. 2003. Responding to and recovering from mistakes during collaboration. In Gheorghe Tecuci, David W. Aha, Mihai Boicu, Michael T. Cox, George Ferguson, and Austin Tate, editors, *Proceedings of the IJCAI Workshop on Mixed-Initiative Intelligent Systems*, pages 59–64, August.

Barbara J. Grosz and Candace L. Sidner. 1986. Attention, intentions, and the structure of discourse. *Computational Linguistics*, 12(3):175–204.

Barbara J. Grosz, Luke Hunsberger, and Sarit Kraus. 1999. Planning and acting together. *AI Magazine*, 20(4):23–34.

James Henderson, Oliver Lemon, and Kallirroi Georgila. 2005. Hybrid reinforcement/supervised learning for dialogue policies from communicator data. In *Proc. IJCAI workshop on Knowledge and Reasoning in Practical Dialogue Systems*, Edinburgh (UK).

Jörg Hoffmann and Bernhard Nebel. 2001. The ff planning system: Fast plan generation through heuristic search. *Journal of Artificial Intelligence Research*, 14:253–302.

Alexander Huber and Bernd Ludwig. 2002. A natural language multi-agent system for controlling model trains. In *Proceedings AI, Simulation, and Planning in High Autonomy Systems (AIS 2002)*, pages 145–149, Lissabon.

Staffan Larsson. 2002. *Issue-based Dialogue Management*. Ph.D. thesis, Department of Linguistics, Göteborg University, Göteborg, Sweden.

Oliver Lemon, Alexander Gruenstein, Alexis Battle, and Stanley Peters. 2002. Multi-tasking and collaborative activities in dialogue systems. In *Proceedings of the 3rd SIGdial Workshop on Discourse and Dialogue*, pages 113–124, Philadelphia.

Henry Lieberman and José Espinosa. 2006. A goal-oriented interface to consumer electronics using planning and commonsene reasoning. In *Proceedings of the 11th International Conference on Intelligent User Interfaces*. ACM, ACM Press.

Bernd Ludwig. 2004. A pragmatics-first approach to the analysis and generation of dialogues. In Susanne Biundo, Rhom Frühwirth, and Günther Palm, editors, *Proc. KI-2004 (27th Annual German Conference on AI (KI-2004)*, pages 82–96, Berlin. Springer.

Tom M. Mitchell. 1997. *Machine Learning*. McGraw-Hill.

Massimo Poesio and David Traum. 1998. Towards an axiomatisation of dialogue acts. In J. Hulstijn and A. Nijholt, editors, *Proceedings of the Twente Workshop on the Formal Semantics and Pragmatics of Dialogues*, pages 207–222, Enschede.

David R. Traum and Elizabeth A. Hinkelman. 1992. Conversation acts in task-oriented spoken dialogue. *Computational Intelligence*, 8(3):575–592.

David Traum. 1994. *A Computational Theory of Grounding in Natural Language Conversation*. Ph.D. thesis, Computer Science Department, University of Rochester.

Alexander Yates, Oren Etzioni, and Daniel Weld. 2003. A reliable natural language interface to household appliances. In *Proceedings of the 8th International Conference on Intelligent User Interfaces*, pages 189–196. ACM, ACM Press.

Claus Zinn. 2004. Flexible dialogue management in natural-language enhanced tutoring. In *Konvens 2004 Workshop on Advanced Topics in Modeling Natural Language Dialog*, pages 28–35, Viena, September.

Semantic and Pragmatic Presupposition in Discourse Representation Theory

Yafa Al-Raheb
National Centre for Language Technology
School of Computing
Dublin City University, Ireland
yafa.alraheb@gmail.com

Abstract

This paper investigates semantic and pragmatic presupposition in Discourse Representation Theory (DRT) and enhances the pragmatic perspective of presupposition in DRT. In doing so, it draws attention to the need to account for agent presupposition (i.e. both speaker and hearer presupposition) when dealing with pragmatic presupposition. Furthermore, this paper links this pragmatic conception of presupposition with the semantic one (sentence presupposition) through using 'information checks' which agents are hypothesized to employ when making and receiving utterances.[1]

1 Introduction

DRT, with its detailed apparatus for the representation of context, offers the most obvious framework for investigating presupposition in depth (Kamp 1984, 1988, 1990, 1995, 2001a, 2001b; Kamp and Reyle 1993; Kamp et al. 2005). However, despite the suitability of DRT for pursuing a detailed account of presupposition, it is argued that in order to enrich our understanding of presupposition within the DRT framework, this framework itself needs to be modified (cf. Al-Raheb 2005). The approach presented in this paper understands presupposition within the parameters of dynamic semantics (van der Sandt 1992), part of which is DRT, but attempts to go beyond that in order to make the understanding of presupposition within DRT more pragmatic. The dynamic semantics view of presupposition is incomplete from a pragmatic standpoint because it neglects the connection between beliefs and presupposition, hence neglecting the connection between pragmatic presupposition and semantic presupposition in DRT.

To account for pragmatic presupposition as well as making presupposition within DRT more pragmatic, presupposition is understood to be a property of the agent. In essence, the effect of presupposition is to give insights about the speaker's beliefs as well as the speaker's beliefs about the hearer's beliefs. Speaker belief leads to presupposition, which indicates the beliefs of the speaker to the hearer. Presupposition is a reflection of the speaker's state of mind. This is stronger than what is generally conceded in the literature. Geurts (1996, 1998, 1999) maintains that a presupposition should not necessarily reflect the beliefs of the speaker, but rather the speaker's commitment to the truth of the presupposition. If, for example, we were to use Stalnaker's (2002) example,

(1) I have to pick my sister up from the airport.

Geurts argues that the speaker does not have to believe she has a sister, but just needs to be 'committed to' the truth of the presupposition that she has a sister. In other words, the speaker need only commit to the presupposition (P) being true. The approach presented here takes a somewhat stronger position than Geurts' position (Geurts 1999) because it assumes that Grice's Cooperative Principle is in place (Grice 1975, 1989). If we make the simplifying assumption that the agents in the dialogue are being cooperative, are not lying, are being relevant, etc., we can take the stronger position that the information introduced by the presupposition, here 'having a sister', is indeed a belief held by the speaker.

[1] I gratefully acknowledge support from Science Foundation Ireland grant 04/IN/I527.

Proceedings of the 7th SIGdial Workshop on Discourse and Dialogue, pages 68–75,
Sydney, July 2006.

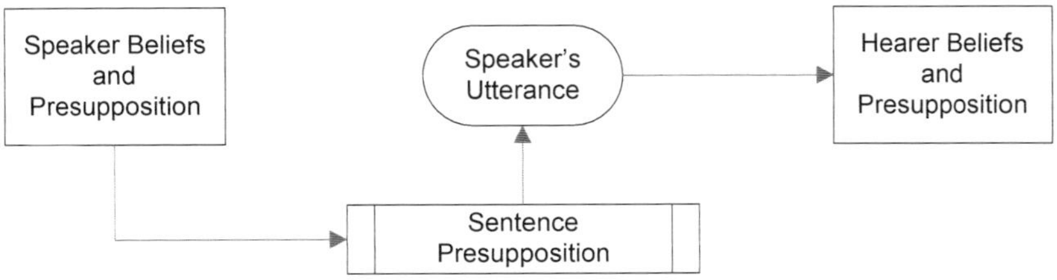

Figure 1: Speaker, Sentence and Hearer Presupposition

Viewing presupposition from the more pragmatic perspective of the agents' point of view in dialogue leads us to viewing presupposition from both the speaker's and the hearer's points of view. Distinguishing speaker presupposition from hearer presupposition helps make the approach to presupposition within DRT more pragmatic, since we are speaking not of truth conditions but of states of mind in communicative interaction. Therefore, this paper deals with two types of agent presupposition, speaker presupposition and hearer presupposition (cf. section 3). This is different from semantic presupposition, i.e. sentence presupposition (cf. section 2). Agent presupposition differs from sentence presupposition in that the latter stems from sentence meaning, whereas the former attaches itself to the beliefs of the speaker and her intentions. It is argued here that the semantic and pragmatic notions of presupposition in DRT can be linked through linking agents' beliefs to the utterance being communicated.

2 Semantic and Pragmatic Presupposition

The literature has mostly considered the hearer's side of receiving the presupposition when dealing with agent presupposition (pragmatics) as opposed to sentence presupposition (semantics). For instance, van der Sandt (1992) deals with accommodation from the hearer's perspective, not distinguishing between speaker and hearer presupposition. However, the relationship between sentence presupposition and agent presupposition can be explained by dividing agent presupposition into speaker presupposition and hearer presupposition.

From the speaker's point of view, speakers make utterances to communicate new information. Generally speaking, to generate a communicatively meaningful utterance, there would be some discrepancy between the speaker's beliefs and the speaker's beliefs about the hearer's beliefs. The discrepancy leads to an assertion, A, which may need presupposed arguments to be understood. First, the speaker decides on the assertion after checking belief discrepancies. Then, the speaker finds the right presuppositions to be able to communicate the assertion.

Hearer presupposition differs in that utterances are split into presupposition and assertion, where possible, and presuppositions are first needed to establish links to objects in order for the new information to be understood by the hearer. For a hearer, assertions build on presupposition and the procedure is bottom-up (assertion is supported by presupposition).[2]

Therefore, in line with linking the speaker's beliefs with the linguistic utterance and the linguistic utterance with the hearer's beliefs, the speaker's presupposition is conveyed through the speaker's utterance (sentence presupposition), and the speaker's utterance leads to the hearer's presupposition. This interaction between the semantic and pragmatic notions of presupposition is a more balanced conception of presupposition (cf. Figure 1).

With regard to the A part of an utterance received by the hearer, the hearer can first 'accept', or 'weakly believe', the new information and later on turn that weak belief into a belief, by adding it to her belief set (Al-Raheb 2005). However, it is worth mentioning that when making an utterance, both the speaker and the hearer focus their attention on A, which can get accepted by the hearer. In such a case, the hearer may later adopt A as a belief and indicate so to the speaker, making A a mutual belief, which may or may not serve as a presupposition afterwards in the dialogue. It is possible for P to be a mutual belief that both agents in the conversation mutually know they hold, or a

[2]It remains for future work to test the psychological reality of these hypotheses.

new piece of information packaged as P. From this discussion, it can be seen that beliefs impose some constraints on making an utterance. The following section distinguishes between agent presupposition (speaker presupposition and hearer presupposition) and links agents presupposition to sentence presupposition.

3 Agent Presupposition

Speaker presupposition differs from hearer presupposition in terms of three 'information checks' agents are hypothesized to perform when introducing or dealing with presupposition. The checks are (1) *clarification check*, (2) *informativity check*, and (3) *consistency check*. The checks are similar in principle to Purver (2004) and van der Sandt (1992). However, they are developed here as a process which distinguishes speaker generation from hearer recognition, allowing us to differentiate speaker presupposition from hearer presupposition, hence establishing the link between speaker presupposition and sentence presupposition, and between sentence presupposition and hearer presupposition. The three checks apply to both speaker and hearer.

The clarification check may be used at the beginning of the process of checking. It corresponds to Grice's maxim of manner on the part of the speaker (1989). Nonetheless, as there are different kinds of clarification requests (Purver et al. 2003), clarification can also be initiated at various stages of the check process, indicating a different kind of clarification.

The purpose of the informativity check is to check whether the presupposition is new or old information to the speaker and the hearer. This check is a modification of Grice's (1989) quality maxim, which has been reworked to include two degrees of beliefs, acceptance and belief (Al-Raheb 2005). In addition, it checks whether the information is new or old to the other agent, based on the beliefs of one agent about the other. The process of checks for the speaker mirrors that of the hearer. However, as the process of recognition is different from the process of generation, the 'information checks' are described for the speaker and hearer individually.

Similarly, the consistency check determines whether the presupposition is consistent with the agents' beliefs – in accordance with Grice's maxim of relevance (1989). For presupposition, as part of the consistency check, another check is performed, more specifically for the hearer's benefit, which checks whether the presupposition is remarkable or unremarkable. Generally, information can be accommodated, so long as it is 'unremarkable' (Geurts 1999: 36). For example,

(2) The car across the street from my house belongs to my neighbour.

is less likely to cause problems than

(3) The small jet across the street from my house belongs to my neighbour,

when the hearer knows that the speaker lives in the city centre.[3]

The process of 'information checks' influences how speakers make their utterances and how hearers recognize those utterances. Section 3.1 follows the information check process for presuppositions for the speaker, whereas section 3.2 demonstrates that process for the hearer.

3.1 Speaker Presupposition

Speaker presupposition differs from hearer presupposition in terms of checks. When a speaker generates a sentence presupposition (via the communicated utterance), we are assuming that the speaker is bound by Grice's Cooperative Principle (1975, 1989). To utter a sentence triggering a presupposition, the speaker needs to have reason to believe that her presupposition is going to be 'clear' and 'consistent'. The speaker may have previous context in memory that shows her presupposition to be consistent with her beliefs about the hearer's beliefs. However, when such evidence is lacking, the speaker may still make presupposition–triggering utterances (sentence presupposition) and then make the judgement that the presupposition is consistent if there is no negative feedback; alternatively, the speaker might receive evidence that shows the presupposition to be contradictory with her beliefs about the hearer's beliefs.

The informativity check comes into play when the speaker elaborates on given or known information by packaging it as a presupposition and focusing attention on the assertion part of her utterance, i.e. on the new information. In this case, the

[3] Of course, anything can be 'out of the ordinary' or its reverse for a specific set of circumstances. The speaker is making assumptions about shared conceptions of the 'ordinary'.

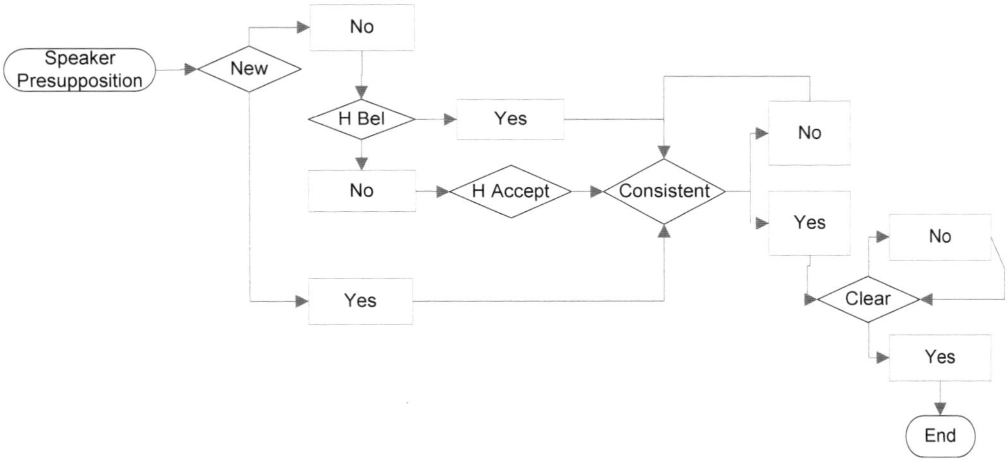

Figure 2: Speaker Presupposition

speaker needs to have reason to believe that the hearer is already aware of this presupposed information, therefore, that it is known. For example,

(4) My grandchild loves horses.

To be consistent, the speaker checks her memory to see if the speaker has record that she, the speaker, has reason to believe that the hearer believes that the speaker has a grandchild. The speaker, being in a retirement home, discussing her grandchildren with the carer, and having had previous conversations with the same carer about her family, has reason to believe that the hearer already knows she has a grandchild. She, therefore, presupposes 'I have a grandchild'.

Another example of elaborating on given information is when the speaker believes the given information has been established, i.e. both the speaker and the hearer believe that the information is part of their mutual or common beliefs. This constitutes a case of strong speaker belief. Consider example (5):

(5) Sylvia's will means we have to move out.

In this case, the speaker and the hearer have been talking about Sylvia's will in their dialogue and both have reason to believe that Sylvia has a will and that they both know the other person has reason to believe Sylvia has a will.

Generally, if the speaker assumes the information presented in the presupposition to be known to the hearer, the speaker would expect the hearer to accept the information provided by the sentence presupposition by default, or even believe it. This process is generally referred to as binding in dynamic semantics.[4] Of course, the hearer may experience some difficulty in understanding and ask for a 'clarification', check 1.

However, the information presented as a sentence presupposition may be new. The speaker may wish to introduce a topic into the dialogue, knowing that the hearer has no previous knowledge of the topic. The new information (speaker presupposition) is then checked by the speaker for consistency, where it may be remarkable or unremarkable. Here, we follow Geurts's (1999) classification of remarkable and unremarkable presupposition.[5] Thus, examples (6) and (7), given a certain situation and agents, are more unusual to accommodate without questioning than example (1), where many people may have sisters.

(6) I have to pick my personal trainer up from the airport.

(7) I have to get the keys for my private jet.

Unremarkable information is information that people may accept without too much questioning,

[4]The lack of feedback about this information is considered 'weak positive feedback' that the hearer has accepted the information (Al-Raheb 2005).

[5]This further subclassification of presupposition is not indicated in the classification of checks for reasons of clarity, but it is incorporated in the DRT model presented in this paper.

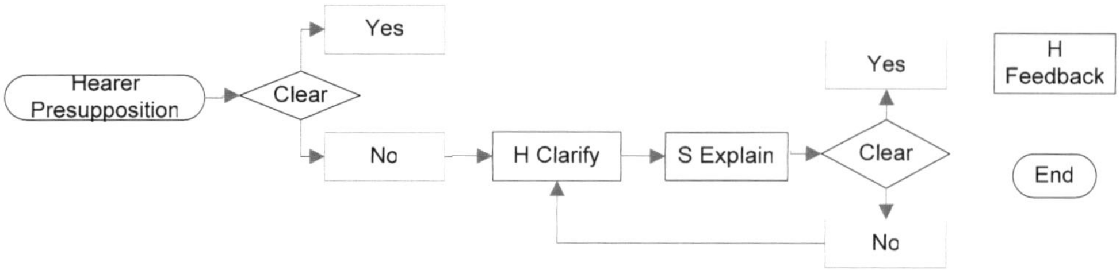

Figure 3: Hearer Presupposition: Check 1 (Clarification Check)

such as having a brother or a sister. An example of remarkable information might be:

(8) My private jet arrives this afternoon.

In social contexts in which it is not expected that everyone owns a private jet, such information will at least raise an eyebrow. Being cooperative, the speaker will assume, unless the hearer indicates otherwise, that the information she provides in the presupposition is unremarkable for the particular hearer in the particular context, and that the hearer will accommodate the information by either accepting it or believing it. Whether something is remarkable depends on the specific participant and type of communicative situation. For example, two film stars talking together would presumably not find example (8) 'remarkable', nor might a journalist interviewing a celebrity.

The speaker has to be prepared for cases when, despite being cooperative, the hearer might perceive sentence presupposition as unclear and/or contradictory. What this means for the present treatment of presupposition is that generally the speaker believes that the new information presented in the presupposition is unremarkable; therefore, the speaker will expect the hearer to accommodate the new information. However, in case the hearer should find the new information unusual or remarkable, the speaker will, we assume, expect the hearer to check whether the presupposition is consistent with her beliefs or not. The speaker may also expect the hearer to ask for clarification if the sentence presupposition is not clear.

If clear, the speaker may expect the hearer to accommodate the sentence presupposition and may safely assume that the information has been accepted, unless it is indicated through 'strong positive feedback' that the information is actually strongly believed (Al-Raheb 2005). However, if the presupposition is not clear, the speaker may expect the hearer to ask for clarification and a clarification process takes place, in which the hearer might ask for more clarification if the information is still not clear. When the information is finally clear, the hearer may provide feedback.

Despite the speaker's best efforts to be cooperative, there are cases where the presupposition contradicts the hearer's previous beliefs. Speakers usually do not expect this to happen, but are generally prepared to produce a clarification or attempt to fix the dialogue when such a problem occurs.

Figure 2 is a flowchart displaying the speaker's expectations in terms of presupposition according to her beliefs and on the assumption that she is being cooperative. According to this treatment of presupposition, whether the speaker believes the information in a presupposition is new or old, the result is the same in terms of how the speaker expects the hearer to act. The only difference is that new information gets accommodated by the hearer, while known information is 'bound' and either already accepted or believed (Asher and Lascarides 1998; van der Sandt and Geurts 1991).[6] It has to be said that this is of course an ideal situation. The speaker does not always have beliefs concerning whether the hearer already believes the presupposed information or not.

To sum up, when initiating the topic of a presupposition, we can conclude the following: bel(S, P), bel(S, clear(P)), bel(S, consistent(P)), and bel(S, accept(H,P)).[7] The speaker may have either the belief bel(S,¬ bel(H,P)) or the belief bel(S,bel(H,P)). However, in our implementation of the pragmatic and semantic notions of presupposition in DRT, the only beliefs represented after S's utterance are: bel(S, P), or accept(S,P) and if

[6]Discourse referents of known presuppositions attach themselves to previous discourse markers referring to the same object or person.

[7]S stands for the speaker, H stands for the hearer and bel stands for believes.

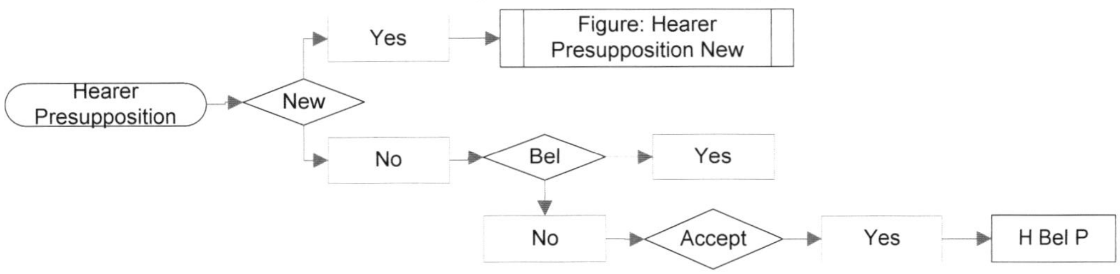

Figure 4: Hearer Presupposition: Check 2 (Informativity Check: Old)

sufficient previous information is available, either bel(S,¬ bel(H,P)) or bel(S,bel(H,P)).

3.2 Hearer Presupposition

As a result of the speaker's initiating the topic of P indicated through sentence presupposition, the hearer acquires the belief that the speaker believes the presupposition. The first information check to apply to hearer presupposition is the clear/ not clear check. That is to say, upon hearing P, the hearer first checks whether the presupposition is clear (e.g. hearer has no problems with perception). As mentioned previously, there are other types of clarification requested when inconsistency arises. However, what we are concerned with here is whether the hearer has been able to receive the message or not. Other clarification checks may take place after the hearer performs the new/old (informativity) check and the consistency check.

If the presupposition is not clear in the above sense, the hearer may ask the speaker to clarify her statement. As a simple example, consider an imaginary dialogue between a customer and customer service assistant about a gas heater:

(9) Customer: How long does it take to fix my gas heater?
Customer Service Assistant: Your what?
Customer: My gas heater needs fixing.

After checking whether the information, sentence presupposition, is clear, the customer service assistant asks the customer to clarify. In this particular case, the lack of clarity may be attributed to, e.g. not hearing very well. The hearer expects the speaker to provide an explanation or clarification. The speaker is then obliged to provide a further explanation. If the information is still not clear, the hearer may ask for more clarification and the hearer needs to provide an explanation. Figure 3 incorporates this potentially iterative loop. This is consistent with conversation analysis research, which assumes that information may be cleared up after an explanation is provided, but also allows for further clarification if needed (Schegloff et al. 1977). If the sentence presupposition is cleared up, then the hearer may provide feedback that the information is clear. However, lack of feedback is also considered a case of 'weak positive feedback' (Al-Raheb 2005). Generally, after providing an explanation, the speaker's assumptions are likely to be that the hearer now has no problems with the sentence presupposition.

Having made sure that the sentence presupposition is clear, the hearer may now move on to perform the informativity check, check 2. If the information the speaker presents as a sentence presupposition is known to the hearer, in the sense of being in his acceptance space, i.e. already a hearer presupposition, the hearer may strengthen that acceptance by now believing the presupposition (cf. Al-Raheb 2005). The hearer may previously hold a strong belief about the presupposition, i.e. the hearer may already believe P. In this case, it is not necessary to add a new belief that P to hearer presupposition. We are assuming here that the hearer's knowledge of a sentence presupposition means that this presupposition does not contradict previous beliefs held by the hearer. Figure 4 shows the hearer's options if the sentence presupposition is already a hearer presupposition, or known to him. The speaker ideally expects the hearer will accept P (i.e. P will have become hearer presupposition), unless negative feedback is provided by the hearer. If strong positive feedback is provided by the hearer, the speaker may thereby form the meta-belief that bel(H,bel(S,bel(H,P))).

If the sentence presupposition provides new information, the hearer then performs the consis-

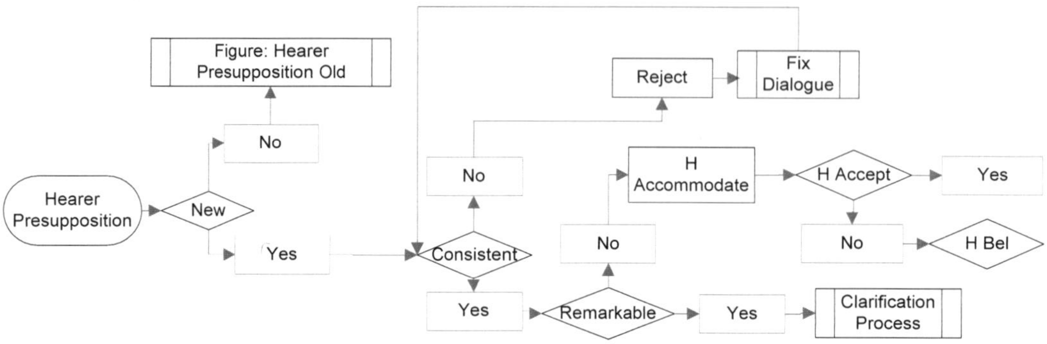

Figure 5: Hearer Presupposition: Check 3 (Consistency and Informativity Check: New)

tency check. If the information provided contradicts previous beliefs, the hearer may reject the sentence presupposition and an attempt would be made to remedy or fix the dialogue. For example, consider:

(10) Speaker: Julia's husband is coming for dinner.
Hearer: This can't be! Julia is widowed!

When the information presented by the sentence presupposition is consistent with the hearer's belief space or acceptance space, the hearer makes a judgement about whether the information is remarkable (odd or unusual) or *unremarkable* (cf. Geurts 1999). If the information is unremarkable, the hearer accommodates the new information by either accepting it or believing it. In other words, it becomes hearer presupposition. Figure 5 shows presupposition processing from the hearer's perspective when the sentence presupposition contains information new to the hearer.

If the presupposition is remarkable, the hearer may check for clarity. This is a different type of clarity check from the one performed initially. Clarification checks can arise from different reasons and not just because of difficulty in hearing. This time the hearer requires an explanation for the *oddness* of the information used as a presupposition. This is when the clarification process starts again. For example,

(11) Speaker: My pet lion requires a lot of attention.
Hearer: Your pet what?
Speaker: Oh sorry, I mean one of those virtual pets you take care of.

Here, we may assume, the hearer has not found the appropriate discourse referent for 'pet lion' and thus goes through 'remarkable' check after the consistency check.[8]

Again, the hearer may provide feedback concerning whether the explanation has been accepted or not. Unless negative feedback is provided, the hearer is expected to at least accept the presupposition bel(S,accept(H,P)). In addition, the other agent (speaker) may assume that the hearer now has no problem with the presupposition, bel(S,clear(H,P)). If the hearer is not convinced by the speaker's explanation, an attempt at repairing the dialogue is needed.[9]

To sum up, at the stage of the hearer's receiving the speaker's utterance, the hearer may make the judgement that the speaker believes the presupposition (speaker presupposition). In addition, unless the hearer gives the speaker reason to think that the hearer disagrees with the presupposition, the speaker assumes that the hearer has no problem understanding the sentence presupposition, and further, that the hearer has now come to accept the presupposition (hearer presupposition). It must be pointed out that generally speaking, unless the speaker has introduced as her presupposition a topic perceived to be new and very unusual, the hearer does not need to go through the clarification process for each presupposition, since generally the presuppositions are not the focus of the speaker's utterance (Levinson 1983).

[8]This example raises a lot of interesting cognitive and pragmatic issues, which will be ignored here so as not to distract from the main focus of this argument.

[9]Fixing a dialogue process is not addressed here. It is assumed that if fixing the dialogue is successful, the agent will then continue with the consistency check in order to carry on with the dialogue, unless one of the agents simply gives up.

4 Conclusion

This paper has enhanced the pragmatic conception of presupposition in DRT by considering presupposition from both the speaker's and the hearer's point of view. It has also linked semantic presupposition with pragmatic presupposition through linking the speaker's presupposition with the presupposition communicated by her utterance (sentence presupposition) on the one hand, and sentence presupposition with hearer presupposition on the other hand. This it was argued is helped by the information checks which both the speaker and the hearer perform.

References

Al-Raheb, Y. 2005. *Speaker/Hearer Representation in a Discourse Representation Theory Model of Presupposition: A Computational-Linguistic Approach*. Phd. University of East Anglia.

Asher, N. and Lascarides, A. 1998b. 'The Semantics and Pragmatics of Presupposition'. *Journal of Semantics* 15, pp. 239–299.

Geurts, B. 1996. 'Local Satisfaction Guaranteed: A Presupposition Theory and Its Problems'. *Linguistics and Philosophy* 19, pp. 259–294.

Geurts, B. 1998. 'Presupposition and Anaphors in Attitude Contexts'. *Linguistics and Philosophy* 21, pp. 545–601.

Geurts, B. 1999. *Presuppositions and Pronouns: Current Research in the Semantics/ Pragmatics Interface*. Oxford: Elsevier.

Grice, P. 1975. 'Logic and Conversation (from the William James Lectures, Harvard University, 1967)'. In: P. Cole and J. Morgan (Eds.). *Syntax and Semantics 3: Speech Acts*. pp. 41-58. New York: Academic Press.

Grice, P. 1989. *Studies in the Way of Words*. Cambridge, MA: Harvard University Press.

Kamp, H. 1984. 'A Theory of Truth and Semantic Representation'. In: J. Groenendijk, T. Janseen, and M. Stokhof (Eds.). *Truth, Interpretation and Information: Selected Papers from the Third Amsterdam Colloquium*. Amsterdam: Foris Publications.

Kamp, H. 1988. 'Comments on Stalnaker'. In: R. Grimm and D. Merrill (Eds.). *Contents of Thought. Proceedings of the 1985 Oberlin Colloquium in Philosophy*. pp. 156–181. Tucson State: The University of Arizona Press.

Kamp, H. 1990. 'Prolegomena to a Structural Account of Belief and Other Attitudes'. In: C. Anderson and J. Owens (Eds.). *Propositional Attitudes: The Role of Content in Logic, Language, and Mind*. Stanford, CA: CSLI Publications.

Kamp, H. 1995. 'Discourse Representation Theory'. In: J. Verschueren, J. Ostman, and J. Bloomaert (Eds.). *Handbook of Pragmatics Manual*. Amsterdam: John Benjamin.

Kamp, H. 2001a. 'Computation and Justification of Presuppositions: One Aspect of the Interpretation of Multi-Sentence Discourse'. In: M. Bras and L. Vieu (Eds.). *Semantics and Pragmatics of Discourse and Dialogue: Experimenting with Current Theories*. pp. 57–84. Oxford: Elsevier Science.

Kamp, H. 2001b. 'The Importance of Presupposition'. In: C. Rohrer and A. Rossdeutscher (Eds.). *Linguistic Form and its Computation: Selected Papers from the SFB 340*. pp. 207-254. Stanford: CSLI.

Kamp, H. and Reyle, U. 1993. *From Discourse to Logic: Introduction to Model Theoretic Semantics of Natural Language, Formal Logic and Discourse Representation Theory*. Boston, Dordrecht: Kluwer.

Kamp, H., van Genabith, J., and Reyle, U. 2005. *The Handbook of Logic*. Unpublished Manuscript. http://www.ims.uni-stuttgart.de/~hans/.

Lambrecht, K. 1994. *Information Structure and Sentence Form: Topic, Focus and the Mental Representations of Discourse Referents*. Cambridge: Cambridge University Press.

Levinson, S. 1983. *Pragmatics*. Cambridge: Cambridge University Press.

Purver, M., Healey, P., King, J., Ginzburg, J., and Mills, G. 2003. 'Answering Clarification Questions'. In: *Proceedings of the 4th SIGdial Workshop on Discourse and Dialogue, Association for Computational Linguistics*. pp. 23–33. Sapporo.

Purver, M. 2004. 'Claire: the Clarification Engine'. In: J. Ginzburg and E. Vallduvi (Eds.). *Proceedings of the Eighth Workshop on the Semantics and Pragmatics of Dialogue. Catalog '04*. pp. 77-84. Universitat Pompeu Fabra: Barcelona.

Schegloff, E., Jefferson, G., and Sacks, H. 1977. 'The Preference for Self-Correction in the Organization of Repair in Conversation'. *Language* 53, pp. 361–382.

Stalnaker, R. 2002. 'Common ground'. *Linguistics and Philosophy* 25(5-6), pp. 701–721.

van der Sandt, R. and Geurts, B. 1991. 'Presupposition, Anaphora, and Lexical Content'. In: O. Herzog and C.-R. Rollinger (Eds.). *Text Understanding in LILOG*. pp. 259–296. Berlin, Heidelberg: Springer Verlag.

van der Sandt, R. 1992. 'Presupposition Projection as Anaphora Resolution'. *Journal of Semantics* 9, pp. 333–377.

Semantic tagging for resolution of indirect anaphora

R. Vieira[1], **E. Bick**[2], **J. Coelho**[1], **V. Muller**[1], **S. Collovini**[1], **J. Souza**[1], **L. Rino**[3]
UNISINOS[1], University of Denmark[2], UFSCAR[3]
renatav@unisinos.br, eckhard.bick@mail.dk, lucia@dc.ufscar.br

Abstract

This paper presents an evaluation of indirect anaphor resolution which considers as lexical resource the semantic tagging provided by the PALAVRAS parser. We describe the semantic tagging process and a corpus experiment.

1 Introduction

Bridging anaphora represents a special part of the general problem of anaphor resolution. As a special case of anaphora, it has been studied and discussed by different authors and for various languages. There are many problems in developing such studies. First, bridging is not a regular class, it seldom contains cases of associative and indirect anaphora (defined in the sequence); lexical resources such as Wordnet are not available for every language, and even when available such resources have proven to be insufficient for the problem. In fact, different sources of lexical knowledge have been evaluated for anaphora resolution (Poesio et al., 2002; Markert and Nissim, 2005; Bunescu, 2003). At last, corpus studies of bridging anaphora usually report results on a reduced number of examples, because this kind of data is scarce. Usually bridging anaphora considers two types: **Associative anaphors** are NPs that have an antecedent that is necessary to their interpretation (the relation between the anaphor and its antecedent is different from identity); and **Indirect anaphor** are those that have an identity relation with their antecedents but the anaphor and its antecedent have different head-nouns. In both associative and indirect anaphora, the semantic relation holding between the anaphor and its antecedent play an essential role for resolution. However, here we present an evaluation of the semantic tagging provided by the Portuguese parser PALAVRAS (Bick, 2000) (http://visl.sdu.dk/visl/pt/parsing/automatic) as a lexical resource for indirect anaphora resolution. We focus on indirect anaphors for two reasons, they are greater in number and they present better agreement features concerning human annotation.

2 Semantic Annotation with Prototype Tags

As a Constraint Grammar system, PALAVRAS encodes all annotational information as word based tags. A distinction is made between morphological, syntactic, valency and semantic tags, and for a given rule module (or level of analysis), one tag type will be regarded as primary (= flagged for disambiguation), while tags from lower levels provide unambiguous context, and tags from higher levels ambiguous lexical potentialities. Thus, semantic tags are regarded as secondary help tags at the syntactic level, but will have undergone some disambiguation at the anaphora resolution level. The semantic noun classes were conceived as *distinctors* rather than semantic definitions, the goal being on the one hand to capture semantically motivated regularities and relations in syntax, on the other hand to allow to distinguish between different senses, or to chose different translation equivalents in MT applications. A limited set of *semantic prototype* classes was deamed ideal for both purposes, since it allows at the same time similarity-based lumping of words (useful in structural analysis, IR, anaphora resolution) and context based polysemy resolution for an individual word (useful in MT, lexicography, alignment). Though we define *class hypernyms* as prototypes in the Roschian sense (Rosch, 1978)

Proceedings of the 7th SIGdial Workshop on Discourse and Dialogue, pages 76–79,
Sydney, July 2006.

as an (idealized) best instance of a given class of entities, we avoided low level prototypes, using <Azo> for four-legged land-animals rather than <dog> and <cat> for dog and cat races etc.). Where possible, systematic sub-classes were established. Semiotic artifacts <sem>, for instance are sub-divided into "readables" <sem-r> (book-prototype: *book, paper, magazine*), "watchables" <sem-w> (*film, show, spectacle*), "listenables" etc. The final category inventory, though developed independently, resembles the ontology used in the multilingual European SIMPLE project (http://www.ub.es/ gilcub/SIMPLE/simple.html). For the sake of rule based inheritance reasoning, semantic prototype classes were bundled using a matrix of 16 *atomic semantic features*. Thus, the atomic feature +MOVE is shared by the different human and animal prototypes as well as the vehicle prototype, but the vehicle prototype lacks the +ANIM feature, and only the bundle on human prototypes (<Hprof>, <Hfam>, <Hideo>,...) shares the +HUM feature (human professional, human family, human follower of a theory/belief/conviction/ideology). In the parser, a rule selecting the +MOVE feature (e.g. for subjects of movement verbs) will help discard competing senses from lemmas with the above prototypes, since they will all inherit choices based on the shared atomic feature. Furthermore, atomic features can themselves be subjected to inheritance rules, e.g. +HUM −> +ANIM −> +CONCRETE, or +MOVE −> +MOVABLE. In Table 1, which contains examples of polysemic institution nouns, positive features are marked with capital letters, negative features with small letters[1]. The words in the Table 1 are ambiguous with regard to the feature H, and since it is only the <inst> prototype that contributes the +HUM feature potential, it can be singled out by a rule selecting 'H' or by discarding 'h'. The parser's about 140 prototypes have been manually implemented for a lexicon of about 35.000 nouns. In addition, the ±HUM category was also introduced as a selection restriction for 2.000 verb senses (subject restriction) and 1.300 adjective senses (head restriction).

While the semantic annotation of common nouns is carried out by disambiguating a given lemma's lexicon-listed prototype potential, this strategy is not sufficient for proper nouns, due

[1]furn=furniture, con=container, inst=institution

Ee = entities (±CONCRETE)	Jj = ±MOVABLE	Hh = ±HUMAN ENTITY	Mm = ±MAS	Ll = ±LOCATION	**polysemy spectrum**
Ee	j	Hh	m	Ll	*faculdade*
E		H		L	<inst> univ. faculty
e		h		l	<f-c> property
Ee	j	Hh	m	Ll	*fundo*
e		h		L	<Labs> bottom
E		H		L	<inst> foundation
e		h		l	<ac> <smP> funds
Ee	j	Hh	Mm	Ll	*indústria*
E		H	m	L	<inst> industry
e		h	M	l	<am> diligence
E	Jj	Hh	m	L	*rede*
	J	h			<con> net
	j	H			<inst> <+n> network
	J	h			<furn> hammock

Table 1: Feature bundles in prototype based polysemy

to the productive nature of this word class. In two recent NER projects, the parser was augmented with a pattern recognition module and a rule-based module for identifying and classifying names. In the first project (Bick, 2003), 6 main classes with about 15 subclasses were used in a lexeme-based approach, while the second adopted the 41 largely functional categories of Linguateca's joint HAREM evaluation in 2005 (http://www.linguateca.com). A lexicon-registered name like *Berlin* would have a stable tag (<civ> = civitas) in the first version, while it would be tagged as either <hum>, <top> or <org> in the second, dependent on context. At the time of writing, we have not yet tagged our anaphora corpus with name type tags, and it is unclear which approach, lexematic or functional, will work best for the resolution of indirect and associative anaphora.

3 Indirect Anaphora Resolution

Our work was based on a corpus formed by 31 newspaper articles, from Folha de São Paulo, written in Brazilian Portuguese. The corpus was automatically parsed using the parser PALAVRAS, and manually annotated for anaphoricity using the MMAX tool(http://mmax.eml-research.de/) . Four subjects annotated the corpus. All annotators agreed on the antecedent in 73% of the cases, in other 22% of the cases there was agreement between three annotators and in 5% of the cases only two annotators agreed. There were 133 cases of definite *Indirect anaphors* (NPs starting with definite articles) from the total of 1454 definite descriptions (near to 10%) and 2267 NPs.

The parser gives to each noun of the text (or to most of them) a semantic tag. For instance, the noun *japonês* [*japanese*] has the following semantic tags *ling* and *Hnat*, representing the features: human nationality and language respectively.

```
<word id="word_28">
 <n can="japonês" gender="M" number="S">
    <secondary_n tag="Hnat"/>
    <secondary_n tag="ling"/>
 </n>
</word>
```

The approach consists in finding relationships with previous nouns through the semantic tags. The chosen antecedent will be the nearest expression with the largest number of equal semantic tags. For instance, in the example below, the anaphor is resolved by applying this resolution principle, to *japonês - a língua*.

O Eurocenter oferece *cursos de japonês* em Kanazawa. Após um mês, o aluno falará modestamente *a língua*.

The Eurocenter offers *Japanese courses* in Kanazawa. After one month, a student can modestly speak *the language*.

As both expressions (japanese and language) hold the semantic tag "ling" the anaphor is resolved. For the experiments, we considered as correct the cases where the antecedent found automatically was the same as in the manual annotation (same), and also the cases in which the antecedent of the manual annotation was found further up in the chain identified automatically (in-chain). We also counted those cases in which the antecedent of the manual annotation was among the group of candidates sharing the same tags (in-candidates), but was not the chosen one (the chosen being the nearest with greater number of equal tags).

	Indirect anaphora	
Results	**#**	**% of Total**
Same	25	19%
In-chain	15	11%
Total Correct	40	30%
In-candidates	9	7%
Unsolved	40	30%
Error	44	33%
Total	**133**	**100%**

Table 2: Indirect anaphor resolution

Table 2 shows the results of the indirect anaphor resolution. In 19% of the cases, the system found the same antecedent as marked in the manual annotation. Considering the chain identified by the system the correct cases go up to 30%. The great number of unsolved cases were related to the fact that proper names were not tagged. Considering mainly the tagged nouns (about 93 cases), the correct cases amount to 43%). This gives us an idea of the quality of the tags for the task. We further tested if increasing the weight of more specific features in opposition to the more general ones would help in the antecedent decision process. A semantic tag that is more specific receives a higher weight The semantic tag set has three levels, level 1, which is more general receives weight 1, level 2 receives 5, and level 3 receives 10. See the example below.

```
<A>      1        Animal, umbrella tag
<AA>     5        Group of animals
<Adom>   10       Domestic    animal
```

In this experiment the chosen candidate is the nearest one whose sum of equal tag values has higher weight. Table 3 shows just a small improvement in the correct cases. If we do not consider unsolved cases, mostly related to proper names, indirect anaphors were correctly identified in 46% of the cases (43/96).

	Indirect anaphora	
Results	**#**	**% of Total**
Same	24	18%
In-chain	19	14%
Total Correct	43	32%
In-candidates	6	5%
Unsolved	40	30%
Error	44	33%
Total	**133**	**100%**

Table 3: Indirect anaphor - weighting schema

Since there is no semantic tagging for proper names as yet, the relationship between pairs such as *São Carlos - a cidade* [*São Carlos - the city*] could not be found. Regarding wrong antecedents, we have seen that some semantic relationships are weaker, having no semantic tags in common, for instance: *a proposta - o aumento* [*the proposal - the rise*]. In some cases the antecedent is not a previous noun phrase but a whole sentence, paragraph or disjoint parts of the text. As we consider only relations holding between noun phrases, these cases could not be resolved. Finally, there are cases of plain heuristic failure. For instance, establishing a relationship between *os professores* [*the teachers*], with the semantic tags *H* and *Hprof*, and *os politicos* [*the politicians*], with the semantic tags *H* and *Hprof*, when the correct antecedent was *os docentes* [*the docents*], with the semantic tags *HH* (group of humans) and *Hprof*.

4 Final Remarks

Previous work on nominal anaphor resolution has used lexical knowledge in different ways. (Poesio et al., 1997) presented results concerning the resolution of bridging definitions, using the WordNet (Fellbaum, 1998), where bridging DDs enclose our *Indirect* and *Associative anaphora*. Poesio et al. reported 35% of recall for synonymy, 56% for hypernymy and 38% for meronymy. (Schulte im Walde, 1997) evaluated the bridging cases presented in (Poesio et al., 1997), on the basis of lexical acquisition from the British National Corpus. She reported a recall of 33% for synonymy, 15% for hypernymy and 18% for meronymy. (Poesio et al., 2002) considering syntactic patterns for lexical knowledge acquisition, obtained better results for resolving meronymy (66% of recall). (Gasperin and Vieira, 2004) tested the use of word similarity lists on resolving indirect anaphora, reporting 33% of recall. (Markert and Nissim, 2005) presented two ways (WordNet and Web) of obtaining lexical knowledge for antecedent selection in coreferent DDs (*Direct* and *Indirect anaphora*). Markert and Nissim achieved 71% of recall using Web-based method and 65% of recall using WordNet-based method. We can say that our results are very satisfactory, considering the related work. Note that usually evaluation of bridging anaphora is made on the basis of a limited number of cases, because the data is sparse. Our study was based on 133 examples, which is not much but surpasses some of the previous related work. Mainly, our results indicate that the semantic tagging provided by the parser is a good resource for dealing with the problem, if compared to other lexical resources such as WordNet and acquired similarity lists. We believe that the results will improve significantly once semantic tags for proper names are provided by the parser. This evaluation is planned as future work.

Acknowledgments

This work was partially funded by CNPq.

References

Eckhard Bick. 2000. *The Parsing System PALAVRAS: Automatic Grammatical Analysis of Protuguese in a Constraint Grammar Framework*. Ph.D. thesis, Arhus University, Arhus.

Eckhard Bick. 2003. Multi-level ner for portuguese in a cg framework. In Nuno J. et al. Mamede, editor, *Computational Processing of the Portuguese Language (Procedings of the 6th International Workshop, PROPOR 2003)*, number 2721 in Lecture Notes in Computer Science, pages 118–125, Faro, Portugal. Springer.

Razvan Bunescu. 2003. Associative anaphora resolution: A web-based approach. In *Proceedings of the Workshop on The Computational Treatment of Anaphora - EACL 2003*, Budapest.

Christiane Fellbaum, editor. 1998. *WordNet: An Electronic Lexical Database*. MIT Press, Cambridge, MA.

Caroline Gasperin and Renata Vieira. 2004. Using word similarity lists for resolving indirect anaphora. In *Proceedings of ACL Workshop on Reference Resolution and its Applications*, pages 40–46, Barcelona.

Katja Markert and Malvina Nissim. 2005. Comparing knowledge sources for nominal anaphora resolution. *Computational Linguistics*, 31(3):367–401.

Massimo Poesio, Renata Vieira, and Simone Teufel. 1997. Resolving bridging descriptions in unrestricted texts. In *Proceedings of the Workshop on Operational Factors In Practical, Robust, Anaphora Resolution for Unrestricted Texts*, pages 1–6, Madrid.

Masimo Poesio, Ishikawa Tomonori, Sabine Shulte im Walde, and Renata Vieira. 2002. Acquiring lexical knowledge for anaphora resolution. In *Proceedings of 3rd Language resources and evaluation conference LREC 2002*, Las Palmas.

Eleanor Rosch. 1978. Principles of categorization. In E. Rosch and B. Lloyd, editors, *Cognition and Categorization*, pages 27–48. Hillsdale, New Jersey: Lawrence Erlbaum Associate.

Sabine Schulte im Walde. 1997. *Resolving Bridging Descriptions in High-Dimensional Space Resolving Bridging Descriptions in High-Dimensional Space*. Ph.D. thesis, Institut für Maschinelle Sprachverarbeitung, Universität Stuttgart, and Center for Cognitive Science, University of Edinburgh, Edinburgh.

An annotation scheme for citation function

Simone Teufel **Advaith Siddharthan** **Dan Tidhar**
Natural Language and Information Processing Group
Computer Laboratory
Cambridge University, CB3 0FD, UK
{Simone.Teufel,Advaith.Siddharthan,Dan.Tidhar}@cl.cam.ac.uk

Abstract

We study the interplay of the discourse structure of a scientific argument with formal citations. One subproblem of this is to classify academic citations in scientific articles according to their rhetorical function, e.g., as a rival approach, as a part of the solution, or as a flawed approach that justifies the current research. Here, we introduce our annotation scheme with 12 categories, and present an agreement study.

1 Scientific writing, discourse structure and citations

In recent years, there has been increasing interest in applying natural language processing technologies to scientific literature. The overwhelmingly large number of papers published in fields like biology, genetics and chemistry each year means that researchers need tools for information access (extraction, retrieval, summarization, question answering etc). There is also increased interest in automatic citation indexing, e.g., the highly successful search tools Google Scholar and CiteSeer (Giles et al., 1998).[1] This general interest in improving access to scientific articles fits well with research on discourse structure, as knowledge about the overall structure and goal of papers can guide better information access.

Shum (1998) argues that experienced researchers are often interested in relations between articles. They need to know if a certain article criticises another and what the criticism is, or if the current work is based on that prior work. This type of information is hard to come by with current search technology. Neither the author's abstract, nor raw citation counts help users in assessing the relation between articles. And even though CiteSeer shows a text snippet around the physical location for searchers to peruse, there is no guarantee that the text snippet provides enough information for the searcher to infer the relation. In fact, studies from our annotated corpus (Teufel, 1999), show that 69% of the 600 sentences stating contrast with other work and 21% of the 246 sentences stating research continuation with other work do not contain the corresponding citation; the citation is found in preceding sentences (i.e., the sentence expressing the contrast or continuation would be outside the CiteSeer snippet). We present here an approach which uses the classification of citations to help provide relational information across papers.

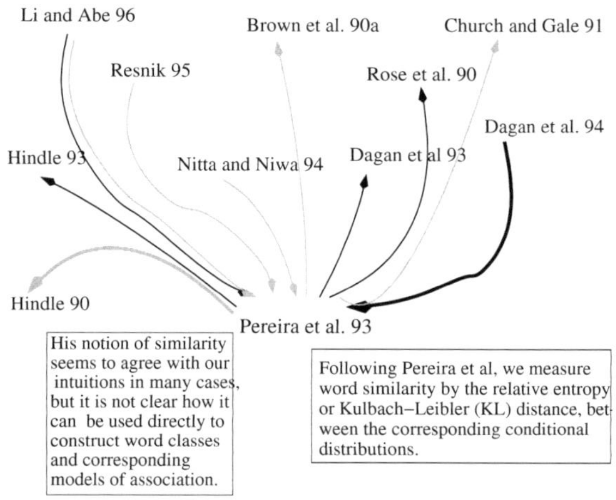

Figure 1: A rhetorical citation map

Citations play a central role in the process of writing a paper. Swales (1990) argues that scientific writing follows a general rhetorical argumentation structure: researchers must justify that their paper makes a contribution to the knowledge in their discipline. Several argumentation steps are required to make this justification work, e.g., the statement of their specific goal in the paper (Myers, 1992). Importantly, the authors also must relate their current work to previous research, and acknowledge previous knowledge claims; this is done with a formal citation, and with language connecting the citation to the argument, e.g., statements of usage of other people's approaches (often near textual segments in the paper where these approaches are described), and statements of contrast with them (particularly in the discussion or related work sections). We argue that the automatic recognition of citation function is interesting for two reasons: a) it serves to build better citation indexers and b) in the long run, it will help constrain interpretations of the overall argumentative structure of a scientific paper.

Being able to interpret the rhetorical status of a citation at a glance would add considerable value to citation indexes, as shown in Fig. 1. Here differences and similarities are shown between the example paper (*Pereira et al., 1993*) and the papers it cites, as well as

[1] CiteSeer automatically citation-indexes all scientific articles reached by a web-crawler, making them available to searchers via authors or keywords in the title.

Proceedings of the 7th SIGdial Workshop on Discourse and Dialogue, pages 80–87,
Sydney, July 2006.

the papers that cite it. *Contrastive* links are shown in grey – links to rival papers and papers the current paper contrasts itself to. *Continuative* links are shown in black – links to papers that are taken as starting point of the current research, or as part of the methodology of the current paper. The most important textual sentence about each citation could be extracted and displayed. For instance, we see which aspect of *Hindle (1990)* the *Pereira et al.* paper criticises, and in which way *Pereira et al.*'s work was used by *Dagan et al.* (1994).

We present an annotation scheme for citations, based on empirical work in content citation analysis, which fits into this general framework of scientific argument structure. It consists of 12 categories, which allow us to mark the relationships of the current paper with the cited work. Each citation is labelled with exactly one category. The following top-level four-way distinction applies:

- Weakness: Authors point out a weakness in cited work
- Contrast: Authors make contrast/comparison with cited work (4 categories)
- Positive: Authors agree with/make use of/show compatibility or similarity with cited work (6 categories), and
- Neutral: Function of citation is either neutral, or weakly signalled, or different from the three functions stated above.

We first turn to the point of how to classify citation function in a robust way. Later in this paper, we will report results for a human annotation experiment with three annotators.

1.	Cited source is mentioned in the introduction or discussion as part of the history and state of the art of the research question under investigation.
2.	Cited source is the specific point of departure for the research question investigated.
3.	Cited source contains the concepts, definitions, interpretations used (and pertaining to the discipline of the citing article).
4.	Cited source contains the data (pertaining to the discipline of the citing article) which are used sporadically in the article.
5.	Cited source contains the data (pertaining to the discipline of the citing particle) which are used for comparative purposes, in tables and statistics.
6.	Cited source contains data and material (from other disciplines than citing article) which is used sporadically in the citing text, in tables or statistics.
7.	Cited source contains the method used.
8.	Cited source substantiated a statement or assumption, or points to further information.
9.	Cited source is positively evaluated.
10.	Cited source is negatively evaluated.
11.	Results of citing article prove, verify, substantiate the data or interpretation of cited source.
12.	Results of citing article disprove, put into question the data as interpretation of cited source.
13.	Results of citing article furnish a new interpretation/explanation to the data of the cited source.

Figure 2: Spiegel-Rüsing's (1977) Categories for Citation Motivations

2 Annotation schemes for citations

In the field of library sciences (more specifically, the field of Content Citation Analysis), the use of information from citations above and beyond simple citation counting has received considerable attention. Bibliometric measures assesses the quality of a researcher's output, in a purely quantitative manner, by counting how many papers cite a given paper (White, 2004; Luukkonen, 1992) or by more sophisticated measures like the h-index (Hirsch, 2005). But not all citations are alike. Researchers in content citation analysis have long stated that the classification of motivations is a central element in understanding the relevance of the paper in the field. Bonzi (1982), for example, points out that *negational* citations, while pointing to the fact that a given work has been *noticed* in a field, do not mean that that work is *received well*, and Ziman (1968) states that many citations are done out of "politeness" (towards powerful rival approaches), "policy" (by name-dropping and argument by authority) or "piety" (towards one's friends, collaborators and superiors). Researchers also often follow the custom of citing some particular early, basic paper, which gives the foundation of their current subject ("paying homage to pioneers"). Many classification schemes for citation functions have been developed (Weinstock, 1971; Swales, 1990; Oppenheim and Renn, 1978; Frost, 1979; Chubin and Moitra, 1975), inter alia. Based on such annotation schemes and hand-analyzed data, different influences on citation behaviour can be determined, but annotation in this field is usually done manually on small samples of text by the author, and not confirmed by reliability studies. As one of the earliest such studies, Moravcsik and Murugesan (1975) divide citations in running text into four dimensions: conceptual or operational use (i.e., use of theory vs. use of technical method); evolutionary or juxtapositional (i.e., own work is based on the cited work vs. own work is an alternative to it); organic or perfunctory (i.e., work is crucially needed for understanding of citing article or just a general acknowledgement); and finally confirmative vs. negational (i.e., is the correctness of the findings disputed?). They found, for example, that 40% of the citations were perfunctory, which casts further doubt on the citation-counting approach.

Other content citation analysis research which is relevant to our work concentrates on relating textual spans to authors' descriptions of other work. For example, in O'Connor's (1982) experiment, *citing statements* (one or more sentences referring to other researchers' work) were identified manually. The main problem encountered in that work is the fact that many instances of citation context are linguistically unmarked. Our data confirms this: articles often contain large segments, particularly in the central parts, which describe other people's research in a fairly neutral way. We would thus expect many citations to be neutral (i.e., not to carry any function relating to the argumentation per se).

Many of the distinctions typically made in content citation analysis are immaterial to the task considered here as they are too sociologically orientated, and can thus be difficult to operationalise without deep knowledge of the field and its participants (Swales, 1986). In particular, citations for general reference (background material, homage to pioneers) are not part of our analytic interest here, and so are citations "in passing", which are only marginally related to the argumentation of the overall paper (Ziman, 1968).

Spiegel-Rüsing's (1977) scheme (Fig. 2) is an example of a scheme which is easier to operationalise than most. In her scheme, more than one category can apply to a citation; for instance positive and negative evaluation (category 9 and 10) can be cross-classified with other categories. Out of 2309 citations examined, 80% substantiated statements (category 8), 6% discussed history or state of the art of the research area (category 1) and 5% cited comparative data (category 5).

Category	Description
Weak	Weakness of cited approach
CoCoGM	Contrast/Comparison in Goals or Methods (neutral)
CoCoR0	Contrast/Comparison in Results (neutral)
CoCo-	Unfavourable Contrast/Comparison (current work is better than cited work)
CoCoXY	Contrast between 2 cited methods
PBas	author uses cited work as starting point
PUse	author uses tools/algorithms/data
PModi	author adapts or modifies tools/algorithms/data
PMot	this citation is positive about approach or problem addressed (used to motivate work in current paper)
PSim	author's work and cited work are similar
PSup	author's work and cited work are compatible/provide support for each other
Neut	Neutral description of cited work, or not enough textual evidence for above categories or unlisted citation function

Figure 3: Our annotation scheme for citation function

Our scheme (given in Fig. 3) is an adaptation of the scheme in Fig. 2, which we arrived at after an analysis of a corpus of scientific articles in computational linguistics. We tried to redefine the categories such that they should be reasonably reliably annotatable; at the same time, they should be informative for the application we have in mind. A third criterion is that they should have some (theoretical) relation to the particular discourse structure we work with (Teufel, 1999).

Our categories are as follows: One category (Weak) is reserved for weakness of previous research, if it is addressed by the authors (cf. Spiegel-Rüsing's categories 10, 12, possibly 13). The next three categories describe comparisons or contrasts between own and other work (cf. Spiegel-Rüsing's category 5). The difference between them concerns whether the comparison is between methods/goals (CoCoGM) or results (CoCoR0). These two categories are for comparisons without explicit value judgements. We use a different category (CoCo-) when the authors claim their approach is better than the cited work.

Our interest in differences and similarities between approaches stems from one possible application we have in mind (the rhetorical citation search tool). We do not only consider differences stated between the current work and other work, but we also mark citations if they are explicitly compared and contrasted with other work (not the current paper). This is expressed in category CoCoXY. It is a category not typically considered in the literature, but it is related to the other contrastive categories, and useful to us because we think it can be exploited for search of differences and rival approaches.

The next set of categories we propose concerns positive sentiment expressed towards a citation, or a statement that the other work is actively used in the current work (which is the ultimate praise). Like Spiegel-Rüsing, we are interested in use of data and methods (her categories 4, 5, 6, 7), but we cluster different usages together and instead differentiate unchanged use (PUse) from use with adaptations (PModi). Work which is stated as the explicit starting point or intellectual ancestry is marked with our category PBas (her category 2). If a claim in the literature is used to strengthen the authors' argument, this is expressed in her category 8, and vice versa, category 11. We collapse these two in our category PSup. We use two categories she does not have definitions for, namely similarity of (aspect of) approach to other approach (PSim), and motivation of approach used or problem addressed (PMot). We found evidence for prototypical use of these citation functions in our texts. However, we found little evidence for her categories 12 or 13 (disproval or new interpretation of claims in cited literature), and we decided against a "state-of-the-art" category (her category 1), which would have been in conflict with our PMot definition in many cases.

Our fourteenth category, Neut, bundles truly neutral descriptions of other researchers' approaches with all those cases where the textual evidence for a citation function was not enough to warrant annotation of that category, and all other functions for which our scheme did not provide a specific category. As stated above, we do in fact expect many of our citations to be neutral.

Citation function is hard to annotate because it in principle requires interpretation of author intentions (what could the author's intention have been in choosing a certain citation?). Typical results of earlier citation function studies are that the sociological aspect of citing is not to be underestimated. One of our most fundamental ideas for annotation is to only mark explicitly signalled citation functions. Our guidelines explicitly state that a general linguistic phrase such as "better" or "used by us" must be present, in order to increase objectivity in finding citation function. Annotators are encouraged to point to textual evidence they have for assigning a particular function (and are asked to type the source of this evidence into the annotation tool for each citation). Categories are defined in terms of certain objective types of statements (e.g., there are 7 cases for `PMot`). Annotators can use general text interpretation principles when assigning the categories, but are not allowed to use in-depth knowledge of the field or of the authors.

There are other problematic aspects of the annotation. Some concern the fact that authors do not always state their purpose clearly. For instance, several earlier studies found that negational citations are rare (Moravcsik and Murugesan, 1975; Spiegel-Rüsing, 1977); MacRoberts and MacRoberts (1984) argue that the reason for this is that they are potentially politically dangerous, and that the authors go through lengths to diffuse the impact of negative references, hiding a negative point behind insincere praise, or diffusing the thrust of criticism with perfunctory remarks. In our data we found ample evidence of this effect, illustrated by the following example:

> *Hidden Markov Models (HMMs)* **(Huang et al. 1990)** *offer a powerful statistical approach to this problem, though it is unclear how they could be used to recognise the units of interest to phonologists.* (9410022, S-24)[2]

It is also sometimes extremely hard to distinguish usage of a method from statements of similarity between a method and the own method. This happens in cases where authors do not want to admit they are using somebody else's method:

> *The same test was used in* **Abney and Light (1999)**. (0008020, S-151)

> *Unification of indices proceeds in the same manner as unification of all other typed feature structures* **(Carpenter 1992)**. (0008023, S-87)

In this case, our annotators had to choose between categories `PSim` and `PUse`.

It can also be hard to distinguish between continuation of somebody's research (i.e., taking somebody's research as starting point, as intellectual ancestry, i.e. `PBas`) and simply using it (`PUse`). In principle, one would hope that annotation of all usage/positive categories (starting with `P`), if clustered together, should result in higher agreement (as they are similar, and as the resulting scheme has fewer distinctions). We would expect this to be the case in general, but as always, cases exist where a conflict between a contrast (`CoCo`) and a change to a method (`PModi`) occur:

> *In contrast to* **McCarthy, Kay and Kiraz**, *we combine the three components into a single projection.* (0006044, S-182)

The markable units in our scheme are a) all full citations (as recognized by our automatic citation processor on our corpus), and b) all names of authors of cited papers anywhere in running text outside of a formal citation context (i.e., without date). Our citation processor recognizes these latter names after parsing the citation list an marks them up. This is unusual in comparison to other citation indexers, but we believe these names function as important referents comparable in importance to formal citations. In principle, one could go even further as there are many other linguistic expressions by which the authors could refer to other people's work: pronouns, abbreviations such as "Mueller and Sag (1990), henceforth M & S", and names of approaches or theories which are associated with particular authors. If we could mark all of these up automatically (which is not technically possible), annotation would become less difficult to decide, but technical difficulty prevent us from recognizing these other cases automatically. As a result, in these contexts it is impossible to annotate citation function directly on the referent, which sometimes causes problems. Because this means that annotators have to consider non-local context, one markable may have different competing contexts with different potential citation functions, and problems about which context is "stronger" may occur. We have rules that context is to be constrained to the paragraph boundary, but for some categories paper-wide information is required (e.g., for `PMot`, we need to know that a praised approach is used by the authors, information which may not be local in the paragraph).

Appendix A gives unambiguous example cases where the citation function can be decided on the basis of the sentence alone, but Fig. 4 shows a more typical example where more context is required to interpret the function. The evaluation of the citation *Hindle (1990)* is contrastive; the evaluative statement is found 4 sentences after the sentence containing the citation[3]. It consists of a positive statement (agreement with authors' view), followed by a weakness, underlined, which is the chosen category. This is marked on the nearest markable (*Hindle*, 3 sentences after the citation).

[2] In all corpus examples, numbers in brackets correspond to the official Cmp_lg archive number, "S-" numbers to sentence numbers according to our preprocessing.

[3] In Fig. 4, markables are shown in boxes, evaluative statements underlined, and referents in bold face.

S-5 **Hindle (1990)/**`Neut` *proposed dealing with the sparseness problem by estimating the likelihood of unseen events from that of "similar" events that have been seen.*
S-6 *For instance, one may estimate the likelihood of a particular direct object for a verb from the likelihoods of that direct object for similar verbs.*
S-7 *This requires a reasonable definition of verb similarity and a similarity estimation method.*
S-8 *In* **Hindle/**`Weak` *'s proposal, words are similar if we have strong statistical evidence that they tend to participate in the same events.*
S-9 **His** *notion of similarity seems to agree with our intuitions in many cases, but it is not clear how it can be used directly to construct word classes and corresponding models of association.* (9408011)

Figure 4: Annotation example: influence of context

A naive view on this annotation scheme could consider the first two sets of categories in our scheme as "negative" and the third set of categories "positive". There is indeed a sentiment aspect to the interpretation of citations, due to the fact that authors need to make a point in their paper and thus have a stance towards their citations. But this is not the whole story: many of our "positive" categories are more concerned with different ways in which the cited work is useful to the current work (which aspect of it is used, e.g., just a definition or the entire solution?), and many of the contrastive statements have no negative connotation at all and simply state a (value-free) difference between approaches. However, if one looks at the distribution of positive and negative adjectives around citations, one notices a (non-trivial) connection between our task and sentiment classification.

There are written guidelines of 25 pages, which instruct the annotators to only assign one category per citation, and to skim-read the paper before annotation. The guidelines provide a decision tree and give decision aids in systematically ambiguous cases, but subjective judgement of the annotators is nevertheless necessary to assign a single tag in an unseen context. We implemented an annotation tool based on XML/XSLT technology, which allows us to use any web browser to interactively assign one of the 12 tags (presented as a pull-down list) to each citation.

3 Data

The data we used came from the CmpLg (Computation and Language archive; 320 conference articles in computational linguistics). The articles are in XML format. Headlines, titles, authors and reference list items are automatically marked up with the corresponding tags. Reference lists are parsed, and cited authors' names are identified. Our citation parser then applies regular patterns and finds citations and other occurrences of the names of cited authors (without a date) in running text and marks them up. Self-citations are detected by overlap of citing and cited authors. The citation processor developped in our group (Ritchie et al., 2006) achieves high accuracy for this task (96% of citations recognized, provided the reference list was error-free). On average, our papers contain 26.8 citation instances in running text[4].

4 Human Annotation: results

In order to machine learn citation function, we are in the process of creating a corpus of scientific articles with human annotated citations, according to the scheme discussed before. Here we report preliminary results with that scheme, with three annotators who are developers of the scheme.

In our experiment, the annotators independently annotated 26 conference articles with this scheme, on the basis of guidelines which were frozen once annotation started[5]. The data used for the experiment contained a total of 120,000 running words and 548 citations.

The relative frequency of each category observed in the annotation is listed in Fig. 5. As expected, the distribution is very skewed, with more than 60% of the citations of category `Neut`.[6] What is interesting is the relatively high frequency of usage categories (`PUse`, `PModi`, `PBas`) with a total of 18.9%. There is a relatively low frequency of clearly negative citations (`Weak`, `CoCoR-`, total of 4.1%), whereas the neutral–contrastive categories (`CoCoGM`, `CoCoR0`, `CoCoXY`) are slightly more frequent at 7.6%. This is in concordance with earlier annotation experiments (Moravcsik and Murugesan, 1975; Spiegel-Rüsing, 1977).

We reached an inter-annotator agreement of K=.72 (n=12;N=548;k=3)[7]. This is comparable to aggreement on other discourse annotation tasks such as dialogue act parsing and Argumentative Zoning (Teufel et al., 1999). We consider the agreement quite good, considering the number of categories and the difficulties (e.g., non-local dependencies) of the task.

The annotators are obviously still disagreeing on some categories. We were wondering to what degree the fine granularity of the scheme is a problem. When we collapsed the obvious similar categories (all `P` categories into one category, and all `CoCo` categories into another) to give four top level categories (`Weak`, `Positive`, `Contrast`, `Neutral`), this only raised kappa to 0.76. This

[4] As opposed to reference list items, which are fewer.

[5] The development of the scheme was done with 40+ different articles.

[6] Spiegel-Rüsing found that out of 2309 citations she examined, 80% substantiated statements.

[7] Following Carletta (1996), we measure agreement in Kappa, which follows the formula $K = \frac{P(A)-P(E)}{1-P(E)}$ where P(A) is observed, and P(E) expected agreement. Kappa ranges between -1 and 1. K=0 means agreement is only as expected by chance. Generally, Kappas of 0.8 are considered stable, and Kappas of .69 as marginally stable, according to the strictest scheme applied in the field.

Neut	PUse	CoCoGM	PSim	Weak	CoCoXY	PMot	PModi	PBas	PSup	CoCo-	CoCoR0
62.7%	15.8%	3.9%	3.8%	3.1%	2.9%	2.2%	1.6%	1.5%	1.1%	1.0%	0.8%

Figure 5: Distribution of the categories

	Weak	CoCo-	CoCoGM	CoCoR0	CoCoXY	PUse	PBas	PModi	PMot	PSim	PSup	Neut
Weak	**5**											3
CoCo-		**1**	3									
CoCoGM			**23**							3		
CoCoR0				**4**								
CoCoXY					**1**							
PUse						**86**	6			2	1	12
PBas							**3**					2
PModi								**3**				
PMot									**13**			4
PSim						3				**20**		5
PSup		1				2					**1**	
Neut	6		10	6	4	17	1		6	4		**287**

Figure 6: Confusion matrix between two annotators

points to the fact that most of our annotators disagreed about whether to assign a more informative category or `Neut`, the neutral fall-back category. Unfortunately, Kappa is only partially sensitive to such specialised disagreements. While it will reward agreement with infrequent categories more than agreement with frequent categories, it nevertheless does not allow us to weight disagreements we care less about (`Neut` vs more informative category) less than disagreements we do care a lot about (informative categories which are mutually exclusive, such as `Weak` and `PSim`).

Fig. 6 shows a confusion matrix between the two annotators who agreed most with each other. This again points to the fact that a large proportion of the confusion involves an informative category and `Neut`. The issue with `Neut` and `Weak` is a point at hand: authors seem to often (deliberately or not) mask their intended citation function with seemingly neutral statements. Many statements of weakness of other approaches were stated in such caged terms that our annotators disagreed about whether the signals given were "explicit" enough.

While our focus is not sentiment analysis, it is possible to conflate our 12 categories into three: *positive*, *weakness* and *neutral* by the following mapping:

Old Categories	New Category
Weak, CoCo-	Negative
PMot, PUse, PBas, PModi, PSim, PSup	Positive
CoCoGM, CoCoR0, CoCoXY, Neut	Neutral

Thus negative contrasts and weaknesses are grouped into `Negative`, while neutral contrasts are grouped into `Neutral`. All the positive classes are conflated into `Positive`. This resulted in kappa=0.75 for three annotators.

Fig. 7 shows the confusion matrix between two annotators for this sentiment classification. Fig. 7 is particularly instructive, because it shows that annotators

	Weakness	Positive	Neutral
Weakness	**9**	1	12
Positive		**140**	13
Neutral	4	30	**339**

Figure 7: Confusion matrix between two annotators; categories collapsed to reflect sentiment

have only one case of confusion between positive and negative references to cited work. The vast majority of disagreements reflects genuine ambiguity as to whether the authors were trying to stay neutral or express a sentiment.

Distinction	**Kappa**
`PMot` v. all others	.790
`CoCoGM` v. all others	.765
`PUse` v. all others	.761
`CoCoR0` v. all others	.746
`Neut` v. all others	.742
`PSim` v. all others	.649
`PModi` v. all others	.553
`CoCoXY` v. all others	.553
`Weak` v. all others	.522
`CoCo-` v. all others	.462
`PBas` v. all others	.414
`PSup` v. all others	.268

Figure 8: Distinctiveness of categories

In an attempt to determine how well each category was defined, we created artificial splits of the data into binary distinctions: each category versus a super-category consisting of all the other collapsed categories. The kappas measured on these datasets are given in Fig. 8. The higher they are, the better the annotators could distinguish the given category from all the other categories. We can see that out of the informative categories, four are defined at least as well as the overall distinction (i.e. above the line in Fig. 8: PMot, PUse, CoCoGM and CoCoR0. This is encouraging, as the application of citation maps is almost entirely centered around usage and contrast. However, the semantics of some categories are less well-understood by our annotators: in particular PSup (where the difficulty lies in what an annotator understands as "mutual support" of two theories), and (unfortunately) PBas. The problem with PBas is that its distinction from PUse is based on subjective judgement of whether the authors *use* a part of somebody's previous work, or *base* themselves entirely on this previous work (i.e., see themselves as following in the same intellectual framework). Another problem concerns the low distinctivity for the clearly negative categories CoCo- and Weak. This is in line with MacRoberts and MacRoberts' hypothesis that criticism is often hedged and not clearly lexically signalled, which makes it more difficult to reliably annotate such citations.

5 Conclusion

We have described a new task: human annotation of citation function, a phenomenon which we believe to be closely related to the overall discourse structure of scientific articles. Our annotation scheme concentrates on contrast, weaknesses of other work, similarities between work and usage of other work. One of its principles is the fact that relations are only to be marked if they are explicitly signalled. Here, we report positive results in terms of interannotator agreement.

Future work on the annotation scheme will concentrate on improving guidelines for currently suboptimal categories, and on measuring intra-annotator agreement and inter-annotator agreement with naive annotators. We are also currently investigating how well our scheme will work on text from a different discipline, namely chemistry. Work on applying machine learning techniques for automatic citation classification is currently underway (Teufel et al., 2006); the agreement of one annotator and the system is currently K=.57, leaving plenty of room for improvement in comparison with the human annotation results presented here.

6 Acknowledgements

This work was funded by the EPSRC projects CITRAZ (GR/S27832/01, "Rhetorical Citation Maps and Domain-independent Argumentative Zoning") and SCIBORG (EP/C010035/1, "Extracting the Science from Scientific Publications").

References

Susan Bonzi. 1982. Characteristics of a literature as predictors of relatedness between cited and citing works. *JASIS*, 33(4):208–216.

Jean Carletta. 1996. Assessing agreement on classification tasks: The kappa statistic. *Computational Linguistics*, 22(2):249–254.

Daryl E. Chubin and S. D. Moitra. 1975. Content analysis of references: Adjunct or alternative to citation counting? *Social Studies of Science*, 5(4):423–441.

Carolyn O. Frost. 1979. The use of citations in literary research: A preliminary classification of citation functions. *Library Quarterly*, 49:405.

C. Lee Giles, Kurt D. Bollacker, and Steve Lawrence. 1998. Citeseer: An automatic citation indexing system. In *Proceedings of the Third ACM Conference on Digital Libraries*, pages 89–98.

Jorge E. Hirsch. 2005. An index to quantify an individual's scientific research output. *Proceedings of the National Academy of Sciences of the United Stated of America (PNAS)*, 102(46).

Terttu Luukkonen. 1992. Is scientists' publishing behaviour reward-seeking? *Scientometrics*, 24:297–319.

Michael H. MacRoberts and Barbara R. MacRoberts. 1984. The negational reference: Or the art of dissembling. *Social Studies of Science*, 14:91–94.

Michael J. Moravcsik and Poovanalingan Murugesan. 1975. Some results on the function and quality of citations. *Social Studies of Science*, 5:88–91.

Greg Myers. 1992. In this paper we report...—speech acts and scientific facts. *Journal of Pragmatics*, 17(4):295–313.

John O'Connor. 1982. Citing statements: Computer recognition and use to improve retrieval. *Information Processing and Management*, 18(3):125–131.

Charles Oppenheim and Susan P. Renn. 1978. Highly cited old papers and the reasons why they continue to be cited. *JASIS*, 29:226–230.

Anna Ritchie, Simone Teufel, and Steven Robertson. 2006. Creating a test collection for citation-based IR experiments. In *Proceedings of HLT-06*.

Simon Buckingham Shum. 1998. Evolving the web for scientific knowledge: First steps towards an "HCI knowledge web". *Interfaces, British HCI Group Magazine*, 39:16–21.

Ina Spiegel-Rüsing. 1977. Bibliometric and content analysis. *Social Studies of Science*, 7:97–113.

John Swales. 1986. Citation analysis and discourse analysis. *Applied Linguistics*, 7(1):39–56.

John Swales, 1990. *Genre Analysis: English in Academic and Research Settings. Chapter 7: Research articles in English*, pages 110–176. Cambridge University Press, Cambridge, UK.

Simone Teufel, Jean Carletta, and Marc Moens. 1999. An annotation scheme for discourse-level argumentation in research articles. In *Proceedings of the Ninth Meeting of the European Chapter of the Association for Computational Linguistics (EACL-99)*, pages 110–117.

Simone Teufel, Advaith Siddharthan, and Dan Tidhar. 2006. Automatic classification of citation function. In *Proceedings of EMNLP-06*.

Simone Teufel. 1999. *Argumentative Zoning: Information Extraction from Scientific Text*. Ph.D. thesis, School of Cognitive Science, University of Edinburgh, UK.

Melvin Weinstock. 1971. Citation indexes. In *Encyclopedia of Library and Information Science*, volume 5, pages 16–40. Dekker, New York, NY.

Howard D. White. 2004. Citation analysis and discourse analysis revisited. *Applied Linguistics*, 25(1):89–116.

John M. Ziman. 1968. *Public Knowledge: An Essay Concerning the Social Dimensions of Science*. Cambridge University Press, Cambridge, UK.

A Annotation examples

Weak	*However,* **Koskenniemi** *himself understood that his initial implementation had significant limitations in handling non-concatenative morphotactic processes.* (0006044, S-4)
CoCoGM	*The goals of the two papers are slightly different:* **Moore** *'s approach is designed to reduce the total grammar size (i.e., the sum of the lengths of the productions), while our approach minimizes the number of productions.* (0008021, S-22)
CoCoR0	*This is similar to results in the literature* **(Ramshaw and Marcus 1995).** (0008022, S-147)
CoCo-	*For the Penn Treebank,* **Ratnaparkhi (1996)** *reports an accuracy of 96.6% using the Maximum Entropy approach, our much simpler and therefore faster HMM approach delivers 96.7%.* (0003055, S-156)
CoCoXY	*Unlike previous approaches* **(Ellison 1994, Walther 1996), Karttunen** *'s approach is encoded entirely in the finite state calculus, with no extra-logical procedures for counting constraint violations.* (0006038, S-5)
PBas	*Our starting point is the work described in* **Ferro et al. (1999)** *, which used a fairly small training set.* (0008004, S-11)
PUse	*In our application, we tried out the Learning Vector Quantization (LVQ)* **(Kohonen et al. 1996).** (0003060, S-105)
PModi	*In our experiments, we have used a conjugate-gradient optimization program adapted from the one presented in* **Press et al.** (0008028, S-72)
PMot	*It has also been shown that the combined accuracy of an ensemble of multiple classifiers is often significantly greater than that of any of the individual classifiers that make up the ensemble (e.g.,* **Dietterich (1997)).** (0005006, S-9)
PSim	*Our system is closely related to those proposed in* **Resnik (1997)** *and* **Abney and Light (1999).** (0008020, S-24)
PSup	*In all experiments the SVM_Light system outperformed other learning algorithms, which confirms* **Yang and Liu** *'s* **(1999)** *results for SVMs fed with Reuters data.* (0003060, S-141)
Neut	*The cosine metric and Jaccard's coefficient are commonly used in information retrieval as measures of association* **(Salton and McGill 1983).** (0001012, S-29)

An Information State-Based Dialogue Manager for Call for Fire Dialogues

Antonio Roque and **David Traum**
USC Institute for Creative Technologies
13274 Fiji Way, Marina Del Rey, CA 90292
roque@ict.usc.edu, traum@ict.usc.edu

Abstract

We present a dialogue manager for "Call for Fire" training dialogues. We describe the training environment, the domain, the features of its novel information state-based dialogue manager, the system it is a part of, and preliminary evaluation results.

1 Overview

Dialogue systems are built for many different purposes, including information gathering (e.g., (Aust et al., 1995)), performing simple transactions (e.g, (Walker and Hirschman, 2000)), collaborative interaction (e.g., (Allen et al., 1996)), tutoring (e.g., (Rose et al., 2003)), and training (e.g. (Traum and Rickel, 2002)). Aspects of the purpose, as well as features of the domain itself (e.g., train timetables, air flight bookings, schedule maintenance, physics, and platoon-level military operations) will have a profound effect on the nature of the dialogue which a system will need to engage in. Issues such as initiative, error correction, flexibility in phrasing and dialogue structure may depend crucially on these factors.

The information state approach to dialogue managers (Larsson and Traum, 2000) has been an attempt to cast some of these differences within the same framework. In this approach, a theory of dialogue is constructed by providing information structure elements, a set of dialogue moves that can be recognized and produced and are used to modify the nature of these elements, a set of update rules that govern the dynamics of how the information is changed as dialogue moves are performed, and an update strategy. Many different dialogue systems have been built according to this general approach (e.g., (Cooper and Larsson, 1999; Matheson et al., 2000; Lemon et al., 2001; Johnston et al., 2002; Traum and Rickel, 2002; Purver, 2002)).

In this paper, we present an information-state based dialogue manager for a new domain: training call for fire dialogues. Like other dialogue systems used as role-players in training applications, the structure of the dialogue is not completely free for a dialogue designer to specify based on issues of dialogue efficiency. The dialogue system must conform as much as possible to the type of dialogue that a trainee would actually encounter in the types of interaction he or she is being trained for. In particular, for military radio dialogues, much of the protocol for interaction is specified by convention (e.g., (Army, 2001)). Still, there is a fair amount of flexibility in how other aspects of the dialogue progress.

This dialogue manager is part of a system we call Radiobot-CFF. Radiobots are a general class of dialogue systems meant to speak over the radio in military simulations. Our most extended effort to date is the Radiobot-CFF system, which engages in "call for fire" dialogues to train artillery observers within a virtual reality training simulation. Our dialogue system can operate according to three different use cases, depending on how much control a human operator/trainer would like to exercise over the dialogue. There is a fully automatic mode in which the Radiobot-CFF system engages unassisted in dialogue with the user, a semi-automatic mode in which the Radiobot-CFF system fills in forms (which can be edited) and the operator can approve or change communication with a simulator or trainee, and a passive mode in which the operator is engaging in the dialogue and the Radiobot-CFF system is just observing.

In section 2, we describe the training applica-

Proceedings of the 7th SIGdial Workshop on Discourse and Dialogue, pages 88–95,
Sydney, July 2006.

tion that our dialogue system has been embedded in as well as the system itself. In section 3, we describe some aspects of "call for fire dialogues", especially the differences in initiative and purposes of different phases in the dialogue. In section 4, we describe the information-state based dialogue model we have developed for this domain. This includes dialogue moves, information components, and update rules. We describe some error handling capabilities in section 5, and evaluation results in section 6.

2 Testbed

Our current testbed, Radiobot-CFF, has been developed in a military training environment, JFETS-UTM, at the U.S. Army base in in Ft. Sill, Oklahoma. JFETS-UTM trains soldiers to make Calls for Fire (CFFs), in which a Forward Observer (FO) team locates an enemy target and requests an artillery fire mission by radio from a Fire Direction Center (FDC). The training room resembles a battle-scarred apartment in a Middle Eastern country. A window shows a virtual city displayed by a rear-projected computer screen, and the soldiers use binoculars with computer displays at their ends to search for targets.

Ordinarily, two trainers control a UTM session. One communicates with the FO via a simulated radio, and the other decides what the artillery fire should be and inputs it to a GUI for the simulator. It is our goal to replace those two trainers with one trainer focusing on assessment while Radiobot-CFF handles the radio communications and interfaces with the virtual world.

Radiobot-CFF is composed of several pipelined components. A Speech Recognition component is implemented using the SONIC speech recognition system (Pellom, 2001) with custom language and acoustic models. An Interpreter component tags the ASR output with its its dialogue move and parameter labels using two separate Conditional Random Field (Sha and Pereira, 2003; McCallum, 2002) taggers trained on hand-annotated utterances. A Dialogue Manager processes the tagged output, sending a reply to the FO (via a template-based Generator) and, when necessary, a message to the artillery simulator FireSim XXI[1] to make decisions on what type of fire to send. The reply to FO and messages to simulator are mediated by GUIs where the trainer can intervene if need be.

[1] http://sill-www.army.mil/blab/sims/FireSimXXI.htm

3 Call for Fire Dialogues

Call for Fire procedures are specified in an Army field manual (Army, 2001) with variations based on a unit's standard operating procedure. Messages are brief and followed by confirmations, where any misunderstandings are immediately corrected. A typical CFF is shown in Figure 1.

1	FO	steel one niner this is gator niner one adjust fire polar over
2	FDC	gator nine one this is steel one nine adjust fire polar out
3	FO	direction five niner four zero distance four eight zero over
4	FDC	direction five nine four zero distance four eight zero out
5	FO	one b m p in the open i c m in effect over
6	FDC	one b m p in the open i c m in effect out
7	FDC	message to observer kilo alpha high explosive four rounds adjust fire target number alpha bravo one zero zero zero over
8	FO	m t o kilo alpha four rounds target number alpha bravo one out
9	FDC	shot over
10	FO	shot out
11	FDC	splash over
12	FO	splash out
13	FO	right five zero fire for effect out over
14	FDC	right five zero fire for effect out
15	FDC	shot over
16	FO	shot out
17	FDC	rounds complete over
18	FO	rounds complete out
19	FO	end of mission one b m p suppressed zero casualties over
20	FDC	end of mission one b m p suppressed zero casualties out

Figure 1: Example Dialogue with Radiobot-CFF

CFFs can generally be divided into three *phases*. In the first phase (utterances 1-6 in Figure 1) the FOs identify themselves and important information about the CFF, including their coordinates, the kind of fire they are requesting, the location of the target, and the kind of target. In utterance 1 in Figure 1 the FO performs an identification, giving his own call sign and that of the FDC he is calling, and also specifies a method of fire ("adjust fire") and a method of targeting ("polar".) Note that when speakers expect a reply, they end their utterance with "over" as in utterance 1, otherwise with "out" as in the confirmation in utterance 2. In utterance 3 the FO gives target coordinates, and in utterance 5 the FO identifies the target as a BMP (a type of light tank) and requests ICM rounds ("improved conventional munitions".) These turns typically follow one another in quick sequence.

In the second phase of a CFF, (utterances 7-12 in Figure 1), after the FDC decides what kind of fire they will send, they inform the FO in a message to observer (MTO) as in utterance 7. This includes the units that will fire ("kilo alpha"), the kind of ammunition ("high explosive"), the number of rounds and method of fire ("4 rounds adjust fire"), and the target number ("alpha bravo one zero zero zero"). CFFs are requests rather than orders, and they may be denied in full or in part. In this example, the FO's request for ICM rounds was denied in favor of High Explosive rounds. Next the FDC informs the FO when the fire mission has been shot, as in utterance 9, and when the fire is about to land, as in utterance 11. Each of these are confirmed by the FO.

In the third phase, (utterances 13-20 in Figure 1) the FO regains dialogue initiative. Depending on the observed results, the FO may request that the fire be repeated with an adjust in location or method of fire. In utterance 13 the FO requests that the shot be re-sent to a location 50 meters to the right of the previous shot as a "fire for effect" all-out bombardment rather than an "adjust fire" targeting fire. This is followed by the abbreviated FDC-initiated phase of utterances 15-18. In utterance 19 the FO ends the mission, describing the results and number of casualties.

Besides the behavior shown, at any turn either participant may request or initiate an intelligence report or request the status of a mission. Furthermore, after receiving an MTO the FO may immediately begin another fire mission and thus have multiple missions active; subsequent adjusts are disambiguated with the target numbers assigned during the MTOs.

4 Dialogue Manager

We have constructed an Information State-based dialogue manager (Larsson and Traum, 2000) on this domain consisting of a set of dialogue moves, a set of informational components with appropriate formal representations, and a set of update rules with an update strategy. We describe each of these in turn.

4.1 Dialogue Moves

We defined a set of dialogue moves to represent the incoming FO utterances based on a study of transcripts of human-controlled JFETS-UTM sessions, Army manuals, and the needs of the simulator. As shown in Figure 2 these are divided into three groups: those that provide information about the FO or the fire mission, those that confirm information that the FDC has transmitted, and those that make requests.

```
Mission Information:
  Observer Coordinates
  Situation Report
  Identification
  Warning Order
  Method of Control
  Method of Engagement
  Target Location
  Target Description
  End of Mission

Confirming Information:
  Message to Observer
  Shot
  Splash
  Rounds Complete
  Intel Report

Other Requests:
  Radio Check
  Say Again
  Status
  Standby
  Command
```

Figure 2: FO Dialogue Moves

The dialogue moves that provide information include those in which the FOs transmit their Observer Coordinates (grid location on a map), a generic Situation Report, or one of the various components of a fire mission request ranging from call sign Identification to final End of Mission. The dialogue moves that confirm information include those that confirm the MTO and other FDC-initiated utterances, or a general report on scenario Intel. The final group includes requests to check radio functionality, to repeat the previous utterance, for status of a shot, to stand by for transmission of information, and finally a set of commands such as "check fire" requesting cancellation of a submitted fire mission.

Each of these dialogue moves contains information important to the dialogue manager. This information is captured by the parameters of the dialogue move, which are enumerated in Figure 3. Each parameter is listed with the dialogue move it usually occurs with, but this assignment is not strict. For example, "number_of_enemies" parameters occur in Target Description as well as End of Mission dialogue moves.

```
Identification-related:
  fdc_id
  fo_id

Warning Order-related:
  method_of_fire
  method_of_control
  method_of_engagement
  method_of_location

Target Location-related:
  grid_location
  direction
  distance
  attitude
  left_right
  left_right_adjust
  add_drop
  add_drop_adjust
  known_point

End Of Mission-related:
  target_type
  target_description
  number_of_enemies
  disposition

Other:
  command
  detail_of_request
  target_number
```

Figure 3: Dialogue Move Parameters

Figure 4 shows how the dialogue moves and parameters act to identify the components of an FO utterance. The example is based on utterance 1 in Figure 1; the Identification move has two parameters representing the call signs of the FDC and the FO, and the Warning Order has two parameters representing the method of fire and method of location. Parameters need to be identified to confirm back to the FO, and in some cases to be sent to the simulator and for use in updating the information state. In the example in Figure 4, the fact that the requested method of fire is an "adjust fire" will be sent to the simulator, and the fact that a method of fire has been given will be updated in the information state.

Identification: steel one nine this is gator niner one
`fdc_id`: steel one nine
`fo_id`: gator niner one
Warning Order: adjust fire polar
`method_of_fire`: adjust fire
`method_of_location`: polar

Figure 4: Example Dialogue Moves and Parameters

4.2 Informational Components

The Radiobot-CFF dialogue manager's information state consists of five classes of informational components, defined by their role in the dialogue and their level of accessibility to the user. These are the Fire Mission Decision components, the Fire Mission Value components, the Post-Fire Value components, the Disambiguation components, and the Update Rule Processing components.

By dividing the components into multiple classes we separate those that are simulator-specific from more general aspects of the domain.

Decisions to fire are based on general constraints of the domain, whereas the exact components to include in a message to simulator will be simulator-specific. Also, the components have been designed such that there is almost no overlap in the update rules that modify them (see section 4.3). This reduces the complexity involved in editing or adding rules; although there are over 100 rules in the information state, there are few unanticipated side-effects when rules are altered.

The first class of components are the Fire Mission Decision components, which are used to determine whether enough information has been collected to send fire. These components are boolean flags, updated by rules based on incoming dialogue moves and parameters. Figure 5 shows the values of these components after utterance 3 in Figure 1 has been processed. The FO has given a warning order, and a target location (which can either be given through a grid location, or through a combination of direction and distance values, and observer coordinates), so the appropriate components are "true". After the FO gives a target description, that component will be true as well, and an update rule will recognize that enough information has been gathered to send a fire mission.

```
has warning order? true
has target location? true
    has grid location? false
    has polar direction? true
    has polar distance? true
    has polar obco? true
has target descr? false
```

Figure 5: Fire Mission Decision Components

The second class of information state components is the set of Fire Mission Value components, which track the value of various information elements necessary for requesting a fire mission. These are specific to the FireSim XXI simulator. Figure 6 shows the values after utterance 3 in Figure 1. Components such as "direction value" take number values, and components such as "method of fire" take values from a finite set of possibilities. Several of these components, such as "attitude" have defaults that are rarely changed. Once the dialogue manager or human trainer decides that it has enough information to request fire, these components are translated into a simulator command and sent to the simulator.

```
method of control: adjust fire
method of fire: adjust fire
method of engagement: none given
target type: -
grid value: -
direction value: 5940
distance value: 480
length: 0
width: 100
attitude: 0
observer coordinate value: 45603595
```

Figure 6: Fire Mission Value Components

Fire Mission Value components are also directly modifiable by the trainer. Figure 7 shows the GUI which the trainer can use to take control of the session, edit any of the Fire Mission Value components, and relinquish control of the session back to Radiobot-CFF. This allows the trainer to correct any mistakes that the Radiobot may have made or test the trainee's adaptability by sending the fire to an unexpected location. The example shown in Figure 7 is after utterance 5 of Figure 1; the system is running in semi-automated mode and the dialogue manager has decided that it has enough information to send a fire. The trainer may send the message or edit it and then send it. A second GUI, not shown, allows the trainer to take control of the outgoing speech of the Radiobot, and, in semi-automated mode, either confirm the sending of a suggested output utterance, alter it before sending, or author new text for the radiobot to say.

The third class of components is the Post-Fire Value components, which are also exposed to the trainer for modification. The example shown in Figure 8 is from after utterance 13 in Figure 1; the FO has requested an "adjust fire" with an indicator of "fire for effect" and a right adjustment of 50. At this point in the dialogue the FO could have instead chosen to end the mission. If the initial fire had been a "fire for effect" it could have been repeated, rather than following up an initial "adjust fire." The adjust fire stage does not have any decision components because typically the adjust information is given in one move.

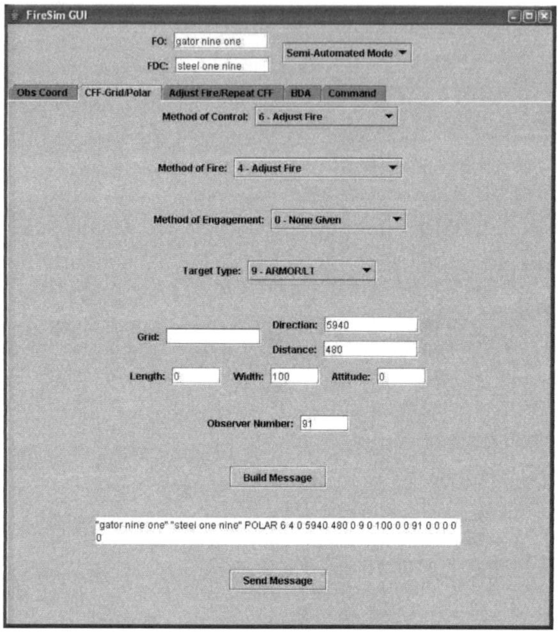

Figure 7: GUI

```
adjust fire: true
  shift indicator: fire for effect
repeat FFE: false

  left-right adjustment: 50
  add-drop adjustment: 0
  vertical adjustment: 0

end of mission: false
  disposition: -
  number of casualties: -
```

Figure 8: Post-Fire Value Components

The fourth class, Disambiguation components, are used by many rules to disambiguate local information based on global dialogue features. The example shown in Figure 9 is from the dialogue in Figure 1, after utterance 1. The "mission is polar" component helps determine the method of target location if speech recognition erroneously detects both polar and grid coordinates. Target numbers allow the FOs to handle multiple missions at the same time (e.g., starting a new call for fire, before the previous mission has been completed). The "missions active" component tracks how many missions are currently being discussed. The "phase" refers to the state of a three-state FSA that tracks which of the three subdialogue phases (described in section 3) the dialogue is in for the most recently-discussed mission.

An example of the use of the Disambiguation components is to determine whether the phrase "fire for effect" refers to an adjustment of a previous mission or the initiation of a new mission. In utterance 13 in Figure 1, "fire for effect" refers to an adjustment of a CFF that began with an "adjust fire" in utterance 1. However, the FO could have started that CFF by calling for a "fire for effect". Furthermore the FO could have started a second CFF in utterance 13 rather than doing an adjust, and might have specified "fire for effect". By using a rule to check the phase of the mission the move can be disambiguated to understand that it is referring to an adjustment, rather than the initiation of a new fire mission.

```
mission is polar?: true
target number: 0
missions active: 0
last method of fire: adjust
phase: Info-Gathering
```

Figure 9: Disambiguation Components

The last class of components, shown in Figure 10, is closely tied to the update rule processing, and is therefore described in the following section.

```
current reply: gator nine one this is
               steel one nine
previous reply: -
understood? true
send EOM? false
send repeat? false
send repeat adjust? false
send repeat ffe? false
```

Figure 10: Update Rule Processing Components

4.3 Update Rules

Update rules update the informational components, build a message to send to the FO, build a message to send to the simulator, and decide whether a message should actually be sent to the FO or simulator.

As an example of rule application, consider the processing of utterance 1 in Figure 1. Figure 4 shows the moves and parameters for this utterance. When the dialogue manager processes this utterance, a set of rules associated with the Identification move are applied, which starts building a response to the FO. This response is built in the "current reply" Update Rule Processing component. Figure 10 shows a reply in the process of being built: a rule has recognized that an Identification move is being given, and has filled in slots in a template with the necessary information and added it to the "current reply" component.

Next, the update rules will recognize that a Warning Order is being given, and will identify that it is an "adjust fire" method of fire, and update the "has warning order" decision component, the "method of control" and "method of fire" value components, and the "last method of fire" disambiguation component. As part of this, the appropriate fields of the GUIs will be filled in to allow the trainer to override the FO's request if need be. Another rule will then fill in the slots of a template to add "adjust fire polar" to the current reply, and later another rule will add "out", thus finishing the reply to the FO. After the reply is finished, it will place it in the "previous reply" component, for reference if the FO requests a repeat of the previous utterance.

Certain rules are specified as achieving comprehension — that is, if they are applied, the "understood" variable for that turn is set. If no reply has been built but the move has been understood, then no reply needs to be sent. This happens, for example, for each of utterances 8, 10, and 12 in Figure 1: because they are confirmations of utterances that the FDC has initiated, they do not need to be replied to. Similarly, no reply needs to be sent if no reply has been built and the incoming message is empty or only contains one or two words indicative of an open mic and background noise. Finally, if no reply has been built and the move has not been understood, then the FO is prompted to repeat the message.

As described above, the Fire Mission Decision components are used to determine whether to send a fire mission. For other communications with the simulator, a simpler approach is possible. The decisions to send an end of mission, a repeat fire, or a repeat fire with the 'adjust' or 'fire for effect' specification can be made with update rules acting on a single boolean, and so these are also part of the Update Rule Processing Components as shown in Figure 10.

Finally, the application of rules follows a specific strategy. A given utterance may contain one or more dialogue moves, each with a set of rules specific to it. The dialogue manager applies the appropriate rules to each dialogue move in the utterance before applying the rules that send the FO messages or simulator commands, as shown in Figure 11. Rules for producing replies and simulator commands are delayed until the end of processing an utterance to allow for utterances that may contain self-corrections or relevant details later in the turn.

```
for each dialogue move in utterance
  apply rules for that dialogue move
end for

apply rules to send reply to FO
apply rules to send simulator commands
```

Figure 11: Update Strategy for Rules

5 Error Handling

Radiobot-CFF is able to handle various kind of problematic input in a number of ways. It can handle partially correct information, as in Figure 12. Speech recognition errors caused the "three casualties" information to be lost, but the update rules were able to handle the essential part of the FO contribution: that the mission was ended, and that the target was neutralized. The domain is forgiving in this particular example, although a strict trainer might want to intervene by the GUI and insist that the FO re-submit the end of mission report.

```
FO Said:     end of mission target
             neutralized estimate three
             casualties over
ASR Output:  in end of mission target
             neutralized as the make three
             catch a these over
Radiobot:    end of mission target
             neutralized out
```

Figure 12: Error Correction

In other cases, such as when giving number coordinates, all information must be fully grounded. An example of this is in Figure 13, where the number "five" is lost by the speech recognition. In this case, the domain-appropriate response is to prompt for a repetition.

```
FO Said:     right five zero over
ASR Output:  right by zero over
Radiobot:    say again over
```

Figure 13: Error Correction - Prompt

6 Evaluation

We conducted an evaluation of the Radiobot-CFF system in fully-automated, semi-automated, and human-controlled conditions. The system performed well in a number of measures; for example, Table 1 shows the scores for median time-to-fire and task-completion rates. Additional measures and further details are available in (Robinson et al., 2006).

Table 1: *Example Evaluation Measures*

Measure	Human	Semi	Fully
Time To Fire	106.2 s	139.4 s	104.3 s
Task Compl.	100%	97.5%	85.9%

Of particular relevance here, we performed an evaluation of the dialogue manager, using the evaluation corpus of 17 missions run on 8 sessions, a total of 408 FO utterances. We took transcribed recordings of the FO utterances, ran them through the Interpreter, and corrected them. For each session, we ran corrected Interpreter output through the Dialogue Manager to print out the values of the informational components at the end of every turn. We then corrected those, and compared the corrections to the uncorrected values to receive precision, accuracy, and f-scores of 0.99 each.[2]

7 Summary

We presented a dialogue manager which can engage in Call for Fire training dialogues, and described the environment and system in which it works. It has an information state-based design with several components accessible to a human operator, and may be controlled either fully, in part, or not at all by that human operator.

8 Acknowledgements

This work has been sponsored by the U.S. Army Research, Development, and Engineering Command (RDECOM). Statements and opinions expressed do not necessarily reflect the position or the policy of the United States Government, and no official endorsement should be inferred.

[2]In this preliminary evaluation, the Interpreter and informational component corrections were all done by a single coder; also, the coder was correcting the informational component output rather than entering informational component information from blank, thus any errors of omission on the part of the coder would work in favor of the system performance.

We would like to thank Charles Hernandez and Janet Sutton of the Army Research Laboratory, and Bill Millspaugh and the Depth & Simultaneous Attack Battle Lab in Fort Sill, Oklahoma, for their efforts on this project. We would also like to thank the other members of the Radiobots project.

References

James F. Allen, Bradford W. Miller, Eric K. Ringger, and Teresa Sikorski. 1996. A robust system for natural spoken dialogue. In *Proceedings of the 1996 Annual Meeting of the Association for Computational Linguistics (ACL-96)*, pages 62–70.

Department of the Army. 2001. Tactics, techniques and procedures for observed fire and fire support at battalion task force and below. Technical Report FM 3-09.30 (6-30), Department of the Army.

H. Aust, M. Oerder, F. Siede, and V. Steinbiss. 1995. A spoken language enquiry system for automatic train timetable information. *Philips Journal of Research*, 49(4):399–418.

Robin Cooper and Staffan Larsson. 1999. Dialogue moves and information states. In H.C. Bunt and E. C. G. Thijsse, editors, *Proceedings of the Third International Workshop on Computational Semantics*.

Michael Johnston, Srinivas Bangalore, Gunaranjan Vasireddy, Amanda Stent, Patrick Ehlen, Marilyn Walker, Steve Whittaker, and Preetam Maloor. 2002. Match: An architecture for multimodal dialogue systems. In *Proceedings of the 40th Annual Meeting of the Association for Computational Linguistics (ACL)*, pages 376–383.

Staffan Larsson and David Traum. 2000. Information state and dialogue management in the TRINDI dialogue move engine toolkit. *Natural Language Engineering*, 6:323–340, September. Special Issue on Spoken Language Dialogue System Engineering.

Oliver Lemon, Anne Bracy, Alexander Gruenstein, and Stanley Peters. 2001. The witas mult-modal dialogue system i. In *Proc. European Conf. on Speech Communication and Tech- nology*, pages 559–1562.

Colin Matheson, Massimo Poesio, and David Traum. 2000. Modelling grounding and discourse obligations using update rules. In *Proceedings of the First Conference of the North American Chapter of the Association for Computational Linguistics*.

Andrew Kachites McCallum. 2002. Mallet: A machine learning for language toolkit. http://mallet.cs.umass.edu.

Bryan Pellom. 2001. Sonic: The university of colorado continuous speech recognizer. Technical Report TR-CSLR-2001-01, University of Colorado.

Matthew Purver. 2002. Processing unknown words in a dialogue system. In *Proceedings of the 3rd ACL SIGdial Workshop on Discourse and Dialogue*, pages 174–183. Association for Computational Linguistics, July.

Susan Robinson, Antonio Roque, Ashish Vaswani, and David Traum. 2006. Evaluation of a spoken dialogue system for military call for fire training. To Appear.

C. Rose, D. Litman, D. Bhembe, K. Forbes, S. Silliman, R. Srivastava, and K. van Lehn. 2003. A comparison of tutor and student behavior in speech versus text based tutoring.

F. Sha and F. Pereira. 2003. Shallow parsing with conditional random fields.

David R. Traum and Jeff Rickel. 2002. Embodied agents for multi-party dialogue in immersive virtual worlds. In *Proceedings of the first International Joint conference on Autonomous Agents and Multiagent systems*, pages 766–773.

M. Walker and L. Hirschman. 2000. Evaluation for darpa communicator spoken dialogue systems.

Automatically Detecting Action Items in Audio Meeting Recordings

William Morgan Pi-Chuan Chang Surabhi Gupta Jason M. Brenier

Department of Computer Science
Stanford University
353 Serra Mall
Stanford, CA 94305-9205
ruby@cs.stanford.edu
pcchang@cs.stanford.edu
surabhi@cs.stanford.edu

Department of Linguistics
Center for Spoken Language Research
Institute of Cognitive Science
University of Colorado at Boulder
594 UCB
Boulder, Colorado 80309-0594
jbrenier@colorado.edu

Abstract

Identification of action items in meeting recordings can provide immediate access to salient information in a medium notoriously difficult to search and summarize. To this end, we use a maximum entropy model to automatically detect action item-related utterances from multi-party audio meeting recordings. We compare the effect of lexical, temporal, syntactic, semantic, and prosodic features on system performance. We show that on a corpus of action item annotations on the ICSI meeting recordings, characterized by high imbalance and low inter-annotator agreement, the system performs at an F measure of 31.92%. While this is low compared to better-studied tasks on more mature corpora, the relative usefulness of the features towards this task is indicative of their usefulness on more consistent annotations, as well as to related tasks.

1 Introduction

Meetings are a ubiquitous feature of workplace environments, and recordings of meetings provide obvious benefit in that they can be replayed or searched through at a later date. As recording technology becomes more easily available and storage space becomes less costly, the feasibility of producing and storing these recordings increases. This is particularly true for audio recordings, which are cheaper to produce and store than full audio-video recordings.

However, audio recordings are notoriously difficult to search or to summarize. This is doubly true of multi-party recordings, which, in addition to the difficulties presented by single-party recordings, typically contain backchannels, elaborations, and side topics, all of which further confound search and summarization processes. Making efficient use of large meeting corpora thus requires intelligent summary and review techniques.

One possible user goal given a corpus of meeting recordings is to discover the *action items* decided within the meetings. Action items are decisions made within the meeting that require post-meeting attention or labor. Rapid identification of action items can provide immediate access to salient portions of the meetings. A review of action items can also function as (part of) a summary of the meeting content.

To this end, we explore the task of applying maximum entropy classifiers to the task of automatically detecting action item utterances in audio recordings of multi-party meetings. Although available corpora for action items are not ideal, it is hoped that the feature analysis presented here will be of use to later work on other corpora.

2 Related work

Multi-party meetings have attracted a significant amount of recent research attention. The creation of the ICSI corpus (Janin et al., 2003), comprised of 72 hours of meeting recordings with an average of 6 speakers per meeting, with associated transcripts, has spurred further annotations for various types of information, including dialog acts (Shriberg et al., 2004), topic hierarchies and action items (Gruenstein et al., 2005), and "hot spots" (Wrede and Shriberg, 2003).

The classification of individual utterances based on their role in the dialog, i.e. as opposed to their semantic payload, has a long history, especially in the context of *dialog act* (DA) classification.

Proceedings of the 7th SIGdial Workshop on Discourse and Dialogue, pages 96–103,
Sydney, July 2006.

Research on DA classification initially focused on two-party conversational speech (Mast et al., 1996; Stolcke et al., 1998; Shriberg et al., 1998) and, more recently, has extended to multi-party audio recordings like the ICSI corpus (Shriberg et al., 2004). Machine learning techniques such as graphical models (Ji and Bilmes, 2005), maximum entropy models (Ang et al., 2005), and hidden Markov models (Zimmermann et al., 2005) have been used to classify utterances from multi-party conversations.

It is only more recently that work focused specifically on action items themselves has been developed. SVMs have been successfully applied to the task of extracting action items from email messages (Bennett and Carbonell, 2005; Corston-Oliver et al., 2004). Bennett and Carbonell, in particular, distinguish the task of action item detection in email from the more well-studied task of text classification, noting the finer granularity of the action item task and the difference of semantics vs. intent. (Although recent work has begun to blur this latter division, e.g. Cohen et al. (2004).)

In the audio domain, annotations for action item utterances on several recorded meeting corpora, including the ICSI corpus, have recently become available (Gruenstein et al., 2005), enabling work on this topic.

3 Data

We use action item annotations produced by Gruenstein et al. (2005). This corpus provides topic hierarchy and action item annotations for the ICSI meeting corpus as well as other corpora of meetings; due to the ready availability of other types of annotations for the ICSI corpus, we focus solely on the annotations for these meetings. Figure 1 gives an example of the annotations.

The corpus covers 54 ICSI meetings annotated by two human annotators, and several other meetings annotated by one annotator. Of the 54 meetings with dual annotations, 6 contain no action items. For this study we consider only those meetings which contain action items and which are annotated by both annotators.

As the annotations were produced by a small number of untrained annotators, an immediate question is the degree of consistency and reliability. Inter-annotator agreement is typically measured by the kappa statistic (Carletta, 1996), defined as:

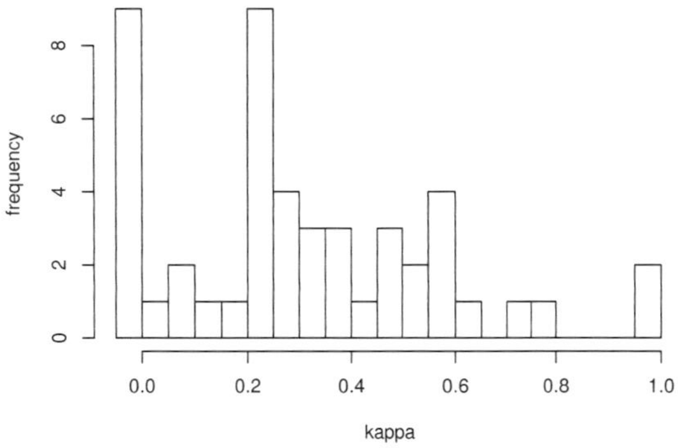

Figure 2: Distribution of κ (inter-annotator agreement) across the 54 ICSI meetings tagged by two annotators. Of the two meetings with $\kappa = 1.0$, one has only two action items and the other only four.

$$\kappa = \frac{P(O) - P(E)}{1 - P(E)}$$

where $P(O)$ is the probability of the observed agreement, and $P(E)$ the probability of the "expected agreement" (i.e., under the assumption the two sets of annotations are independent). The kappa statistic ranges from -1 to 1, indicating perfect disagreement and perfect agreement, respectively.

Overall inter-annotator agreement as measured by κ on the action item corpus is poor, as noted in Purver et al. (2006), with an overall κ of 0.364 and values for individual meetings ranging from 1.0 to less than zero. Figure 2 shows the distribution of κ across all 54 annotated ICSI meetings.

To reduce the effect of poor inter-annotator agreement, we focus on the top 15 meetings as ranked by κ; the minimum κ in this set is 0.435. Although this reduces the total amount of data available, our intention is that this subset of the most consistent annotations will form a higher-quality corpus.

While the corpus classifies related action item utterances into action item "groups," in this study we wish to treat the annotations as simply binary attributes. Visual analysis of annotations for several meetings outside the set of chosen 15 suggests that the union of the two sets of annotations yields the most consistent resulting annotation; thus, for this study, we consider an utterance to be an action item if at least one of the annotators marked it as such.

The 15-meeting subset contains 24,250 utter-

A1	A2	
X	X	So that will be sort of the assignment for next week, is to—
X	X	to—for slides and whatever net you picked and what it can do and—and how far you've gotten. Pppt!
X	-	Well, I'd like to also,
X	X	though, uh, ha- have a first cut at what the
X	X	belief-net looks like.
-	X	Even if it's really crude.
-	-	OK? So, you know,
-	-	here a- here are—
-	X	So we're supposed to @@ about features and whatnot, and—

Figure 1: Example transcript and action item annotations (marked "X") from annotators A1 and A2. "@@" signifies an unintelligible word. This transcript is from an ICSI meeting recording and has $\kappa = 0.373$, ranking it 16th out of 54 meetings in annotator agreement.

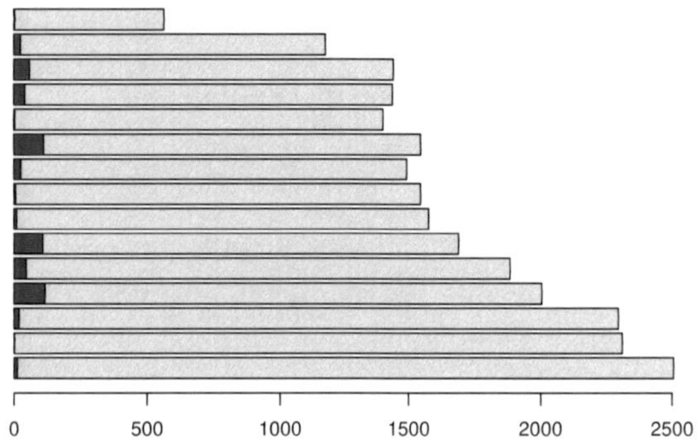

Figure 3: Number of total and action item utterances across the 15 selected meetings. There are 24,250 utterances total, 590 of which (2.4%) are action item utterances.

ances total; under the union strategy above, 590 of these are action item utterances. Figure 3 shows the number of action item utterances and the number of total utterances in the 15 selected meetings.

One noteworthy feature of the ICSI corpus underlying the action item annotations is the "digit reading task," in which the participants of meetings take turns reading aloud strings of digits. This task was designed to provide a constrained-vocabulary training set of speech recognition developers interested in multi-party speech. In this study we did not remove these sections; the net effect is that some portions of the data consist of these fairly atypical utterances.

4 Experimental methodology

We formulate the action item detection task as one of binary classification of utterances. We apply a maximum entropy (maxent) model (Berger et al., 1996) to this task.

Maxent models seek to maximize the conditional probability of a class c given the observations X using the exponential form

$$P(c|X) = \frac{1}{Z(X)} \exp\left[\sum_i \lambda_{i,c}\, f_{i,c}(X)\right]$$

where $f_{i,c}(X)$ is the ith feature of the data X in class c, $\lambda_{i,c}$ is the corresponding weight, and $Z(X)$ is a normalization term. Maxent models choose the weights $\lambda_{i,c}$ so as to maximize the entropy of the induced distribution while remaining consistent with the data and labels; the intuition is that such a distribution makes the fewest assumptions about the underlying data.

Our maxent model is regularized by a quadratic prior and uses quasi-Newton parameter optimization. Due to the limited amount of training data (see Section 3) and to avoid overfitting, we employ 10-fold cross validation in each experiment.

To evaluate system performance, we calculate the F measure (F) of precision (P) and recall (R), defined as:

$$\begin{aligned} P &= \frac{|A \cap C|}{|A|} \\ R &= \frac{|A \cap C|}{|C|} \\ F &= \frac{2PR}{P+R} \end{aligned}$$

where A is the set of utterances marked as action items by the system, and C is the set of (all) correct action item utterances.

The use of precision and recall is motivated by the fact that the large imbalance between positive and negative examples in the corpus (Section 3) means that simpler metrics like accuracy are insufficient—a system that simply classifies every utterance as negative will achieve an accuracy of 97.5%, which clearly is not a good reflection of desired behavior. Recall and F measure for such a system, however, will be zero.

Likewise, a system that flips a coin weighted in proportion to the number of positive examples in the entire corpus will have an accuracy of 95.25%, but will only achieve $P = R = F = 2.4\%$.

5 Features

As noted in Section 3, we treat the task of producing action item annotations as a binary classification task. To this end, we consider the following sets of features. (Note that all real-valued features were range-normalized so as to lie in $[0, 1]$ and that no binning was employed.)

5.1 Immediate lexical features

We extract word unigram and bigram features from the transcript for each utterance. We normalize for case and for certain contractions; for example, "I'll" is transformed into "I will".

Note that these are oracle features, as the transcripts are human-produced and not the product of automatic speech recognizer (ASR) system output.

5.2 Contextual lexical features

We extract word unigram and bigram features from the transcript for the previous and next utterances across all speakers in the meeting.

5.3 Syntactic features

Under the hypothesis that action item utterances will exhibit particular syntactic patterns, we use a conditional Markov model part-of-speech (POS) tagger (Toutanova and Manning, 2000) trained on the Switchboard corpus (Godfrey et al., 1992) to tag utterance words for part of speech. We use the following binary POS features:

- Presence of UH tag, denoting the presence of an "interjection" (including filled pauses, unfilled pauses, and discourse markers).
- Presence of MD tag, denoting presence of a modal verb.
- Number of NN* tags, denoting the number of nouns.
- Number of VB* tags, denoting the number of verbs.
- Presence of VBD tag, denoting the presence of a past-tense verb.

5.4 Prosodic features

Under the hypothesis that action item utterances will exhibit particular prosodic behavior—for example, that they are emphasized, or are pitched a certain way—we performed pitch extraction using an auto-correlation method within the sound analysis package Praat (Boersma and Weenink, 2005). From the meeting audio files we extract the following prosodic features, on a per-utterance basis: (pitch measures are in Hz; intensity in energy; normalization in all cases is z-normalization)

- Pitch and intensity range, minimum, and maximum.
- Pitch and intensity mean.
- Pitch and intensity median (0.5 quantile).
- Pitch and intensity standard deviation.
- Pitch slope, processed to eliminate halving/doubling.
- Number of voiced frames.
- Duration-normalized pitch and intensity ranges and voiced frame count.
- Speaker-normalized pitch and intensity means.

5.5 Temporal features

Under the hypothesis that the length of an utterance or its location within the meeting as a whole will determine its likelihood of being an action item—for example, shorter statements near the end of the meeting might be more likely to be action items—we extract the duration of each utterance and the time from its occurrence until the end of the meeting. (Note that the use of this feature precludes operating in an online setting, where the end of the meeting may not be known in advance.)

5.6 General semantic features

Under the hypothesis that action item utterances will frequently involve temporal expressions—e.g. "Let's have the paper written by *next Tuesday*"—we use Identifinder (Bikel et al., 1997) to mark temporal expressions ("TIMEX" tags) in utterance transcripts, and create a binary feature denoting the existence of a temporal expression in each utterance.

Note that as Identifinder was trained on broadcast news corpora, applying it to the very different domain of multi-party meeting transcripts may not result in optimal behavior.

5.7 Dialog-specific semantic features

Under the hypothesis that action item utterances may be closely correlated with specific dialog act tags, we use the dialog act annotations from the ICSI Meeting Recorder Dialog Act Corpus. (Shriberg et al., 2004) As these DA annotations do not correspond one-to-one with utterances in the ICSI corpus, we align them in the most liberal way possible, i.e., if at least one word in an utterance is annotated for a particular DA, we mark the entirety of that utterance as exhibiting that DA.

We consider both fine-grained and coarse-grained dialog acts.[1] The former yields 56 features, indicating occurrence of DA tags such as "appreciation," "rhetorical question," and "task management"; the latter consists of only 7 classes—"disruption," "backchannel," "filler," "statement," "question," "unlabeled," and "unknown."

6 Results

The final performance for the maxent model across different feature sets is given in Table 1. F measures scores range from 13.81 to 31.92. Figure 4 shows the interpolated precision-recall curves for several of these feature sets; these graphs display the level of precision that can be achieved if one is willing to sacrifice some recall, and vice versa.

Although ideally, all combinations of features should be evaluated separately, the large number of features in this precludes this strategy. The combination of features explored here was chosen so as to start from simpler features and successively add more complex ones. We start with transcript features that are immediate and context-independent ("unigram", "bigram", "TIMEX"); then add transcript features that require context ("temporal", "context"), then non-transcript (i.e. audio signal) features ("prosodic"), and finally add features that require both the transcript and the audio signal ("DA").

[1]We use the map_01 grouping defined in the MRDA corpus to collapse the tags.

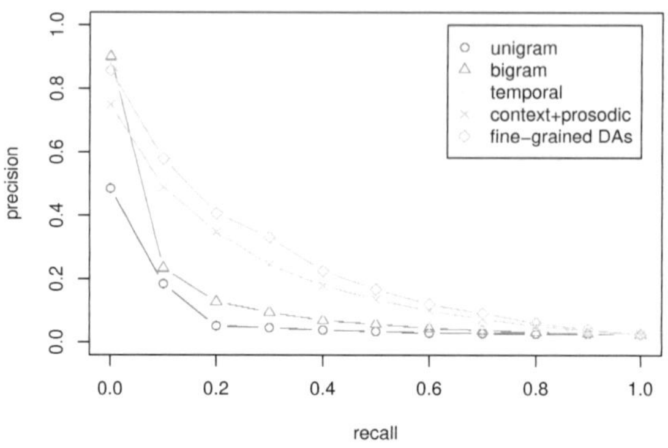

Figure 4: Interpolated precision-recall curve for several (cumulative) feature sets. This graph suggests the level of precision that can be achieved if one is willing to sacrifice some recall, and vice versa.

In total, nine combinations of features were considered. In every case except that of syntactic and coarse-grained dialog act features, the additional features improved system performance and these features were used in succeeding experiments. Syntactic and coarse-grained DA features resulted in a drop in performance and were discarded from succeeding systems.

7 Analysis

The unigram and bigram features provide significant discriminative power. Tables 2 and 3 give the top features, as determined by weight, for the models trained only on these features. It is clear from Table 3 that the detailed end-of-utterance punctuation in the human-generated transcripts provide valuable discriminative power.

The performance gain from adding TIMEX tagging features is small and likely not statistically significant. Post-hoc analysis of the TIMEX tagging (Section 5.6) suggests that Identifinder tagging accuracy is quite plausible in general, but exhibits an unfortunate tendency to mark the digit-reading (see Section 3) portion of the meetings as temporal expressions. It is plausible that removing these utterances from the meetings would allow this feature a higher accuracy.

Based on the low feature weight assigned, utterance length appears to provide no significant value to the model. However, the time until the meeting is over ranks as the highest-weighted feature in the unigram+bigram+TIMEX+temporal feature set. This feature is thus responsible for the 39.25%

features	number	F	% imp.
unigram	6844	13.81	
unigram+bigram	61281	16.72	21.07
unigram+bigram+TIMEX	61284	16.84	0.72
unigram+bigram+TIMEX+temporal	61286	23.45	39.25
unigram+bigram+TIMEX+temporal+syntactic	*61291*	*21.94*	*-6.44*
unigram+bigram+TIMEX+temporal+context	183833	25.62	9.25
unigram+bigram+TIMEX+temporal+context+prosodic	183871	27.44	7.10
unigram+bigram+TIMEX+temporal+context+prosodic+coarse DAs	*183878*	*26.47*	*-3.53*
unigram+bigram+TIMEX+temporal+context+prosodic+fine DAs	183927	31.92	16.33

Table 1: Performance of the maxent classifier as measured by F measure, the relative improvement from the preceding feature set, and the number of features, across all feature sets tried. Italicized lines denote the addition of features which do not improve performance; these are omitted from succeeding systems.

feature	+/-	λ
"pull"	+	2.2100
"email"	+	1.7883
"needs"	+	1.7212
"added"	+	1.6613
"mm-hmm"	-	1.5937
"present"	+	1.5740
"nine"	-	1.5019
"!"	-	1.5001
"five"	-	1.4944
"together"	+	1.4882

Table 2: Features, evidence type (positive denotes action item), and weight for the top ten features in the unigram-only model. "Nine" and "five" are common words in the digit-reading task (see Section 3).

feature	+/-	λ
"- $"	-	1.4308
"i will"	+	1.4128
", $"	-	1.3115
"uh $"	-	1.2752
"w- $"	-	1.2419
". $"	-	1.2247
"email"	+	1.2062
"six $"	-	1.1874
"* in"	-	1.1833
"so $"	-	1.1819

Table 3: Features, evidence type and weight for the top ten features in the unigram+bigram model. The symbol * denotes the beginning of an utterance and $ the end. All of the top ten features are bigrams except for the unigrams "email".

feature	+/-	λ
mean intensity (norm.)	-	1.4288
mean pitch (norm.)	-	1.0661
intensity range	+	1.0510
"i will"	+	0.8657
"email"	+	0.8113
reformulate/summarize (DA)	+	0.7946
"just go" (next)	+	0.7190
"i will" (prev.)	+	0.7074
"the paper"	+	0.6788
understanding check (DA)	+	0.6547

Table 4: Features, evidence type and weight for the top ten features on the best-performing model. Bigrams labeled "prev." and "next" correspond to the lexemes from previous and next utterances, respectively. Prosodic features labeled as "norm." have been normalized on a per-speaker basis.

boost in F measure in row 3 of Table 1.

The addition of part-of-speech tags actually decreases system performance. It is unclear why this is the case. It may be that the unigram and bigram features already adequately capture any distinctions these features make, or simply that these features are generally not useful for distinguishing action items.

Contextual features, on the other hand, improve system performance significantly. A post-hoc analysis of the action item annotations makes clear why: action items are often split across multiple utterances (e.g. as in Figure 1), only a portion of which contain lexical cues sufficient to distinguish them as such. Contextual features thus allow utterances immediately surrounding these "obvious" action items to be tagged as well.

Prosodic features yield a 7.10% increase in F measure, and analysis shows that speaker-normalized intensity and pitch, and the range in intensity of an utterance, are valuable discriminative features. The subsequent addition of coarse-grained dialog act tags does not further improve system performance. It is likely this is due to reasons similar to those for POS tags—either the categories are insufficient to distinguish action item utterances, or whatever usefulness they provide is subsumed by other features.

Table 4 shows the feature weights for the top-ranked features on the best-scoring system. The addition of the fine-grained DA tags results in a significant increase in performance.The F measure of this best feature set is 31.92%.

8 Conclusions

We have shown that several classes of features are useful for the task of action item annotation from multi-party meeting corpora. Simple lexical features, their contextual versions, the time until the end of the meeting, prosodic features, and fine-grained dialog acts each contribute significant increases in system performance.

While the raw system performance numbers of Table 1 are low relative to other, better-studied tasks on other, more mature corpora, we believe the relative usefulness of the features towards this task is indicative of their usefulness on more consistent annotations, as well as to related tasks.

The Gruenstein et al. (2005) corpus provides a valuable and necessary resource for research in this area, but several factors raise the question of annotation quality. The low κ scores in Section 3 are indicative of annotation problems. Post-hoc error analysis yields many examples of utterances which are somewhat difficult to imagine as possible, never mind desirable, to tag. The fact that the extremely useful oracular information present in the fine-grained DA annotation does *not* raise performance to the high levels that one might expect further suggests that the annotations are not ideal—or, at the least, that they are inconsistent with the DA annotations.[2]

This analysis is consistent with the findings of Purver et al. (2006), who achieve an F measure of less than 25% when applying SVMs to the classification task to the same corpus, and motivate the development of a new corpus of action item annotations.

9 Future work

In Section 6 we showed that contextual lexical features are useful for the task of action item detection, at least in the fairly limited manner employed in our implementation, which simply looks at immediate previous and immediate next utterances. It seems likely that applying a sequence model such as an HMM or conditional random field (CRFs) will act as a generalization of this feature and may further improve performance.

Addition of features such as speaker change and "hot spots" (Wrede and Shriberg, 2003) may also aid classification. Conversely, it is possible that feature selection techniques may improve performance by helping to eliminate poor-quality features. In this work we have followed an "everything but the kitchen sink" approach, in part because we were curious about which features would prove useful. The effect of adding POS and coarse-grained DA features illustrates that this is not necessarily the ideal strategy in terms of ultimate system performance.

In general, the features evaluated in this work are an indiscriminate mix of human- and automatically-generated features; of the human-generated features, some are plausible to generate automatically, at some loss of quality (e.g. transcripts) while others are unlikely to be automatically generated in the foreseeable future (e.g. fine-grained dialog acts). Future work may focus on the effects that automatic generation of the former has on overall system performance (although this may require higher-quality annotations to be useful.) For example, the detailed end-of-utterance punctuation present in the human transcripts provides valuable discriminative power (Table 3), but current ASR systems are not likely to be able to provide this level of detail. Switching to ASR output will have a negative effect on performance.

One final issue is that of utterance segmentation. The scheme used in the ICSI meeting corpus does not necessarily correspond to the ideal segmentation for other tasks. The action item annotations were performed on these segmentations, and in this study we did not attempt resegmentation, but in the future it may prove valuable to collapse,

[2]Which is not to say they are devoid of significant value—training and testing our best system on the corpus with the 590 positive classifications randomly shuffled across all utterances yields an F measure of only 4.82.

for example, successive un-interrupted utterances from the same speaker into a single utterance.

In conclusion, while overall system performance does not approach levels typical of better-studied classification tasks such as named-entity recognition, we believe that this is a largely a product of the current action item annotation quality. We believe that the feature analysis presented here is useful, for this task and for other related tasks, and that, provided with a set of more consistent action item annotations, the current system can be used as is to achieve better performance.

Acknowledgments

The authors wish to thank Dan Jurafsky, Chris Manning, Stanley Peters, Matthew Purver, and several anonymous reviewers for valuable advice and comments.

References

Jeremy Ang, Yang Liu, and Elizabeth Shriberg. 2005. Automatic dialog act segmentation and classification in multiparty meetings. In *Proceedings of the ICASSP*.

Paul N. Bennett and Jaime Carbonell. 2005. Detecting action-items in e-mail. In *Proceedings of SIGIR*.

Adam Berger, Stephen Della Pietra, and Vincent Della Pietra. 1996. A maximum entropy approach to natural language processing. *Computational Linguistics*, 22(1):39–71.

D. Bikel, S. Miller, R. Schwartz, and R. Weischedel. 1997. Nymble: a high-performance learning name-finder. In *Proceedings of the Conference on Applied NLP*.

Paul Boersma and David Weenink. 2005. Praat: doing phonetics by computer v4.4.12 (computer program).

J. Carletta. 1996. Assessing agreement on classification tasks: The kappa statistic. *Computational Linguistics*, 22(2):249–254.

William W. Cohen, Vitor R. Carvalho, and Tom M. Mitchell. 2004. Learning to classify email into "speech acts". In *Proceedings of EMNLP*.

Simon Corston-Oliver, Eric Ringger, Michael Gamon, and Richard Campbell. 2004. Task-focused summarization of email. In *Text Summarization Branches Out: Proceedings of the ACL Workshop*.

J. Godfrey, E. Holliman, and J.McDaniel. 1992. SWITCHBOARD: Telephone speech corpus for research and development. In *Proceedings of ICAASP*.

Alexander Gruenstein, John Niekrasz, and Matthew Purver. 2005. Meeting structure annotation: Data and tools. In *Proceedings of the 6th SIGDIAL Workshop on Discourse and Dialogue*.

Adam Janin, Don Baron, Jane Edwards, Dan Ellis, David Gelbart, Nelson Morgan, Barbara Peskin, Thilo Pfau, Elizabeth Shriberg, Andreas Stolcke, and Chuck Wooters. 2003. The ICSI meeting corpus. In *Proceedings of the ICASSP*.

Gang Ji and Jeff Bilmes. 2005. Dialog act tagging using graphical models. In *Proceedings of the ICASSP*.

Marion Mast, R. Kompe, S. Harbeck, A. Kießling, H. Niemann, E. Nöth, E.G. Schukat-Talamazzini, and V. Warnke. 1996. Dialog act classification with the help of prosody. In *Proceedings of the ICSLP*.

Matthew Purver, Patrick Ehlen, and John Niekrasz. 2006. Detecting action items in multi-party meetings: Annotation and initial experiments. In *Proceedings of the 3rd Joint Workshop on MLMI*.

Elizabeth Shriberg, Rebecca Bates, Andreas Stolcke, Paul Taylor, Daniel Jurafsky, Klaus Ries, Noah Coccaro, Rachel Martin, Marie Meteer, and Carol Van EssDykema. 1998. Can prosody aid the automatic classification of dialog acts in conversational speech? *Language and Speech*, 41(3–4):439–487.

Elizabeth Shriberg, Raj Dhillon, Sonali Bhagat, Jeremy Ang, and Hannah Carvey. 2004. The ICSI meeting recorder dialog act (MRDA) corpus. In *Proceedings of the 5th SIGDIAL Workshop on Discourse and Dialogue*.

Andreas Stolcke, Elizabeth Shriberg, Rebecca Bates, Noah Coccaro, Daniel Jurafsky, Rachel Martin, Marie Meteer, Klaus Ries, Paul Taylor, and Carol Van EssDykema. 1998. Dialog act modeling for conversational speech. In *Proceedings of the AAAI Spring Symposium on Applying Machine Learning to Discourse Processing*.

Kristina Toutanova and Christopher D. Manning. 2000. Enriching the knowledge sources used in a maximum entropy part-of-speech tagger. In *Proceedings of EMNLP*.

Britta Wrede and Elizabeth Shriberg. 2003. Spotting "hot spots" in meetings: Human judgments and prosodic cues. In *Proceedings of the European Conference on Speech Communication and Technology*.

Matthias Zimmermann, Yang Liu, Elizabeth Shriberg, and Andreas Stolcke. 2005. Toward joint segmentation and classification of dialog acts in multiparty meetings. In *Proceedings of the 2nd Joint Workshop on MLMI*.

Empirical Verification of Adjacency Pairs Using Dialogue Segmentation

T. Daniel Midgley **Shelly Harrison**
Discipline of Linguistics,
University of Western Australia
(dmidgley, shelley)@cyllene.uwa.edu.au

Cara MacNish
School of Computer Science and Software Engineering,
University of Western Australia
cara@csse.uwa.edu.au

Abstract

A problem in dialogue research is that of finding and managing expectations. Adjacency pair theory has widespread acceptance, but traditional classification features (in particular, 'previous-tag' type features) do not exploit this information optimally. We suggest a method of dialogue segmentation that verifies adjacency pairs and allows us to use dialogue-level information within the entire segment and not just the previous utterance. We also use the χ^2 test for statistical significance as 'noise reduction' to refine a list of pairs. Together, these methods can be used to extend expectation beyond the traditional classification features.

1 Introduction

Adjacency pairs have had a long history in dialogue research. The pairs of question/answer, inform/backchannel, and others have been well-known ever since they were proposed by Sacks and Schegloff in 1973. They have been used by dialogue researchers to assist in knowing 'what comes next' in dialogue.

Unfortunately, this dialogue information has been difficult to leverage. Most dialogue act (DA) classification research uses some kind of dialogue history, but this usually takes the form of some kind of 'previous tag' feature, perhaps even 'two-previous tag'. Dialogue information from three or more utterances previous is not normally used because, in the words of one researcher, "[n]o benefit was found from using higher-order dialog grammars" (Venkataraman et al. 2002). This could be due to the sparse data problem; more permutations means fewer repetitions.

Part of the problem, then, may lie in the way the 'previous tag' feature is used. Consider the following example from the Verbmobil-2 corpus (Verbmobil 2006)[1]:

A:	how does does November fourteenth and fifteenth look	SUGGEST
B:	no	REJECT

Here, the second pair part occurs directly after the first pair part that occasioned it. But sometimes performance factors intervene as in the following example, where B is engaging in floor-holding using a dialogue act annotated here as DELIBERATE:

A:	so that maybe I if I need to if I need to order like a limo or something	SUGGEST
B:	<hes> let us see	DELIBERATE
B:	the this is the <hes> wrong month	DELIBERATE
B:	the third	DELIBERATE
B:	let us see	DELIBERATE
B:	I don't have anything scheduled that morning and we are leaving at one	INFORM

The response (INFORM) finally comes, but the forgetful 'previous tag' feature is now looking for what comes after DELIBERATE.

What is needed is a way to not only determine what is likely to happen next, but to retain that expectation over longer distances when unfulfilled, until that expectation is no longer needed. Such information would conform more closely to this description of a conversational game (but which could be applied to any communicative subgoal):

[1]For a full description of the Verbmobil speech acts, see Alexandersson 1997.

Proceedings of the 7th SIGdial Workshop on Discourse and Dialogue, pages 104–108,
Sydney, July 2006. ©2006 Association for Computational Linguistics

> A conversational game is a sequence of moves starting with an initiation and encompassing all moves up *until that initiation's purpose is either fulfilled or abandoned*. (Carletta 1997, italics mine.)

2 Dialogue segmentation

This work grew out of related research into finding expectations in dialogue, but we were also interested in dialogue segmentation. Dialogues taken as a whole are very different from each other, so segmentation is necessary to derive meaningful information about their parts. The question is, then, how best to segment dialogues so as to reveal dialogue information or to facilitate some language task, such as DA classification?

Various schemes for dialogue segmentation have been tried, including segmentation based on fulfilment of expectation (Ludwig et al. 1998), and segmenting by propositionality (Midgley 2003).

One answer to the question of how to segment dialogue came from the pioneering work of Sacks and Schegloff (1973) article.

> A basic rule of adjacency pair operation is: given the recognizable production of a *first pair part*, on its first possible completion its speaker should stop and a next speaker should start and produce a *second pair part* from the same pair type of which the first is recognizably a member. (p. 296, italics mine.)

Thus, if a speaker stops speaking, it is likely that such a handover has just taken place. The last utterance of a speaker's turn, then, will be the point at which the first speaker has issued a first pair part, and is now expecting a second pair part from the other speaker. This suggests a natural boundary.

This approach was also suggested by Wright (1998), who used a "most recent utterance by previous speaker" feature in her work on DA tagging. This feature alone has boosted classification accuracy by about 2% in our preliminary research, faring better than the traditional 'previous tag' feature used in much DA tagging work.

We collected a training corpus of 40 English-speaking dialogues from the Verbmobil-2 corpus, totalling 5,170 utterances. We then segmented the dialogues into *chunks*, where a chunk included everything from the last utterance of one speaker's turn to the last-but-one utterance of the next speaker.

3 Results of segmentation

This segmentation revealed some interesting patterns. When ranked by frequency, the most common chunks bear a striking resemblance to the adjacency pairs posited by Schegloff and Sacks.

Here are the 25 most common chunks in our training corpus, with the number of times they appeared. The full list can be found at http://www.csse.uwa.edu.au/~fontor/research/chi/fullseg.txt

SUGGEST:ACCEPT	176
INFORM:FEEDBACK_POSITIVE	166
FEEDBACK_POSITIVE:FEEDBACK_POSITIVE	104
FEEDBACK_POSITIVE:INFORM	97
ACCEPT:FEEDBACK_POSITIVE	65
FEEDBACK_POSITIVE:SUGGEST	60
INFORM:INFORM	57
REQUEST:INFORM	46
INFORM:BACKCHANNEL	41
INFORM:SUGGEST	40
REQUEST_COMMENT:FEEDBACK_POSITIVE	40
INIT:FEEDBACK_POSITIVE	35
BYE:NONE	34
ACCEPT:INFORM	32
BYE:BYE	31
REQUEST:FEEDBACK_POSITIVE	30
POLITENESS_FORMULA:FEEDBACK_POSITIVE	29
REQUEST_CLARIFY:FEEDBACK_POSITIVE	28
BACKCHANNEL:INFORM	28
NOT_CLASSIFIABLE:INFORM	28
REQUEST_SUGGEST:SUGGEST	28
NONE:GREET	27
SUGGEST:SUGGEST	27
ACCEPT:SUGGEST	26
SUGGEST:REQUEST_CLARIFY	26

The data suggest a wide variety of language behaviour, including traditional adjacency pairs (e.g. `SUGGEST: ACCEPT`), acknowledgement (`INFORM: BACKCHANNEL`), formalised exchanges (`POLITENESS_FORMULA: FEEDBACK_POSITIVE`) offers and counter-offers (`SUGGEST: SUGGEST`), and it even hints at negotiation subdialogues (`SUGGEST: REQUEST_CLARIFY`).

However, there are some drawbacks to this list. Some of the items are not good examples of adjacency pairs because the presence of the first does not create an expectation for the second half (e.g. `NOT_CLASSIFIABLE: INFORM`). In some cases they appear backwards (ACCEPT: SUGGEST). Legitimate pairs appear further down the list than more-common bogus ones. For example, SUGGEST: REJECT is a well-known adjacency pair, but it does not appear on the list until after several less-worthy-seeming pairs. Keeping the less-intuitive chunks may help us with classification, but it falls short of providing empirical verification for pairs.

What we need, then, is some kind of noise reduction that will strain out spurious pairs and bring legitimate pairs closer to the top of the list.

We use the well-known χ^2 test for statistical significance.

4 The χ^2 test

The χ^2 test tells how the observed frequency of an event compares with the expected frequency. For our purposes, it tells whether the observed frequency of an event (in this case, one kind of speech act following a certain other act) can be attributed to random chance. The test has been used for such tasks as feature selection (Spitters 2000) and translation pair identification (Church and Gale 1991).

The χ^2 value for any two speech acts *A* and *B* can be calculated by counting the times that an utterance marked as tag A (or not) is followed by an utterance marked as tag B (or not), as in Table 1.

	$U_i = A$	$U_i \neq A$
$U_{i+1} = B$	AB	$\neg AB$
$U_{i+1} \neq B$	$A\neg B$	$\neg A\neg B$

Table 1. Obtaining counts for χ^2.

These counts (as well as *N*, the total number of utterances) are plugged into a variant of the χ^2 equation used for 2x2 tables, as in Schütze et al. (1995).

$$\chi^2 = \frac{N(AB \cdot \neg A\neg B - A\neg B \cdot \neg AB)}{(AB + A\neg B)(AB + \neg AB)(A\neg B + \neg A\neg B)(\neg AB + \neg A\neg B)}$$

We trained the χ^2 method on the aforementioned chunks. Rather than restrict our focus to only adjacent utterances, we allowed a match for pair A:B if B occurred *anywhere* within the chunk started by A. By doing so, we hoped to reduce any acts that may have been interfering with the adjacency pairs, especially hesitation noises (usually classed as DELIBERATE) and abandoned utterances (NOT_CLASSIFIABLE).

5 Results for χ^2

Here are the 25 pairs with the highest χ^2 scores. With tail probability $p = .0001$, a χ^2 value > 10.83 is statistically significant. The full list can be found at http://www.csse.uwa.edu.au/~fontor/research/chi/fullchi.txt.

NONE:GREET	1576.87
BYE:NONE	949.89
SUGGEST:ACCEPT	671.81
BYE:BYE	488.60
NONE:POLITENESS_FORMULA	300.46
POLITENESS_FORMULA: POLITENESS_FORMULA	272.95
GREET:GREET	260.69
REQUEST_CLARIFY:CLARIFY	176.63
CLARIFY:CLARIFY	165.76
DEVIATE_SCENARIO: DEVIATE_SCENARIO	159.45
SUGGEST:FEEDBACK_POSITIVE	158.12
COMMIT:COMMIT	154.46
GREET:POLITENESS_FORMULA	111.19
INFORM:FEEDBACK_POSITIVE	84.82
REQUEST_SUGGEST:SUGGEST	83.17
SUGGEST:REJECT	83.11
THANK:THANK	76.25
SUGGEST:EXPLAINED_REJECT	69.31
POLITENESS_FORMULA:INIT	67.76
NONE:INIT	59.97
FEEDBACK_POSITIVE:ACCEPT	59.41
DEFER:ACCEPT	56.07
THANK:BYE	51.82
POLITENESS_FORMULA:THANK	50.21
POLITENESS_FORMULA:GREET	45.17

Using χ^2 normalises the list; low-frequency acts like REJECT and EXPLAINED_REJECT now appear as a part of their respective pairs.

These results give empirical justification for Sacks and Schegloff's adjacency pairs, and reveals more not mentioned elsewhere in the literature, such as DEFER:ACCEPT. As such, it gives a good idea of what kinds of speech acts are expected within a chunk.

In addition, these results can be plotted into a directed acyclic graph (seen in Figure 1). This graph can be used as a sort of conversational map.

6 Conclusions and Future Work

We can draw some tentative conclusions from this work. First of all, the dialogue segmentation combined with the χ^2 test for significance yields information about what is likely to happen, not just for the next utterance, but somewhere in the next chunk. This will help to overcome the limitations imposed by the traditional 'previous tag' feature. We are working to implement this information into a model where the expectations inherent in a first pair part are retained when not immediately fulfilled. The expectations will also decay with time.

Second, this approach provides empirical evidence for adjacency pairs mentioned in the literature on conversation analysis. The noise reduction feature of the χ^2 test gives more weight to legitimate adjacency pairs where they appear in the data.

An intriguing possibility for the chunked data is that of *chunk matching*. Nearest-neighbour algorithms are already used for classification tasks (including DA tagging for individual utterances), but once segmented, the dialogue chunks could be compared against each other as a classification tool as in a nearest-neighbour algorithm.

References

J. Alexandersson, B. Buschbeck-Wolf, T. Fujinami, E. Maier, N. Reithinger, B. Schmitz, and M. Siegel. 1997. *Dialogue acts in Verbmobil-2*. Verbmobil Report 204.

J. Carletta, A. Isard, S. Isard, J. C. Kowtko, G. Doherty-Sneddon, and A. H. Anderson. 1997. The reliability of a dialogue structure coding scheme. *Computational Linguistics*, 23(1):13--31.

K. W. Church and W. A. Gale. 1991. Concordances for parallel text. In *Proceedings of the Seventh Annual Conference of the UW Centre for the New OED and Text Research*, pages 40–62, Oxford.

D. Midgley. 2003. Discourse chunking: a tool for dialogue act tagging. In *ACL-03 Companion Volume to the Proceedings of the Conference*, pages 58–63, Sapporo, Japan.

E. A. Schegloff. and H. Sacks. 1973. Opening up closings. *Semiotica*, 8(4):289–327.

H. Schütze, D. Hull, and J. Pedersen. 1995. A comparison of classifiers and document representations for the routing problem. In *Proceedings of SIGIR '95*, pages 229–237.

M. Spitters. 2000. "Comparing feature sets for learning text categorization." In *Proceedings of RIAO 2000*, April, 2000.

A. Venkataraman, A. Stolcke, E. Shriberg. Automatic dialog act labeling with minimal supervision. In *Proceedings of the 9th Australian International Conference on Speech Science and Technology*, Melbourne, Australia, 2002.

Verbmobil. 2006. "Verbmobil" [online]. Available <http://verbmobil.dfki.de/>.

H. Wright. 1998. Automatic utterance type detection using suprasegmental features. In *ICSLP (International Conference on Spoken Language Processing) '98*. Sydney, Australia.

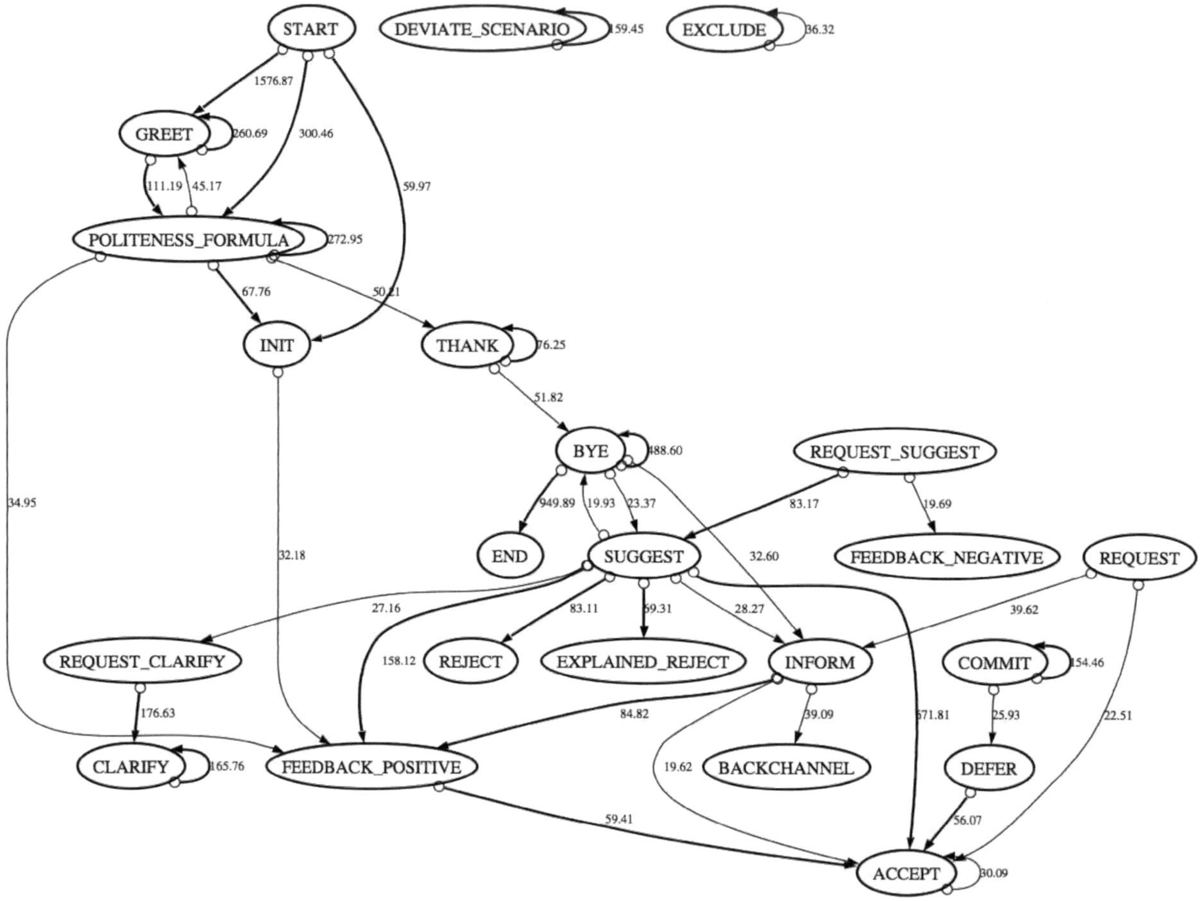

Figure 1. A directed acyclic graph using the χ^2 data for the 40 highest pairs. For any pair of connected nodes, the first node represents the last utterance in a speaker's turn, and the second could be any utterance in the other speaker's turn. The numbers are χ^2 scores. For illustrative purposes, higher χ^2 values are shown by bold lines. The complete graph can be found at http://www.csse.uwa.edu.au/~fontor/research/chi/fullchart.jpg

Multimodal Dialog Description Language for Rapid System Development

Masahiro Araki **Kenji Tachibana**
Kyoto Institute of Technology
Graduate School of Science and Technology, Department of Information Science
Matsugasaki Sakyo-ku Kyoto 606-8585 Japan
araki@dj.kit.ac.jp

Abstract

In this paper, we explain a rapid development method of multimodal dialogue sys-tem using MIML (Multimodal Interaction Markup Language), which defines dialogue patterns between human and various types of interactive agents. The feature of this language is three-layered description of agent-based interactive systems which separates task level description, interaction description and device dependent realization. MIML has advantages in high-level interaction description, modality extensibility and compatibility with standardized technologies.

1 Introduction

In recent years, various types of interactive agents, such as personal robots, life-like agents (Kawamoto et al. 2004), and animated agents are developed for many purposes. Such interactive agents have an ability of speech communication with human by using automatic speech recognizer and speech synthesizer as a main modality of communication. The purpose of these interactive agents is to realize a user-friendly interface for information seeking, remote operation task, entertainment, etc.

Each agent system is controlled by different description language. For example, Microsoft agent is controlled by JavaScript / VBScript embedded in HTML files, Galatea (Kawamoto et al.. 2004) is controlled by extended VoiceXML (in Linux version) and XISL (Katsurada et al. 2003) (in Windows version). In addition to this difference, these languages do not have the ability of higher level task definition because the main elements of these languages are the control of modality functions for each agent. These make rapid development of multimodal system difficult.

In order to deal with these problems, we propose a multimodal interaction description language, MIML (Multimodal Interaction Markup Language), which defines dialogue patterns between human and various types of interactive agents by abstracting their functions. The feature of this language is three-layered description of agent-based interactive systems.

The high-level description is a task definition that can easily construct typical agent-based interactive task control information. The middle-level description is an interaction description that defines agent's behavior and user's input at the granularity of dialogue segment. The low-level description is a platform dependent description that can override the pre-defined function in the interaction description.

The connection between task-level and interaction-level is realized by generation of interaction description templates from the task level description. The connection between interaction-level and platform-level is realized by a binding mechanism of XML.

The rest of this paper consists as follows. Section 2 describes the specification of the proposed language. Section 3 explains a process of rapid multimodal dialogue system development. Section 4 gives a comparison with existing multimodal languages. Section 5 states conclusions and future works.

Proceedings of the 7th SIGdial Workshop on Discourse and Dialogue, pages 109–116,
Sydney, July 2006. ©2006 Association for Computational Linguistics

2 Specification of MIML

2.1 Task level markup language

2.1.1 Task classification

In spoken dialogue system development, we proposed task classification based on the direction of information flow (Araki et al. 1999). We consider that the same analysis can be applied to agent based interactive systems (see Table 1).

Table 1: Task classification of agent-based interactive systems

Class	Direction of Info. flow	Typical task
Information assistant	user ← agent	Interactive presentation
User agent	user → agent	control of home network equipments
Question and Answer	user ↔ agent	daily life information query

In the information assistant class, the agent has information to be presented to the user. Typically, the information contents are Web pages, an instruction of consumer product usage, an educational content, etc. Sometimes the contents are too long to deliver all the information to the user. Therefore, it needs user model that can manage user's preference and past interaction records in order to select or filter out the contents.

In the user agent class, the user has information to be delivered to the agent in order to achieve a user's goal. Typically, the information is a command to control networked home equipments, travel schedule to reserve a train ticket, etc. The agent mediates between user and target application in order to make user's input appropriate and easy at the client side process (e.g. checking a mandatory filed to be filled, automatic filling with personal data (name, address, e-mail, etc.)).

In the Question and Answer class, the user has an intention to acquire some information from the agent that can access to the Web or a database. First, the user makes a query in natural language, and then the agent makes a response according to the result of the information retrieval. If too much information is retrieved, the agent makes a narrowing down subdialogue. If there is no information that matches user's query, the agent makes a request to reformulate an initial query. If the amount of retrieved information is appropriate to deliver to the user by using current modality, the agent reports the results to the user. The appropriate amount of information differs in the main interaction modality of the target device, such as small display, normal graphic display or speech. Therefore, it needs the information of media capability of the target device.

2.1.2 Overview of task markup language

As a result of above investigation, we specify the task level interaction description language shown in Figure 1.

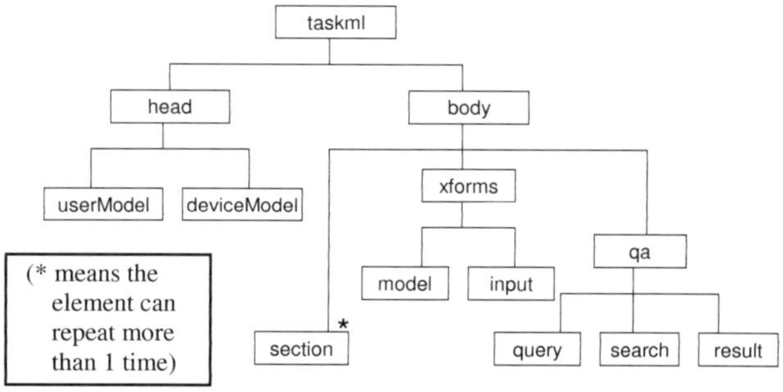

Figure. 1 Structure of the Task Markup Language.

The features of this language are (1) the ability to model each participant of dialogue (i.e. user and agent) and (2) to provide an execution framework of each class of task.

The task markup language <taskml> consists of two parts corresponding to above mentioned features: <head> part and <body> part. The <head> part specifies models of the user (by <userModel> element) and the agent (by <deviceModel> element). The content of each model is described in section 2.1.3. The <body> part specifies a class of interaction task. The content of each task is declaratively specified under the <section>, <xforms> and <qa> elements, which are explained in section 2.1.4.

2.1.3 Head part of task markup language

In the <head> element of the task markup language, the developer can specify user model in <userModel> element and agent model in <deviceModel> element.

In the <userModel> element, the developer declares variables which represent user's information, such as expertise to domain, expertise to dialogue system, interest level to the contents, etc.

In the <deviceModel> element, the developer can specify the type of interactive agent and main modality of interaction. This information is used for generating template from this task description to interaction descriptions.

2.1.4 Body part of task markup language

According to the class of the task, the <body> element consists of a sequence of <section> elements, a <xforms> element or a <qa> element.

The <section> element represents a piece of information in the task of the information assistant class. The attributes of this element are id, start time and end time of the presentation material and declared user model variable which indicates whether this section meets the user's needs or knowledge level. The child elements of the <section> element specify multimodal presentation. These elements are the same set of the child elements of <output> element in the interaction level description explained in the next subsection. Also, there is a <interaction> element as a child element of the <section> element which specifies agent interaction pattern description as an external pointer. It is used for additional comment generated by the agent to the presented contents. For the sake of this separation of contents and additional comments, the developer can easily add agent's behavior in accordance with the user model. The interaction flow of this class is shown in Figure 2.

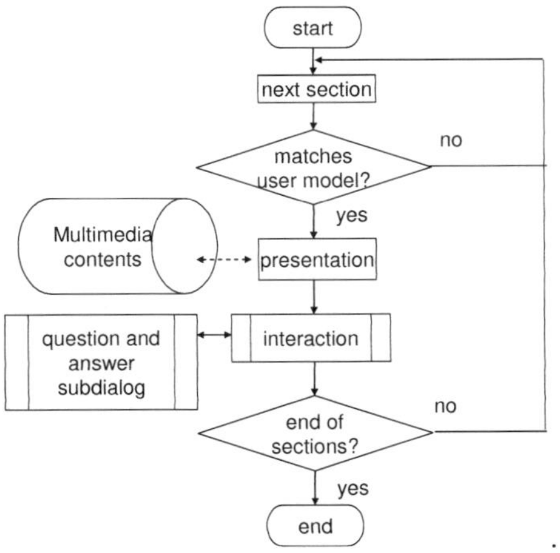

Figure. 2 Interaction flow of Information Assist class

The <xforms> element represents a group of information in the task of the user agent class. It specifies a data model, constraint of the value and submission action following the notation of XForms 1.0.

In the task of user agent class, the role of interactive agent is to collect information from the user in order to achieve a specific task, such as hotel reservation. XForms is designed to separate the data structure of information and the appearance at the user's client, such as using text field input, radio button, pull-down menu, etc. because such interface appearances are different in devices even in GUI-based systems. If the developer wants to use multimodal input for the user's client, such separation of the data structure and the appearance, i.e. how to show the necessary information and how to get user's input, is very important.

In MIML, such device dependent 'appearance' information is defined in interaction level. Therefore, in this user agent class, the task description is only to define data structure because interaction flows of this task can be limited to the typical patterns. For example, in hotel reservation, as a result of AP (application) access, if there is no available room at the requested date, the user's reservation request is rejected. If the system recommends an alternative choice to the user, the interaction branches to subdialogue of recommendation, after the first user's request is processed (see Figure 3). The interaction pattern of each subdialogue is described in the interaction level markup language.

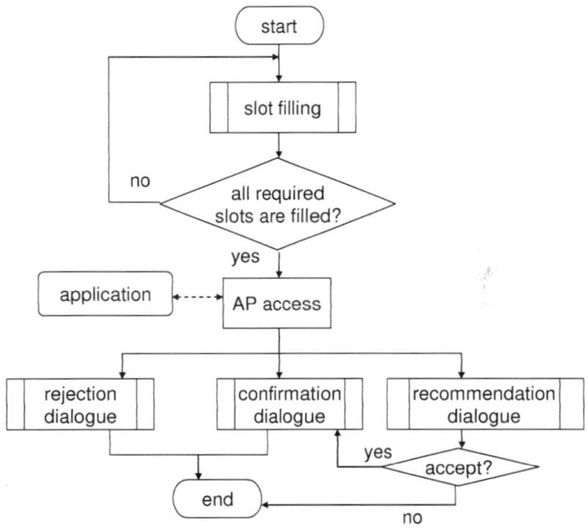

Figure. 3 Interaction flow of User Agent class

The <qa> element consists of three children: <query>, <search> and <result>.

The content of <query> element is the same as the <xforms> element explained above. However, generated interaction patterns are different in user agent class and question and answer class. In user agent class, all the values (except for optional slots indicated explicitly) are expected to be filled. On the contrary, in question and answer class, a subset of slots defined by form description can make a query. Therefore, the first exchange of the question and answer class task is system's prompt and user's query input.

The <search> element represents application command using the variable defined in the <query> element. Such application command can be a database access command or SPARQL (Simple Protocol And RDF Query Language)[1] in case of Semantic Web search.

The <result> element specifies which information to be delivered to the user from the query result. The behavior of back-end application of this class is not as simple as user agent class. If too many results are searched, the system transits to narrowing down subdialogue. If no result is searched, the system transits to subdialogue that relaxes initial user's query. If appropriate number (it depends on presentation media) of results are searched, the presentation subdialogue begins. The flow of interaction is shown in Figure 4.

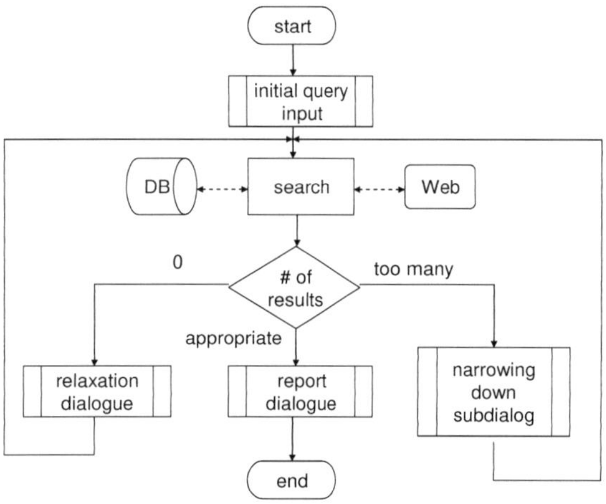

Figure. 4 Interaction flow of Question and Answer class

2.2 Interaction level markup language

2.2.1 Overview of interaction markup language

Previously, we proposed a multimodal interaction markup language (Araki et al. 2004) as an extension of VoiceXML[2]. In this paper, we modify the previous proposal for specializing human-agent interaction and for realizing interaction pattern defined in the task level markup language.

The main extension is a definition of modality independent elements for input and output. In VoiceXML, system's audio prompt is defined in <prompt> element as a child of <field> element that defines atomic interaction acquiring the value of the variable. User's speech input pattern is defined by <grammar> element under <field> element. In our MIML, <grammar> element is replaced by the <input> element which specifies active input modalities and their input pattern to be bund to the variable that is indicated as name attribute of the <field> element. Also, <prompt> element is replaced by the <output> element which specifies active output modalities and a source media file or contents to be presented to the user. In <output> element, the developer can specify agent's behavior by using <agent> element. The outline of this interaction level markup language is shown in Figure 5.

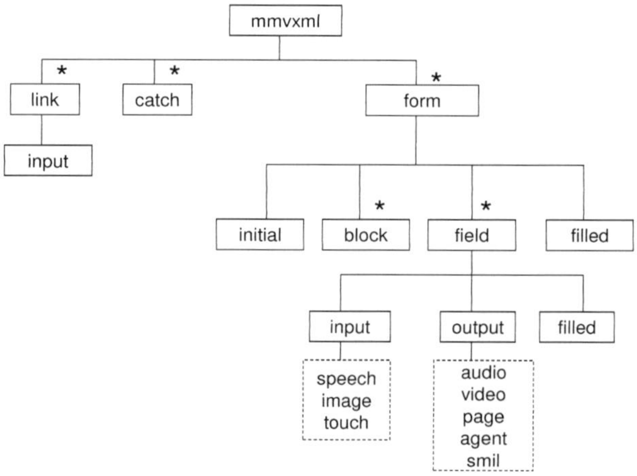

Figure. 5 Structure of Interaction level Markup Language

2.2.2 Input and output control in agent

The <input> element and the <output> element are designed for implementing various types of interactive agent systems.

The <input> element specifies the input processing of each modality. For speech input, grammar attribute of <speech> element specifies user's input pattern by SRGS (Speech Recognition Grammar Specification)[3], or alternatively, type attribute specifies built-in grammar such as Boolean, date, digit, etc. For image input, type attribute of <image> element specifies built-in behavior for camera input, such as nod, faceRecognition, etc. For touch input, the value of the variable is given by referring external definition of the relation between displayed object and its value.

The <output> element specifies the output control of each modality. Each child element of

[1] http://www.w3.org/TR/rdf-sparql-query/
[2] http://www.w3.org/TR/voicexml20/
[3] http://www.w3.org/TR/speech-grammar/

this element is performed in parallel. If the developer wants to make sequential output, it should be written in <smil> element (Synchronized Multimedia Integration Language)[4], For audio output, <audio> element works as the same way as VoiceXML, that is, the content of the element is passed to TTS (Text-to-Speech module) and if the audio file is specified by the src attribute, it is a prior output. In <video>, <page> (e.g. HTML) and <smil> (for rich multimedia presentation) output, each element specifies the contents file by src attribute. In <agent> element, the agent's behavior definition, such as move, emotion, status attribute specifies the parameter for each action.

2.3 Platform level description

The differences of agent and other devices for input/output are absorbed in this level. In interaction level markup language, <agent> element specifies agent's behavior. However, some agent can move in a real world (e.g. personal robot), some agent can move on a computer screen (e.g. Microsoft Agent), and some cannot move but display their face (e.g. life-like agent).

One solution for dealing with such variety of behavior is to define many attributes at <agent> element, for example, move, facial expression, gesture, point, etc. However, the defects of this solution are inflexibility of correspondence to progress of agent technology (if an agent adds new ability to its behavior, the specification of language should be changed) and interference of reusability of interaction description (description for one agent cannot apply to another agent).

Our solution is to use the binding mechanism in XML language between interaction level and platform dependent level. We assume default behavior for each value of the move, emotion and status attributes of the <agent> element. If such default behavior is not enough for some purpose, the developer can override the agent's behavior using binding mechanism and the agent's native control language. As a result, the platform level description is embedded in binding language described in next section.

3 Rapid system development

3.1 Usage of application framework

Each task class has a typical execution steps as investigated in previous section. Therefore a system developer has to specify a data model and specific information for each task execution. Web application framework can drive interactive task using these declarative parameters.

As an application framework, we use Struts[5] which is based on Model-View-Controller (MVC) model. It clearly separates application logic (model part), transition of interaction (controller part) and user interface (view part). Although MVC model is popular in GUI-based Web application, it can be applied in speech-based application because any modality dependent information can be excluded from the view part. Struts provides (1) a controller mechanism and (2) integration mechanism with the back-end application part and the user interface part. In driving Struts, a developer has to (1) define a data class which stores the user's input and responding results, (2) make action mapping rules which defines a transition pattern of the target interactive system, and (3) make the view part which defines human-computer interaction patterns. The process of Struts begins by the request from the user client (typically in HTML, form data is submitted to the Web server via HTTP post method).

The controller catches the request and stores the submitted data to the data class, and then calls the action class specified by the request following the definition of action mapping rules.

The action class communicates with the back-end application, such as database management system or outside Web servers by referring the data class, and returns the status of the processing to the controller. According to the status, the controller refers the action mapping rules and selects the view file which is passed to the user's client. Basically, this view file is written in Java Server Pages, which can be any XML file that includes Java code or useful tag libraries. Using this embedded programming method, the results of the application processing is reflected to the response. The flow of processing in the Struts is shown in Figure 6.

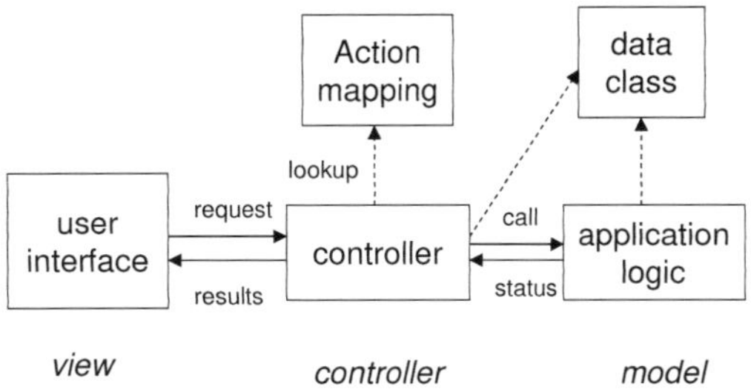

Figure. 6 MVC model.

[4] http://www.w3.org/AudioVideo/

[5] http:// struts.apache.org

The first step of rapid development is to prepare backend application (Typically using Database Management System) and their application logic code. The action mapping file and data class file are created automatically from the task level description described next subsection.

3.2 Task definition

Figure 7 shows an example description of the information assistant task. In this task setting, video contents which are divided into sections are presented to the user one by one. At the end of a section, a robot agent put in a word in order to help user's understanding and to measure the user's preference (e.g. by the recognition of acknowledging, nodding, etc.) . If low user's preference is observed, unimportant parts of the presentation are skipped and comments of the robot are adjusted to beginner's level. The importance of the section is indicated by interestLevel attribute and knowledgeLevel attribute that are introduced in the <userModel> element. If one of the values of these attribute is below the current value of the user model, the relevant section is skipped. The skipping mechanism using user model variables is automatically inserted into an interaction level description.

```
<taskml type="infoAssist">
 <head>
  <userModel>
   <interestLevel/>
   <knowledgeLevel/>
  </userModel>
  <deviceModel
     mainMode="speech" agentType="robot"/>
 </head>
 <body>
  <section id="001"
     s_time="00:00:00" e_time="00:00:50"
     intersetLevel="1"  knowledgeLevel="1">
    <video src="vtr1.avi" />
    <interaction name="interest1.mmi"
         s_time="00:00:30"/>
  </section>
   ...
 </body>
</taskml>
```

Figure. 7 An Example of Task Markup Language.

3.3 Describing Interaction

The connection between task-level and interaction-level is realized by generation of interaction description templates from the task level description. The interaction level description corresponds to the view part of the MVC model on which task level description is based. From this point of view, task level language specification gives higher level parameters over MVC framework which restricts behavior of the model for typical interactive application patterns. Therefore, from this pattern information, the skeletons of the view part of each typical pattern can be generated based on the device model information in task markup language.

For example, by the task level description shown in Figure 7, data class is generated from <userModel> element by mapping the field of the class to user model variable, and action mapping rule set is generated using the sequence information of <section> elements. The branch is realized by calling application logic which compares the attribute variables of the <section> and user model data class. Following action mapping rule, the interaction level description is generated for each <section> element. In information assistant class, a <section> element corresponds to two interaction level descriptions: the one is presenting contents which transform <video> element to the <output> elements and the other is interacting with user, such as shown in Figure 8.

The latter file is merely a skeleton. Therefore, the developer has to fill the system's prompt, specify user's input and add corresponding actions.

Figure 8 describes an interaction as follows: at the end of some segment, the agent asks the user whether the contents are interesting or not. The user can reply by speech or by nodding gesture. If the user's response is affirmative, the global variable of interest level in user model is incremented.

```
<mmvxml>
 <form>
  <field name="question">
   <input>
     <speech type="boolean"/>
     <image type="nod"/>
   </input>
   <output>
     <audio> Is it interesting? </audio>
   </output>
   <filled>
     <if cond="question==true">
        <assign name="intersestLevel"
                expr=" intersestLevel+1"/>
     </if>
     <submit src="http://localhost:8080/step2/>
   </filled>
  </field>
 </form>
</mmvxml>
```

Figure. 8 An Example of Interaction level Markup Language.

3.4 Adaptation to multiple interaction devices

The connection between interaction-level and platform-level is realized by binding mechanism of XML. XBL (XML Binding Language)[6] was originally defined for smart user interface description, extended for SVG afterwards, and furthermore, for general XML language. The concept of binding in XBL is a tree extension by inheriting the value of attributes to the sub tree (see Figure 9). As a result of this mechanism, the base language, in this the case interaction markup language, can keep its simplicity but does not loose flexibility.

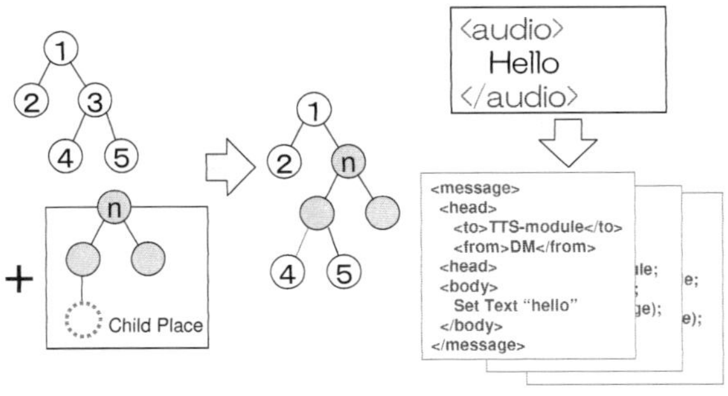

Figure. 9 Concept of XML binding.

By using this mechanism, we implemented various types of weather information system, such as Microsoft agent (Figure 10), Galatea (Figure 11) and a personal robot. The platform change is made only by modifying agentType attribute of <deviceModel> element of taskML.

Figure. 10 Interaction with Microsoft agent.

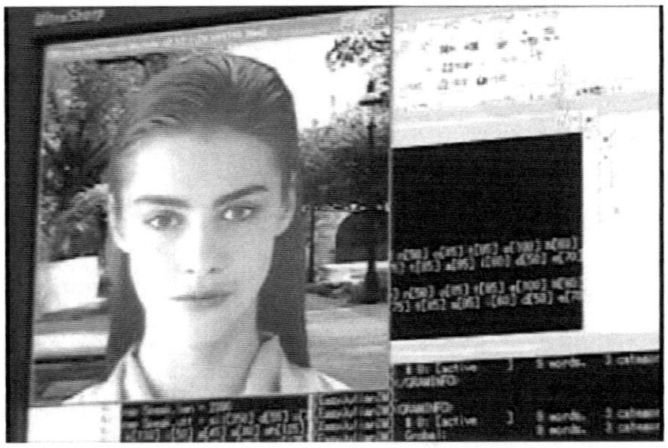

Figure. 11 Interaction with Galatea.

4 Comparison with existing multimodal language

There are several multimodal interaction systems, mainly in research level (López-Cózar and Araki 2005). XHTML+Voice[7] and SALT[8] are most popular multimodal interaction description languages. These two languages concentrate on how to add speech interaction on graphical Web pages by adding spoken dialogue description to (X)HTML codes. These are not suitable for a description of virtual agent interactions.

(Fernando D'Haro et al. 2005) proposes new multimodal languages for several layers. Their proposal is mainly on development environment which supports development steps but for language itself. In contrary to that, our proposal is a

[6] http://www.w3.org/TR/xbl/

[7] http://www-306.ibm.com/software/pervasive/multimodal/x%2Bv/11/spec.htm

[8] http://www.saltforum.org/

simplified language and framework that automate several steps for system development.

5 Conclusion and future works

In this paper, we explained a rapid development method of multimodal dialogue system using MIML. This language can be extended for more complex task settings, such as multi-scenario presentation and multiple-task agents. Although it is difficult to realize multi-scenario presentation by the proposed filtering method, it can be treated by extending filtering concept to discrete variable and enriching the data type of <userModel> variables. For example, if the value of <knowledgeLevel> variable in Figure 7 can take one of "expert", "moderate" and "novice", and each scenario in multi-scenario presentation is marked with these values, multi-scenario presentation can be realized by filtering with discrete variables. In case of multiple-task agents, we can implement such agents by adding one additional interaction description which guides to branch various tasks.

Acknowledgments

Authors would like to thank the members of ISTC/MMI markup language working group for their useful discussions.

References

M. Araki, K. Komatani, T. Hirata and S. Doshita. 1999. *A Dialogue Library for Task-oriented Spoken Dialogue Systems*, Proc. IJCAI Workshop on Knowledge and Reasoning in Practical Dialogue Systems, pp.1-7.

M. Araki, K. Ueda, M. Akita, T. Nishimoto and Y. Niimi. 2002. *Proposal of a Multimodal Dialogue Description Language*, In Proc. of PRICAI 02.

L. Fernando D'Haro et al. 2005. An advanced platform to speed up the design of multilingual dialog applications for multiple modalities, Speech Communication, *in Press*.

R. López-Cózar Delgado, M Araki. 2005. *Spoken, Multilingual and Multimodal Dialogue Systems: Development and Assessment,* Wiley.

K. Katsurada, Y. Nakamura, H. Yamada, T. Nitta. 2003. *XISL: A Language for Describing Multimodal Interaction Scenarios*, Proc. of ICMI'03, pp.281-284.

S. Kawamoto, H. Shimodaira, T. Nitta, T. Nishimoto, S. Nakamura, K. Itou, S. Morishima, T. Yotsukura, A. Kai, A. Lee, Y. Yamashita, T. Kobayashi, K. Tokuda, K. Hirose, N. Minematsu, A. Yamada, Y. Den, T. Utsuro and S. Sagayama. 2004. *Galatea: Open-Source Software for Developing Anthropomorphic Spoken Dialog Agents*, In Life-Like Characters. Tools, Affective Functions, and Applications. ed. H. Prendinger and M. Ishizuka, pp.187-212, Springer.

Classification of Discourse Coherence Relations: An Exploratory Study using Multiple Knowledge Sources

Ben Wellner[†*], **James Pustejovsky**[†], **Catherine Havasi**[†],
Anna Rumshisky[†] and **Roser Saurí**[†]
[†]Department of Computer Science
Brandeis University
Waltham, MA USA
[*]The MITRE Corporation
202 Burlington Road
Bedford, MA USA
{wellner,jamesp,havasi,arum,roser}@cs.brandeis.edu

Abstract

In this paper we consider the problem of identifying and classifying discourse coherence relations. We report initial results over the recently released Discourse GraphBank (Wolf and Gibson, 2005). Our approach considers, and determines the contributions of, a variety of syntactic and lexico-semantic features. We achieve 81% accuracy on the task of discourse relation type classification and 70% accuracy on relation identification.

1 Introduction

The area of modeling discourse has arguably seen less success than other areas in NLP. Contributing to this is the fact that no consensus has been reached on the inventory of discourse relations nor on the types of formal restrictions placed on discourse structure. Furthermore, modeling discourse structure requires access to considerable prior linguistic analysis including syntax, lexical and compositional semantics, as well as the resolution of entity and event-level anaphora, all of which are non-trivial problems themselves.

Discourse processing has been used in many text processing applications, most notably text summarization and compression, text generation, and dialogue understanding. However, it is also important for general text understanding, including applications such as information extraction and question answering.

Recently, Wolf and Gibson (2005) have proposed a graph-based approach to representing informational discourse relations.[1] They demonstrate that tree representations are inadequate for modeling coherence relations, and show that many discourse segments have multiple parents (incoming directed relations) and many of the relations introduce crossing dependencies – both of which preclude tree representations. Their annotation of 135 articles has been released as the GraphBank corpus.

In this paper, we provide initial results for the following tasks: (1) automatically classifying the *type* of discourse coherence relation; and (2) identifying whether any discourse relation *exists* on two text segments. The experiments we report are based on the annotated data in the Discourse GraphBank, where we assume that the discourse units have already been identified.

In contrast to a highly structured, compositional approach to discourse parsing, we explore a simple, flat, feature-based methodology. Such an approach has the advantage of easily accommodating many knowledge sources. This type of detailed feature analysis can serve to inform or augment more structured, compositional approaches to discourse such as those based on Segmented Discourse Representation Theory (SDRT) (Asher and Lascarides, 2003) or the approach taken with the D-LTAG system (Forbes et al., 2001).

Using a comprehensive set of linguistic features as input to a Maximum Entropy classifier, we achieve 81% accuracy on classifying the correct type of discourse coherence relation between two segments.

2 Previous Work

In the past few years, the tasks of discourse segmentation and parsing have been tackled from different perspectives and within different frameworks. Within Rhetorical Structure Theory (RST), Soricut and Marcu (2003) have developed two

[1]The relations they define roughly follow Hobbs (1985).

Proceedings of the 7th SIGdial Workshop on Discourse and Dialogue, pages 117–125,
Sydney, July 2006.

probabilistic models for identifying clausal elementary discourse units and generating discourse trees at the sentence level. These are built using lexical and syntactic information obtained from mapping the discourse-annotated sentences in the RST Corpus (Carlson et al., 2003) to their corresponding syntactic trees in the Penn Treebank.

Within SDRT, Baldridge and Lascarides (2005b) also take a data-driven approach to the tasks of segmentation and identification of discourse relations. They create a probabilistic discourse parser based on dialogues from the Redwoods Treebank, annotated with SDRT rhetorical relations (Baldridge and Lascarides, 2005a). The parser is grounded on headed tree representations and dialogue-based features, such as turn-taking and domain specific goals.

In the Penn Discourse TreeBank (PDTB) (Webber et al., 2005), the identification of discourse structure is approached independently of any linguistic theory by using discourse connectives rather than abstract rhetorical relations. PDTB assumes that connectives are binary discourse-level predicates conveying a semantic relationship between two abstract object-denoting arguments. The set of semantic relationships can be established at different levels of granularity, depending on the application. Miltsakaki, et al. (2005) propose a first step at disambiguating the sense of a small subset of connectives (*since, while*, and *when*) at the paragraph level. They aim at distinguishing between the temporal, causal, and contrastive use of the connective, by means of syntactic features derived from the Penn Treebank and a MaxEnt model.

3 GraphBank

3.1 Coherence Relations

For annotating the discourse relations in text, Wolf and Gibson (2005) assume a clause-unit-based definition of a discourse segment. They define four broad classes of coherence relations:

(1) 1. Resemblance: similarity (par), contrast (contr), example (examp), generalization (gen), elaboration (elab);
2. Cause-effect: explanation (ce), violated expectation (expv), condition (cond);
3. Temporal (temp): essentially narration;
4. Attribution (attr): reporting and evidential contexts.

The textual evidence contributing to identifying the various resemblance relations is heterogeneous at best, where, for example, *similarity* and *contrast* are associated with specific syntactic constructions and devices. For each relation type, there are well-known lexical and phrasal cues:

(2) a. *similarity*: and;
b. *contrast*: by contrast, but;
c. *example*: for example;
d. *elaboration*: also, furthermore, in addition, note that;
e. *generalization*: in general.

However, just as often, the relation is encoded through lexical coherence, via semantic association, sub/supertyping, and accommodation strategies (Asher and Lascarides, 2003).

The cause-effect relations include conventional *causation* and *explanation* relations (captured as the label *ce*), such as (3) below:

(3) **cause:** SEG1: crash-landed in New Hope, Ga.,
effect: SEG2: and injuring 23 others.

It also includes *conditionals* and *violated expectations*, such as (4).

(4) **cause:** SEG1: an Eastern Airlines Lockheed L-1011 en route from Miami to the Bahamas lost all three of its engines,
effect: SEG2: and land safely back in Miami.

The two last coherence relations annotated in GraphBank are *temporal (temp)* and *attribution (attr)* relations. The first corresponds generally to the *occasion* (Hobbs, 1985) or *narration* (Asher and Lascarides, 2003) relation, while the latter is a general annotation over attribution of source.[2]

3.2 Discussion

The difficulty of annotating coherence relations consistently has been previously discussed in the literature. In GraphBank, as in any corpus, there are inconsistencies that must be accommodated for learning purposes. As perhaps expected, annotation of attribution and temporal sequence relations was consistent if not entirely complete. The most serious concern we had from working with

[2]There is one non-rhetorical relation, *same*, which identifies discontiguous segments.

the corpus derives from the conflation of diverse and semantically contradictory relations among the *cause-effect* annotations. For canonical causation pairs (and their violations) such as those above, (3) and (4), the annotation was expectedly consistent and semantically appropriate. Problems arise, however when examining the treatment of purpose clauses and rationale clauses. These are annotated, according to the guidelines, as cause-effect pairings. Consider (5) below.

(5) **cause:** SEG1: to upgrade lab equipment in 1987.
effect: SEG2: The university spent $ 30,000

This is both counter-intuitive and temporally false. The rationale clause is annotated as the cause, and the matrix sentence as the effect. Things are even worse with purpose clause annotation. Consider the following example discourse:[3]

(6) John pushed the door to open it, but it was locked.

This would have the following annotation in GraphBank:

(7) **cause:** to open it
effect: John pushed the door.

The guideline reflects the appropriate intuition that the intention expressed in the purpose or rationale clause must precede the implementation of the action carried out in the matrix sentence. In effect, this would be something like

(8) [INTENTION TO SEG1] CAUSES SEG2

The problem here is that the cause-effect relation conflates real event-causation with *telos*-directed explanations, that is, action directed towards a goal by virtue of an intention. Given that these are semantically disjoint relations, which are furthermore triggered by distinct grammatical constructions, we believe this conflation should be undone and characterized as two separate coherence relations. If the relations just discussed were annotated as *telic*-causation, the features encoded for subsequent training of a machine learning algorithm could benefit from distinct syntactic environments. We would like to automatically generate temporal orderings from cause-effect relations from the events directly annotated in the text.

[3]This specific example was brought to our attention by Alex Lascarides (p.c).

Splitting these classes would preserve the soundness of such a procedure, while keeping them lumped generates inconsistencies.

4 Data Preparation and Knowledge Sources

In this section we describe the various linguistic processing components used for classification and identification of GraphBank discourse relations.

4.1 Pre-Processing

We performed tokenization, sentence tagging, part-of-speech tagging, and shallow syntactic parsing (chunking) over the 135 GraphBank documents. Part-of-speech tagging and shallow parsing were carried out using the Carafe implementation of Conditional Random Fields for NLP (Wellner and Vilain, 2006) trained on various standard corpora. In addition, full sentence parses were obtained using the RASP parser (Briscoe and Carroll, 2002). Grammatical relations derived from a single top-ranked tree for each sentence (headword, modifier, and relation type) were used for feature construction.

4.2 Modal Parsing and Temporal Ordering of Events

We performed both modal parsing and temporal parsing over *events*. Identification of events was performed using EvITA (Saurí et al., 2006), an open-domain event tagger developed under the TARSQI research framework (Verhagen et al., 2005). EvITA locates and tags all event-referring expressions in the input text that can be temporally ordered. In addition, it identifies those grammatical features implicated in temporal and modal information of events; namely, tense, aspect, polarity, modality, as well as the event class. Event annotation follows version 1.2.1 of the TimeML specifications.[4]

Modal parsing in the form of identifying subordinating verb relations and their type was performed using SlinkET (Saurí et al., 2006), another component of the TARSQI framework. SlinkET identifies subordination constructions introducing modality information in text; essentially, infinitival and *that*-clauses embedded by factive predicates (*regret*), reporting predicates (*say*), and predicates referring to events of attempting (*try*), volition (*want*), command (*order*), among others.

[4]See http://www.timeml.org.

SlinkET annotates these subordination contexts and classifies them according to the modality information introduced by the relation between the embedding and embedded predicates, which can be of any of the following types:

- **factive:** The embedded event is presupposed or entailed as true (e.g., *John managed to leave the party*).
- **counter-factive:** The embedded event is presupposed as entailed as false (e.g., *John was unable to leave the party*).
- **evidential:** The subordination is introduced by a reporting or perception event (e.g., *Mary saw/told that John left the party*).
- **negative evidential:** The subordination is a reporting event conveying negative polarity (e.g., *Mary denied that John left the party*).
- **modal:** The subordination creates an intensional context (e.g., *John wanted to leave the party*).

Temporal orderings between events were identified using a Maximum Entropy classifier trained on the TimeBank 1.2 and Opinion 1.0a corpora. These corpora provide annotated events along with temporal links between events. The link types included: *before* (e_1 occurs before e_2) , *includes* (e_2 occurs sometime during e_1), *simultaneous* (e_1 occurs over the same interval as e_2), *begins* (e_1 begins at the same time as e_2), *ends* (e_1 ends at the same time as e_2).

4.3 Lexical Semantic Typing and Coherence

Lexical semantic types as well as a measure of lexical similarity or coherence between words in two discourse segments would appear to be useful for assigning an appropriate discourse relationship. *Resemblance* relations, in particular, require similar entities to be involved and lexical similarity here serves as an approximation to definite nominal coreference. Identification of lexical relationships between words across segments appears especially useful for *cause-effect* relations. In example (3) above, determining a (potential) cause-effect relationship between *crash* and *injury* is necessary to identify the discourse relation.

4.3.1 Corpus-based Lexical Similarity

Lexical similarity was computed using the Word Sketch Engine (WSE) (Killgarrif et al., 2004) similarity metric applied over British National Corpus. The WSE similarity metric implements the word similarity measure based on grammatical relations as defined in (Lin, 1998) with minor modifications.

4.3.2 The Brandeis Semantic Ontology

As a second source of lexical coherence, we used the Brandeis Semantic Ontology or BSO (Pustejovsky et al., 2006). The BSO is a lexically-based ontology in the Generative Lexicon tradition (Pustejovsky, 2001; Pustejovsky, 1995). It focuses on contextualizing the meanings of words and does this by a rich system of types and qualia structures. For example, if one were to look up the phrase RED WINE in the BSO, one would find its type is WINE and its type's type is ALCOHOLIC BEVERAGE. The BSO contains ontological qualia information (shown below). Using the BSO, one

wine
CONSTITUTIVE = **Alcohol**
HAS ELEMENT = **Alcohol**
MADE OF = **Grapes**
INDIRECT TELIC = **drink activity**
INDIRECT AGENTIVE = **make alcoholic beverage**

is able to find out where in the ontological type system WINE is located, what RED WINE's lexical neighbors are, and its full set of part of speech and grammatical attributes. Other words have a different configuration of annotated attributes depending on the type of the word.

We used the BSO typing information to semantically tag individual words in order to compute lexical paths between word pairs. Such lexical associations are invoked when constructing cause-effect relations and other implicatures (e.g. between *crash* and *injure* in Example 3).

The type system paths provide a measure of the connectedness between words. For every pair of head words in a GraphBank document, the shortest path between the two words within the BSO is computed. Currently, this metric only uses the type system relations (i.e., inheritance) but preliminary tests show that including qualia relations as connections is promising. We also computed the earliest common ancestor of the two words. These metrics are calculated for every possible sense of the word within the BSO.

The use of the BSO is advantageous compared to other frameworks such as Wordnet because it focuses on the connection between words and their semantic relationship to other items. These connections are captured in the qualia information and the type system. In Wordnet, qualia-like information is only present in the glosses, and they do not provide a definite semantic path between any two lexical items. Although synonymous in some ways, synset members often behave differently in many situations, grammatical or otherwise.

5 Classification Methodology

This section describes in detail how we constructed features from the various knowledge sources described above and how they were encoded in a Maximum Entropy model.

5.1 Maximum Entropy Classification

For our experiments of classifying relation types, we used a Maximum Entropy classifier[5] in order to assign labels to each pair of discourse segments connected by some relation. For each instance (i.e. pair of segments) the classifier makes its decision based on a set of *features*. Each feature can query some arbitrary property of the two segments, possibly taking into account external information or knowledge sources. For example, a feature could query whether the two segments are adjacent to each other, whether one segment contains a discourse connective, whether they both share a particular word, whether a particular syntactic construction or lexical association is present, etc. We make strong use of this ability to include very many, highly interdependent features[6] in our experiments. Besides binary-valued features, feature values can be real-valued and thus capture frequencies, similarity values, or other scalar quantities.

5.2 Feature Classes

We grouped the features together into various *feature classes* based roughly on the knowledge source from which they were derived. Table 1 describes the various feature classes in detail and provides some actual example features from each class for the segment pair described in Example 5 in Section 3.2.

[5]We use the Maximum Entropy classifier included with Carafe available at http://sourceforge.net/projects/carafe

[6]The total maximum number of features occurring in our experiments is roughly 120,000.

6 Experiments and Results

In this section we provide the results of a set of experiments focused on the task of discourse relation classification. We also report initial results on relation *identification* with the same set of features as used for classification.

6.1 Discourse Relation Classification

The task of discourse relation classification involves assigning the correct label to a pair of discourse segments.[7] The pair of segments to assign a relation to is provided (from the annotated data). In addition, we assume, for asymmetric links, that the nucleus and satellite are provided (i.e., the *direction* of the relation). For the *elaboration* relations, we ignored the annotated subtypes (person, time, location, etc.). Experiments were carried out on the full set of relation types as well as the simpler set of coarse-grained relation categories described in Section 3.1.

The GraphBank contains a total of 8755 annotated coherence relations. [8] For all the experiments in this paper, we used 8-fold cross-validation with 12.5% of the data used for testing and the remainder used for training for each fold. Accuracy numbers reported are the average accuracies over the 8 folds. Variance was generally low with a standard deviation typically in the range of 1.5 to 2.0. We note here also that the inter-annotator agreement between the two GraphBank annotators was 94.6% for relations *when they agreed on the presence of a relation*. The majority class baseline (i.e., the accuracy achieved by calling all relations *elaboration*) is 45.7% (and 66.57% with the collapsed categories). These are the upper and lower bounds against which these results should be based.

To ascertain the utility of each of the various feature classes, we considered each feature class independently by using only features from a single class in addition to the Proximity feature class which serve as a baseline. Table 2 illustrates the result of this experiment.

We performed a second set of experiments shown in Table 3 that is essentially the converse of the previous batch. We take the union of all the

[7]Each segment may in fact consist of a sequence of segments. We will, however, use the term *segment* loosely to refer to segments or segment sequences.

[8]All documents are doubly annotated; we used the *annotator1* annotations.

Feature Class	Description	Example
C	Words appearing at beginning and end of the two discourse segments - these are often important discourse cue words.	first1-is-*to*; first2-is-*The*
P	Proximity and direction between the two segments (in terms of segments) - binary features such as *distance less than 3*, *distance greater than 10* were used in addition to the distance value itself; the distance from beginning of the document using a similar binning approach	adjacent; dist-less-than-3; dist-less-than-5; direction-reverse; samesentence
BSO	Paths in the BSO up to length 10 between non-function words in the two segments.	ResearchLab → EducationalActivity → University
WSE	WSE word-pair similarities between words in the two segments were binned as (> 0.05, > 0.1, > 0.2). We also computed sentence similarity as the sum of the word similarities divided by the sum of their sentence lengths.	WSE-greater-than-0.05; WSE-sentence-sim = 0.005417
E	Event head words and event head word pairs between segments as identified by EvITA.	event1-is-*upgrade*; event2-is-*spent*; event-pair-*upgrade-spent*
SlinkET	Event attributes, subordinating links and their types between event pairs in the two segments	seg1-class-is-*occurrence*; seg2-class-is-*occurrence*; seg1-tense-is-*infinitive*; seg2-tense-is-*past*; seg2-*modal*-seg1
C-E	Cuewords of one segment paired with events in the other.	first1-is-*to*-event2-is-*spent*; first2-is-*The*-event1-is-*upgrade*
Syntax	Grammatical dependency relations between two segments as identified by the RASP parser. We also conjoined the relation with one or both of the headwords associated with the grammatical relation.	gr-*ncmod*; gr-*ncmod*-head1-*equipment*; gr-*ncmod*-head-2-*spent*; etc.
Tlink	Temporal links between events in the two segments. We included both the link types and the number of occurrences of those types between the segments	seg2-*before*-seg1

Table 1: Feature classes, their descriptions and example feature instances for Example 5 in Section 3.2.

Feature Class	Accuracy	Coarse-grained Acc.
Proximity	60.08%	69.43%
P+C	76.77%	83.50%
P+BSO	62.92%	74.40%
P+WSE	62.20%	70.10%
P+E	63.84%	78.16%
P+SlinkET	69.00%	75.91%
P+CE	67.18%	78.63%
P+Syntax	70.30%	80.84%
P+Tlink	64.19%	72.30%

Table 2: Classification accuracy over standard and coarse-grained relation types with each feature class added to Proximity feature class.

feature classes and perform ablation experiments by removing one feature class at a time.

Feature Class	Accuracy	Coarse-grain Acc.
All Features	81.06%	87.51%
All-P	71.52%	84.88%
All-C	75.71%	84.69%
All-BSO	80.65%	87.04%
All-WSE	80.26%	87.14%
All-E	80.90%	86.92%
All-SlinkET	79.68%	86.89%
All-CE	80.41%	87.14%
All-Syntax	80.20%	86.89%
All-Tlink	80.30%	87.36%

Table 3: Classification accuracy with each feature class removed from the union of all feature classes.

6.2 Analysis

From the ablation results, it is clear that overall performance is most impacted by the *cue-word* features (C) and *proximity* (P). Syntax and SlinkET also have high impact improving accuracy by roughly 10 and 9 percent respectively as shown in Table 2. From the ablation results in Table 3, it is clear that the utility of most of the individual features classes is lessened when all the other feature classes are taken into account. This indicates that multiple feature classes are responsible for providing evidence any given discourse relations. Removing a single feature class degrades performance, but only slightly, as the others can compensate.

Overall precision, recall and F-measure results for each of the different link types using the set of all feature classes are shown in Table 4 with the corresponding confusion matrix in Table A.1. Performance correlates roughly with the frequency of the various relation types. We might therefore expect some improvement in performance with more annotated data for those relations with low frequency in the GraphBank.

Relation	Precision	Recall	F-measure	Count
elab	88.72	95.31	91.90	512
attr	91.14	95.10	93.09	184
par	71.89	83.33	77.19	132
same	87.09	75.00	80.60	72
ce	78.78	41.26	54.16	63
contr	65.51	66.67	66.08	57
examp	78.94	48.39	60.00	31
temp	50.00	20.83	29.41	24
expv	33.33	16.67	22.22	12
cond	45.45	62.50	52.63	8
gen	0.0	0.0	0.0	0

Table 4: Precision, Recall and F-measure results.

6.3 Coherence Relation Identification

The task of identifying the presence of a relation is complicated by the fact that we must consider all $\binom{n}{2}$ potential relations where n is the number of segments. This presents a troublesome, highly-skewed binary classification problem with a high proportion of negative instances. Furthermore, some of the relations, particularly the *resemblance* relations, are transitive in nature (e.g. $parallel(s_i, s_j) \wedge parallel(s_j, s_k) \rightarrow parallel(s_i, s_k)$). However, these transitive links are not provided in the GraphBank annotation - such segment pairs will therefore be presented incorrectly as negative instances to the learner, making this approach infeasible. An initial experiment considering all segment pairs, in fact, resulted in performance only slightly above the majority class baseline.

Instead, we consider the task of identifying the presence of discourse relations between segments within the same sentence. Using the same set of all features used for relation classification, performance is at 70.04% accuracy. Simultaneous identification and classification resulted in an accuracy of 64.53%. For both tasks the baseline accuracy was 58%.

6.4 Modeling Inter-relation Dependencies

Casting the problem as a standard classification problem where each instance is classified independently, as we have done, is a potential drawback. In order to gain insight into how collective, dependent modeling might help, we introduced additional features that model such dependencies: For a pair of discourse segments, s_i and s_j, to classify the relation between, we included features based on the *other* relations involved with the two segments (from the gold standard annotations): $\{R(s_i, s_k) | k \neq j\}$ and $\{R(s_j, s_l) | l \neq i\}$. Adding these features improved classification accuracy to 82.3%. This improvement is fairly significant (a 6.3% reduction in error) given that this dependency information is only encoded weakly as features and not in the form of model constraints.

7 Discussion and Future Work

We view the accuracy of 81% on coherence relation classification as a positive result, though room for improvement clearly remains. An examination of the errors indicates that many of the remaining problems require making complex lexical associations, the establishment of entity and event anaphoric links and, in some cases, the exploitation of complex world-knowledge. While important lexical connections can be gleaned from the BSO, we hypothesize that the current lack of word sense disambiguation serves to lessen its utility since lexical paths between *all* word sense of two words are currently used. Additional feature engineering, particularly the crafting of more specific *conjunctions* of existing features is another avenue to explore further - as are automatic feature selection methods.

Different types of relations clearly benefit from different feature types. For example, resemblance relations require similar entities and/or events, indicating a need for robust anaphora resolution, while cause-effect class relations require richer lexical and world knowledge. One promising approach is a pipeline where an initial classifier assigns a coarse-grained category, followed by separately engineered classifiers designed to model the finer-grained distinctions.

An important area of future work involves incorporating additional *structure* in two places. First, as the experiment discussed in Section 6.4 shows, classifying discourse relations collectively shows potential for improved performance. Secondly, we believe that the tasks of: 1) identifying which segments are related and 2) identifying the discourse segments themselves are probably best approached by a parsing model of discourse. This view is broadly sympathetic with the approach in (Miltsakaki et al., 2005).

We furthermore believe an extension to the GraphBank annotation scheme, with some minor changes as we advocate in Section 3.2, layered on top of the PDTB would, in our view, serve as an interesting resource and model for informational discourse.

Acknowledgments

This work was supported in part by ARDA/DTO under grant number NBCHC040027 and MITRE Sponsored Research. Catherine Havasi is supported by NSF Fellowship # 2003014891.

References

N. Asher and A. Lascarides. 2003. *Logics of Conversation*. Cambridge University Press, Cambridge, England.

J. Baldridge and A. Lascarides. 2005a. Annotating discourse structures for robust semantic interpretation. In *Proceedings of the Sixth International Workshop on Computational Semantics*, Tilburg, The Netherlands.

J. Baldridge and A. Lascarides. 2005b. Probabilistic head-driven parsing for discourse structure. In *Proceedings of the Ninth Conference on Computational Natural Language Learning*, Ann Arbor, USA.

T. Briscoe and J. Carroll. 2002. Robust accurate statistical annotation of general text. *Proceedings of the Third International Conference on Language Resources and Evaluation (LREC 2002), Las Palmas, Canary Islands, May 2002*, pages 1499–1504.

L. Carlson, D. Marcu, and M. E. Okurowski. 2003. Building a discourse-tagged corpus in the framework of rhetorical structure theory. In Janvan Kuppelvelt and Ronnie Smith, editors, *Current Directions in Discourse and Dialogue*. Kluwer Academic Publishers.

K. Forbes, E. Miltsakaki, R. Prasad, A. Sakar, A. Joshi, and B. Webber. 2001. D-LTAG system: Discourse parsing with a lexicalized tree adjoining grammar. In *Proceedings of the ESSLLI 2001: Workshop on Information Structure, Discourse Structure and Discourse Semantics*.

J. Hobbs. 1985. On the coherence and structure of discourse. In *CSLI Technical Report 85-37*, Stanford, CA, USA. Center for the Study of Language and Information.

A. Killgarrif, P. Rychly, P. Smrz, and D. Tugwell. 2004. The sketch engine. In *Proceedings of Euralex, Lorient, France*, pages 105–116.

D. Lin. 1998. Automatic retrieval and clustering of similar words. In *Proceedings of COLING-ACL*, Montreal, Canada.

E. Miltsakaki, N. Dinesh, R. Prasad, A. Joshi, and B. Webber. 2005. Experiments on sense annotation and sense disambiguation of discourse connectives. In *Proceedings of the Fourth Workshop on Treebanks and Linguistic Theories (TLT 2005)*, Barcelona, Catalonia.

J. Pustejovsky, C. Havasi, R. Saurí, P. Hanks, and A. Rumshisky. 2006. Towards a Generative Lexical resource: The Brandeis Semantic Ontology. In *Language Resources and Evaluation Conference, LREC 2006*, Genoa, Italy.

J. Pustejovsky. 1995. *The Generative Lexicon*. MIT Press, Cambridge, MA.

J. Pustejovsky. 2001. Type construction and the logic of concepts. In *The Language of Word Meaning*. Cambridge University Press.

R. Saurí, M. Verhagen, and J. Pustejovsky. 2006. Annotating and recognizing event modality in text. In *The 19th International FLAIRS Conference, FLAIRS 2006*, Melbourne Beach, Florida, USA.

R. Soricut and D. Marcu. 2003. Sentence level discourse parsing using syntactic and lexical information. In *Proceedings of the HLT/NAACL Conference*, Edmonton, Canada.

M. Verhagen, I. Mani, R. Saurí, R. Knippen, J. Littman, and J. Pustejovsky. 2005. Automating temporal annotation within TARSQI. In *Proceedings of the ACL 2005*.

B. Webber, A. Joshi, E. Miltsakaki, R. Prasad, N. Dinesh, A. Lee, and K. Forbes. 2005. A short introduction to the penn discourse TreeBank. In *Copenhagen Working Papers in Language and Speech Processing*.

B. Wellner and M. Vilain. 2006. Leveraging machine readable dictionaries in discriminative sequence models. In *Language Resources and Evaluation Conference, LREC 2006*, Genoa, Italy.

F. Wolf and E. Gibson. 2005. Representing discourse coherence: A corpus-based analysis. *Computational Linguistics*, 31(2):249–287.

A Appendix

A.1 Confusion Matrix

	elab	par	attr	ce	temp	contr	same	examp	expv	cond	gen
elab	488	3	7	3	1	0	2	4	0	3	1
par	6	110	2	2	0	8	2	0	0	2	0
attr	4	0	175	0	0	1	2	0	1	1	0
ce	18	9	3	26	3	2	2	0	0	0	0
temp	6	8	2	0	5	3	0	0	0	0	0
contr	4	12	0	0	0	38	0	0	3	0	0
same	3	9	2	2	0	2	54	0	0	0	0
examp	15	1	0	0	0	0	0	15	0	0	0
expv	3	1	1	0	1	4	0	0	2	0	0
cond	3	0	0	0	0	0	0	0	0	5	0
gen	0	0	0	0	0	0	0	0	0	0	0

A.2 SlinkET Example

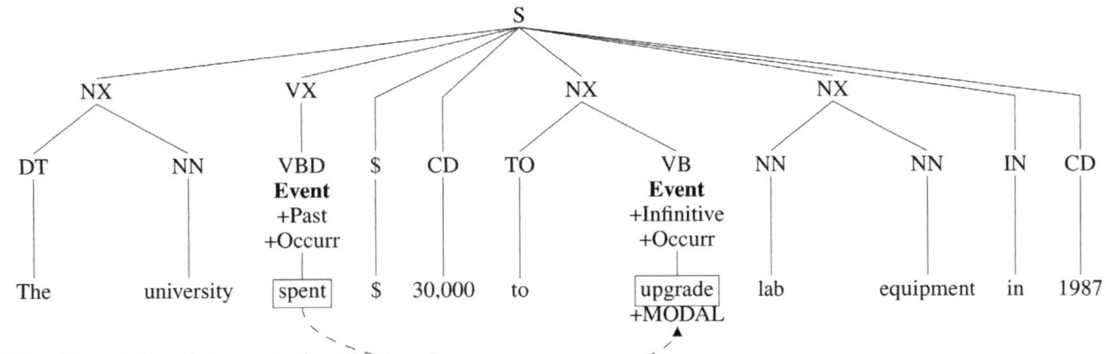

A.3 GraphBank Annotation Example

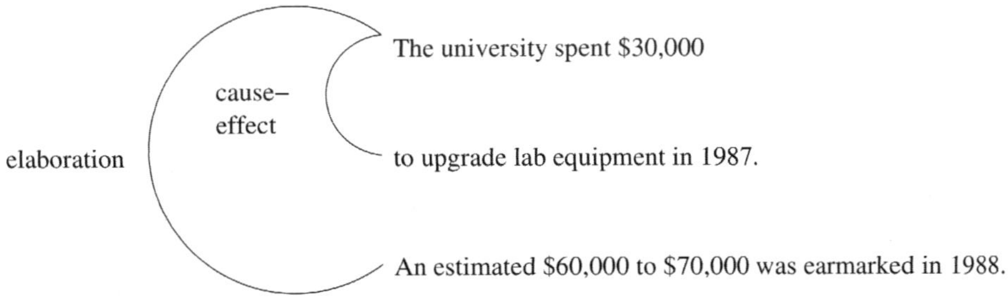

Measuring annotator agreement in a complex hierarchical dialogue act annotation scheme

Jeroen Geertzen and Harry Bunt
Language and Information Science
Tilburg University, P.O. Box 90153
NL-5000 LE Tilburg, The Netherlands
{j.geertzen,h.bunt}@uvt.nl

Abstract

We present a first analysis of inter-annotator agreement for the DIT^{++} tagset of dialogue acts, a comprehensive, layered, multidimensional set of 86 tags. Within a dimension or a layer, subsets of tags are often hierarchically organised. We argue that especially for such highly structured annotation schemes the well-known kappa statistic is not an adequate measure of inter-annotator agreement. Instead, we propose a statistic that takes the structural properties of the tagset into account, and we discuss the application of this statistic in an annotation experiment. The experiment shows promising agreement scores for most dimensions in the tagset and provides useful insights into the usability of the annotation scheme, but also indicates that several additional factors influence annotator agreement. We finally suggest that the proposed approach for measuring agreement per dimension can be a good basis for measuring annotator agreement over the dimensions of a multidimensional annotation scheme.

1 Introduction

The DIT^{++} tagset (Bunt, 2005) was designed to combine in one comprehensive annotation scheme the communicative functions of dialogue acts distinguished in Dynamic Interpretation Theory (DIT, (Bunt, 2000; Bunt and Girard, 2005)), and many of those in DAMSL (Allen and Core, 1997) and in other annotation schemes. An important difference between the DIT^{++} and DAMSL schemes is the more elaborate and fine-grained set of functions for feedback and other aspects of dialogue control that is available in DIT, partly inspired by the work of Allwood (Allwood et al., 1993). As it is often thought that more elaborate and fine-grained annotation schemes are difficult for annotators to apply consistently, we decided to address this issue in an annotation experiment on which we report in this paper. A frequently used way of evaluating human dialogue act classification is inter-annotator agreement. Agreement is sometimes measured as percentage of the cases on which the annotators agree, but more often expected agreement is taken into account in using the kappa statistic (Cohen, 1960; Carletta, 1996), which is given by:

$$\kappa = \frac{p_o - p_e}{1 - p_e} \quad (1)$$

where p_o is the observed proportion of agreement and p_e is the proportion of agreement expected by chance. Ever since its introduction in general (Cohen, 1960) and in computational linguistics (Carletta, 1996), many researchers have pointed out that there are quite some problems in using κ (e.g. (Di Eugenio and Glass, 2004)), one of which is the discrepancy between p_0 and κ for skewed class distribution.

Another is that the degree of disagreement is not taken into account, which is relevant for any non-nominal scale. To address this problem, a weighted κ has been proposed (Cohen, 1968) that penalizes disagreement according to their degree rather than treating all disagreements equally. It would be arguable that in a similar way, characteristics of dialogue acts in a particular taxonomy and possible pragmatic similarity between them should be taken into account to express annotator agreement. For dialogue act taxonomies which are structured in a meaningful way, such as those that

Proceedings of the 7th SIGdial Workshop on Discourse and Dialogue, pages 126–133,
Sydney, July 2006.

express hierarchical relations between concepts in the taxonomy, the taxonomic structure can be exploited to express how much annotators disagree when they choose different concepts that are directly or indirectly related. Recent work that accounts for some of these aspects is a metric for automatic dialogue act classification (Lesch et al., 2005) that uses distance in a hierarchical structure of multidimensional labels.

In the following sections of this paper, we will first briefly consider the dimensions in the DIT^{++} scheme and highlight the taxonomic characteristics that will turn out to be relevant in later stage. We will then introduce a variant of weighted κ for inter-annotator agreement called κ_{tw} that adopts a taxonomy-dependent weighting, and discuss its use.

2 Annotation using DIT

DIT is a context-change (or information-state update) approach to the analysis of dialogue, which describes utterance meaning in terms of context update operations called 'dialogue acts'. A dialogue act in DIT has two components: (1) the semantic content, being the objects, events, properties, relations, etc. that are considered; and (2) the communicative function, that describes how the addressee is intended to use the semantic content for updating his context model when he understands the utterance correctly. DIT takes a multidimensional view on dialogue in the sense that speakers may use utterances to address several aspects of the communication simultaneously, as reflected in the multifunctionality of utterances. One such aspect is the performance of the task or activity for which the dialogue takes place; another is the monitoring of each other's attention, understanding and uptake through feedback acts; others include for instance the turn-taking process and the timing of communicative actions, and finally yet another aspect is formed by the social obligations that may arise such as greeting, apologising, or thanking. The various aspects of communication that can be addressed independently are called *dimensions* (Bunt and Girard, 2005; Bunt, 2006). The DIT^{++} tagset distinguishes 11 dimensions, which all contain a number of communicative functions that are specific to that dimension, such as TURN GIVING, PAUSING, and APOLOGY.

Besides dimension-specific communicative functions, DIT also distinguishes a layer of communicative functions that are not specific to any particular dimension but that can be used to address any aspect of communication. These functions, which include questions, answers, statements, and commissive as well as directive acts, are called *general purpose functions*. A dialogue act falls within a specific dimension if it has a communicative function specific for that dimension or if it has a general-purpose function and a semantic content relating to that dimension. Dialogue utterances can in principle have a function (but never more than one) in each of the dimensions, so annotators using the DIT^{++} scheme can assign at most one tag for each of the 11 dimensions to any given utterance.

Both within the set of general-purpose communicative function tags and within the sets of dimension-specific tags, tags can be hierarchically related in such a way that a label lower in a hierarchy is more specific than a label higher in the same hierarchy. Tag F_1 is more specific than tag F_2 if F_1 defines a context update operation that includes the update operation corresponding to F_2. For instance, consider a part of the taxonomy for general purpose functions (Figure 1).

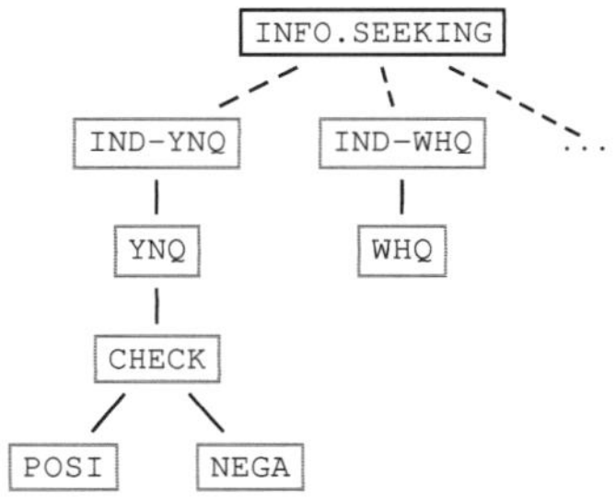

Figure 1: Two hierarchies in the information seeking general purpose functions.

For an utterance to be assigned a YN-QUESTION, we assume the speaker believes that the addressee knows the truth value of the proposition presented. For an utterance to be assigned a CHECK, we assume the speaker *additionally* has a weak belief that the proposition that forms the semantic content is true. And for a POSI-CHECK, there is the additional assumption that the speaker believes (weakly) that the hearer also believes that the proposition is true.[1]

Similar to the hierarchical relations between YN-Question, CHECK, and POSI-CHECK, other parts

[1]For a formal description of each function in the DIT^{++} tagset see http://ls0143.uvt.nl/dit/

of the annotation scheme contain hierarchically related functions.

The following example illustrates the use of DIT^{++} communicative functions for a very simple translated) dialogue fragment[2].

1	S	at what time do you want to travel today? TASK = WH-Q, TURN-MANAGEMENT = GIVE
2	U	at ten. TASK = WH-A, TURN-MANAGEMENT = GIVE
3	S	so you want to leave at ten in the morning? TASK = POSI-CHECK, TURN-MANAGEMENT = GIVE
4	U	yes that is right. TASK = CONFIRM, TURN-MANAGEMENT = GIVE

3 Agreement using κ

3.1 Related work

Inter-annotator agreements have been calculated with the purpose of qualitatively evaluating tagsets and individual tags. For DAMSL, the first agreement results were presented in (Core and Allen, 1997), based on the analysis of TRAINS 91-93 dialogues (Gross et al., 1993; Heeman and Allen, 1995). In this analysis, 604 utterances were tagged by mostly two annotators. Following the suggestions in (Carletta, 1996), Core et al. consider kappa scores above 0.67 to indicate significant agreement and scores above 0.8 reliable agreement. Another more recent analysis was performed for 8 dialogues of the MONROE corpus (Stent, 2000), counting 2897 utterances in total, processed by two annotators for 13 DAMSL dimensions. Other analyses apply DAMSL derived schemes (such as SWITCHBOARD-DAMSL) to various corpora (e.g. (Di Eugenio et al., 1998; Shriberg et al., 2004)). For the comprehensive DIT^{++} taxonomy, the work reported here represents the first investigation of annotator agreement.

3.2 Experiment outline

As noted, existing work on annotator agreement analysis has mostly involved only two annotators. It may be argued that especially for annotation of concepts that are rather complex, an odd number of annotators is desirable. First, it allows having majority agreement unless all annotators choose entirely different. Second, it allows to deal better with the undesirable situation that one annotator chooses quite differently from the others. The agreement scores reported in this paper are all calculated on the basis of the annotations of three annotators, using the method proposed in (Davies and Fleiss, 1982).

The dialogues that were annotated are task-oriented and are all in Dutch. To account for different complexities of interaction, both human-machine and human-human dialogues are considered. Moreover, the dialogues analyzed are drawn from different corpora: OVIS (Strik et al., 1997), DIAMOND (Geertzen et al., 2004), and a collection of Map Task dialogues (Caspers, 2000); see Table 1, where the number of annotated utterances is also indicated.

corpus	domain	type	#utt
OVIS	TRAINS like interactions on train connections	H-M	193
DIAMOND1	interactions on how to operate a fax device	H-M	131
DIAMOND2	interactions on how to operate a fax device	H-H	114
MAPTASK	HCRC Map Task like interaction	H-H	120
			558

Table 1: Characteristics of the utterances considered

Six undergraduate students annotated the selected dialogue material. They had been introduced to the DIT^{++} annotation scheme and the underlying theory while participating in a course on pragmatics. During this course they were exposed to approximately four hours of lecturing and few small annotation exercises. For all dialogues, the audio recordings were transcribed and the annotators annotated presegmented utterances for which full agreement was established on segmentation level beforehand. During the annotation sessions the annotators had — apart from the transcribed speech — access to the audio recordings, to the on-line definitions of the communicative functions in the scheme and to a very brief, 1-page set of annotation guidelines[3]. The task was facilitated by the use of an annotation tool that had been built for this occasion; this tool allowed the subjects to assign each utterance one DIT^{++} tag for each dimension without any further constraints. In total 1,674 utterances were annotated.

3.3 Problems with standard κ

If we were to apply the standard κ statistic to DIT^{++} annotations, we would not do justice to an important aspect of the annotation scheme concerning the differences between alternative tags,

[2]Drawn from the OVIS corpus (Strik et al., 1997): OVIS2:104/001/001:008-011

[3]See http://ls0143.uvt.nl/dit

and hence the possible differences in the disagreement between annotators using alternative tags. An aspect in which the DIT^{++} scheme differs from other taxonomies for dialogue acts is that, as noted in Section 2, communicative functions (CFs) within a dimension as well as general-purpose CFs are often structured into hierarchies in which a difference in level represents a relation of specificity. When annotators differ in that they assign tags which both belong to the same hierarchy, they may differ in the degree of specificity that they want to express, but they agree to the extent that these tags inherit the same elements from tags higher in the hierarchy. Inter-annotator disagreement is in such a case much less than if they would choose two unrelated tags. This is for instance obvious in the following example of the annotations of two utterances by two annotators:

1	S	what do you want to know?	WHQ	YNQ
2	U	can I print now?	YNQ	CHECK

With utterance 1, the annotators should be said simply to disagree (in fact, annotator 2 incorrectly assigns a YNQ function). Concerning utterance 2 the annotators also disagree, but Figure 1 and the definitions given in Section 2 tell us that the disagreement in this case is quite small, as a CHECK inherits the properties of a YNQ. We therefore should not use a black-and-white measure of agreement, like the standard κ, but we should have a measure for *partial annotator agreement*.

In order to measure partial (dis-)agreement between annotators in an adequate way, we should not just take into account whether two tags are hierarchically related or not, but also how far they are apart in the hierarchy, to reflect that two tags which are only one level apart are semantically more closely related than tags that are several levels apart. We will take this additional requirement into account when designing a weighted disagreement statistic in the next section.

4 Agreement based on structural taxonomic properties

The agreement coefficient we are looking for should in the first place be *weighted* in the sense that it takes into account the magnitude of disagreement. Two such coefficients are weighted kappa (κ_w, (Cohen, 1968)) and alpha (Krippendorff, 1980). For our purposes, we adopt κ_w for its property to take into account a probability distribution typical for each annotator, generalize it to the case for multiple annotators by taking the average over the scores of annotator pairs, and define a function to be used as distance metric.

4.1 Cohen's weighted κ

Assuming the case of two annotators, let p_{ij} denote the proportion of utterances for which the first and second annotator assigned categories i and j, respectively. Then Cohen defines κ_w in terms of *disagreement* rather than *agreement* where $q_o = 1 - p_o$ and $q_e = 1 - p_e$ such that Equation 1 can be rewritten to:

$$\kappa = 1 - \frac{q_o}{q_e} \qquad (2)$$

To arrive at κ_w, the proportions q_o and q_e in Equation 2 are replaced by weighted functions over all possible category pairs:

$$\kappa_w = 1 - \frac{\sum v_{ij} \cdot p_{oij}}{\sum v_{ij} \cdot p_{eij}} \qquad (3)$$

where v_{ij} denotes the disagreement weight. To calculate this weight we need to specify a distance function as metric.

4.2 A taxonomic metric

The task of defining a function in order to calculate the difference between a pair of categories requires us to determine semantic-pragmatic relatedness between the CFs in the taxonomy. For any annotation scheme, whether it is hierarchically structured or not, we could assign for each possible pair of categories a value that expresses the semantic-pragmatic relatedness between the two categories compared to all other possible pairs. However, it seems quite difficult to find universal characteristics for CFs to be used to express relatedness on a rational scale. When we consider a taxonomy that is structured in a meaningful way, in this case one that expresses hierarchical relations between CF based on their effect on information states, the taxonomic structure can be exploited to express in a systematic fashion how much annotators disagree when they choose different concepts that are directly or indirectly related.

The assignment of different CFs to a specific utterance by two annotators represents full disagreement in the following cases:

1. the two CFs belong to different dimensions;

2. one of the two CFs is general-purpose; the other is dimension-specific;[4]

3. the two CFs belong to the same dimension but not to the same hierarchy;

4. the two CFs belong to the same hierarchy but are not located in the same branch. Two CFs are said to be located in the same branch when one of the two CFs is an ancestor of the other.

If, by contrast, the two CFs take part in a parent-child relation within a hierarchy (either within a dimension or among the general-purpose CFs), then the CFs are related and this assignment represents partial disagreement. A distance metric that measures this disagreement, which we denote as δ, should have the following properties:

1. δ should be a real number normalized in the range $[0 \ldots 1]$;

2. Let C be the (unordered) set of CFs.[5] For every two CFs $c_1, c_2 \in C$, $\delta(c_1, c_2) = 0$ when c_1 and c_2 are not related;

3. Let C be the (unordered) set of CFs. For every communicative function $c \in C$, $\delta(c, c) = 1$;

4. Let C be the (unordered) set of CFs. For every two CFs $c_1, c_2 \in C$, $\delta(c_1, c_2) = \delta(c_2, c_1)$.

Furthermore, when c_1 and c_2 are related, we should specify how distance between them in the hierarchy should be expressed in terms of partial disagreement. For this, we should take the following aspects into account:

1. The distance in levels between c_1 and c_2 in the hierarchy is proportional to the magnitude of the disagreement;

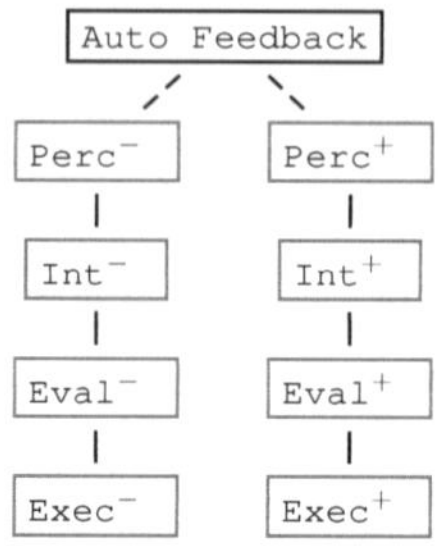

Figure 2: Hierarchical structures in the auto feedback dimension.

2. The magnitude of disagreement between c_1 and c_2 being located in two different levels of depths n and $n+1$ *might* be considered to be more different than that between to levels of depth $n+1$ and $n+2$. If this would be the case, the deeper two levels are located in the tree, the smaller the differences between the nodes on those levels. For the hierarchies in DIT, we keep the magnitude of disagreement linear with the difference in levels, and independent of level depth;

Given the considerations above, we propose the following metric:

$$\delta(c_i, c_j) = a^{\Delta(c_i, c_j)} \cdot b^{\Gamma(c_i, c_j)} \tag{4}$$

where:

- a is a constant for which $0 < a < 1$, expressing how much distance there is between two adjacent levels in the hierarchy; a plausible value for a could be 0.75;

- Δ is a function that returns the difference in depth between the levels of c_i and c_j;

- b is a constant for which $0 < b \leq 1$, expressing in what rate differences should become smaller when the depth in the hierarchy gets larger. If there is no reason to assume that differences on a higher depth in the hierarchy are of less magnitude than differences on a lower depth, then $b = 1$;

- $\Gamma(c_i, c_j)$ is a function that returns the minimal depth of c_i and c_j.

To provide some examples of how δ would be calculated, let us consider the general purpose functions in Figure 1. Consider also Figure 2, that represents two hierarchies of CFs in the auto

[4]This is in fact a simplification. For instance, an INFORM act of which the semantic content conveys that the speaker did not understand the previous utterance forms an act in the Auto-Feedback dimension (see Note 6), and a tagging to this effect should perhaps not be considered to express full disagreement with the assignment of the dimension-specific tag AUTO-FEEDBACK-Int$^-$. See also the next footnote.

[5]Strictly speaking, in DIT a dialogue act annotation tag is either (a) the name of a dimension-specific function, or (b) a pair consisting of the name of a general-purpose function and the name of a dimension. However, in view of the simplification mentioned in the previous note, for the sake of this paper we may as well consider tags containing a general-purpose function as simply consisting of that function.

feedback dimension[6], and let us assume the values of the various parameters those that are suggested above. We then get the following calculations:

$$\begin{array}{lll} \delta(IND-YNQ, CHECK) & = 0.75^2 \cdot 1 & = 0.563 \\ \delta(YNQ, CHECK) & = 0.75^1 \cdot 1 & = 0.75 \\ \delta(Perc^+, Perc^+) & = 0.75^0 \cdot 1 & = 1 \\ \delta(Perc^+, Eval^+) & = 0.75^2 \cdot 1 & = 0.563 \\ \delta(Int^-, Int^+) & & = 0 \\ \delta(POSI, NEGA) & & = 0 \end{array}$$

To conclude, we can simply take δ to be the weighting in Cohen's κ_w and come to a coefficient which we will call *taxonomically weighted kappa*, denoted by κ_{tw}:

$$\kappa_{tw} = 1 - \frac{\sum(1-\delta(i,j)) \cdot p_{oij}}{\sum(1-\delta(i,j)) \cdot p_{eij}} \quad (5)$$

4.3 κ_{tw} statistics for DIT

Considering the DIT^{++} taxonomy, it may be argued that due to the many hierarchies in the topology of the general-purpose functions, this is the part where most is to be gained by employing κ_{tw}.

Table 2 shows the statistics for each dimension, averaged over all annotation pairs. With *annotation pair* is understood the pair of assignments an utterance received by two annotators for a particular dimension. The figures in the table are based on those cases in which both annotators assigned a function to a specific utterance for a specific dimension. Cases where either one annotator does not assign a function while the other does, or where both annotators do not assign a function, are not considered. Scores for standard κ and κ_{tw} can be found in the first two columns. The column *#pairs* indicates on how many annotation pairs the statistics are based. The last column shows the *ap-ratio*. This figure indicates which fraction of all annotated functions in that dimension are represented by annotation pairs. When $\#ap$ denotes the number of annotation pairs and $\#pa$ denotes the number of partial annotations (annotations in which one annotator assigned a function and the other did not), then the ap-ratio is calculated as $\#ap/(\#pa + \#ap)$. We can observe that due to the use of the taxonomic weighting both *feedback* dimensions and the *task* dimension gained substantially in annotator agreement.

[6]Auto-feedback: feedback on the processing (perception, understanding, evaluation,..) of previous utterances by the speaker. DIT also distinguishes allo-feedback, where the speaker provides or elicits information about the addressee's processing.

Dimension	κ	κ_{tw}	#pairs	ap-ratio
task	0.47	0.71	848	0.87
task:action discussion	0.61	0.61	91	0.37
auto feedback	0.21	0.57	127	0.34
allo feedback	0.42	0.58	17	0.14
turn management	0.82	0.82	115	0.18
time management	0.58	0.58	68	0.72
contact management	1.00	1.00	8	0.17
topic management	nav	nav	2	0.08
own com. management	1.00	1.00	2	0.08
partner com. management	nav	nav	1	0.07
dialogue struct. management	0.74	0.74	15	0.31
social obl. management	1.00	1.00	61	0.80

Table 2: Scores for corrected κ and κ_{tw} per DIT dimension.

When we look at the agreement statistics and consider κ scores above 0.67 to be significant and scores above 0.8 considerably reliable, as is usual for κ statistics, we can find the dimensions `TURN-MANAGEMENT`, `CONTACT MANAGEMENT`, and `SOCIAL-OBLIGATIONS-MANAGEMENT` to be reliable and `DIALOGUE STRUCT. MANAGEMENT` to be significant. For some dimensions, the occurences of functions in these dimensions in the annotated dialogue material were too few to draw conclusions. When we also take the ap-ratio into account, only the dimensions `TASK`, `TIME MANAGEMENT`, and `SOCIAL-OBLIGATIONS-MANAGEMENT` combine a fair agreement on functions with fair agreement on whether or not to annotate in these dimensions. Especially for the other dimensions, the question should be raised for which cases and for what reasons the ap-ratio is low. This question asks for further qualitative analysis, which is beyond the scope of this paper[7].

5 Discussion

In the previous sections, we showed how the taxonomically weighted κ_{tw} that we proposed can be more suitable for taxonomies that contain hierarchical structures, like the DIT$^+$+) taxonomy. However, there are some specific and general issues that deserve more attention.

A question that might be raised in using κ_{tw} as opposed to ordinary κ, is if the assumption that the interpretations of κ proposed in literature in terms of reliability is also valid for κ_{tw} statistics. This is ultimately an empirical issue, to be decided by which κ_{tw} scores researchers find to correspond to fair or near agreement between annotators.

Another point of discussion is the arbitrariness of the values of the parameters that can be chosen in δ. In this paper we proposed $a = 0.75$ and $\beta = 0.5$. Choosing different values may change

[7]See (Geertzen, 2006) for more details.

the disagreement of two distinct CFs located in the same hierarchy considerably. Still, we think that by interpolating smoothly between the intuitively clear cases at the two extreme ends of the scale, it is possible to choose reasonable values for the parameters that scale well, given the average hierarchy depth.

A more general problem, inherent in almost any (dialogue act) annotation activity is that when we consider the possible factors that influence the agreement scores, we find that they can be numerous. Starting with the tagset, unclear definitions and vague concepts are a major source of disagreement. Other factors are the quality and extensiveness of annotation instructions, and the experience of the annotators. These were kept constant throughout the experiment reported in this paper, but clearly the use of more experienced or better trained annotators could have a great influence. Then there is the influence that the use of an annotation tool can have. Does the tool gives hints on annotation consistency (e.g. an `ANSWER` should be preceded by a `QUESTION`), does it enforce consistency, or does it not consider annotation consistency at all? Are the possible choices for annotators presented in such a way that each choice is equally well visible and accessible? Clearly, when we do not control these factors sufficiently, we run the risk that what we measure does not express what we try to quantify: (dis)agreement among annotators about the description of what happens in a dialogue.

6 Conclusion and future work

In this paper we have presented agreement scores for Cohen's unweighted κ and claimed that for annotation schemes with hierarchically related tags, a weighted κ gives a better indication of (dis)agreement than unweighted κ. The κ scores for some dimensions seem not particularly spectacular but become more interesting when looking at semantic-pragmatic differences between dialogue acts or CFs. Even though there are somewhat arbitrary aspects in weighting, when parameters are carefully chosen a weighted metric gives a better representation of the inter-annotator agreements. More generally, we propose that semantic-pragmatic relatedness between taxonomic concepts should be taken into account when calculating inter-annotator (dis)agreement. While we used DIT^{++} as tagset, the weighting function we proposed can be employed in any taxonomy containing hierarchically related concepts, since we only used *structural* properties of the taxonomy.

We have also quantitatively[8] evaluated the DIT^{++} tagset per dimension, and obtained an indication of its usability. We focussed on agreement per dimension, but when we desire a global indication of the difference in semantic-pragmatic interpretation of a complete utterance it requires us to consider other aspects. A truly multidimensional study of inter-annotator agreement should not only take intra-dimensional aspects into account but also relate the dimensions to each other. In (Bunt and Girard, 2005; Bunt, 2006) it is argued that dimensions should be *orthogonal*, meaning that an utterance can have a function in one dimension independent of functions in other dimensions. This is a somewhat utopical condition, since there are some functions that show correlations and dependencies with across dimensions. For this reason it makes sense to try to express the effect of the presence of strong correlations, dependencies and possible entailments in a multidimensional notion of (dis)agreement. Additionally, it may be desirable to take into account the importance that a CF can have. It is widely acknowledged that utterances are often multifunctional, but it could be argued that in many cases an utterance has a *primary* function and *secondary functions*; for instance, if an utterance has both a task-related function and one or more other functions, the task-related function is typically felt to be more important than the other functions, and disagreement about the task-related function is therefore felt to be more serious than disagreement about one of the other functions. This might be taken into account by adding a weighting function when combining agreement measures over multiple dimensions.

Other future work we plan is more methodological in nature, quantifying the relative effect of the factors that may have influenced the scores that we have found. This would create a situation in which there is more insight in *what* exactly is evaluated. As for evaluating the tagset, we for instance plan to further analyze co-occurence matrices to identify frequent misannotations, and to have annotators thinking aloud while performing the annotation task.

[8] Kappa statistics are indicative. To get a full understanding of what the figures represent, qualitative analysis by using e.g. co-occurence matrices is required, which is beyond the scope of this paper.

Acknowledgements

The authors thank three anonymous reviewers for their helpful comments on an earlier version of this paper.

References

James Allen and Mark Core. 1997. Draft of DAMSL: Dialog act markup in several layers. Unpublished manuscript.

J. Allwood, J. Nivre, and E. Ahlsén. 1993. Manual for coding interaction management. Technical report, Göteborg University. Project report: Semantik och talspråk.

Harry C. Bunt and Yann Girard. 2005. Designing an open, multidimensional dialogue act taxonomy. In *Proceedings of the 9th Workshop on the Semantics and Pragmatics of Dialogue (DIALOR 2005)*, pages 37–44, Nancy, France, June.

Harry C. Bunt. 2000. Dialogue pragmatics and context specification. In Harry C. Bunt and William Black, editors, *Abduction, Belief and Context in Dialogue; Studies in Computational Pragmatics*, pages 81–150. John Benjamins, Amsterdam, The Netherlands.

Harry C. Bunt. 2005. A framework for dialogue act specification. In *Joint ISO-ACL Workshop on the Representation and Annotation of Semantic Information*, Tilburg, The Netherlands, January.

Harry C. Bunt. 2006. Dimensions in dialogue annotation. In *Proceedings of the 5th International Conference on Language Resources and Evaluation (LREC 2006)*, Genova, Italy, May.

Jean Carletta. 1996. Assessing agreement on classification tasks: The kappa statistic. *Computational Linguistics*, 22(2):249–254.

Johanneke Caspers. 2000. Pitch accents, boundary tones and turn-taking in dutch map task dialogues. In *Proceedings of the 6th International Conference on Spoken Language Processing (ICSLP 2000)*, volume 1, pages 565–568, Beijing, China.

Jacob Cohen. 1960. A coefficient of agreement for nominal scales. *Education and Psychological Measurement*, 20:37–46.

Jacob Cohen. 1968. Weighted kappa: Nominal scale agreement with provision for scaled disagreement or partial credit. *Psychological Bulletin*, 70:213–220.

Mark G. Core and James F. Allen. 1997. Coding dialogues with the DAMSL annotation scheme. In David Traum, editor, *Working Notes: AAAI Fall Symposium on Communicative Action in Humans and Machines*, pages 28–35, Menlo Park, CA, USA. American Association for Artificial Intelligence.

Mark Davies and J.L. Fleiss. 1982. Measuring agreement for multinomial data. *Biometrics*, 38:1047–1051.

Barbara Di Eugenio and Michael Glass. 2004. The kappa statistic: a second look. *Computational Linguistics*, 30(1):95–101.

Barbara Di Eugenio, Pamela W. Jordan, Johanna D. Moore, and Richmond H. Thomason. 1998. An empirical investigation of proposals in collaborative dialogues. In *Proceedings of the 17th International Conference on Computational Linguistics and the 36th Annual Meeting of the Association for Computational Linguistics (COLING-ACL 1998)*, pages 325–329, Montreal, Canada.

Jeroen Geertzen, Yann Girard, Roser Morante, Ielka van der Sluis, Hans Van Dam, Barbara Suijkerbuijk, Rintse van der Werf, and Harry Bunt. 2004. The diamond project (poster,project description). In *The 8th Workshop on the Semantics and Pragmatics of Dialogue (Catalog'04)*. Barcelona, Spain.

Jeroen Geertzen. 2006. Inter-annotator agreement within dit^{++} dimensions. Technical report, Tilburg University, Tilburg, The Netherlands.

Derek Gross, James F. Allen, and David R. Traum. 1993. The TRAINS 91 dialogues. Technical Report TN92-1, University of Rochester, Rochester, NY, USA.

Peter A. Heeman and James F. Allen. 1995. The TRAINS 93 dialogues. Technical Report TN94-2, University of Rochester, Rochester, NY, USA.

Klaus Krippendorff. 1980. *Content Analysis: An Introduction to its Methodology*. Sage Publications, Beverly Hills, CA, USA.

Stephan Lesch, Thomas Kleinbauer, and Jan Alexandersson. 2005. A new metric for the evaluation of dialog act classification. In *Proceedings of the 9th Workshop on the Semantics and Pragmatics of Dialogue (DIALOR 2005)*, pages 143–146, Nancy, France, june.

Elizabeth Shriberg, Raj Dhillon, Sonali Bhagat, Jeremy Ang, and Hannah Carvey. 2004. The ICSI meeting recorder dialog act (MRDA) corpus. In *Proceedings of the 5th SIGdial Workshop on Discourse and Dialogue*, pages 97–100, Boston, USA, April-May.

Amanda J. Stent. 2000. The monroe corpus. Technical Report TR728/TN99-2, University of Rochester, Rochester, UK.

Helmer Strik, Albert Russel, Henk van den Heuvel, Catia Cucchiarini, and Lou Boves. 1997. A spoken dialog system for the dutch public transport information service. *International Journal of Speech Technology*, 2(2):119–129.

Balancing Conflicting Factors in Argument Interpretation

Ingrid Zukerman, Michael Niemann and Sarah George
Faculty of Information Technology
Monash University
Clayton, VICTORIA 3800, AUSTRALIA
{ingrid,niemann,sarahg}@csse.monash.edu.au

Abstract

We present a probabilistic approach for the interpretation of arguments that casts the selection of an interpretation as a model selection task. In selecting the best model, our formalism balances conflicting factors: model complexity against data fit, and structure complexity against belief reasonableness. We first describe our basic formalism, which considers interpretations comprising inferential relations, and then show how our formalism is extended to suppositions that account for the beliefs in an argument, and justifications that account for the inferences in an interpretation. Our evaluations with users show that the interpretations produced by our system are acceptable, and that there is strong support for the postulated suppositions and justifications.

1 Introduction

The source-channel approach has been often used for word-based language tasks, such as speech recognition and machine translation (Epstein, 1996; Och and Ney, 2002). According to this approach, an addressee receives a noisy channel (language or speech wave), and decodes this channel to derive the source (idea). The selected source is that with the maximum posterior probability.

In this paper, we apply the source-channel approach to the interpretation of arguments. This approach enables us to cast argument interpretation as a trade-off between conflicting factors, viz model complexity against data fit, and structure complexity against belief reasonableness. This trade-off is inspired by the Minimum Message Length (MML) Criterion – a model selection method that is the basis for several machine learning techniques (Wallace, 2005). According to this trade-off, a more complex model might fit the data better, but the plausibility (priors) of the model must be taken into account to avoid over-fitting.[1]

Our argument interpretation mechanism has been implemented in a system called BIAS (Bayesian Interactive Argumentation System). BIAS presents to a user a set of facts about the world (evidence), and the user constructs an argument about a particular goal proposition in light of this evidence. BIAS then generates an interpretation of the user's argument, i.e., it tries to understand the argument. When people try to understand an interlocutor's discourse, their interpretation is in terms of their own beliefs and inference patterns. Likewise, our system's interpretations are in terms of its underlying knowledge representation – a Bayesian network (BN). The interpretations generated by BIAS include *inferences* that connect the propositions in a user's argument, *suppositions* that postulate a user's beliefs that are necessary to make sense of the argument, and *explanatory extensions* that justify the inferences in the interpretation (and in the argument). BIAS does *not* generate its own arguments, rather, it integrates these components to make sense of the user's argument.

In this paper, we first describe our basic formalism, which is used to calculate the probability of interpretations that include only inferences, and then show how progressive enhancements of this formalism are used for more informative interpretations.

In Section 2, we explain what is an argument interpretation, and describe briefly the interpretation process. Next, we discuss our probabilistic formalism for selecting an interpretation, which is the focus of this paper. In Section 4, we present

[1]Other model selection criteria such as Akaike Information Criterion (AIC) and Bayes Information Criterion (BIC) (Box et al., 1994) also argue for model parsimony, but they do so by penalizing models with more free parameters.

Proceedings of the 7th SIGdial Workshop on Discourse and Dialogue, pages 134–143,
Sydney, July 2006.

the results of our evaluations, followed by a discussion of related work, and concluding remarks.

ARGUMENT
Mr Green *probably* being in the garden at 11 implies that
he *possibly* had the opportunity to kill Mr Body, but
he *possibly* did *not* murder Mr Body.

EXCERPT OF DOMAIN BN

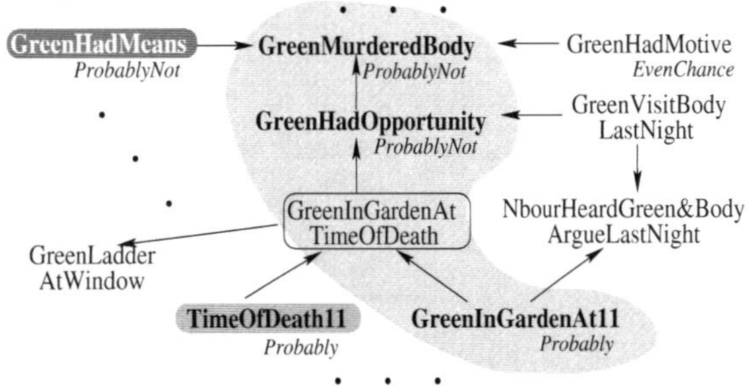

INTERPRETATION
Mr Green *probably* being in the garden at 11, and
supposing that the time of death is 11 implies that
Mr Green probably was in the garden at the time of death.
Hence, he *possibly* had the opportunity to kill Mr Body, but
Mr Green probably did not have the means.
Therefore, he *possibly* did *not* murder Mr Body.

Figure 1: Sample argument, BN excerpt and interpretation

2 Argument interpretation

We define an interpretation of a user's argument as the tuple $\{SC, IG, EE\}$, where SC is a *supposition configuration*, IG is an *interpretation graph*, and EE are *explanatory extensions*.

- A **Supposition Configuration** is a set of suppositions attributed to the user (in addition to or instead of shared beliefs) to account for the beliefs in his or her argument.
- An **Interpretation Graph** is a domain structure, in our case a subnet of the domain BN, that connects the nodes mentioned in the argument. The nodes and arcs that are included in an interpretation graph but were not mentioned by the user fill in additional detail from the BN, bridging inferential leaps in the argument.
- **Explanatory Extensions** are domain structures (subnets of the domain BN) that are added to an interpretation graph to justify an inference. Contrary to suppositions, these explanations contain propositions believed by the user and the system. The presentation of these explanations is motivated by the results of our early trials, where people objected to *belief discontinuities* between the antecedents and the consequent of inferences, i.e., increases in certainty or large changes in certainty (Zukerman and George, 2005).

To illustrate these components, consider the example in Figure 1. The top segment contains a short argument, and the bottom segment contains its interpretation. The middle segment contains an excerpt of the domain BN which includes the interpretation; the probabilities of some nodes are indicated with linguistic terms.[2] The *interpretation graph*, which appears inside a light gray bubble in the BN excerpt, includes the extra node *GreenInGardenAtTimeOfDeath* (boxed). Note that the propagated beliefs in this interpretation graph do not match those in the argument. To address this problem, the system *supposes* that the user believes that *TimeOfDeath11*=TRUE, instead of the BN belief of *Probably* (boldfaced and gray-boxed). This fixes the mismatch between the probabilities in the argument and those in the interpretation, but one problem remains: in early trials we found that people objected to belief discontinuities, such as the "jump in belief" from *possibly* having opportunity to *possibly not* murdering Mr Body (this jump appears both in the original argument and in the interpretation, whose beliefs now match those in the argument as a result of the supposition). This prompts the generation of the explanatory extension *GreenHadMeans[ProbablyNot]* (white boldfaced and dark-gray boxed). The three elements added during the interpretation process – the extra node in the interpretation graph, the supposition and the explanatory extension – appear in boldface italics in the interpretation at the bottom of the figure.

2.1 Proposing Interpretations

The problem of finding the best interpretation is exponential. In previous work, we proposed an *anytime* algorithm to propose interpretation graphs and supposition configurations until time runs out (George et al., 2004). Here we apply our algorithm to generate interpretations comprising supposition configurations (SC), interpretation graphs (IG) and explanatory extensions (EE) (Figure 2).

Supposition configurations are proposed first, as instantiated beliefs affect the plausibility of inter-

[2]We use the terms *Very Probable, Probable, Possible* and their negations, and *Even Chance*. These terms, which are similar to those used in (Elsaesser, 1987), are most consistently understood by people according to our user surveys.

Algorithm *GenerateInterpretations(Arg)*
while {there is time}
{
1. Propose a supposition configuration SC that accounts for the beliefs stated in the argument.
2. Propose an interpretation graph IG that connects the nodes in *Arg* under supposition configuration SC.
3. Propose explanatory extensions EE for interpretation graph IG under supposition configuration SC if necessary.
4. Calculate the probability of interpretation $\{SC, IG, EE\}$.
5. Retain the top N (=6) most probable interpretations.

}

Figure 2: Anytime algorithm for generating interpretations

pretation graphs, which in turn affect the need for explanatory extensions. The proposal of supposition configurations, interpretation graphs and explanatory extensions is driven by the probability of these components. In each iteration, we generate candidates for a component, calculate the probability of these candidates *in the context of the selections made in the previous steps*, and probabilistically select one of these candidates. That is, higher probability candidates have a better chance of being selected than lower probability ones (our selection procedures are described in George et al., 2004). For example, say that in Step 1, we selected supposition configuration SC_a. Next, in Step 2, the probability of candidate IGs is calculated *in the context of the domain BN and* SC_a, and one of the IGs is probabilistically selected, say IG_b. Similarly, in Step 3, one of the candidate EEs is selected *in the context of* SC_a *and* IG_b. In the next iteration, we probabilistically select an SC (which could be a previously chosen one), and so on. To generate diverse interpretations, if SC_a is selected again, a different IG will be chosen.

3 Probabilistic formalism

Following (Wallace, 2005), our approach requires the specification of three elements: *background knowledge, model* and *data*. **Background knowledge** is everything known to the system prior to interpreting a user's argument, e.g., domain knowledge, shared beliefs with the user, and dialogue history; the **data** is the argument; and the **model** is the interpretation.

We posit that the best interpretation is that with the highest posterior probability.

$IntBest = \text{argmax}_{i=1,\ldots,q}\Pr(SC_i, IG_i, EE_i|Arg)$

where q is the number of interpretations.

After applying Bayes rule, this probability is represented as follows.[3]

$$\Pr(SC_i, IG_i, EE_i|Arg) = \alpha \Pr(SC_i, IG_i, EE_i) \times \Pr(Arg|SC_i, IG_i, EE_i) \quad (1)$$

where α is a normalizing constant that ensures that the probabilities of the interpretations sum to 1 $\left(\alpha = \frac{1}{\sum_{j=1}^{n}\Pr(SC_j, IG_j, EE_j)\times\Pr(Arg|SC_j, IG_j, EE_j)}\right)$.

The first factor represents *model complexity*, and the second factor represents *data fit*.

- Model complexity measures how difficult it is to produce the model (interpretation) from the background knowledge. The higher/lower the complexity of a model, the lower/higher its probability.
- Data fit measures how well the data (argument) matches the model (interpretation). The better/worse the match between the argument and an interpretation, the higher/lower the probability that the speaker intended this interpretation when he or she uttered the argument.

Model Complexity

Model complexity is a function $\{\mathcal{B}, \mathcal{M}\}\rightarrow[0, 1]$ that represents the prior probability of the model $\mathcal{M}$ (i.e., the interpretation) in terms of the background knowledge $\mathcal{B}$. The calculation of model complexity depends on the type of the model: numerical or structural.

The probability of a ***numerical model*** depends on the similarity between the numerical values (or distributions) in the model and those in the background knowledge. The higher/lower this similarity, the higher/lower the probability of the model. For instance, a supposition configuration SC comprising beliefs that differ significantly from those in the background knowledge will lower the probability of an interpretation. One of the functions we have used to calculate belief probabilities is the Zipf distribution, where the parameter is the difference between beliefs, e.g., between the supposed

[3] In principle, $\Pr(SC_i, IG_i, EE_i|Arg)$ can be calculated directly. However, it is not clear how to incorporate the priors of an interpretation in the direct calculation.

beliefs and the corresponding beliefs in the background knowledge (Zukerman and George, 2005). That is, the probability of a supposed belief in proposition P according to model $\mathcal{M}$ (bel $_M(P)$), in light of the belief in P according to background knowledge $\mathcal{B}$ (bel $_B(P)$), is

$$\Pr(\text{bel}_M(P)|\text{bel}_B(P)) = \frac{\theta}{|\text{bel}_M(P) - \text{bel}_B(P)|^\gamma}$$

where θ is a normalizing constant, and γ determines the penalty assigned to the discrepancy between the beliefs in P. For example,
$\Pr(\text{bel}_M(P) = \text{TRUE}|\text{bel}_B(P) = \textit{Probable}) >$
$\Pr(\text{bel}_M(P) = \text{TRUE}|\text{bel}_B(P) = \textit{EvenChance})$
as TRUE is closer to *Probable* than to *EvenChance*.

The probability of a ***structural model*** (e.g., an interpretation graph) is obtained from the probabilities of the elements in the structure (e.g., nodes and arcs) in light of the background knowledge. The simplest calculation assumes that the probability of including nodes and arcs in an interpretation graph is uniform. That is, the probability of an interpretation graph comprising n nodes and a arcs is a function of

- the probability of n,
- the probability of selecting n particular nodes from N nodes in the domain BN: $\binom{N}{n}^{-1}$,
- the probability of a, and
- the probability of selecting a particular arcs from the arcs that connect the n selected nodes.

This calculation generally prefers small models to larger models.[4]

Data fit

Data fit is a function $\{\mathcal{M}, \mathcal{D}\} \rightarrow [0, 1]$ that represents the probability of the data $\mathcal{D}$ (argument) given the model $\mathcal{M}$ (interpretation). This probability hinges on the similarity between the model and the data – the closer the data is to the model, the higher is the probability of the data.

The calculation of the similarity between ***numerical data*** and a numerical model is the same as the calculation of the similarity between a numerical model and background knowledge.

The similarity between ***structural data*** and a structural model is a function of the number and type of operations required to convert the model into the data, e.g., node and arc insertions and deletions. For the example in Figure 1, to convert the interpretation graph into the argument, we must delete one node (*GreenInGardenAtTimeOfDeath*) and its incident arcs. The more operations need to be performed, the lower the similarity between the data and the model, and the lower the probability of the data given the model.

We now discuss our basic probabilistic formalism, which accounts for interpretation graphs, followed by two enhancements: (1) a more complex model that accounts for suppositions; and (2) increases in background knowledge that yield a preference for larger interpretation graphs under certain circumstances, and account for explanatory extensions.

3.1 Basic formalism: Interpretation graphs

In the basic formalism, the model contains only an interpretation graph. Thus, Equation 1 is simply

$$\Pr(IG_i|\textit{Arg}) = \alpha \Pr(IG_i) \times \Pr(\textit{Arg}|IG_i) \quad (2)$$

The difference in the calculations of model complexity and data fit for numerical and structural information warrants the separation of structure and belief, which yields

$$\Pr(IG_i|\textit{Arg}) = \alpha \Pr(\text{bel } IG_i, \text{struc } IG_i) \times \Pr(\text{bel } \textit{Arg}, \text{struc } \textit{Arg}|\text{bel } IG_i, \text{struc } IG_i)$$

After applying the chain rule of probability

$$\begin{aligned}\Pr(IG_i|\textit{Arg}) = \\ &\alpha \Pr(\text{bel } IG_i|\text{struc } IG_i) \times \Pr(\text{struc } IG_i) \times \\ &\Pr(\text{bel } \textit{Arg}|\text{struc } \textit{Arg}, \text{bel } IG_i, \text{struc } IG_i) \times \\ &\Pr(\text{struc } \textit{Arg}|\text{bel } IG_i, \text{struc } IG_i)\end{aligned}$$

Note that $\Pr(\text{bel } IG_i|\text{struc } IG_i)$ does *not* calculate the probability of (or belief in) the nodes in IG_i. Rather, it calculates how probable are these beliefs in light of the structure of IG_i and the expectations from the background knowledge. For instance, if the belief in a node is p, it calculates the probability of p. This probability depends on the closeness between the beliefs in IG_i and the expected ones. Since the beliefs in IG_i are obtained algorithmically by means of Bayesian propagation from the background knowledge, they match precisely the expectations. Hence, $\Pr(\text{bel } IG_i|\text{struc } IG_i) = 1$.

We also make the following simplifying assumptions for situations where the interpretation is known (given): (1) the probability of the beliefs in the argument depends only on the beliefs in the

[4]In the rare cases where $n > N/2$, smaller models do not yield lower probabilities.

Table 1: Probability – Basic formalism

Model complexity (against background)	
$\downarrow$ Pr(struc IG_i)	$\uparrow$ structural complexity (model size)
Data fit with model	
$\uparrow$ Pr(struc *Arg*|struc IG_i)	$\downarrow$ structural discrepancy
Pr(bel *Arg*|bel IG_i)	numerical discrepancy

Table 2: Probability – More informed model

Model complexity (against background)	
Pr(struc IG_i|$\mathbf{SC_i}$)	structural complexity
$\downarrow$ Pr($\mathbf{SC_i}$)	$\uparrow$numerical discrepancy
Data fit with model	
Pr(struc *Arg*|struc IG_i)	structural discrepancy
$\uparrow$ Pr(bel *Arg*|$\mathbf{SC_i}$,bel IG_i)	$\downarrow$numerical discrepancy

interpretation (and not on its structure or the argument's structure), and (2) the probability of the argument structure depends only on the interpretation structure (and not on its beliefs). This yields

$$\Pr(IG_i|Arg) = \alpha \Pr(\text{struc } IG_i)\times \Pr(\text{bel } Arg|\text{bel } IG_i) \times \Pr(\text{struc } Arg|\text{struc } IG_i) \quad (3)$$

Table 1 summarizes the calculation of these probabilities separated according to model complexity and data fit. It also shows the trade-off between structural model complexity and structural data fit. As seen at the start of Section 3, smaller structures generally have a lower model complexity than larger ones. However, an increase in structural model complexity (indicated by the $\uparrow$ next to the structural complexity and the $\downarrow$ next to the resultant probability of the model) may reduce the structural discrepancy between the argument structure and the structure of the interpretation graph (indicated by the $\downarrow$ next to the structural discrepancy and the $\uparrow$ next to the probability of the structural data-fit). For instance, the smallest possible interpretation for the argument in Figure 1 consists of a single node, but this interpretation has a very poor data fit with the argument.

3.2 A more informed model

In order to postulate suppositions that account for the beliefs in an argument, we expand the basic model to include supposition configurations (beliefs attributed to the user in addition to or instead of the beliefs shared with the system). Now the model comprises the pair $\{SC_i, IG_i\}$, and Equation 2 becomes

$$\Pr(SC_i, IG_i|Arg) = \alpha \Pr(SC_i, IG_i) \times \Pr(Arg|SC_i, IG_i) \quad (4)$$

Similar probabilistic manipulations to those performed in Section 3.1 yield

$$\Pr(SC_i, IG_i|Arg) = \alpha \Pr(\text{struc } IG_i|SC_i) \times \Pr(SC_i) \times \Pr(\text{bel } Arg|SC_i, \text{bel } IG_i) \times \Pr(\text{struc } Arg|\text{struc } IG_i) \quad (5)$$

(Recall that suppositions pertain to beliefs only, i.e., they don't have a structural component.)

Table 2 summarizes the calculation of these probabilities separated according to model complexity and data fit (the elements that differ from the basic model are **boldfaced**). It also shows the trade-off between belief model complexity and belief data fit. Making suppositions has a higher model complexity (lower probability) than not making suppositions (where SC_i matches the beliefs in the domain BN). However, as seen in the example in Figure 1, making a supposition that reduces or eliminates the discrepancy between the beliefs in the argument and those in the interpretation increases the belief data-fit considerably, at the expense of a more complex belief model.

3.3 Additional background knowledge

An increase in our background knowledge means that we take into account additional factors about the world. This extra knowledge in turn may cause us to prefer interpretations that were previously discarded. We have considered two additions to background knowledge: dialogue history, and users' preferences regarding inference patterns.

Dialogue history

Dialogue history influences the salience of a node, and hence the probability that it was included in a user's argument. We have modeled salience by means of an activation function that decays with time (Anderson, 1983), and used this function to moderate the probability of including a node in an interpretation (instead of using a uniform distribution). We have experimented with two activation functions: (1) a function where the level of activation of a node is based on the frequency and recency of the direct activation of this node; and (2) a function where the level of activation of a node depends on its similarity with all the (activated) nodes, together with the frequency and recency of their activation (Zukerman and George,

2005).

To illustrate the influence of salience, compare the preferred interpretation graph in Figure 1 (in the light gray bubble) with an alternative path through *NbourHeard-Green&BodyArgueLastNight* and *GreenVisit-BodyLastNight*. The preferred path has 4 nodes, while the alternative one has 5 nodes, and hence a lower probability. However, if the nodes in the longer path had been recently mentioned, their salience could overcome the size disadvantage. Thus, although the chosen interpretation graph may have a worse data fit than the smallest graph, it still may have the best overall probability in light of the additional background knowledge.

Inference patterns

In a formative evaluation of an earlier version of our system, we found that people objected to inferences that had increases in certainty or large changes in certainty (Zukerman and George, 2005). An example of an increase in certainty is
A [Probably] implies B [VeryProbably].
A large change in certainty is illustrated by
A [VeryProbably] implies B [EvenChance].

We then conducted another survey to determine the types of inferences considered acceptable by people (from the standpoint of the beliefs in the antecedents and the consequent). The results from our preliminary survey prompted us to distinguish between three types of inferences: *BothSides, SameSide* and *AlmostSame.*

- *BothSides* inferences have antecedents with beliefs on both "sides" of the consequent (in favour and against), e.g.,
  A[VeryProbably] & B[ProbablyNot] implies C[EvenChance].
- All the antecedents in *SameSide* inferences have beliefs on "one side" of the consequent, but at least one antecedent has the same belief level as the consequent, e.g.,
  A[VeryProbably] & B[Possibly] implies C[Possibly].
- All the antecedents in *AlmostSame* inferences have beliefs on one side of the consequent, but the closest antecedent is one level "up" from the consequent, e.g.,
  A[VeryProbably] & B[Possibly] implies C[EvenChance].

Our survey contained six evaluation sets, which were done by 50 people. Each set contained an initial statement (we varied the polarity of the statement in the various sets), three alternative arguments that explain this statement, and the option to say that no argument is a good explanation. The respondents were asked to rank these options in order of preference.

All the evaluation sets contained one argument that was objectionable according to our preliminary survey (there was an increase in belief or a large change in belief from the antecedent to the consequent). The two other arguments, each of which comprises a single inference, were distributed among the six evaluation sets as follows.

- Three sets had one *BothSides* inference and one *SameSide* inference, each with two antecedents.
- Two sets had one *SameSide* inference, and one *AlmostSame* inference, each with two antecedents.
- One set had one *SameSide* inference with two antecedents, and one *BothSides* inference comprising three antecedents.

In order to reduce the effect of the respondents' domain bias, we generated two versions of the survey, where for each evaluation set we swapped the antecedent propositions in one of the inferences with the antecedent propositions in the other.

Our survey showed that people prefer *BothSides* inferences (which contain antecedents for and against the consequent). They also prefer *Same-Side* to *AlmostSame* for antecedents with beliefs in the negative range (*VeryProbNot, ProbNot* and *PossNot*); and they did not distinguish between *SameSide* and *AlmostSame* for antecedents with beliefs in the positive range. Further, *BothSides* inferences with three antecedents were preferred to *SameSide* inferences with two antecedents. This indicates that persuasiveness carries more weight than parsimony.

These general preferences are incorporated into our background knowledge as expectations for a range of acceptable beliefs in the consequents of inferences in light of their antecedents. The farther the actual beliefs in the consequents are from the expectations, the lower the probability of these beliefs. Hence, it is no longer true that Pr(bel $IG_i|SC_i$, struc IG_i) $= 1$ (Section 3.1), as we now have a belief expectation that goes beyond Bayesian propagation. As done at the start of Section 3, the probability of the beliefs in an interpretation is a function of the discrepancy between these beliefs and expected beliefs. We calculate this probability using a variant of the Zipf distribution adjusted for ranges of beliefs.

Explanatory extensions are added to an interpretation in order to overcome these belief discrepancies, yielding an expanded model that comprises the tuple $\{SC_i, IG_i, EE_i\}$. Equation 2 now becomes

$$\text{Pr}(SC_i, IG_i, EE_i|Arg) = \alpha\,\text{Pr}(SC_i, IG_i, EE_i) \times \text{Pr}(Arg|SC_i, IG_i, EE_i) \quad (6)$$

We make simplifying assumptions similar to those made in Section 3.1, i.e., given the interpretation graph and supposition configuration, the beliefs in the argument depend only on the beliefs in the interpretation, and the argument structure depends only on the interpretation structure. These assumptions, together with probabilistic manipulations similar to those performed in Section 3.1, yield

$$\begin{aligned}&\text{Pr}(SC_i, IG_i, EE_i|Arg) = \quad (7)\\ &\alpha\,\text{Pr}(\text{struc } IG_i|SC_i) \times \text{Pr}(SC_i) \times\\ &\text{Pr}(\text{bel } IG_i|SC_i, \text{struc } IG_i, \text{bel } EE_i, \text{struc } EE_i) \times\\ &\text{Pr}(\text{struc } EE_i|SC_i, \text{struc } IG_i, \text{bel } EE_i) \times\\ &\text{Pr}(\text{bel } EE_i|SC_i, \text{struc } IG_i, \text{struc } EE_i) \times\\ &\text{Pr}(\text{bel } Arg|SC_i, \text{bel } IG_i) \times \text{Pr}(\text{struc } Arg|\text{struc } IG_i)\end{aligned}$$

The calculation of the probability of an explanatory extension is the same as the calculation for structural model complexity at the start of Section 3. However, the nodes in an explanatory extension are selected from the nodes directly connected to the interpretation graph. In addition, as for the basic model (Section 3.1), the beliefs in the nodes in explanatory extensions are obtained algorithmically by means of Bayesian propagation. Hence, there is no discrepancy with expected beliefs, i.e., $\text{Pr}(\text{bel } EE_i|SC_i, \text{struc } IG_i, \text{struc } EE_i) = 1$.

Table 3 summarizes the calculation of these probabilities (the elements that differ from the basic model and the enhanced model are **boldfaced**). It also shows the trade-off between structural and belief model complexity. Presenting explanatory extensions has a higher structural complexity (lower probability) than not presenting them. However, explanatory extensions can reduce the numerical discrepancy between the beliefs in an interpretation and the beliefs expected from the background knowledge, thereby increasing the belief probability of the interpretation. For instance, in the example in Figure 1, the added explanatory extension eliminates the unacceptable jump in belief.

Table 3: Probability – Additional background knowledge

Model complexity (against background)	
$\text{Pr}(\text{struc } IG_i\|SC_i)$	structural complexity
$\text{Pr}(SC_i)$	numerical discrepancy
$\downarrow$ $\text{Pr}(\text{struc } \mathbf{EE_i}\|\mathbf{SC_i}, \text{struc } \mathbf{IG_i}, \text{bel } \mathbf{EE_i})$ $\uparrow$	structural complexity
$\uparrow$ $\text{Pr}(\text{bel } IG_i\|SC_i, \text{struc } IG_i, \text{bel } \mathbf{EE_i}, \text{struc } \mathbf{EE_i})$ $\downarrow$	numerical discrepancy
Data fit with model	
$\text{Pr}(\text{struc } Arg\|\text{struc } IG_i)$	structural discrepancy
$\text{Pr}(\text{bel } Arg\|SC_i, \text{bel } IG_i)$	numerical discrepancy

Table 4: Summary of Trade-offs

$\downarrow$ Pr model structure (IG)	$\Rightarrow$	$\uparrow$ Pr struct. data fit
$\downarrow$ Pr model belief (SC)	$\Rightarrow$	$\uparrow$ Pr belief data fit
$\downarrow$ Pr model structure (EE)	$\Rightarrow$	$\uparrow$ Pr model belief

Table 4 summarizes the trade-offs discussed in this section.

4 Evaluation

We evaluated separately each component of an interpretation – interpretation graph, supposition configuration and explanatory extensions.

4.1 Interpretation graph

We prepared four evaluation sets, each of which was done by about 20 people (Zukerman and George, 2005). In three of the sets, the participants were given a simple argument and a few candidate interpretations (ranked highly by our system). The fourth set featured a complex argument, and only one interpretation (other candidates had much lower probabilities). The participants were asked to give each interpretation a score between 1 (Very UNreasonable) and 5 (Very reasonable). Table 5 shows the results obtained for the interpretation selected by our formalism for each set, which was the top scoring interpretation. The first

Table 5: Evaluation results: Interpretation graph

Set #	**1**	**2**	**3**	**4**
Avg. score	3.38	3.68	3.35	4.00
Std. dev.	1.45	1.11	1.39	1.02
Stat. sig. (p)	0.08	0.15	0.07	NA

row shows the average score given by our subjects to this interpretation, the second row shows the standard deviation, and the third row the statistical significance, derived using a paired Z-test against alternative options (no alternatives were presented for the fourth set). Our results show that the interpretations generated by our system were generally acceptable, but that some people gave low scores. Our subjects' feedback indicated that these scores were mainly due to mismatches between beliefs in the argument and in its interpretation, and due to belief discontinuities. This led to the addition of suppositions and explanatory extensions.

4.2 Supposition configuration

We prepared four evaluation sets, each of which was done by 34 people (George et al., 2005). Each set consisted of a short argument, plus a list of supposition options as follows: (a) four suppositions that had a reasonably high probability according to our formalism, (b) the option to make a free-form supposition in line with the domain BN, and (c) the option to suppose nothing. We then asked our subjects to indicate which of these options was required for the argument to make sense. Specifically, they had to rank their preferred options in order of preference (but they did not have to rank options they disliked). Overall, there was strong support for the supposition preferred by our formalism. In three of the evaluation sets, it was ranked first by most of the trial subjects (30/34, 19/34, 20/34), with no other option a clear second. Only in the fourth set, the supposition preferred by our formalism was equal-first with another option, but still was ranked first 10 times (out of 34).

4.3 Explanatory extensions

We constructed two evaluation sets, each of which was done by 20 people. Each set consisted of a short argument and two alternative interpretations (with and without explanatory extensions). There was strong support for the explanatory extensions proposed by our formalism, with 57.5% of our trial subjects favouring the interpretations with explanatory extensions, compared to 37.5% of the subjects who preferred the interpretations without such extensions, and 5% who were indifferent.

5 Related Research

An important aspect of discourse understanding involves filling in information that was omitted by the interlocutor. In this paper, we have presented a probabilistic formalism that balances conflicting factors when filling in three types of information omitted from an argument. Interpretation graphs fill in details in the argument's inferences, supposition configurations make sense of the beliefs in the argument, and explanatory extensions overcome belief discontinuities.

Our approach resembles the work of Hobbs et al. (1993) in several respects. They employed an abductive approach where a model (interpretation) is inferred from evidence (sentence); they made assumptions as necessary; and used guiding criteria pertaining to the model and the data for choosing between candidate models. There are also significant differences between our work and theirs. Their interpretation focused on problems of reference and disambiguation in single sentences, while ours focuses on a longer discourse and the relations between the propositions therein. This distinction also determines the nature of the task, as they try to find a concise model that explains as much of the data as possible (e.g., one referent that fits many clues), while we try to find a representation for a user's argument. Additionally, their domain knowledge is logic-based, while ours is Bayesian; and they used weights to apply their hypothesis selection criteria, while our criteria are embodied in a probabilistic framework.

Plan recognition systems also generate one or more interpretations of a user's utterances, employing different resources to fill in information omitted by the user, e.g., (Allen and Perrault, 1980; Litman and Allen, 1987; Carberry and Lambert, 1999; Raskutti and Zukerman, 1991). These plan recognition systems used a plan-based approach to propose interpretations. The first three systems applied different types of heuristics to select an interpretation, while the fourth system used a probabilistic approach moderated by heuristics to select the interpretation with the highest probability. We use a probabilistic domain representation in the form of a BN (rather than plan libraries), and apply a probabilistic mechanism that represents explicitly the contribution of background knowledge, model complexity and data fit to the generation of an interpretation. Our mechanism, which can be applied to other domain representations, balances different types of complexities and discrepancies to select the interpretation with the highest posterior probability.

Several researchers used maximum posterior

probability as the criterion for selecting an interpretation (Charniak and Goldman, 1993; Gertner et al., 1998; Horvitz and Paek, 1999). They used BNs to represent a probability distribution over the set of possible explanations for the observed facts, and selected the explanation (a node in the BN or a value of a node) with the highest probability. We also use BNs as our domain representation, but our "explanation" of the facts (the user's argument) is a Bayesian subnet (rather than a single node) supplemented by suppositions. Additionally, we calculate the probability of an interpretation on the basis of the fit between the argument and the interpretation, and the complexity of the interpretation in light of the background knowledge.

Our work on positing suppositions is related to research on presuppositions (Kaplan, 1982; Gurney et al., 1997) – a type of supposition implied by the wording of a statement. Like our suppositions, presuppositions are necessary to make sense of what is being said, but they operate at a different knowledge level than our suppositions. This aspect of our work is also related to research on the recognition of flawed plans (Quilici, 1989; Pollack, 1990; Chu-Carroll and Carberry, 2000). These researchers used a plan-based approach to identify erroneous beliefs that account for a user's statements or plan, while we use a probabilistic approach. Our approach supports the consideration of many possible options, and integrates suppositions into a broader reasoning context.

Finally, the research reported in (Joshi et al., 1984; van Beek, 1987; Zukerman and McConachy, 2001) considers the addition of information to planned discourse to prevent a user's erroneous inferences from this discourse. Our mechanism adds explanatory extensions to an interpretation to prevent inferences that are objectionable due to discontinuities in belief. Since such non-sequiturs may also be present in system-generated arguments, the approach presented here may be incorporated into argument-generation systems.

6 Conclusion

We have offered a probabilistic approach to the interpretation of arguments that casts the selection of an interpretation as a model selection task. In so doing, our formalism balances conflicting factors: model complexity against data fit, and structure complexity against belief reasonableness. We have demonstrated the use of our basic formalism for the selection of an interpretation graph, and shown how a more complex model and additional background knowledge account respectively for the inclusion of suppositions and explanatory extensions in an interpretation. Our user evaluations show that the interpretation graphs produced by our formalism are generally acceptable, and that there is strong support for the suppositions and explanatory extensions it proposes.

References

J.F. Allen and C.R. Perrault. 1980. Analyzing intention in utterances. *Artificial Intelligence*, 15(3):143–178.

J. R. Anderson. 1983. *The Architecture of Cognition*. Harvard University Press, Cambridge, Massachusetts.

G.E.P. Box, G.M. Jenkins, and G.C. Reinsel. 1994. *Time Series Analysis: Forecasting and Control*. Prentice Hall.

S. Carberry and L. Lambert. 1999. A process model for recognizing communicative acts and modeling negotiation subdialogues. *Computational Linguistics*, 25(1):1–53.

E. Charniak and R. Goldman. 1993. A Bayesian model of plan recognition. *Artificial Intelligence*, 64(1):53–79.

J. Chu-Carroll and S. Carberry. 2000. Conflict resolution in collaborative planning dialogues. *International Journal of Human Computer Studies*, 6(56):969–1015.

C. Elsaesser. 1987. Explanation of probabilistic inference for decision support systems. In *Proceedings of the AAAI-87 Workshop on Uncertainty in Artificial Intelligence*, pages 394–403, Seattle, Washington.

M.E. Epstein. 1996. *Statistical Source Channel Models for Natural Language Understanding*. Ph.D. thesis, Department of Computer Science, New York University, New York, New York.

S. George, I. Zukerman, and M. Niemann. 2004. An anytime algorithm for interpreting arguments. In *PRICAI2004 – Proceedings of the Eighth Pacific Rim International Conference on Artificial Intelligence*, pages 311–321, Auckland, New Zealand.

S. George, I. Zukerman, and M. Niemann. 2005. Modeling suppositions in users' arguments. In *UM05 – Proceedings of the 10th International Conference on User Modeling*, pages 19–29, Edinburgh, Scotland.

A. Gertner, C. Conati, and K. VanLehn. 1998. Procedural help in Andes: Generating hints using a

Bayesian network student model. In *AAAI98 – Proceedings of the Fifteenth National Conference on Artificial Intelligence*, pages 106–111, Madison, Wisconsin.

J. Gurney, D. Perlis, and K. Purang. 1997. Interpreting presuppositions using active logic: From contexts to utterances. *Computational Intelligence*, 13(3):391–413.

J. R. Hobbs, M. E. Stickel, D. E. Appelt, and P. Martin. 1993. Interpretation as abduction. *Artificial Intelligence*, 63(1-2):69–142.

E. Horvitz and T. Paek. 1999. A computational architecture for conversation. In *UM99 – Proceedings of the Seventh International Conference on User Modeling*, pages 201–210, Banff, Canada.

A. Joshi, B. L. Webber, and R. M. Weischedel. 1984. Living up to expectations: Computing expert responses. In *AAAI84 – Proceedings of the Fourth National Conference on Artificial Intelligence*, pages 169–175, Austin, Texas.

S. J. Kaplan. 1982. Cooperative responses from a portable natural language query system. *Artificial Intelligence*, 19:165–187.

D. Litman and J.F. Allen. 1987. A plan recognition model for subdialogues in conversation. *Cognitive Science*, 11(2):163–200.

F.J. Och and H. Ney. 2002. Discriminative training and maximum entropy models for statistical machine translation. In *ACL'02 – Proceedings of the Annual Meeting of the Association for Computational Linguistics*, pages 295–302, Philadelphia, Pennsylvania.

M.E. Pollack. 1990. Plans as complex mental attitudes. In P. Cohen, J. Morgan, and M.E. Pollack, editors, *Intentions in Communication*, pages 77–103. MIT Press.

A. Quilici. 1989. Detecting and responding to plan-oriented misconceptions. In A. Kobsa and W. Wahlster, editors, *User Models in Dialog Systems*, pages 108–132. Springer-Verlag.

B. Raskutti and I. Zukerman. 1991. Generation and selection of likely interpretations during plan recognition. *User Modeling and User Adapted Interaction*, 1(4):323–353.

P. van Beek. 1987. A model for generating better explanations. In *Proceedings of the Twenty-Fifth Annual Meeting of the Association for Computational Linguistics*, pages 215–220, Stanford, California.

C.S. Wallace. 2005. *Statistical and Inductive Inference by Minimum Message Length*. Springer, Berlin, Germany.

I. Zukerman and S. George. 2005. A probabilistic approach for argument interpretation. *User Modeling and User-Adapted Interaction, Special Issue on Language-Based Interaction*, 15(1-2):5–53.

I. Zukerman and R. McConachy. 2001. WISHFUL: A discourse planning system that considers a user's inferences. *Computational Intelligence*, 1(17):1–61.

An Analysis of Quantitative Aspects in the Evaluation of Thematic Segmentation Algorithms

Maria Georgescul
ISSCO/TIM, ETI
University of Geneva
1211 Geneva, Switzerland
maria.georgescul@eti.unige.ch

Alexander Clark
Department of Computer Science
Royal Holloway University of London
Egham, Surrey TW20 0EX, UK
alexc@cs.rhul.ac.uk

Susan Armstrong
ISSCO/TIM, ETI
University of Geneva
1211 Geneva, Switzerland
susan.armstrong@issco.unige.ch

Abstract

We consider here the task of linear thematic segmentation of text documents, by using features based on word distributions in the text. For this task, a typical and often implicit assumption in previous studies is that a document has just one topic and therefore many algorithms have been tested and have shown encouraging results on artificial data sets, generated by putting together parts of different documents. We show that evaluation on synthetic data is potentially misleading and fails to give an accurate evaluation of the performance on real data. Moreover, we provide a critical review of existing evaluation metrics in the literature and we propose an improved evaluation metric.

1 Introduction

The goal of thematic segmentation is to identify boundaries of topically coherent segments in text documents. Giving a rigorous definition of the notion of topic is difficult, but the task of discourse/dialogue segmentation into thematic episodes is usually described by invoking an "intuitive notion of topic" (Brown and Yule, 1998). Thematic segmentation also relates to several notions such as speaker's intention, topic flow and cohesion.

Since it is elusive what mental representations humans use in order to distinguish a coherent text, different surface markers (Hirschberg and Nakatani, 1996; Passonneau and Litman, 1997) and external knowledge sources (Kozima and Furugori, 1994) have been exploited for the purpose of automatic thematic segmentation. Halliday and Hasan (1976) claim that the text meaning is realised through certain language resources and they refer to these resources by the term of cohesion. The major classes of such text-forming resources identified in (Halliday and Hasan, 1976) are: substitution, ellipsis, conjunction, reiteration and collocation. In this paper, we examine one form of lexical cohesion, namely lexical reiteration.

Following some of the most prominent discourse theories in literature (Grosz and Sidner, 1986; Marcu, 2000), a hierarchical representation of the thematic episodes can be proposed. The basis for this is the idea that topics can be recursively divided into subtopics. Real texts exhibit a more intricate structure, including 'semantic returns' by which a topic is suspended at one point and resumed later in the discourse. However, we focus here on a reduced segmentation problem, which involves identifying non-overlapping and non-hierarchical segments at a coarse level of granularity.

Thematic segmentation is a valuable initial tool in information retrieval and natural language processing. For instance, in information access systems, smaller and coherent passage retrieval is more convenient to the user than whole-document retrieval and thematic segmentation has been shown to improve the passage-retrieval performance (Hearst and Plaunt, 1993). In cases such as collections of transcripts there are no headers or paragraph markers. Therefore a clear separation of the text into thematic episodes can be used together with highlighted keywords as a kind of 'quick read guide' to help users to quickly navigate through and understand the text. Moreover automatic thematic segmentation has been shown to play an important role in automatic summarization (Mani, 2001), anaphora resolution and dis-

Proceedings of the 7th SIGdial Workshop on Discourse and Dialogue, pages 144–151,
Sydney, July 2006.

course/dialogue understanding.

In this paper, we concern ourselves with the task of linear thematic segmentation and are interested in finding out whether different segmentation systems can perform well on artificial and real data sets without specific parameter tuning. In addition, we will refer to the implications of the choice of a particular error metric for evaluation results.

This paper is organized as follows. Section 2 and Section 3 describe various systems and, respectively, different input data selected for our evaluation. Section 4 presents several existing evaluation metrics and their weaknesses, as well as a new evaluation metric that we propose. Section 5 presents our experimental set-up and shows comparisons between the performance of different systems. Finally, some conclusions are drawn in Section 6.

2 Comparison of Systems

Combinations of different features (derived for example from linguistic, prosodic information) have been explored in previous studies like (Galley et al., 2003) and (Kauchak and Chen, 2005). In this paper, we selected for comparison three systems based merely on the lexical reiteration feature: TextTiling (Hearst, 1997), C99 (Choi, 2000) and TextSeg (Utiyama and Isahara, 2001). In the following, we briefly review these approaches.

2.1 *TextTiling* Algorithm

The *TextTiling* algorithm was initially developed by Hearst (1997) for segmentation of expository texts into multi-paragraph thematic episodes having a linear, non-overlapping structure (as reflected by the name of the algorithm). TextTiling is widely used as a de-facto standard in the evaluation of alternative segmentation systems, e.g. (Reynar, 1998; Ferret, 2002; Galley et al., 2003). The algorithm can briefly be described by the following steps.

Step 1 includes stop-word removal, lemmatization and division of the text into 'token-sequences' (i.e. text blocks having a fixed number of words).

Step 2 determines a score for each gap between two consecutive token-sequences, by computing the *cosine similarity* (Manning and Schütze, 1999) between the two vectors representing the frequencies of the words in the two blocks.

Step 3 computes a 'depth score' for each token-sequence gap, based on the local minima of the score computed in step 2.

Step 4 consists in smoothing the scores.

Step 5 chooses from any potential boundaries those that have the scores smaller than a certain 'cutoff function', based on the average and standard deviation of score distribution.

2.2 *C99* Algorithm

The *C99* algorithm (Choi, 2000) makes a linear segmentation based on a divisive clustering strategy and the cosine similarity measure between any two minimal units. More exactly, the algorithm consists of the following steps.

Step 1: after the division of the text into minimal units (in our experiments, the minimal unit is an utterance[1]), stop words are removed and a stemmer is applied.

The second step consists of constructing a similarity matrix $S_{m \times m}$, where m is the number of utterances and an element s_{ij} of the matrix corresponds to the cosine similarity between the vectors representing the frequencies of the words in the i-th utterance and the j-th utterance.

Step 3: a 'rank matrix' $R_{m \times m}$ is computed, by determining for each pair of utterances, the number of neighbors in $S_{m \times m}$ with a lower similarity value.

In the final step, the location of thematic boundaries is determined by a divisive top-down clustering procedure. The criterion for division of the current segment B into $b_1, ...b_m$ subsegments is based on the maximisation of a 'density' D, computed for each potential repartition of boundaries as

$$D = \frac{\sum_{k=1}^{m} sum_k}{\sum_{k=1}^{m} area_k},$$

where sum_k and $area_k$ refers to the sum of rank and area of the k-th segment in B, respectively.

2.3 *TextSeg* Algorithm

The *TextSeg* algorithm (Utiyama and Isahara, 2001) implements a probabilistic approach to determine the most likely segmentation, as briefly described below.

The segmentation task is modeled as a problem of finding the minimum cost $\mathcal{C}(\mathcal{S})$ of a segmentation $\mathcal{S}$. The segmentation cost is defined as:

$$\mathcal{C}(\mathcal{S}) \equiv -logPr(\mathcal{W}|\mathcal{S})Pr(\mathcal{S}),$$

[1]Occasionally within this document we employ the term utterance to denote either a sentence or an utterance in its proper sense.

where $\mathcal{W} = w_1 w_2 ... w_n$ represents the text consisting of n words (after applying stop-words removal and stemming) and $\mathcal{S} = S_1 S_2 ... S_m$ is a potential segmentation of $\mathcal{W}$ in m segments. The probability $Pr(\mathcal{W}|\mathcal{S})$ is defined using Laplace law, while the definition of the probability $Pr(\mathcal{S})$ is chosen in a manner inspired by information theory.

A directed graph $\mathcal{G}$ is defined such that a path in $\mathcal{G}$ corresponds to a possible segmentation of $\mathcal{W}$. Therefore, the thematic segmentation proposed by the system is obtained by applying a dynamic programming algorithm for determining the minimum cost path in $\mathcal{G}$.

3 Input Data

When evaluating a thematic segmentation system for an application, human annotators should provide the gold standard. The problem is that the procedure of building such a reference corpus is expensive. That is, the typical setting involves an experiment with several human subjects, who are asked to mark thematic segment boundaries based on specific guidelines and their intuition. The inter-annotator agreement provides the reference segmentation. This expense can be avoided by constructing a synthetic reference corpus by concatenation of segments from different documents. Therefore, the use of artificial data for evaluation is a general trend in many studies, e.g. (Ferret, 2002; Choi, 2000; Utiyama and Isahara, 2001).

In our experiment, we used artificial and real data, i.e. the algorithms have been tested on the following data sets containing English texts.

3.1 Artificially Generated Data

Choi (2000) designed an artificial dataset, built by concatenating short pieces of texts that have been extracted from the Brown corpus. Any test sample from this dataset consists of ten segments. Each segment contains the first n sentences (where $3 \leq n \leq 11$) of a randomly selected document from the Brown corpus. From this dataset, we randomly chose for our evaluation 100 test samples, where the length of a segment varied between 3 and 11 sentences.

3.2 TDT Data

One of the commonly used data sets for topic segmentation emerged from the Topic Detection and Tracking (TDT) project, which includes the task of story segmentation, i.e. the task of segmenting a stream of news data into topically cohesive stories. As part of the TDT initiative several datasets of news stories have been created. In our evaluation, we used a subset of 28 documents randomly selected from the TDT Phase 2 (TDT2) collection, where a document contains an average of 24.67 segments.

3.3 Meeting Transcripts

The third dataset used in our evaluation contains 25 meeting transcripts from the ICSI-MR corpus (Janin et al., 2004). The entire corpus contains high-quality close talking microphone recordings of multi-party dialogues. Transcriptions at word level with utterance-level segmentations are also available. The gold standard for thematic segmentations has been kindly provided by (Galley et al., 2003) and has been chosen by considering the agreement between at least three human annotations. Each meeting is thus divided into contiguous major topic segments and contains an average of 7.32 segments.

Note that thematic segmentation of meeting data is a more challenging task as the thematic transitions are subtler than those in TDT data.

4 Evaluation Metrics

In this section, we will look in detail at the error metrics that have been proposed in previous studies and examine their inadequacies. In addition, we propose a new evaluation metric that we consider more appropriate.

4.1 P_k Metric

(Passonneau and Litman, 1996; Beeferman et al., 1999) underlined that the standard evaluation metrics of precision and recall are inadequate for thematic segmentation, namely by the fact that these metrics did not account for how far away is a hypothesized boundary (i.e. a boundary found by the automatic procedure) from a reference boundary (i.e. a boundary found in the reference data). On the other hand, it is desirable that an algorithm that places for instance a boundary just one utterance away from the reference boundary to be penalized less than an algorithm that places a boundary two (or more) utterances away from the reference boundary. Hence (Beeferman et al., 1999) proposed a new metric, called P_D, that allows for a slight vagueness in where boundaries lie. More specifically, (Beeferman et al., 1999) define P_D as follows[2]:

$P_D(ref, hyp) = \sum_{1 \le i \le j \le N} D(i,j)[\delta_{ref}(i,j) \oplus \delta_{hyp}(i,j)]$.

N is the number of words in the reference data. The function $\delta_{ref}(i,j)$ is evaluated to one if the two reference corpus indices specified by its parameters i and j belong in the same segment, and zero otherwise. Similarly, the function $\delta_{hyp}(i,j)$ is evaluated to one, if the two indices are hypothesized by the automatic procedure to belong in the same segment, and zero otherwise. The $\oplus$ operator is the XNOR function 'both or neither'. $D(i,j)$ is a "distance probability distribution over the set of possible distances between sentences chosen randomly from the corpus". In practice, a distribution D having "all its probability mass at a fixed distance k" (Beeferman et al., 1999) was adopted and the metric P_D was thus renamed P_k.

In the framework of the TDT initiative, (Allan et al., 1998) give the following formal definition of P_k and its components:

$$P_k = P_{Miss} \cdot P_{seg} + P_{FalseAlarm} \cdot (1 - P_{seg}),$$

where:

$$P_{Miss} = \frac{\sum_{i=1}^{N-k} [\delta_{hyp}(i,i+k)] \cdot [1-\delta_{ref}(i,i+k)]}{\sum_{i=1}^{N-k} [1-\delta_{ref}(i,i+k)]},$$

$$P_{FalseAlarm} = \frac{\sum_{i=1}^{N-k} [1-\delta_{hyp}(i,i+k)] \cdot [\delta_{ref}(i,i+k)]}{\sum_{i=1}^{N-k} \delta_{ref}(i,i+k)},$$

and P_{seg} is the *a priori* probability that in the reference data a boundary occurs within an interval of *k* words. Therefore P_k is calculated by moving a window of a certain width k, where k is usually set to half of the average number of words per segment in the gold standard.

Pevzner and Hearst (2002) highlighted several problems of the P_k metric. We illustrate below what we consider the main problems of the P_k metric, based on two examples.

Let $r(i,k)$ be the number of boundaries between positions i and $i+k$ in the gold standard segmentation and $h(i,k)$ be the number of boundaries between positions i and $i+k$ in the automatic hypothesized segmentation.

- Example 1: If $r(i,k) = 2$ and $h(i,k) = 1$ then obviously a missing boundary should be counted in P_k, i.e. P_{Miss} should be increased.
- Example 2: If $r(i,k) = 1$ and $h(i,k) = 2$ then obviously $P_{FalseAlarm}$ should be increased.

However, considering the first example, we will obtain $\delta_{ref}(i,i+k) = 0$, $\delta_{hyp}(i,i+k) = 0$ and consequently P_{Miss} is not increased. By taking the case from the second example we obtain $\delta_{ref}(i,i+k) = 0$ and $\delta_{hyp}(i,i+k) = 0$, involving no increase of $P_{FalseAlarm}$.

In (TDT, 1998), a slightly different definition is given for the P_k metric: the definition of *miss* and *false alarm* probabilities is replaced with:

$$P'_{Miss} = \frac{\sum_{i=1}^{N-k} [1-\Omega_{hyp}(i,i+k)] \cdot [1-\delta_{ref}(i,i+k)]}{\sum_{i=1}^{N-k} [1-\delta_{ref}(i,i+k)]},$$

$$P'_{FalseAlarm} = \frac{\sum_{i=1}^{N-k} [1-\Omega_{hyp}(i,i+k)] \cdot [\delta_{ref}(i,i+k)]}{\sum_{i=1}^{N-k} \delta_{ref}(i,i+k)},$$

where:

$$\Omega_{hyp}(i, i+k) = \begin{cases} 1, & if\ r(i,k) = h(i,k), \\ 0, & otherwise. \end{cases}$$

We will refer to this new definition of P_k by P'_k. Therefore, by taking the definition of P'_k and the first example above, we obtain $\delta_{ref}(i,i+k) = 0$ and $\Omega_{hyp}(i,i+k) = 0$ and thus P'_{Miss} is correctly increased. However for the case of example 2 we will obtain $\delta_{ref}(i,i+k) = 0$ and $\Omega_{hyp}(i,i+k) = 0$, involving no increase of $P'_{FalseAlarm}$ and erroneous increase of P'_{Miss}.

4.2 *WindowDiff* metric

Pevzner and Hearst (2002) propose the alternative metric called *WindowDiff*. By keeping our notations concerning $r(i,k)$ and $h(i,k)$ introduced in the subsection 4.1, *WindowDiff* is defined as:

$$WindowDiff = \frac{\sum_{i=1}^{N-k} [|r(i,k) - h(i,k)| > 0]}{N-k}.$$

Similar to both P_k and P'_k, *WindowDiff* is also computed by moving a window of fixed size across the test set and penalizing the algorithm misses or erroneous algorithm boundary detections. However, unlike P_k and P'_k, *WindowDiff* takes into account how many boundaries fall within the window and is penalizing in "how many discrepancies occur between the reference and the system results" rather than "determining how often two units of text are incorrectly labeled

[2] Let *ref* be a correct segmentation and *hyp* be a segmentation proposed by a text segmentation system. We will keep this notations in equations introduced below.

as being in different segments" (Pevzner and Hearst, 2002).

Our critique concerning *WindowDiff* is that misses are less penalised than false alarms and we argue this as follows. *WindowDiff* can be rewritten as:

$WindowDiff = WD_{Miss} + WD_{FalseAlarm}$,
where:

$WD_{Miss} = \frac{\sum_{i=1}^{N-k} [r(i,k)>h(i,k)]}{N-k}$,

$WD_{FalseAlarm} = \frac{\sum_{i=1}^{N-k} [r(i,k)<h(i,k)]}{N-k}$.

Hence both misses and false alarms are weighted by $\frac{1}{N-k}$.

Note that, on the one hand, there are indeed (N-k) equiprobable possibilities to have a false alarm in an interval of k units. On the other hand, however, the total number of equiprobable possibilities to have a miss in an interval of k units is smaller than (N-k) since it depends on the number of reference boundaries (i.e. we can have a miss in the interval of k units only if in that interval the reference corpus contains at least one boundary). Therefore misses, being weighted by $\frac{1}{N-k}$, are less penalised than false alarms.

Let B_{ref} be the number of thematic boundaries in the reference data. Let's say that the reference data contains about 20% boundaries and 80% non-boundaries from the total number of potential boundaries. Therefore, since there are relatively few boundaries compared with non-boundaries, a strategy introducing no false alarms, but introducing a maximum number of misses (i.e. $k \cdot B_{ref}$ misses) can be judged as being around 80% correct by the *WindowDiff* measure. On the other hand, a segmentation with no misses, but with a maximum number of false alarms (i.e. $(N-k)$ false alarms) is judged as being 100% erroneous by the *WindowDiff* measure. That is, misses and false alarms are not equally penalised.

Another issue regarding *WindowDiff* is that it is not clear "how does one interpret the values produced by the metric" (Pevzner and Hearst, 2002).

4.3 Proposal for a New Metric

In order to address the inadequacies of P_k and *WindowDiff*, we propose a new evaluation metric, defined as follows:

$Pr_{error} = C_{miss} \cdot Pr_{miss} + C_{fa} \cdot Pr_{fa}$,
where:

C_{miss} $(0 \leq C_{miss} \leq 1)$ is the cost of a miss, C_{fa} $(0 \leq C_{fa} \leq 1)$ is the cost of a false alarm,

$Pr_{miss} = \frac{\sum_{i=1}^{N-k} [\Theta_{ref\_hyp}(i,k)]}{\sum_{i=1}^{N-k} [\Delta_{ref}(i,k)]}$,

$Pr_{fa} = \frac{\sum_{i=1}^{N-k} [\Psi_{ref\_hyp}(i,k)]}{N-k}$,

$$\Theta_{ref\_hyp}(i,k) = \begin{cases} 1, & if\ r(i,k) > h(i,k) \\ 0, & otherwise \end{cases}$$

$$\Psi_{ref\_hyp}(i,k) = \begin{cases} 1, & if\ r(i,k) < h(i,k) \\ 0, & otherwise. \end{cases}$$

$$\Delta_{ref}(i,k) = \begin{cases} 1, & if\ r(i,k) > 0 \\ 0, & otherwise. \end{cases}$$

Pr_{miss} could be interpreted as the probability that the hypothesized segmentation contains less boundaries than the reference segmentation in an interval of k units[3], conditioned by the fact that the reference segmentation contains at least one boundary in that interval. Analogously Pr_{fa} is the probability that the hypothesized segmentation contains more boundaries than the reference segmentation in an interval of k units.

For certain applications where misses are more important than false alarms or vice versa, the Pr_{error} can be adjusted to tackle this trade-off via the C_{fa} and C_{miss} parameters. In order to have $Pr_{error} \in [0,1]$, we suggest that C_{fa} and C_{miss} be chosen such that $C_{fa} + C_{miss} = 1$. By choosing C_{fa}=C_{miss}=$\frac{1}{2}$, the penalization of misses and false alarms is thus balanced. In consequence, a strategy that places no boundaries at all is penalized as much as a strategy proposing boundaries everywhere (i.e. after every unit). In other words, both such degenerate algorithms will have an error rate Pr_{error} of about 50%. The worst algorithm, penalised as having an error rate Pr_{error} of 100% when $k = 2$, is the algorithm that places boundaries everywhere except the places where reference boundaries exist.

5 Results

5.1 Test Procedure

For the three datasets we first performed two common preprocessing steps: common words are eliminated using the same stop-list and remaining words are stemmed by using Porter's algorithm (1980). Next, we ran the three segmenters described in Section 2, by employing the default values for any system parameters and by letting the

[3]A unit can be either a word or a sentence / an utterance.

systems estimate the number of thematic boundaries.

We also considered the fact that C99 and TextSeg algorithms can take into account a fixed number of thematic boundaries. Even if the number of segments per document can vary in TDT and meeting reference data, we consider that in a real application it is impossible to provide to the systems the exact number of boundaries for each document to be segmented. Therefore, we ran C99 and TextSeg algorithms (for a second time), by providing them only the average number of segments per document in the reference data, which gives an estimation of the expected level of segmentation granularity.

Four additional naive segmentations were also used for evaluation, namely: *no boundaries*, where the whole text is a single segment; *all boundaries*, i.e. a thematic boundary is placed after each utterance; *random known*, i.e. the same number of boundaries as in gold standard, distributed randomly throughout text; and *random unknown*: the number of boundaries is randomly selected and boundaries are randomly distributed throughout text. Each of the segmentations was evaluated with P_k, P'_k and *WindowDiff*, as described in Section 4.

5.2 Comparative Performance of Segmentation Systems

The results of applying each segmentation algorithm to the three distinct datasets are summarized in Figures 1, 2 and 3. Percent error values are given in the figures and we used the following abbreviations: *WD* to denote *WindowDiff* error metric; *TextSeg_KA* to denote the TextSeg algorithm (Utiyama and Isahara, 2001) when the average number of boundaries in the reference data was provided to the algorithm; *C99_KA* to denote the C99 algorithm (Choi, 2000) when the average number of boundaries in the reference data was provided to the algorithm; *N0* to denote the algorithm proposing a segmentation with no boundaries; *All* to denote the algorithm proposing the degenerate segmentation *all boundaries*; *RK* to denote the algorithm that generates a *random known* segmentation; and *RU* to denote the algorithm that generates a *random unknown* segmentation.

5.2.1 Comparison of System Performance from Artificial to Realistic Data

From the artificial data to the more realistic data, we expect to have more noise and thus the algorithms to constantly degrade, but as our experiments show a reversal of the assessment can appear. More exactly: as can be seen from Figure 1, both C99 and TextSeg algorithms significantly outperformed TextTiling algorithm on the artificially created dataset, when the number of segments was determined by the systems. A comparison between the error rates given in Figure 1 and Figure 2 show that C99 and TextSeg have a similar trend, by significantly decreasing their performance on TDT data, but still giving better results than TextTiling on TDT data. When comparing the systems by Pr_{error}, C99 has similar performance with TextTiling on meeting data (see Figure 3). Moreover, when assessment is done by using *WindowDiff*, P_k or P'_k, both C99 and TextSeg came out worse than TextTiling on meeting data. This demonstrates that rankings obtained when evaluating on artificial data are different from those obtained when evaluating on realistic data. An alternative interpretation can be given by taking into account that the degenerative *no boundaries* segmentation has an error rate of only 30% by the *WindowDiff*, P_k and P'_k metrics on meeting data. That is, we could interpret that all three systems give completely wrong segmentations on meeting data (due to the fact that topic shifts are subtler and not as abrupt as in TDT and artificial data). Nevertheless, we tend to adopt the first interpretation, given the weaknesses of P_k, P'_k and *WindowDiff* (where misses are less penalised than false alarms), as discussed in Section 4.

5.2.2 The Influence of the Error Metric on Assessment

By following the quantitative assessment given by the *WindowDiff* metric, we observe that the algorithm labeled *N0* is three times better than the algorithm *All* on meeting data (see Figure 3), while the same algorithm *N0* is considered only two times better than *All* on the artificial data (see Figure 1). This verifies the limitation of the *WindowDiff* metric discussed in Section 4.

The four error metrics described in detail in Section 4 have shown that the effect of knowing the average number of boundaries on C99 is positive when testing on meeting data. However if we want to take into account all the four error met-

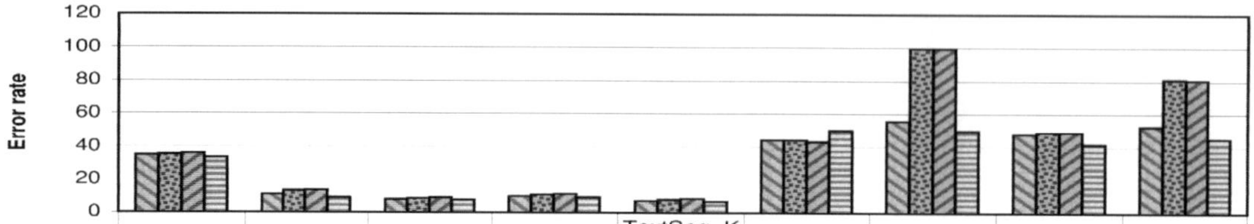

	TextTiling	C99	TextSeg	C99_KA	TextSeg_KA	NO	All	RK	RU
Pk	34.75	11.01	7.89	10	7.15	44.12	55.5	47.71	52.51
P'k	35.1	13.21	8.55	10.94	7.87	44.13	99.58	48.85	80.84
WD	35.73	13.58	9.21	11.34	8.59	43.1	99.59	48.89	80.63
Pr_error	33.33	9.1	7.71	9.34	6.87	49.87	49.79	41.61	45.01

Figure 1: Error rates of the segmentation systems on artificial data, where $k = 42$ and $P_{seg} = 0.44$.

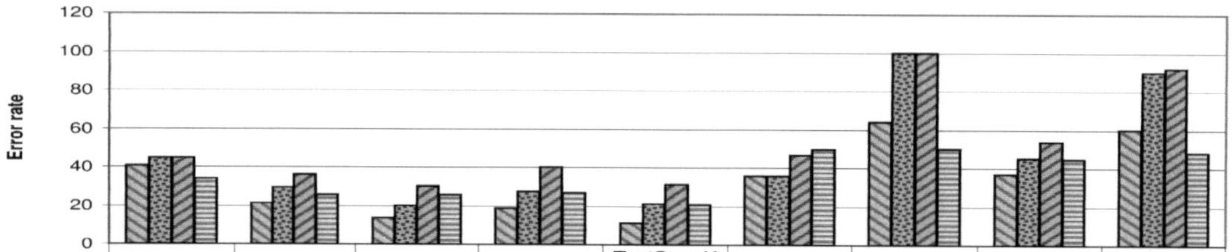

	TextTiling	C99	TextSeg	C99_KA	TextSeg_KA	NO	All	RK	RU
Pk	40.7	21.36	13.97	18.83	11.33	36.02	63.93	37.03	60.04
P'k	44.92	29.5	20.37	27.69	21.4	36.04	100	45.28	89.93
WD	44.76	36.28	30.3	40.26	31.46	46.69	100	53.75	91.92
Pr_error	34.09	25.69	25.62	27.17	21.05	49.96	50	44.89	48.31

Figure 2: Error rates of the segmentation systems on TDT data, where $k = 55$ and $P_{seg} = 0.3606$.

rics, it is difficult to draw definite conclusions regarding the influence of knowing the average number of boundaries on TextSeg and C99 algorithms. For example, when tested on TDT data, C99_KA seems to work better than C99 by P_k and P'_k metrics, while the *WindowDiff* metric gives a contradictory assessment.

6 Conclusions

By comparing the performance of three systems for thematic segmentation on different kinds of data, we address two important issues in a quantitative evaluation. Strong emphasis was put on the kind of data used for evaluation and we have demonstrated experimentally that evaluation on synthetic data is potentially misleading. The second major issue addressed in this paper concerns the choice of a valuable error metric and its side effects on the evaluation assessment.

Acknowledgments

This work is supported by the Interactive Multimodal Information Management project (http://www.im2.ch/). Many thanks to Andrei Popescu-Belis and the anonymous reviewers for their valuable comments. We are grateful to the International Computer Science Institute (ICSI), University of California for sharing the data with us. We also wish to thank Michael Galley who kindly provided us the thematic annotations of ICSI data.

References

James Allan, Jaime Carbonell, George Doddington, Jonathan Yamron, and Yiming Yang. 1998. Topic Detection and Tracking Pilot Study: Final Report. In *DARPA Broadcast News Transcription and Understanding Workshop*, pages 194–218, Landsdowne, VA. Morgan Kaufmann.

Doug Beeferman, Adam Berger, and John Lafferty. 1999. Statistical Models for Text Segmentation. *Machine Learning*, 34(Special Issue on Natural Language Learning):177–210.

Gillian Brown and George Yule. 1998. *Discourse Analysis*. (Cambridge Textbooks in Linguistics), Cambridge.

Freddy Choi. 2000. Advances in Domain Independent Linear Text Segmentation. In *Proceedings of the 1st*

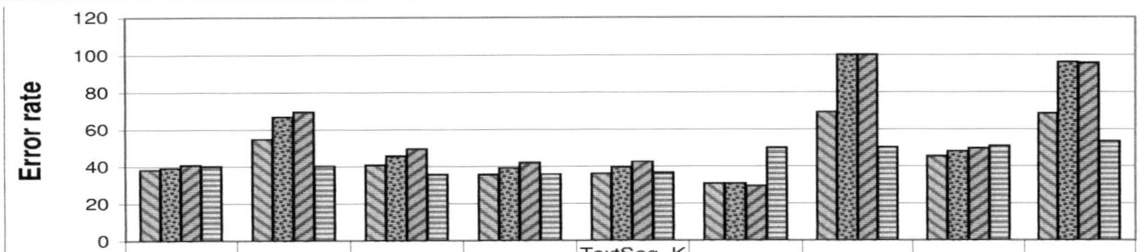

	TextTiling	C99	TextSeg	C99_KA	TextSeg_KA	NO	All	RK	RU
P_k	38.22	54.62	40.82	35.65	35.94	30.82	69.09	45.42	68.48
P'_k	39.12	66.78	45.66	39.04	39.6	30.89	100	47.97	95.99
WD	40.82	69.41	49.27	41.98	42.48	29.31	100	49.64	95.48
Pr_error	40.17	40.27	35.45	35.83	36.61	49.8	50	50.7	53.38

Figure 3: Error rates of the segmentation systems on meeting data, where $k = 85$ and $P_{seg} = 0.3090$.

Conference of the North American Chapter of the Association for Computational Linguistics, Seattle, USA.

Olivier Ferret. 2002. Using Collocations for Topic Segmentation and Link Detection. In *The 19th International Conference on Computational Linguistics*, Taipei, Taiwan.

Michael Galley, Kathleen McKeown, Eric Fosler-Luissier, and Hongyan Jing. 2003. Discourse Segmentation of Multy-Party Conversation. In *Annual Meeting of the Association for Computational Linguistics*, pages 562–569.

Barbara J. Grosz and Candace L. Sidner. 1986. Attention, Intentions and the Structure of Discourse. *Computational Linguistics*, 12:175–204.

Michael A. K. Halliday and Ruqaiya Hasan. 1976. *Cohesion in English*. Longman, London.

Marti Hearst and Christian Plaunt. 1993. Subtopic Structuring for Full-Length Document Access. In *Proceedings of the 16th Annual International ACM/SIGIR Conference*, pages 59–68, Pittsburgh, Pennsylvania, United States.

Marti Hearst. 1997. TextTiling: Segmenting Text into Multi-Paragraph Subtopic Passages. *Computational Linguistics*, 23(1):33–64.

Julia Hirschberg and Christine Nakatani. 1996. A Prosodic Analysis of Discourse Segments in Direction-Giving Monologues. In *Proceedings of the 34th Annual Meeting on Association for Computational Linguistics*, pages 286 – 293, Santa Cruz, California.

Adam Janin, Jeremy Ang, Sonali Bhagat, Rajdip Dhillon, Jane Edwards, Javier Macias-Guarasa, Nelson Morgan, Barbara Peskin, Elizabeth Shriberg, Andreas Stolcke, Chuck Wooters, and Britta Wrede. 2004. The ICSI Meeting Project: Resources and Research. In *ICASSP 2004 Meeting Recognition Workshop (NIST RT-04 Spring Recognition Evaluation)*, Montreal.

David Kauchak and Francine Chen. 2005. Feature-based segmentation of narrative documents. In *Proceedings of the ACL Workshop on Feature Engineering for Machine Learning in Natural Language Processing*, pages 32–39, Ann Arbor; MI; USA.

Hideki Kozima and Teiji Furugori. 1994. Segmenting Narrative Text into Coherent Scenes. *Literary and Linguistic Computing*, 9:13–19.

Inderjeet Mani. 2001. *Automatic Summarization*. John Benjamins Pub Co.

Chris Manning and Hinrich Schütze. 1999. *Foundations of Statistical Natural Language Processing*. MIT Press Cambridge, MA, USA.

Daniel Marcu. 2000. *The Theory and Practice of Discourse Parsing and Summarization*. MIT Press Cambridge, MA, USA.

Rebecca J. Passonneau and Diane J. Litman. 1996. Empirical Analysis of Three Dimensions of Spoken Discourse: Segmentation, Coherence and Linguistic Devices.

Rebecca J. Passonneau and Diane J. Litman. 1997. Discourse Segmentation by Human and Automated Means. *Computational Linguistics*, 23(1).

Lev Pevzner and Marti Hearst. 2002. A Critique and Improvement of an Evaluation Metric for Text Segmentation. *Computational Linguistics*, 16(1):19–36.

Martin Porter. 1980. An Algorithm for Suffix Stripping. *Program*, 14:130 – 137.

Jeffrey Reynar. 1998. *Topic Segmentation: Algorithms and Applications*. Ph.D. thesis, University of Pennsylvania.

TDT. 1998. The Topic Detection and Tracking - Phase 2 Evaluation Plan. Available from World Wide Web: http://www.nist.gov/speech/tests/tdt/tdt98/index.htm.

Masao Utiyama and Hitoshi Isahara. 2001. A Statistical Model for Domain-Independent Text Segmentation. In *ACL/EACL*, pages 491–498.

Invited Talk

Discourse and Dialogue Processing in Spoken Intelligent Tutoring Systems

Diane J. Litman
Computer Science Department &
Learning Research and Development Center
University of Pittsburgh
Pittsburgh, PA USA 15260
email: litman@cs.pitt.edu

Abstract

In recent years, the development of intelligent tutoring dialogue systems has become more prevalent, in an attempt to close the performance gap between human and computer tutors. Tutoring applications differ in many ways, however, from the types of applications for which spoken dialogue systems are typically developed. This talk will illustrate some of the opportunities and challenges in this area, focusing on issues such as affective reasoning, discourse and dialogue analysis, and performance evaluation.

Proceedings of the 7th SIGdial Workshop on Discourse and Dialogue, page 152,
Sydney, July 2006.

A computational model of multi-modal grounding for human robot interaction

Shuyin Li, Britta Wrede, and Gerhard Sagerer
Applied Computer Science, Faculty of Technology
Bielefeld University, 33594 Bielefeld, Germany
shuyinli, bwrede, sagerer@techfak.uni-bielefeld.de

Abstract

Dialog systems for mobile robots operating in the real world should enable mixed-initiative dialog style, handle multi-modal information involved in the communication and be relatively independent of the domain knowledge. Most dialog systems developed for mobile robots today, however, are often system-oriented and have limited capabilities. We present an agent-based dialog model that are specially designed for human-robot interaction and provide evidence for its efficiency with our implemented system.

1 Introduction

Natural language is the most intuitive way to communicate for human beings (Allen et al., 2001). It is, therefore, very important to enable dialog capability for personal service robots that should help people in their everyday life. However, the interaction with a robot as a mobile, autonomous device is different than with many other computer controlled devices which affects the dialog modeling. Here we want to first clarify the most essential requirements for dialog management systems for human-robot interaction (HRI) and then outline state-of-the-art dialog modeling approaches to position ourselves.

The first requirement results from the *situatedness* (Brooks, 1986) of HRI. A mobile robot is situated "here and now" and cohabits the same physical world as the user. Environmental changes can have massive influence on the task execution. For example, a robot should fetch a cup from the kitchen but the door is locked. Under this circumstance the dialog system *must* support mixed-initiative dialog style to receive user commands on the one side and to report on the perceived environmental changes on the other side. Otherwise the robot had to break up the task execution and there is no way for the user to find out the reason.

The second challenge for HRI dialog management is the *embodiment* of a robot which changes the way of interaction. Empirical studies show that the visual access to the interlocutor's body affects the conversation in the way that non-verbal behaviors are used as communicative signals (Nakano et al., 2003). For example, to refer to a cup that is visible to both dialog partners, the speaker tends to say "this cup" while pointing to it. The same strategy is considerably ineffective during a phone call. This example shows, an HRI dialog system must account for multi-modal communication.

The third, probably the unique challenge for HRI dialog management is the implication of the learning ability of such a robot. Since a personal service robot is intended to help human in their individual household it is impossible to hard-code all the knowledge it will need into the system, e.g., where the cup is and what should be served for lunch. Thus, it is essential for such a robot to be able to learn new knowledge and tasks. This ability, however, has the implication for the dialog system that it can not rely on comprehensive, hard-coded knowledge to do dialog planning. Instead, it must be designed in a way that it has a loose relationship with the domain knowledge.

Many dialog modeling approaches already exist. McTear (2002) classified them into three main types: *finite state-based*, *frame-based*, and *agent-based*. In the first two approaches the dialog structure is closely coupled with pre-defined task steps and can therefore only handle well-structured tasks for which one-side led dialog styles are sufficient. In the agent-based approach, the com-

Proceedings of the 7th SIGdial Workshop on Discourse and Dialogue, pages 153–160,
Sydney, July 2006.

munication is viewed as a *collaboration between two intelligent agents*. Different approaches inspired by psychology and linguistics are in use within this category. For example, within the TRAINS/TRIPS project several complex dialog systems for collaborative problem solving have been developed (Allen et al., 2001). Here the dialog system is viewed as a conversational agent that performs communicative acts. During a conversation, the dialog system selects the communicative goal based on its current belief about the domain and general conversational obligations. Such systems make use of communication and domain model to enable mixed-initiative dialog style and to handle more complex tasks. In the HRI field, due to the complexity of the overall systems, usually the finite-state-based strategy is employed (Matsui et al., 1999; Bischoff and Graefe, 2002; Aoyama and Shimomura, 2005). As to the issue of multi-modality, one strand of the research concerns the fusion and representation of multi-modal information such as (Pfleger et al., 2003) and the other strand focuses on the generalisation of human-like conversational behaviors for virtual agents. In this strand, Cassell (2000) proposes a general architecture for multi-modal conversation and Traum (2002) extends his information-state based dialog model by adding more conversational layers to account for multi-modality.

In this paper we present an agent-based dialog model for HRI. As described in section 2, the two main contributions of this model are the new modeling approach of Clark's grounding mechanism and the extension of this model to handle multi-modal grounding. In section 3 we outline the capabilities of the implemented system and present some quantitative evaluation results.

2 Dialog Model

We view a dialog as a collaboration between two agents. Agents are subject to common conversational rules and participate in a conversation by issuing multi-modal contributions (e.g., by saying something or displaying a facial expression). In subsection 2.1 we show how we handle conversational tasks by modeling the conversational rules based on grounding and in subsection 2.2 we present how we model individual contributions to tackle the issue of multi-modality. In subsection 2.3 we put these two things together to complete the model description. In this section, we also put concrete examples from the robot domain to clarify the relatively abstract model.

2.1 Grounding

One of the most influential theories on the collaborative nature of dialog is the common ground theory of Clark (1992). In his opinion, agents need to coordinate their mental states based on their mutual understanding about the current tasks, intentions, and goals during a conversation. Clark termed this process as *grounding* and proposed a contribution model. In this model, "contributions" from conversational agents are considered to be the basic component of a conversation. Each contribution has two phases: a *Presentation* phase and an *Acceptance* phase. In the Presentation phase the speaker presents an utterance to the listener, in the Acceptance phase the listener issues an evidence of understanding to the speaker. The speaker can only be sure that the utterance she presented previously has become a part of their common ground if this evidence is available.

Although this well established theory provides comprehensive insight into human conversation two issues in this theory remain critical when being applied to model dialog. The first one is the recursivity of Acceptance. Clark claimed, since everything said by one agent needs to be understood by her interlocutor, each Acceptance should also play the role of Presentation which needs to be accepted, too. The contributions are thus to be organized as a graph. However, this implies that the grounding process may never really end (Traum, 1994). The second critical issue is taking contributions as the most basic *grounding units*. In Clark's view, the basic grounding unit, i.e., the unit of conversation at which grounding takes place, is the contribution. To provide Acceptance for a contribution agents may need to issue clarification questions or repair. But when modeling a dialog, especially a task-oriented dialog, it is hard to map one single contribution from one agent to a domain task since tasks are always cooperately done by the two agents (Cahn and Brennan, 1999). Traum (1994) addressed the first issue by introducing a finite-state based grounding mechanism and Cahn and Brennan (1999) used "exchanges"' as the basic grounding unit to tackle the second critical issue. We combine the advantages of their work and present a grounding mechanism based on an augmented push-down automaton as described below.

Basic grounding unit: As Cahn and Brennan we take *exchange* as the most basic grounding unit. An exchange is a pair of contributions initiated by the two conversational agents. They represent the idea of *adjacency pairs* (Schegloff and Sacks, 1973). The first contribution of the exchange is the Presentation and the second contribution is the Acceptance, e.g., if one asks a question and the other answers it, then the question is the Presentation and the answer is the Acceptance. In our model, a contribution only represents *one* speech act. For example, if an agent says "Hello, my name is Tom, what is your name?" this utterances is segmented into three Presentations (a greeting, a statement, and a question) although they occur in one turn. These three Presentations initiate three exchanges and each of them needs to be accepted by the interlocutor.

Changing status of grounding units: Also as proposed by Cahn and Brennan, an exchange has two states: *not (yet) grounded* and *grounded*. An exchange is grounded if the Acceptance of the Presentation is available. Note, the Acceptance can be an implicit one, e.g, in form of "continued attention" in Clark's term. Taking the example above, the other agent would reply "Hello, my name is Jane." without explicitely commenting Tom's name, yet the three exchanges that Tom initiated were all accepted.

Organization of grounding units: In accordance with Traum we do not think that the Presentation of one exchange should play the role of the Acceptance of its previous exchange. Instead, we organize exchanges in a stack. The stack represents the whole ungrounded discourse: ungrounded exchanges are pushed onto it and the grounded ones are popped out of it. One major question of this representation is: *What has the grounding status of individual exchange to do with the grounding status of the whole stack?* Jane's Acceptance of Tom's greeting has no apparent relation to the remaining two still ungrounded exchanges initiated by Tom. But in the *center embedding* example in Fig. 1, the Acceptance of B1 (utterance A2) contributes to the Acceptance of A1 (utterance B2). These examples show that the grounding status of the whole discourse depends on (1) the grounding status of the individual exchanges and (2) the relationship between these exchanges, the *grounding relation*. These relations are introduced by the Presentation of each exchange because they start an exchange. We identified 4 types of grounding relations: *Default*, *Support*, *Correct*, and *Delete*. In the following we look at these relations in more detail and refer to exchanges with relation x to its *immediately preceding exchange* (IPE) as "x exchange", e.g., Support exchange:

Default: The current Presentation introduces a new account that is independent of the previous exchange in terms of grounding, e.g., what Tom said to Jane constructs three Presentations that initiate three default exchanges. Such exchanges can be grounded independently of each other.

Support: If an agent can not provide Acceptance for the given Presentation she will initiate a new exchange to support the grounding process of the ungrounded exchange. A typical example of such an exchange is a clarification question like "I beg your pardon?". If a Support exchange is grounded its initiator will try to ground the IPE again with the newly collected information through the supporting exchange.

Correct: Some exchanges are created to correct the content of the IPE, e.g., in case that the listener misunderstood the speaker and the speaker corrects it. Similar to Support, after such an exchange is grounded its IPE is updated with new information and has to be grounded again.

Delete: Agents can give up their effort to build a common ground with her interlocutor, e.g., by saying "Forget it.". If the interlocutor agrees, such exchanges have the effect that all the ungrounded exchanges from the initial Default exchange up to the current state are no longer relevant and the agents do not need to ground them any more.

Note, once an exchange is grounded it is *immediately* removed from the stack so that its IPE becomes the IPE of the next exchange. This model is described as an augmented push-down automaton (Fig. 2). It is augmented in so far that transitions can trigger actions and a variable number of exchanges can be popped or pushed in one step. There are five states in this APDA and they represent the fact what kind of ungrounded exchange is on the top of the stack. Along the arrows that connect the states the input (denoted as I), the resulting stack operation (denoted as S) and the possible action that is triggered (denoted as A) are given. The input of this automaton includes Presentation (e.g., "defaultP" stands for "Default Presentation") and Acceptance.

A1: What do you think about Mr. Watton?
B1: Mr. Watton? our music teacher?
A2: Yes. (accept B1)
B2: Well, he is OK. (accept A1)

Figure 1: An example of center embedding

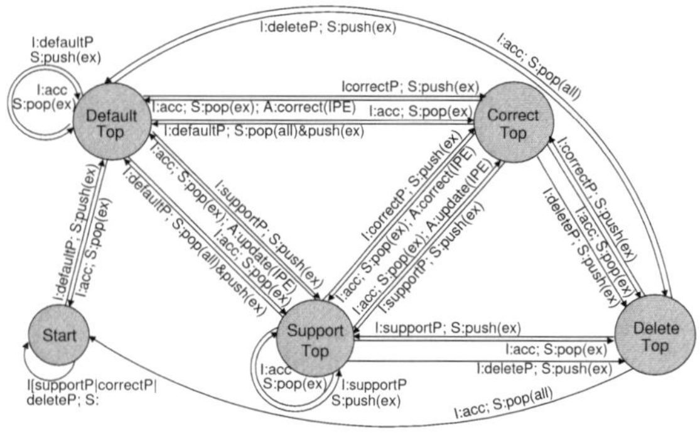

Figure 2: Augmented push-down automaton for grounding (ex: exchange)

As long as there is an ungrounded exchange at the top of the stack, the addressee will try to ground it by providing Acceptance, unless its validity is deleted. For the reason of space, we only explain the APDA with the center embedding example in Fig. 1. Contribution A1 introduces a question into the discourse which initiates a Default exchange, say Ex1. This exchange is pushed onto the stack. Instead of providing Acceptance to A1, contribution B1 initiates a new exchange, say Ex2, with grounding relation Support to Ex1 and is pushed onto the stack. Then contribution A2 acknowledges B1 so that Ex2 is grounded and popped out of the stack. The top element of the stack is now the ungrounded Ex1. Since Ex2 supported Ex1, the Ex1 is updated with the information contained in Ex2 (The music teacher was meant) and B2 then successfully grounds this updated Ex1.

In our model, every exchange can be individually grounded and contributes to the grounding of the whole ungrounded discourse by acting on the IPE according to their grounding relations. This way we can organize the discourse in a sequence without losing the local grounding flexibility. For an implemented system, this means that both the user and the system can easily take initiative or issue clarification questions. To implement this model, however, two points are crucial. The first one is the recognition of the user's contribution type: for every user contribution, the dialog system needs to decide whether it is a Presentation or an Acceptance. If it is a Presentation, the system needs further to decide whether it initiates a new account, corrects or supports the current one, or deletes it. This issue of intention recognition is a classical challenge for dialog systems. We present our solution in section 3. The second point is that the dialog system needs to know when to create an exchange of certain grounding relation by generating an appropriate Presentation and when to create an Acceptance. For that we need to first look at the structure of individual contributions more closely in the next subsection.

2.2 The structure of agents' contributions

To represent the structure of the individual contributions we take into account the whole language generation process which enables us to come up with a powerful solution as described below.

The layers of a contribution: What we can observe in a conversation are only exchanges of agents' contributions in verbal or non-verbal form. But in fact the contributions are the end-product of a complex cognitive process: language production. Levelt (1989) identified three phases of language production: *conceptualization*, *formulation*, and *articulation*. The production of an utterance starts from the conception of a *communicative intention* and the semantic organization in the conceptualization phase before the utterance can be formulated and articulated in the next two phases. Intentions can arise from the previous discourse or from other motivations such as needs for help or information. This finding motivates us to set up a two-layered structure of contributions. One layer is the so-called *intention layer* where communication intentions are conceived. For a robot the communication intentions come from the analysis of the previous discourse or from the robot control system. The other layer is the *conversation layer*. The communication intentions are formulated and articulated here[1]. These two layers represent the intention conception and the language generation process, respectively. We term this two-layered structure of contribution *interaction unit* (IU).

The issue of multi-modality: Face-to-face conversations are multi-modal. Speech and body language (e.g., gesture) can happen simultaneously. McNeill (1992) stated that gesture and speech arise from the same semantic source, the

[1] Since most robot systems use speech synthesizer to generate acoustic output which replaces the articulation process, only formulation is performed on this layer.

so-called "idea unit" and are co-expressive. Since semantic representation is created out of communicative intentions (Levelt, 1989) we assume the communication intentions are the modality independent base that governs the multi-modal language production. We, therefore, extend our structure above by introducing two generators on the conversation layer: one *verbal* and one *non-verbal* generator that represent the verbal and non-verbal language generation mechanism based on the communication intentions created on the intention layer. The relationship between these two generators is variable. For example, Iverson et al. (1999) identified three types of *informational* relationship between speech and gesture: *reinforcement* (gesture reinforces the message conveyed in speech, e.g., emphatic gesture), *disambiguation* (gesture serves as the precise referent of the speech, e.g., deictic gesture accompanying the utterance "this cup"), and *adding-information* (e.g., saying "The ball is so big." and shaping the size with hands). In our work, when processing users' multi-modal contributions we focus on the disambiguation relation; when creating multi-modal contributions for the robot we are also interested in other informational relations [2]. The structure of an IU is illustrated in Fig. 3.

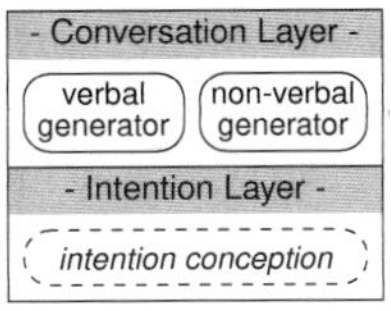

Figure 3: IU

Operation flow within an interaction unit: During a conversation an agent either initiates an account or replies to the interlocutor's account. The communication intentions can thus be *self-motivated* or *other-motivated.* For a robot, self-motivated intentions can be triggered by the robot control system, e.g., observed environmental changes. In this case, an IU is created with its intention layer importing the message from the robot control system and exporting an intention. This intention is transfered to the conversation layer which then formulates a verbal message with the verbal generator and/or constructs a body language expression with the non-verbal generator. Other-motivated intentions can be triggered by the needs of the on-going conversation, e.g., the need to answer a question, or be triggered by robot's execution results of the tasks specified previously by the user. The operation flow is similar to that of the self-motivation apart from the fact that, in case of intentions motivated by conversational needs, the intention layer of the IU does not import any robot control system message but creates an intention directly. Note, the IUs that are initiated by the robot and by the user have identical structure. But in case of user initiated IUs we do not make any assumption of their underlying intention building process and the intention layer of their IUs are thus always empty.

With the IUs, we can integrate the non-verbal behavior systematically into the communication process and model multi-modal dialog. Although it is not the focus of our work, our model can also handle purely non-verbal contributions, since the verbal generator does not always need to be activated if the non-verbal generator already provides enough information about the speaker's intention. Possible scenarios are: the user looks tired (presentation) and the robot offers "I can do that for you." (acceptance) or the user says something (presentation) and robot nods (acceptance).

2.3 Putting things together

Till now we have discussed our concept of using a grounding mechanism to organize contributions and of representing individual contributions as IU. Now it is time to look at the still open point at the end of the section 2.1: when to create an IU as Presentation and when an IU as Acceptance.

Self-motivated intentions usually trigger the creation of an IU as Presentation with Default relation to its IPE. For example, if the robot needs to report something to the user it can create a Default exchange by generating an IU as its Presentation. The user is then expected to signal her Acceptance. Other-motivated intentions can, according to the context, result in either Presentation or Acceptance. To make the correct decision we developed criteria based on the *joint intention theory* of Levesque et al. (1990) which predicts that during a collaboration the partners are committed to a joint goal that they will always try to conform till they reach the goal or give up. Note, this does not mean that one will always agree with her interlocutor, but they will behave in the way that they think is the best to achieve the goal. This theory can be applied to human-robot dialog in a twofold sense: Firstly, a dialog can be generally seen as a collaboration as Clark proposed. Secondly, the human-robot dialog is mostly task-oriented, i.e.,

[2] This policy has a practical reason: it is much more difficult in computer science to correctly recognize and interpret human motion than to simulate it.

the human and the robot work towards the same goal. With this theory in mind we describe how we process other-motivated contributions below.

The precondition of language production based on other-motivated intentions is language perception. Before reacting, i.e., before creating her own IU, an agent first needs to understand the intention conveyed by her interlocutor's IU by studying its conversation layer. Since we focus on disambiguation function of non-verbal behavior we assume that agents first study the generated verbal information, if the intention can not be fully recognized here, one will further study the information provided by the non-verbal generator (e.g., a gesture) and fuse the verbal and non-verbal information. If the intention recognition is still unsuccessful, the agent can not provide Acceptance for the given IU. If she is still committed to the dialog she will issue a clarification question, i.e., she generates an IU as Presentation that initiates a Support exchange to the current ungrounded exchange. If the intention of her interlocutor is successfully recognized the language perception process ends and the agent tries to create her own IU. As described in subsection 2.2 the creation of the IU starts from the creation of an intention on the intention layer. In case of a robot, the dialog system accesses the robot control system and awaits its reaction to the conveyed information (e.g., a user instruction). Usually, a robot is designated to do something for the user, i.e., the robot is committed to the goal proposed by the user, so we define *the robot can only provide acceptance if the task is successfully executed.* In this case, the robot completes the current IU with the filled intention layer by generating an confirmation on its conversation layer. Afterwards, this grounded exchange can be popped from the stack. If the robot can not execute the task for some reasons, then the current exchange can not be grounded and the robot will take the current IU with the filled intention layer as another Presentation that initiates a Support or Correct exchange to the current ungrounded exchange, similar as the case in Fig. 1. The conversation layer of this IU can thus formulate something like "Sorry, I can't do that because..." and present a sorrowful face. This new Support or Correct exchange is pushed onto the stack. Figure 4 illustrates this process as a UML activity diagram.

In our model we only do general conversational planning instead of domain specific task planning.

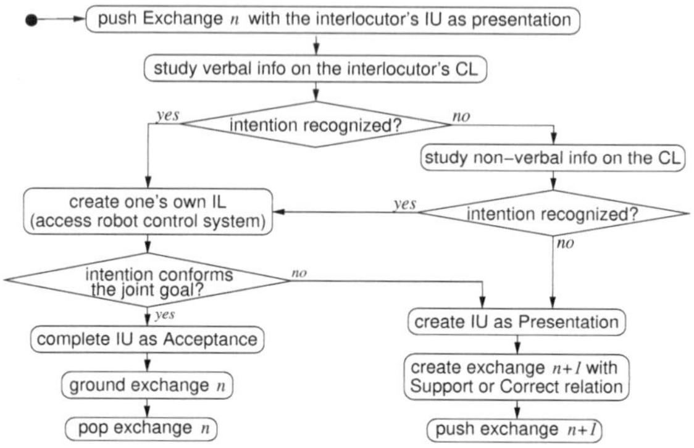

Figure 4: Handling other-motivated contribution (CL: Conversation layer; IL: Intention Layer)

What the dialog system needs to know from the robot control system is what processing results it can produce. The association of these results with robot intentions in terms of whether they start a new account, support or correct one, or delete it, can be configured externally and thus easily updated or replaced. Based on this configuration IUs are generated that operate according to the grounding mechanism as described in section 2.1.

3 Implementation

This dialog model was implemented for our robot BIRON, a personal robot with learning abilities. It can detect and follow persons, focus on objects (according to human deictic gestures) and store collected information into a memory. Our implementation scenario is the so-called *home tour*: a user shows a new robot her home to prepare it for future tasks. The robot should be able to learn and remember features of objects that the user mentions and it "sees", e.g., name, color, images etc. Besides, our system was also successfully ported to a humanoid robot BARTHOC for studies of emotional and social factors of HRI (see. Fig. 5).

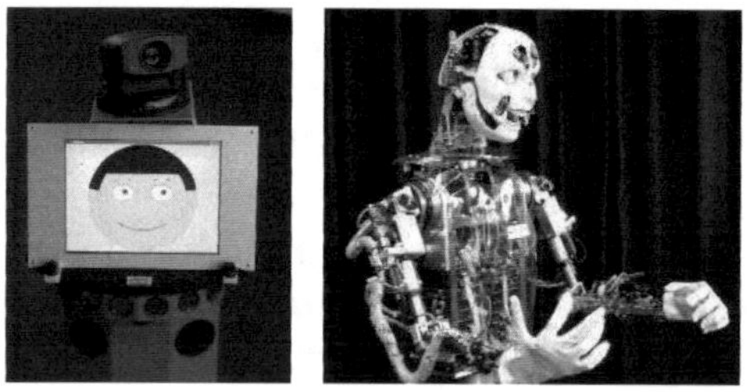

Figure 5: Robots BIRON and BARTHOC

The dialog manager is linked to a speech understanding system which transforms parts of speech from a speech recognizer into a speech-act-based form. To recognize the user's intention, the dialog system classifies this input into 10 categories of three groups according to heuristics, e.g., *instruction*, *description*, and *query* initiate new tasks and thus a new Default exchange; *deletion* and *correction* initiate Delete and Correct exchanges that are related to early exchanges; and *confirmation*, *negation*, etc. can only be responses and are, therefore, viewed as user's Acceptance of exchanges that the robot initiates. The main part of the dialog system is the Dialog Manager that carries out grounding analysis and stack operations. The Robot Control Manager receives messages from the robot control system and calls the Dialog Manager to do relevant operations. This dialog system enables multi-modal, mixed-initiative dialog style and can handle complex repair behaviors. With the example dialog in Fig. 6, which is transcripted from a real interaction session between a user and BIRON, we discuss the two most important features of our system.

Ex1 R1: Hello human! *(looking friendly)*
U1: Hello!
Ex2 Who are you?
R2: My name is BIRON, if you show me something I can remember it. *(looking friendly)*
Ex3 U2: OK, um, look, this is a mug.
Ex4 R3: I beg your pardon? *(looking puzzled)*
U3: This is a mug, umm, here.
Ex5 R4: Sorry, can you use some other words? *(looking sad)*
U4: This is a mug!
Ex6 R5: Sorry, I can't find it. Are you pointing to it with your finger? *(looking sad)*
U5: Yes!
Ex7 R6: I know it is sometimes difficult with me, but don't feel discouraged! *(looking ashamed)*
U6: (laugh)
R7: OK, I've found it, it is really nice! *(looking happily)*

Figure 6: A dialog example with the extrovert BIRON. (U: user, R: robot, Ex: Exchange)

Taking Initiative and robot personality: Initiatives that a dialog system can take often depends on its back-end application. Since BIRON does not have a task planner which would be ideal to demonstrate this ability we implemented an *extrovert* personality for it (additionally to its *basic* personality) that takes communication-related initiatives. The basic BIRON behaves in a rather passive way and only says something when addressed by the user. In contrast, the extrovert BIRON greets persons actively (R1 in Table 6) and remarks on its own performance (R6). When the robot control system detects a person the dialog system initiates a Default exchange to greet her. BIRON can also measure its own performance by counting the number of Support exchanges it has initiated for the current topic. Since the Support exchanges are only created if BIRON can not provide Acceptance to the user's Presentation (because it does not understand the user or it can not execute a task), the amount of the Support exchanges thus has direct correlation to the robot's overall performance. On the other hand, the more Default exchanges there are, the better is the performance because the agents can proceed to another topic only if the current one is grounded (or deleted). Based on this performance indication BIRON does remarks to motivate users.

Resolving multi-modal object references: It happens quite frequently in the home tour scenario that the user points to some objects and says "This is a *z*". BIRON needs to associate its symbolic name (and eventually other features) mentioned by the user with the image of the object. The resolution of such multi-modal object references (U4-R7 in Table 6) is solved as following: the Dialog Manager creates an IU for the user-initiated utterance (e.g., "this is a cup") and studies the verbal and non-verbal generator on its conversation layer. In the verbal generator, what the pronoun "this" refers to is unclear, but it indicates that the user might be using a gesture. Therefore, the Dialog Manager further studies the non-verbal generator. The responsible robot vision module is activated here to search for a gesture and to identify the object cup. If the cup is found in the scene, this module assigns an ID to the image and stores it in the memory. After the Dialog Manager receives this ID, the processing of the conversation layer of the user IU ends, the Dialog Manager proceeds to create its own IU to react to the user's IU. Problems with the object identification indicate failure of the intention recognition process on the user conversation layer. In this case, the Dialog Manager creates a Support exchange to ask the user which object she refers to and retries it if she does not oppose (R5-R7). This process and the associated multimodality fusion and representation are described in (Li et al., 2005) in detail.

The evaluation of dialog systems for human robot interaction is still an open issue. A robot system is usually a complex system including a large number of modules that claim plenty of processing time or are subject to environmental conditions. For the dialog system, this means that the correct interpretation and transaction of user utterances is by no means a guaranty for a prompt response or successful task execution. Thus, the performance of the dialog system can not be directly measured with the performance of the overall system like most desktop dialog applications. We are still working at evaluation metrics for HRI dialog systems (Green et al., 2006). But the efficiency of our system is already visible in the small effort associated with the porting of this system to another robot platform and in the pilot user study with BIRON. In this study, each of the 14 users interacted with BIRON twice. In the total 28 runs the dialog system generated 903 exchanges for the 813 user utterances. Among these exchanges, 34% initiated clarification questions. This result correlated with the evaluation result of our speech understanding system which fully understood 65% of all the user utterances. 18.6% of the exchanges were Support exchanges created due to execution failure of the robot control system which corresponds to the performance of the robot control system. The average processing time of the dialog system was 11 msec.

4 Conclusion

In this paper we presented an agent-based dialog model for HRI. The implemented system enables multi-modal, mixed-initiative dialog style and is relatively domain independent. The real-time testing of the system proves its efficiency. We will work out detailed evaluation metrics for our system to be able to draw more general conclusion about the strength and weakness of our model.

References

J. Allen, D. K. Byron, M. Dzikovska, G. Ferguson, L. Galescu, and A. Stent. 2001. Towards conversational human-computer interaction. *AI Magazine*, 22(4).

K. Aoyama and H. Shimomura. 2005. Real world speech interaction with a humanoid robot on a layered robot behavior control architecture. In *Proc. Int. Conf. on Robotics and Automation*.

R. Bischoff and V. Graefe. 2002. Dependable multimodal communication and interaction with robotic assistants. In *Proc. Int. Workshop on Robot-Human Interactive Communication (ROMAN)*.

R. A. Brooks. 1986. A robust layered control system for a mobile robot. *IEEE Journal of Robotics and Automation*, 2(1):14–23.

J. E. Cahn and S. E. Brennan. 1999. A psychological model of grounding and repair in dialog. In *Proc. Fall 1999 AAAI Symposium on Psychological Models of Communication in Collaborative Systems*.

J. Cassell, T. Bickmore, L. Campbell, and H. Vilhjalmsson. 2000. Human conversation as a system framework: Designing embodied conversational agents. In J. Cassell, J. Sullivan, S. Prevost, and E. Churchill, editors, *Embodied conversational agents*. MIT Press.

H. H. Clark, editor. 1992. *Arenas of Language Use*. University of Chicago Press.

A. Green, K. Severinson-Eklundh, B. Wrede, and S. Li. 2006. Integrating miscommunication analysis in natural language interface design for a service robot. In *Proc. Int. Conf. on Intelligent Robots and Systems*. submitted.

J. M. Iverson, O. Capirci, E. Longobardi, and M. C. Caselli. 1999. Gesturing in mother-child interactions. *Cognitive Develpment*, 14(1):57–75.

W. Levelt. 1989. *Speaking: From intention to articulation*. Cambridge, MA: MIT Press.

H. J. Levesque, P. R. Cohen, and J. H. T. Nunnes. 1990. On acting together. In *Proc. Nat. Conf. on Artificial Intelligence (AAAI)*.

S. Li, A. Haasch, B. Wrede, J. Fritsch, and G. Sagerer. 2005. Human-style interaction with a robot for cooperative learning of scene objects. In *Proc. Int. Conf. on Multimodal Interfaces*.

T. Matsui, H. Asoh, J. Fry, Y. Motomura, F. Asano, T. Kurita, I. Hara, and N. Otsu. 1999. Integrated natural spoken dialogue system of jijo-2 mobile robot for office services,. In *Proc. AAAI Nat. Conf. and Innovative Applications of Artificial Intelligence Conf.*

D. McNeill. 1992. *Hand and Mind: What Gesture Reveal about Thought*. University of Chicago Press.

M. F. McTear. 2002. Spoken dialogue technology: enabling the conversational interface. *ACM Computing Surveys*, 34(1).

Y. I. Nakano, G. Reinstein, T. Stocky, and J. Cassell. 2003. Towards a model of face-to-face grounding. In *Proc. Annual Meeting of the Association for Computational Linguistics*.

N. Pfleger, J. Alexandersson, and T. Becker. 2003. A robust and generic discourse model for multimodal dialogue. In *Proc. 3rd Workshop on Knowledge and Reasoning in Practical Dialogue Systems*.

E. A. Schegloff and H. Sacks. 1973. Opening up closings. *Semiotica*, pages 289–327.

D. Traum and J. Rickel. 2002. Embodied agents for multiparty dialogue in immersive virtual world. In *Proc. 1st Int. Conf on Autonomous Agents and Multi-agent Systems*.

D. Traum. 1994. *A Computational Theory of Grounding in Natural Language Conversation*. Ph.D. thesis, University of Rochester.

Relationship between Utterances and "Enthusiasm" in Non-task-oriented Conversational Dialogue

Ryoko TOKUHISA
Toyota Central R&D Labs., INC.
Nagakute Aichi JAPAN
tokuhisa@mosk.tytlabs.co.jp

Ryuta TERASHIMA
Toyota Central R&D Labs., INC.
Nagakute Aichi JAPAN
ryuta@mosk.tytlabs.co.jp

Abstract

The goal of this paper is to show how to accomplish a more enjoyable and enthusiastic dialogue through the analysis of human-to-human conversational dialogues. We first created a conversational dialogue corpus annotated with two types of tags: one type indicates the particular aspects of the utterance itself, while the other indicates the degree of enthusiasm. We then investigated the relationship between these tags. Our results indicate that affective and cooperative utterances are significant to enthusiastic dialogue.

1 Introduction

For a non-task-oriented conversational dialogue system (e.g. home robots), we should strive for a dialogue strategy that is both enjoyable and enthusiastic, as well as efficient. Many studies have been conducted on efficient dialogue strategies (Walker et al., 1998; Litman et al., 2000; Komatani et al., 2002), but it is not clear how to accomplish a more "human-like enthusiasm" for a conversational dialogue. The goal of this paper is to show the types of utterances that contribute to enthusiasm in conversational dialogues.

2 Corpus Annotation

We created a conversational corpus annotated with two types of tags: one type indicates particular aspects of the utterance itself, while the other indicates the degree of enthusiasm in the dialogue. This section describes our corpus and tagging scheme in detail.

2.1 Corpus Collection

As a result of previous works, several conversational dialogue corpora have been collected with various settings (Graff and Bird, 2000; TSENG, 2001). The largest conversational dialogue corpus is the Switchboard Corpus, which consists of about 2400 conversational English dialogues between two unfamiliar speakers over the telephone on one of 70 topics (e.g. pets, family life, education, gun control, etc.).

Our corpus was collected from face-to-face interaction between two unfamiliar speakers. The reasons were 1) face-to-face interaction increases the number of enthusiastic utterances, relative to limited conversational channel interaction such as over the telephone; 2) the interaction between unfamiliar speakers reduces the enthusiasm resulting from unobserved reasons during the recording; 3) the exchange in a twoparty dialogue will be simpler than that of a multiparty dialogue.

We created a corpus containing ten conversational dialogues that were spoken by an operator (thirties, female) and one of ten subjects (twenties to sixties, equal numbers of males and females). Before beginning the recording session, the subject chose three cards from fifteen cards on the following topics:

Food, Travel, Sport, Hobbies, Movies, Prizes,
TV Programs, Family, Books, School, Music,
Pets, Shopping, Recent Purchases, Celebrities

Straying from the selected topic was permitted, because these topic cards were only ever intended as a prompt to start the dialogue. Thus, we collected ten dialogues, each about 20 minutes long. For convenience, in this paper, we refer to the operator as **speaker1**, and the subject as **speaker2**.

Proceedings of the 7th SIGdial Workshop on Discourse and Dialogue, pages 161–167,
Sydney, July 2006.

2.2 Annotation of DAs and RRs

2.2.1 Definition of tagging scheme

Dialogue Acts (DAs) and Rhetorical Relations (RRs) are well-known tagging schemes for annotating an utterance or a sentence. DAs are tags that pertain to the function of an utterance itself, while RRs indicate the relationship between sentences or utterances. We adopted both tags to allow us to analyze the aspects of utterances in various ways, but adapted them slightly for our particular needs.

The DA annotations were based on SWBD-DAMSL and MRDA (Jurafsky et al., 1997; Dhillon et al., 2004). The SWBD-DAMSL is the DA tagset for labeling a conversational dialogue. The Switchboard Corpus mentioned above was annotated with SWBD-DAMSL. On the other hand, MRDA is the DA tagset for labeling the dialogue of a meeting between multiple participants. Table 1 shows the correspondence between SWBD-DAMSL/MRDA and our DAs[1]. We describe some of the major adaptations below.

The tags pertaining to questions: In SWBD-DAMSL and MRDA, the tags pertaining to questions were classified by the type of their form (e.g. *Wh-question*). We re-categorized them into request and confirm in terms of the "act" for Japanese.

The tags pertaining to responses: We subdivided *Accept* and *Reject* into objective responses (*accept,denial*) and subjective responses (*agree, disagree*).

The emotional tags: We added tags that indicate the expression of *admiration* and *interest*.

The overlap tags with the RRs definition: We did not use any tags (e.g. *Summary*), that overlapped the RR definition.

Consequently, we defined 47 DAs for analyzing a conversational dialogue.

The RR annotations were based on the rhetorical relation defined in Rhetorical Structure Theory (RST) (Mann and Thompson, 1988; Stent and Allen, 2000). Our RR definition was based only on informational level relation defined in RST because we annotated the intentional level with DAs. Table 2 shows the correspondence between the informational relation of RST and our RRs. We describe some of the major adaptations below.

Subdivide evaluation: The evaluation reflects the degree of enthusiasm in the dialogue, so we divided the *Evaluation* into three types of *evaluation (positive/negative/neutral)*.

Integrate the causal relations: We use a directed graph representation for RR annotations, so that we integrate *Non-volitional cause* and *Non-volitional result* into *non-volitional cause-effect*, and *Volitional cause* and *Volitional result* into *volitional cause-effect*.

Add addition relation: The RRs initially represent the structure of the written text, segmented into clause-like units. Therefore, they do not cover those cases in which one clause is uttered by one speaker, but communicatively completed by another. So, we added an *addition* to our RRs. The following is an example of *addition*.

speaker A: the lunch in our company cafeteria

speaker B: is good value for money

We defined 16 RRs as a result of these adaptations.

Table 1: Dialogue Act Definition

SWBD-DAMSL/MRDA	Our DAs	Definition
Statement non opinion	inform objective fact	inform non opinion
Statement opinion	inform subjective element	inform opinion
Wh-Question	request objective fact	request non opinion
Yes-No-question	request agreement	request agreement opinion
Open-Question	confirm objective fact	confirm non opinion
Or-Question	confirm agreement	confirm agreement opinion
Accept	accept	accept non opinion
	agree	accept opinion
Reject	denial	denial non opinion
	disagree	denial opinion
not marked	express admiration	inform admiration
Summary	DEL. (mark as RR)	———

Table 2: Rhetorical Relation Definition

Mann's RST	Our RRs	definition
Evaluation	evaluation (positive)	U2 is a positive evaluation about U1
	evaluation (negative)	U2 is a negative evaluation about U1
	evaluation (neutral)	U2 is neutral evaluation about U1
Volitional cause	volitional cause-effect	U2 is a volitional action, and U1 cause U2
Volitional result		
No Definition	addition	U2 consists of a part of U1

[1]The tags listed in *italics* are based on SWBD-DAMSL while those in **boldface** are based on MRDA.

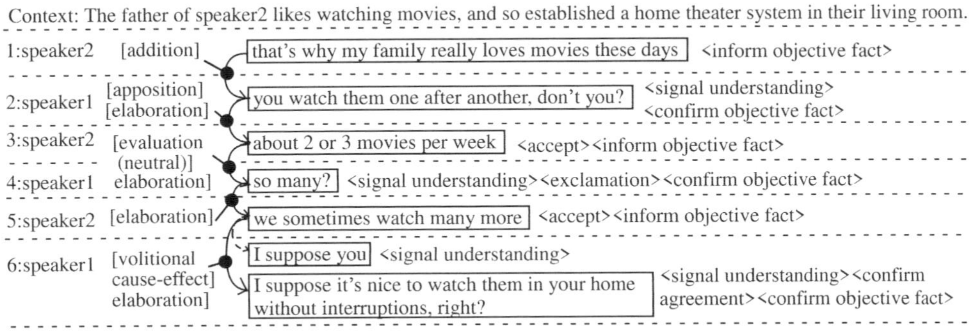

Figure 1: Example of Dialogue annotated with DAs and RRs (Originally in Japanese)

2.2.2 Annotation of DAs and RRs

DAs and RRs are annotated using the MMAX2 Annotation Tool [2] (Muller and Strube, 2003). Figure 1 shows an example of our corpus annotated with DAs and RRs. The ⟨ ⟩ symbol in Figure 1 indicates a DA, while the [ ] symbol indicates an RR. Below, we describe our annotation process for DAs and RRs.

Step 1. Utterance Segmentation: All the utterances in the dialogue are segmented into DA segments, each of which we define as an *utterance*. In Figure 1, the utterance is surrounded with a square. In this step, we also eliminated backchannels from the exchange.

Step 2. Annotation of DAs: DAs are annotated to all utterances. In those cases in which one DA alone cannot represent an utterance, two or more DAs are used (see Figure 1 line 2).

Step 3. Annotation of Adjacency Pairs: Adjacency pairs (APs) are labeled. An AP consists of two utterances where each part is produced by a different speaker. In Figure 1, the solid and dotted lines correspond to links between the APs.

Step 4. Annotation of RRs: RRs on APs are labeled. A solid line indicates an AP that is labeled with RRs, while a dotted line indicates an AP that is not labeled with RRs. If a single RR cannot represent the type of the relationship, two or more RRs are used.

2.3 Annotation of *Enthusiasm*

2.3.1 Related Work on Annotating the degree of enthusiasm

Wrede et al. annotated *Involvement* to the ICSI Meeting Recorder Corpus (Wrede and Shriberg, 2003b; Wrede and Shriberg, 2003a). In their method, a rater judges *involvement (agreement, disagreement, other)* or *Not especially involved* or *Don't Know*, by listening to each utterance without the context of the dialogue. In the experiment, nine raters provided ratings on 45 utterances. Inter-rater agreement between *Involved* and *Not especially involved* yielded a Kappa of κ=.59 ($p<.01$), but 13 of the 45 utterances (28.9%) were rated as *Don't Know* by at least one of the raters. For automatic detection, it is certainly effective to rate *Involvement* without context. However, the results indicate that it is quite difficult to recognize *Involvement* from a single utterance. Moreover, the fluctuation of *Involvement* can not be recognized by this method because *Involvement* is categorized into five categories only.

[2]This supports multilevel annotation and the creation of a relationship between utterances. http://www.eml-research.de/english/research/nlp/down-load/mmax.php

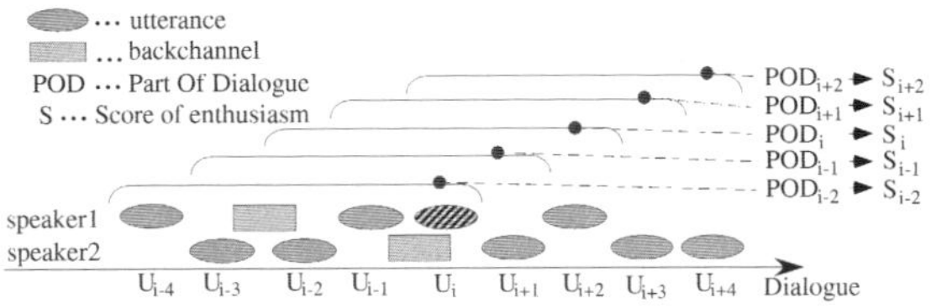

Figure 2: Rating the score of the enthusiasm

2.3.2 Our Method of Annotating *Enthusiasm*

In this section, we propose a method for evaluating the degree of enthusiasm. We describe the process for evaluating the degree of enthusiasm.

Step 1. Rating the score of enthusiasm for POD

A rater estimates a score of the enthusiasm corresponding to the part of dialogue (POD), which is a series of five utterances. As mentioned above, the backchannels are not regarded as utterances. In Figure 2, S_i denotes the score for the enthusiasm of POD_i. The value of the score can be from 10 to 90.

90 ... Extreme
70 ... Moderate
50 ... Neutral
30 ... Low
10 ... No

When rating the score, a rater must obey the following four rules.

1. Listen to each POD more than three times.
2. Perform estimation based on the entire POD and not just part of the POD.
3. Be sure that own ratings represented a consistent continuum.
4. Estimate as participants, not as side-participants.

We did not give any definitions or examples to rate the enthusiasm, a rater estimated a score based on their subjective determination.

Step 2. Calculate the score of enthusiasm for an utterance

The score of enthusiasm for an utterance U_i is given by the average of the scores of the PODs that contain utterance U_i.

$$V(U_i) = \frac{1}{5} \sum_{j=i-2}^{i+2} S_j \tag{1}$$

Step 3. Calculate the degree of enthusiasm for an utterance and an adjacency pair

In this paper, we deal with all the degrees of enthusiasm as a normalized score, which we call *Enthusiasm*, because different raters may have different absolute levels of enthusiasm. Then, *Enthusiasm* for U_i is given as follows:

$$E(U_i) = \frac{V(U_i) - \overline{V(U)}}{\sigma} \tag{2}$$

where

$$\overline{V(U)} = \frac{1}{n} \sum_{i=1}^{n} V(U_i)$$

$$\sigma = \sqrt{\frac{1}{n} \sum_{i=1}^{n} \{V(U_i) - \overline{V(U)}\}^2}$$

n denotes the number of utterances in the dialogue.

In addition, *Enthusiasm* for AP_i is given by the average of *Enthusiasms* of the utterances where are AP_i.

$$E(AP_i) = \frac{1}{2}\{E(U_j) + E(U_k)\} \tag{3}$$

U_j and U_k denote the utterances in AP_i.

3 Estimation of Annotated Corpus

3.1 Reliability of DAs and RRs

We examined the inter-annotator reliability for two annotators[3] for DAs, RRs and APs, using four dialogues mentioned above. Before the start of the investigation, one annotator segmented a dialogue into utterances. The number of segmented utterances was 697. The annotaters annotated them as described in steps 2 to 4 of Section 2.2.2.

DAs annotation: We can not apply the Kappa statistics since it cannot be applied to multiple tag annotations. We then apply formula 4 to examine the reliability.

$$ag. = \frac{(Agreed\,DAs) \times 2}{Total\,of\,DAs\,annotated\,by\,A1\,and\,A2} \times 100 \tag{4}$$

The result of agreement was 1542 DAs (65.5%) from a total of 2355 DAs. The major reasons for the disagreement were as follows.

- Disagreement of subjective/objective ... 124(15.3%)
- Disagreement of request/confirm ... 112(13.8%)
- Disagreement of partial/whole ... 72(8.9%)

Building APs: We examined the agreement of building APs between utterances. The result of agreement was 536 APs (85.2%) from the total of the 629 APs that were built by the annotators. This result shows that the building of APs is reliable.

RRs annotation: We also examined the agreement of RRs annotation. We applied formula 5 to this examination.

$$ag. = \frac{(Agreed\,RRs) \times 2}{Total\,of\,RRs\,annotated\,by\,A1\,and\,A2} \times 100 \tag{5}$$

As a result, we found agreement for 576 RRs (59.6%) out of a total of 967 RRs.

[3] We refer to these annotators as A1 and A2. A1 is one of the authors of this paper.

Table 3: Correlation between random rating and sequential rating

	correlation coefficient	
	speaker1	speaker2
twenties,female	0.833	0.881
twenties,male	0.971	0.950
sixties,female	0.972	0.973
sixties,male	0.971	0.958

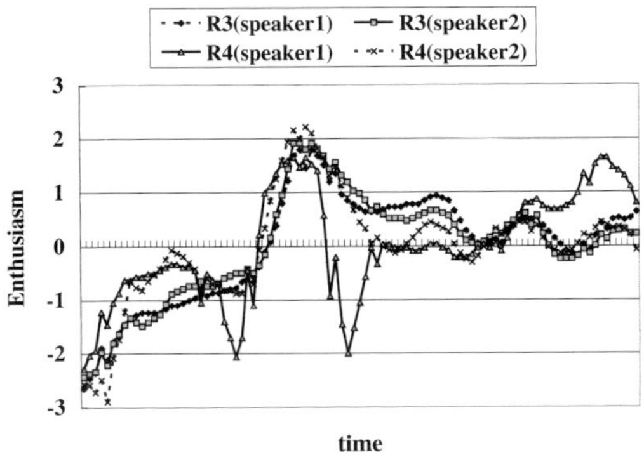

Figure 3: *Enthusiasm* of dialogue of speaker1 and speaker2(thirties,female)

3.2 Estimation Context Influence on the rating of *Enthusiasm*

In order to examine the influence of the context on the rating of *Enthusiasm*, one rater noted *Enthusiasm* under two conditions: 1) Listening to PODs randomly, and 2) Listening to PODs sequentially as dialogue. Table 3 shows the correlation between the random rating and the sequential rating. The correlation coefficient was calculated for the *Enthusiasm* of each of the two participants. The "speaker1" shows the correlation of the *Enthusiasm* rated as speaker1, and "speaker2" shows the correlation of the *Enthusiasm* rated as speaker2. This was found to be approximately 0.9 in both cases. These results show that *Enthusiasm* can be estimated stably and that the context has little influence.

4 Relationship between DAs/RRs and *Enthusiasm*

We investigated the relationship between DAs/RRs and *Enthusiasm*, using four dialogues. The DAs/RRs corpus annotated by A1 was used in this analysis because A1 is one of the authors of this paper and has a better knowledge of the DAs and RRs tagging scheme than A2. The *Enthusiasm* corpus annotated by R3 was used because we found that R4 rated *Enthusiasm* based on non-subjective reasons: after the examination of the rating, R4 said that speaker1 spoke enthusiastically but that it seemed unnatural because speaker1 had to manage the recording of the dialogue, which appears in the results as speaker1's *Enthusiasm* as annotated by R4 as a notable difference (see Figure 3).

Figure 4 and 5 show the ratio of the frequency of DAs and RRs in each of the levels of *Enthusiasm* over a range of 0.5. If DAs and RRs were evenly annotated for any level of *Enthusiasm*, the graph will be completely even. However, the graph shows the right side as being higher if the DAs and RRs increase as *Enthusiasm* increases. Conversely, the graph shows the left side as being higher if the DAs and RRs fall as *Enthusiasm* increases. The number in Figure 4 and 5 indicates the average *Enthusiasm* for each DA and RR. If the average is positive, it means that the frequency of the DAs and RRs is high in that part in which *Enthusiasm* is positive. In contrast, if the average is negative, it means that the frequency of the DAs and RRs is high in that part in which *Enthusiasm* is negative.

We determined the following two points about the tendency of the DAs frequency.

Tendency of subjective and objective DAs: The ratio of the frequency of those DAs related to *subjective elements* tends to increase as *Enthusiasm* increases (see *1 in Figure 4). In contrast, the ratio of the frequency of those DAs pertaining to *objective matters* tends to decrease (see *2 in Figure 4) or equilibrate as *Enthusiasm* increases (see *3 in Figure 4) . We can thus conclude that those exchanges related to subjective elements increases in the enthusiastic dialogue, but those related to objective elements decrease or equilibrate.

Tendency of affective DAs: The ratio of the frequency of those DAs related to the *affective contents* tends to increase as *Enthusiasm* increases (see *4 in Figure 4). However, *express admiration*, which is also related to affective contents, tends to decrease (see *5 in Figure 4). We then analyzed several instances of *admiration*. As a result, we found that the prosodic characteristic of *admiration* utterance will cause this tendency.

Furthermore, we noted the following two points about the tendency of the RRs frequency.

Tendency of additional utterances: The ratio of the frequency of *addition*, which completes the

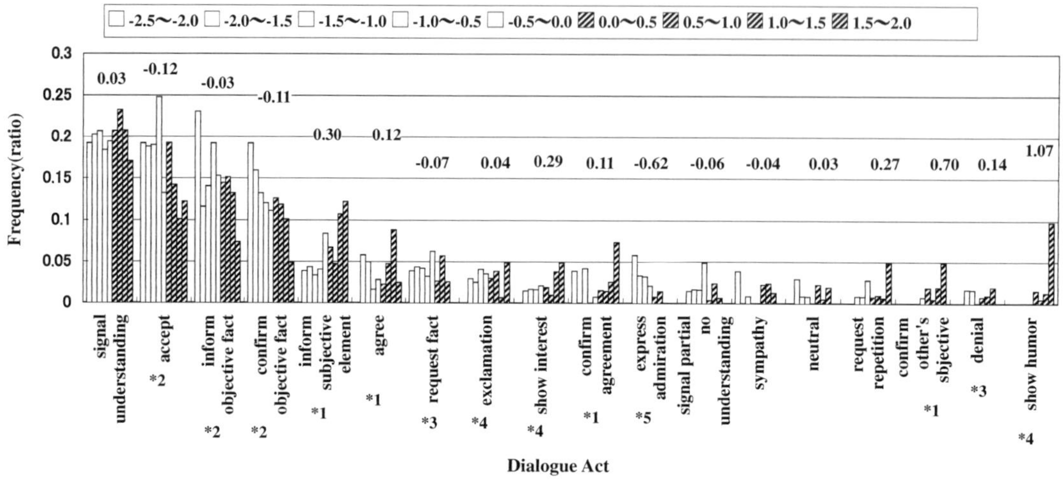

Figure 4: Frequency of DAs per *Enthusiasm*

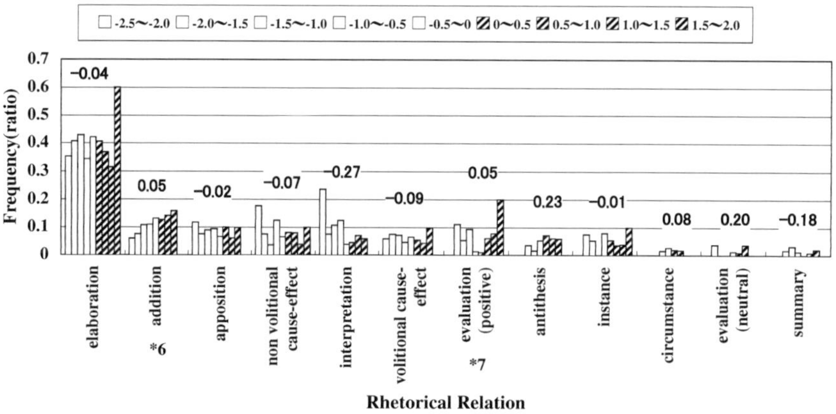

Figure 5: Frequency of RRs per *Enthusiasm*

Context:Mother of speaker2 does not cook dinner when the father is out.
1 speaker1: but if he's there then she
2 speaker2: cooks a really delicious dinner
3 speaker1: wow

Figure 6: Example of *addition*

other participant's utterance, tends to increase as *Enthusiasm* increases (see *6 in Figure 5). Figure 6 shows a dialogue example. There are *addition* relations between lines 1 and 2. This shows that the participant makes an utterance cooperatively by completing the other's utterances in enthusiastic dialogues. Such cooperative utterance is a significant component of enthusiastic dialogues.

Tendency of positive evaluation: The ratio of the frequency of *positive evaluation* tends to increase at lower *Enthusiasm* and higher *Enthusiasm* (see *7 in Figure 5). We analyzed some instances of

Context:About a hamster and its exercise instrument.
1 speaker2: two hamsters run together in their exercise wheel
2 speaker2: they run up and down and side by side
3 speaker1: but surely they can't they run together if they aren't getting along very well?
4 speaker2: exactly
5 speaker2: one gets carried along if it stops when the other continues to run
6 speaker1: is it? does it lean forward?
7 speaker2: yes
8 speaker2: sometimes it falls out
9 speaker1: that's so cute

Figure 7: Example of *positive evaluation*

positive evaluation, we then found that the speaker tries to arouse the dialogue by an utterance of *positive evaluation* at lower *Enthusiasm*, and the speaker summarizes the previous discourse with a *positive evaluation* at higher *Enthusiasm*. Figure 7 shows an example of *positive evaluation* in the enthusiastic dialogue. In this case, speaker1 expresses *positive evaluation* on line 9 about the element on line 8. The utterance on line 9 also has the function of expressing an overall *positive evaluation* of the previous discourse.

5 Conclusion and Future Research

We analyzed the relationship between utterances and the degree of enthusiasm in human-to-human conversational dialogue. We first created a conversational dialogue corpus annotated with two types of tags: DAs/RRs and *Enthusiasm*. The DA and RR tagging scheme was adapted from the definition given in a previous work, and an *Enthusiasm* tagging scheme is proposed. Our method of rating *Enthusiasm* enables the observation of the fluctuation of *Enthusiasm*, which enables the detailed analysis of the relationship between utterances and *Enthusiasm*. The result of the analysis shows the frequency of objective and subjective utterances related to the level of *Enthusiasm*. We also found that affective and cooperative utterances are significant in an enthusiastic dialogue.

In this paper, we only analyzed the relationship between DAs/RRs and *Enthusiasm*, but we expect the non-linguistic-feature related with *Enthusiasm* so that we would analyze the relationship in future research. And, we try to achieve more reliable annotation by reviewing our tagging scheme. Furthermore, we would apply the results of the analysis to our conversational dialogue system.

References

Rajdip Dhillon, Sonali Bhagat, Hannah Carvey, and Elizabeth Shriberg. 2004. Meeting Recorder Project: Dialog Act Labeling Guide. *ICSI Technical Report*, (TR-04-002).

David Graff and Steven Bird. 2000. Many Uses, Many Annotations for Large Speech Corpora: Switchboard and TDT as Case Studies. *LREC2000*.

Dan Jurafsky, Liz Shriberg, and Debra Biasca. 1997. Switchboard SWBD-DAMSL Shallow-Discourse-Function Annotation Coders Manual. *www.dcs.shef.ac.uk/nlp/amities/files/bib/ics-tr-97-02.pdf*.

Kazunori Komatani, Tatsuya Kawahara, Ryosuke Ito, and Hiroshi Okuno. 2002. Efficient Dialogue Strategy to Find Users' Intended Items from Information Query Results. *In Proceedings of the COLING*.

Diane Litman, Satinder Singh, Michael Kearns, and Marilyn Walker. 2000. NJFun: A Reinforcement Learning Spoken Dialogue System. *In Proceedings of the ANLP/NAACL*.

William C. Mann and Sandra A. Thompson. 1988. Rhetorical Structure Theory: Toward a Functional Theory of Text Organization. *Text*, 8(3):243–281.

Christoph Muller and Michael Strube. 2003. Multi-Level Annotation in MMAX. *In Proceedings of the 4th SIGdial Workshop on Discourse and Dialogue*.

Amanda Stent and James Allen. 2000. Annotating Argumentation Acts in Spoken Dialog. *Technical Report 740*.

Shu-Chuan TSENG. 2001. Toward a Large Spontaneous Mandarin Dialogue Corpus. *In Proceedings of the 2nd SIGdial Workshop on Discourse and Dialogue*.

Marilyn A. Walker, Jeanne C. Fromer, and Shrikanth Narayanan. 1998. Learning Optimal Dialogue Strategies: A Case Study of a Spoken Dialogue Agent for Email. *In Proceedings of COLING/ACL*.

Britta Wrede and Elizabeth Shriberg. 2003a. Spotting "Hot Spots" in Meetings: Human Judgements and Prosodic Cues. *Eurospeech-03*, pages 2805–2808.

Britta Wrede and Elizabeth Shriberg. 2003b. The Relationship between Dialogue Acts and Hot Spots in Meetings. *IEEE ASRU Workshop*.

Author Index

Association for Computational Linguistics
209 N. Eighth Street
Stroudsburg, Pennsylvania 18360